# COLLECTOR'S ENCYCLOPEDIA OF

# *Pickard China*

## WITH ADDITIONAL SECTIONS ON OTHER CHICAGO CHINA STUDIOS

**ALAN B. REED**

**COLLECTOR BOOKS**

*A Division of Schroeder Publishing Co., Inc.*

Searching for a Publisher?

We are always looking for knowledgeable people considered to be experts within their fields. If you feel that there is a real need for a book on your collectible subject and have a large comprehensive collection, contact COLLECTOR BOOKS.

## DEDICATION

To Betty, Mary Beth, Michael, Mary Therese, Mark, and Colin

Cover design: Beth Summers
Book design: Michelle Dowling
Photography: Alan B. Reed

Additional copies of this book may be ordered from:

COLLECTOR BOOKS          Alan B. Reed, Firstlight, Inc.
P.O. Box 3009      OR          P.O. Box 6014
Paducah, KY 42002–3009          River Forest, IL 60305–6014

@ $24.95. Add $2.00 for postage and handling.

Printed by IMAGE GRAPHICS, INC., Paducah, Kentucky

# CONTENTS

**Acknowledgments** .........................................................................5

**Foreword** ........................................................................................6

**Preface** ...........................................................................................6

**Notes** .............................................................................................7

**Introduction** ................................................................................7

**Pickard, Inc.** .................................................................................9

  The Early Years 1857–1897 ........................................................9

    Sun Prairie, Wisconsin .............................................................9

    Chicago, Illinois........................................................................9

    The Pauline Pottery ................................................................10

      Chicago 1882–1887 ...........................................................10

      Edgerton 1888–1893 .........................................................10

  The Edgerton Art Studio 1894 ...............................................12

  The Flood Home 1895–1897 ...................................................13

  The Pickard Home 1898–1903 ...............................................14

  The Carriage Barn 1903–1905 ...............................................20

  The Ravenswood Studio 1905–1910 ......................................22

  Etched Gold 1910–1912 ..........................................................31

  War and Transition 1912–1919................................................32

  Postwar and New Directions 1919–1922 ...............................40

  Toward Simplicity 1922–1925.................................................42

  Pickard Studios, Inc. 1925–1930 ...........................................43

  Pickard, Inc. The Great Depression 1930–1938....................44

  Pickard, Inc. Antioch, 1938–Present ......................................46

  Pickard Artist Biographies .....................................................50

  Pickard Artists with Multiple Studio Affiliations...................70

  Pickard Trademarks ................................................................71

  Pickard Patents .......................................................................73

  Pickard Advertising.................................................................75

  Pickard Plates .........................................................................97

  Pickard Pattern Names ...........................................................241

**Julius H. Brauer Studio** ..........................................................244

  Kay-Bee China Works .............................................................244

**Dominick Campana Studio** .....................................................254

  D.M. Campana Art Company ...................................................254

**Edward W. Donath Studio**.......................................................254

  American Hand-Painted China Company.................................254

**France Studios** ..........................................................................262

**A. Heidrich Studios** .................................................................262

**Humboldt Art Studio**...............................................................263

**International Art Studios** ........................................................264

**Kalita Studio**................................................................265

**Keates Art Studio**......................................................266

**J.R. Kittler**................................................................267

**C.F. Koenig Studios**..................................................267

**LeRoy Art Studios**....................................................268

**Luken Art Studios**....................................................268

**Osborne Art Studio**..................................................269

**Parsche Studios**........................................................276

**Rogers-Martini**..........................................................277

    Rogers China Company........................................277

    E. D. Rogers Company........................................277

**Seidel Studio**..............................................................278

    Marmorstein & Seidel........................................278

    H. Marmorstein's Art Studio..............................278

**J. H. Stouffer Company**.............................................278

**Tolpin Studios**............................................................299

    Tolpin Art Studio...............................................299

    Illinois China Decorating Company....................299

    Progressive China Decorating Company............299

    Rivir Studios......................................................299

    China Decorating Company................................299

    Roosevelt China Studio......................................299

    Deluxe China Studios........................................299

    Tolpin Products Manufacturing Company..........299

**White & White**............................................................301

    White's Art Company........................................301

**Wight Art Studio**........................................................305

**Yeschek, Inc.**.............................................................305

    Ceramic Artcraft Studios..................................305

**China Decorating Associations**................................308

    National League of Mineral Painters..................308

    Chicago Ceramic Arts Association......................308

    Atlan Ceramic Arts Club....................................308

**The Decorator-Wholesalers**......................................321

    Burley & Co. .....................................................321

        Burley & Tyrrell.............................................321

    Pitkin & Brooks.................................................322

    Western Decorating Works ...............................325

**Appendices**................................................................325

    A. Chicago China Studios Family Tree...............325

    B. Listing of all listed Chicago China Decorating Studios...................326

    C. Select Bibliography .......................................331

**End Notes**..................................................................332

**Index**.........................................................................334

# ACKNOWLEDGMENTS

We are indebted to the following collectors and dealers for allowing us to photograph their collections: Gary Adams, Patrick and Lavonne Barrett, Tim Ingram, Dorothy Kamm, S. Kellogg, Terrie Kempe, Janet Kendziora, Tom Neale and Glen Schlotfeldt, Joan Poulos, Drs. Harry and Cathy Poulos, Glenda Ridgway, Garrett and Lee Smith, Carlyn Whitehand, and the museum at Pickard, Inc.—Pete Pickard and Eben Morgan.

We are also indebted to Evelyn Bachmann for her background on her father, Max Bachmann, and other artists; Dorothy Bero for background on Albert Bero; Vera and Rolf Beutlich and Katherine Lund for their reminiscences of Anton Beutlich; Patty Meyers Burchfield for her background and photo of Jacob Stouffer; Virginia Carlson for reminiscences of her father, Robert Hessler; Pete, Alice, and Edith Challinor for their reminiscences of the Challinor family; Sharon S. Darling for the gift of her notes on Chicago china artists; C. Gerald DeBolt for his research on Ravenwood china; Mr. and Mrs. Charles Donath for photos and background on Edward Donath and Max Rost; Dale and Chelsea Downey for their background on the J. H. Stouffer Company and for their searches for additional artists; Pickard artist, John Eustice for his anecdotal reminiscences on Pickard and other studios for which he worked and for his explanations of the china decorating art; Robert Goler, former Curator of Decorative Arts at the Chicago Historical Society for his research assistance; Mary Hamilton, Head Librarian of the Edgerton Public Library, for her assistance in our marathon reading of the *Wisconsin Tobacco Reporter* (and for all the welcome cups of coffee); Herbert Hiecke for photos and background on his father, Gustav Hiecke; Claudia Fallert and Mrs. James Rutson for background on George and Bertha Irsch and other independent artists; Mark Hilton, former Vice President of Development at the Chicago Historical Society for his support and assistance; Tim Ingram for his *Keramic Studio* and miscellaneous document research and for searching out additional artist signatures and trademarks; George H. Jamison for his background on Ravenwood China and the Sinclaire Glass Company; Zenon Kalita for his reminiscences of his father, Waclaw Kalita, the Kalita studio, and its artists; Dorothy Kamm for sharing her own research on numerous artists and studios; Terrie Kempe for locating many artists' descendants for us; Matylde Kreller for her girlhood memories of the Ravenswood Studio and her father, John Fuchs, and other artists; Helen Lindberg for background on her mother, Emma Stone, at the Ravenswood studio; Olivia Mahoney, Assistant Curator of Decorative Arts at the Chicago Historical Society for her research assistance; Eben Morgan for his personal background on Pickard, Inc.; Mary Newman for her background on her mother, Ester Samuelson and other artists; Don Parsche for his background on the Parsche Studio; Otto and Glenna Podlaha for the use of many photographs and paper references and valuable background on their father, Otto Podlaha; Dr. Harry and Dr. Cathy Poulos for the use of many old photographs and documents on the Yeschek family and the Pickard and Yeschek studios and for sharing their genealogical research; Claire Burleigh Reed for her reminiscences of her employment as a china artist; Clara Reid for her research in magazine archives; Marie and Al Schrautemeyer for their reminiscences and documents of the Yeschek studios; Adolph G. "Si" Simon for his reminiscences of the Ravenswood Studio; Garrett Smith for his search for unusual artists' signatures and the use of his old printed material; Mrs. Walter Wiard, Dorothy Freund, and Ann Leffler for their background on Charles Wiard and other independent artists.

We are most indebted, of course, to the three grandchildren of Wilder A. Pickard: to Wilder Pickard for sharing his reminiscences of his grandfather with us; to Sherry Shellenbach for the use of all the reference materials from her mother's book, for sharing the Pickard genealogy with us, and for allowing us to interview her and her father, Sherwood K. Platt; and to Pete Pickard for his patient response to all our questions, for the use of all the company's catalog references, and for his valuable comments and corrections.

This book would probably never have been started without the suggestion and assistance of Wendell Freeman who shared his extensive knowledge of hand-painted china with us. By the time we became acquainted with him, his wife, Ruby, was already deceased, and though we never knew her, many of her notes are incorporated into this book. Her collection of Pickard china was said to have numbered over 1,000 pieces at one time. We trust that many of Wendell's and Ruby's friends will see some of their love of hand-painted china reflected in these pages.

# FOREWORD

When Alan Reed called me a few years ago and introduced himself over the phone, he said he was working on a book about the early days of Pickard China and wanted to ask me a few questions. I considered that my aunt, Dorothy Pickard Platt, already had written the definitive work on this subject, but I told Alan I would be happy to meet with him. I supposed that he had in mind some sort of supplementary pamphlet.

As our meeting progressed, it became apparent to me that although his research was far from complete, he already knew much more about the early history of our company than I did. I was able to fill in a few gaps for him, but that was about all.

I'm overwhelmed by the thoroughness of Alan's completed work and by the ingenuity and perseverance it took to unearth and verify all the information contained in it. Without question this book now becomes the bible for Pickard collectors.

It has further significance on a personal basis for me. I was a young boy when my grandfather Wilder died, and unfortunately I never got to know him very well. These pages enhance my understanding of him. And the detailed account of the company's growth and development through the first three decades is fascinating to me.

Pickard China now is entering its second century as an independent, family-owned business. Our continuing viability hinges on maintaining two of the driving forces which were at the core of my grandfather's philosophy. On the one hand, we must be flexible and continually try new ideas. On the other hand, we must maintain the tradition of quality and craftsmanship for which the name Pickard always has stood.

Henry A. Pickard, Jr.
Antioch, Illinois
November 9, 1994

# PREFACE

When my wife, Betty, and I acquired our first pieces of Pickard china, we searched for a reference that could provide information on these unique and beautiful pieces. Eventually we discovered two sources: *The Story of Pickard China* by the founder's daughter, Dorothy Pickard Platt, and *Chicago Ceramics and Glass* by the former Curator of Decorative Arts at the Chicago Historical Society, Sharon S. Darling. Unfortunately, both books are now out of print.

By the time we had acquired these books, however, our interest had widened because we had discovered that many Pickard artists had come from, and/or moved to, many other studios. We were again at a loss for sources of information. Thus we began a search that has taken approximately ten years, including more than 12,000 look-ups in scores of old newspapers, census records, and directories in a score of libraries and museums in six states.

But along with the endless hours of searching we encountered many occasions of unexpected pleasure and excitement. One incident in particular is worth recounting: We had made an appointment with Olivia Mahoney, the Assistant Curator of Decorative Arts at the Chicago Historical Society to examine some materials. She asked us to meet her at the CHS Annex on North Ravenswood Avenue. The address was identical to that of Pickard's Ravenswood Studio and when we arrived, it was indeed the old china studio! A subsequent owner had deeded the property to the Society. It was an eerie experience to examine the photograph of Max Klipphahn decorating a piece of china (Fig. 32) while seated at the same window. The Society later sold the premises, but not before we were permitted a basement-to-attic examination of the old building, thereby giving us valuable insight into the arrangement of the studio.

This book is an attempt to draw all the significant information on Pickard together under one cover while expanding the scope to include other significant Chicago decorating studios, plus many additional artists, patterns, and trademarks not previously identified. Possessors of the Platt book will notice some differences in artist's names and trademark dates. These changes have only been made after very careful research and database matching.

We interviewed many collectors and dealers who offered much helpful information. But where the information was only verbal and no "hard" corroboration has been forth-coming, it is generally not included in this book. In a few instances some unsubstantiated information seemed to have high merit, and it has been included with an appropriate caveat. We also recognize that in a book of this nature some degree of error is unavoidable, and for such incidents we apologize and earnestly seek correction. Most importantly, this book does not end our research on the subject, and we solicit comments and additions. (Correspondence should be accompanied by a stamped, self-addressed envelope.)

# NOTES

Addresses given in the text are those used during the respective years under discussion. All Chicago street addresses were renumbered, exclusive of the downtown area as of September 1, 1909. Downtown addresses were renumbered as of April 1, 1911.

Beyond the personal interviews, letters, and papers we were able to obtain, much of the authentication in this book derives from U. S. Census records, newspapers, and city directories of the period. The listings in the directories were typeset from hand-written notes obtained by door-to-door canvassers. Temporary neighborhood directory offices checked and confirmed the work of the canvassers, and for an age without computers, the publishers produced a remarkably accurate compilation in an even more remarkably short time. Although some errors in spelling and street numbering were inevitable (Wilder A. Pickard became Wiley A. Pickard in 1908), the occupational descriptions were furnished by the listees themselves or by a household member, and changes in occupations can therefore be traced with considerable accuracy.

# CONVENTIONS AND ABBREVIATIONS

This book lists all the known antique pattern names. Of the total population of antique Pickard china, this leaves a substantial number of patterns unidentified. After much internal debate and many conversations with other collectors, the author has selected the more popular designs from this anonymity and applied names that it is hoped will facilitate their identification.

- **Official pattern names are** UNDERLINED SMALL CAPITALS.
- **Author-applied pattern names are** *ITALICIZED SMALL CAPITALS*.

  Atlan—Atlan Ceramic Arts Club
  CCAA—Chicago Ceramic Arts Association
  c., circa—about, approximately
  CHS—Chicago Historical Society
  NLMP—National League of Mineral Painters
  WTR—the Wisconsin Tobacco Reporter

# INTRODUCTION

The development of china painting as an art form in the United States is said to have had its roots in the Arts and Crafts Movement. But whereas in Europe this movement took the form of a rebellion against the Industrial Revolution and in particular, the mechanized production of such art forms as jewelry, pottery, and furniture, the American counter-part was an introspective reaction to the end of an era. By the 1880s America had no more patches of terra incognita on its maps, and exploring minds focused inward upon invention, arts, and crafts.

Another aspect that was largely lacking in the American version of the movement were the social philosophies that flourished in the Utopian guilds and communes of William Morris, John Ruskin, Charles Ashbee, and others. This does not mean that the social benefits associated with the movement never settled on the American artist. In Pickard's studio, they did, but as we shall see, the benefits derived not only from humanitarian considerations, but from sound business fundamentals as well.

The first "China Decorators" appeared in the classified listings of the Chicago Business Directory in 1880, but the famous European pottery and porcelain manufacturers at Staffordshire, Meissen, Dresden, Limoges, and a host of others were all well-established exporters to the North American continent by that time.

In addition to hand painting, the application of designs through paper transfers had reached a high degree of development in Europe. Thus, quantities of mass-produced designs as well as combination transfer and hand-painted items monopolized the American market.

But the American woman, both as consumer and producer was changing that market preference. The popularization of American hand-painted china had been abetted by the country's growing interest in its own arts and crafts. But of no less importance was the increasingly active role in the arts which American women were embracing. China painting was an occupation in which the middle class woman could engage without compromising her husband's or her own social standing. Here too, was an occupation that the woman who truly needed income could pursue without descending into a sweat-shop environment. And for both classes of women, it offered a hitherto unavailable opportunity for artistic expression.

Foremost among nineteenth century women china artists was Susan S. Frackleton. Originally situated in Milwaukee, she eventually relocated to the South Side of Chicago. Her book, *Tried by Fire*, first published in 1886, was the definitive work on china decorating for the amateur as well as the advanced china artist.

Susan Frackleton displayed an independent and entrepreneurial spirit that was exceptional for the unenfranchised woman of the nineteenth century. Like many china decorators, male and female, Susan Frackleton had a strong background in pottery, and china decorating seems to have evolved from it without displacing it. To her artistic offerings, she also added a commercial venture in the form of artist's supplies: paints, brushes, and a wide selection of china blanks. And for those china artists without the means, she also offered firing services in her own kilns.

One sequence in her book provides interesting insight into the problems of china decorating for the nineteenth century woman. She states, "The drawing of the fire (from the kiln) demanded the assistance of a man.... The heat from a bushel or more of live coals is intense, and the light drapery of a woman's skirts make it extremely dangerous. After having seen one woman burned to death from her dress catching fire, I may perhaps be excused for having an exaggerated horror of such danger...."

She not only recognized this problem, she capitalized on it through another business venture, the Frackleton Portable Gas-Kiln.

One more element contributed to the rise in popularity of hand-painted china: as the volume increased and many amateurs put their wares on the market, it became an affordable bit of elegance, even to those of modest means. The wife of the paperhanger or the lamplighter now found it within her means to display a cheaply-made lemonade set on her sideboard or a fruit-encrusted charger on her plate rail. By 1905 it was estimated that there were some 20,000 professional china decorators, nation-wide, who were supplying various levels of this market.

Pickard was the first commercial studio devoted to volume production of fine hand-painted china for the specialty and giftware markets. Pickard's ambition was to raise china decoration into the realm of fine art. Whether he succeeded can be debated at length, but that he made a substantial contribution to china decorating as one of the decorative arts, cannot be denied. In 1898, the first year in which Pickard is listed in the Chicago Business Directory under "China Decorators," his was one of seven such studios. By 1916 that number had risen to one hundred and two. By 1929 the number had retreated to fifteen, and today, of all those studios, only Pickard, Incorporated remains in business. The purpose of this book is to document and illustrate the "golden era" of hand-painted china as produced in Chicago's many china decorating studios between 1894 and 1925. For the sake of completeness (but in lesser detail) some text and china photos follow the more prominent studios beyond 1925 to their ultimate demise, or, as in the case of Pickard, through its present-day successes. Although commercial hand-painted china began well before 1894, and continued in some form well beyond 1925, this span of years constitutes the time-focus of this book.

# PICKARD, INC.

## The Early Years 1857–1897
### Sun Prairie, Wisconsin

Wilder A. Pickard was born on January 12, 1857, to William and Emma Yerxa Pickard on a farm near Sun Prairie, Wisconsin, just northeast of Madison, the state capitol. He had two older sisters, Mary and Anna. Anna was seven years older, and while Wilder was still a boy, Anna attended the University of Wisconsin where she received her bachelor's degree in philosophy. There was a strong appreciation for the Arts in the family, for Anna later went to Europe for further study, acquiring a background in art history that was to allow her to play a major role in Pickard's success.

By the time Wilder Pickard was ready for a higher education, however, his father's circumstances had changed dramatically. Since the end of the Civil War, grain prices had been dropping steadily, trapping farmers into over-producing to pay off their mortgages. The increased production forced prices even lower, compelling the cycle to repeat itself. In September of 1873, the worst financial panic the country had ever known struck Wall Street. (It would be second only to the Great Depression of 1929.) All across America, the panic drew banks and businesses down with it. Like many farmers throughout the country, William Pickard lost everything, including his farm—and Wilder lost all prospect of attending the university.

The ensuing depression lasted six years, and it is unclear whether the family initially moved into the town of Sun Prairie where Emma Pickard's sister lived, but by 1880, the Pickards had taken up residence in Marshall, a small town eight miles east of Sun Prairie.

A year later, Wilder Pickard moved to Chicago. By that time, his sister Anna's marriage to Frank Atkins had taken her to Milwaukee where her husband pursued a career as a "commissioned merchant"—or commodities broker in today's terms— while his sister Mary's marriage to Samuel Junkin had taken her to Chicago.

### Chicago, Illinois

Pickard came to Chicago in 1881, living as a boarder in a home ½ block west of the Newberry

*Figure 1. Wilder A. Pickard, 1857–1939*

Photo courtesy S. Shellenbach.

Library at 267 Oak Street.[1] It seems probable that it was here that he met his future wife, Minnie Verna Flood, since she and her family lived almost directly across the street.[2] His first job was that of a clerk at a retail store on Wabash Avenue just east of Marshall Field's department store. His employer is not identified, but three large china and Queensware retailers were located in the same vicinity at that time. The following year he was a salesman for a produce company on South Water Street. In the meantime, his sister Mary's husband, Samuel F. Junkin, had become manager of the Chicago office of the Cincinnati-based Hubbard Brothers Publishing Company on LaSalle Street. In late 1883 or early 1884 Pickard moved in with the Junkins in a house at 174 State Street,[3] becoming a book salesman for his brother-in-law.

In 1885 the Junkin family moved to California. Pickard remained at the State Street address, and at age twenty-eight, took over as office manager, thereby acquiring some sales and management experience that would serve him well in later years.

By 1886 the publishing company no longer listed him, and there is no record of his activities through 1888. He reappeared early in 1889, when he was said to have been attracted to a piece of Pauline Pottery while walking through Marshall Field's department store. The pottery had been operating in Edgerton, Wisconsin, for just about a year, and his inquiries resulted in his appointment as the pottery's midwest representative.

Pickard's years with the Pauline Pottery were to equip him with a marketing advantage that would ensure his growth and success as Chicago's largest professional china decorating studio, so a step back to the beginnings of the Pauline Pottery will be helpful in understanding subsequent events.

## The Pauline Pottery
### Chicago 1882–1887

The Pauline Pottery was founded in Chicago, in 1882, by Oscar I. Jacobus and his wife, Pauline. She had done some china decorating in the late 1870s, but by 1881, due primarily to the influence of a local exhibition of pottery by Sarah Bernhardt, she had developed an avid interest in the new wave of art pottery. Her early experiments were frustrating, and in 1882 she went to study with Maria Longworth Nichols at Nichols' recently established Rookwood Studio in Cincinnati.

In the fall of that year, Pauline's husband wrote to Rookwood, informing her of a proposed art pottery exhibition by a group of Chicago women. Enlisting the aid of a Rookwood kiln-builder and a teacher, Laura Fry,[4] Pauline hurried back to Chicago where she and her husband opened a pottery at 36th Street and Wabash Avenue. She hired two art-student decorators and a presser (for pressing the clay into the molds), and before the year was out, she had produced an array of art pottery and placed it on exhibition in advance of the other women. The Pauline Art Pottery thus became Chicago's first commercial art pottery.

The Pauline Art Pottery grew quickly and by 1884, the Jacobus's son, Allen, was managing their second retail store on Wabash Avenue behind the Palmer House.

Pauline's decorations were applied underglaze on a great variety of bisque forms—bowls, vases, jardinieres, ewers, tea and coffee sets, planters, and large tiles—that were molded, cast, or thrown. Both red[5] and yellow clays were used, and some of the forms also incorporated incised or low relief decora-

tions. Field flowers, daffodils, and roses rendered in soft earth tones and muted yellows, greens, and even pinks were predominant subjects. These were invariably outlined in very dark greens or black with occasional geometric borders in dark blue and green. Yellow clay forms often received a wash of transparent yellow glaze that further softened the design. Designs on red bisque were sometimes stippled with gold; the gold was also applied to handles and edges of pieces in a style that allowed the brush strokes to become part of the effect.

By 1887, Pauline's customer list included such prestigious firms as Marshall Field in Chicago, Tiffany in New York, and Pitts, Kimball & Lewis in Boston.[6]

But by 1887, the Pauline Art Pottery was no longer just producing art ware. Oscar Jacobus was a bookkeeper by profession, working successively for several commissioned merchants, and his management skills and business connections were major factors in the success of the pottery. Through these connections he had obtained sizable contracts for ceramic battery cups for the growing telephone industry. Early in 1887, an additional pottery, four times the size of the original, began operation under Allen Jacobus's supervision.

Pauline could price her art ware to cover the cost of transporting clay all the way from Ohio, but battery cups could not command any premium for artistic merit, and Oscar Jacobus at once began a search for a more proximate source. In late 1887, some clay samples from Edgerton, Wisconsin, passed Mr. Jacobus's tests, and he quickly set to work, soliciting stock subscriptions from the wealthier residents of Edgerton for the establishment of his new pottery.

### Edgerton 1888–1893

Even by today's standards Oscar Jacobus opened his new pottery with incredible speed. The Pauline Pottery Company held its first annual meeting of shareholders on February 2, 1888, in Edgerton (the word "Art" was now absent from the company name). By March 2 the company had purchased a vacant tobacco warehouse and negotiated for the placement of its kilns along the St. Paul Railroad Company's right-of-way.

Construction of the kilns began on March 22 under the supervision of John Sargeant from Rookwood. Just eight weeks later, all six kilns were complete, a boiler and a 40 horsepower steam engine had been erected in a separately constructed engine house, and two clay washers, a presser, a pug mill, three jiggers, and three lathes had all been installed!

By the middle of May, the first battery cups (Fig. 2) were drawn from the kilns, but the more seasonal decorated wares in the form of pitchers, candle sticks, bouquet holders, puff boxes, vases, fluted bowls, and rose jars followed quickly and were available in quantity in time for the Christmas season. Effectively, the pottery operated for only five months in 1888, yet Oscar Jacobus's astute management overcame the start-up deficit and showed a profit by year-end.

On March 15, 1889, the following paragraph appeared in the Edgerton weekly newspaper, *The Wisconsin Tobacco Reporter*:

*Figure 2. Battery cup, 5¼" high, produced by Pauline Pottery for the Western Electric Company.*

"The Pauline Pottery Co. have contracted with Mr. W. A. Pickard, of Chicago, to sell the decorated ware manufactured by the Pottery in the states of Ind., Mich., Ill., Mo., Ia., Wis., and Minn. and a fine line of sample goods have been prepared for him. Heretofore the pottery has manufactured only upon orders, but now propose to canvass the larger cities with a traveling agent."

By this time, Pickard was living with the Flood family at 276 Oak Street,[7] and he then described himself as a "manufacturer's representative." In April, Allen Jacobus visited Chicago, St. Louis, Indianapolis, Detroit, and Milwaukee, apparently introducing Pickard to the pottery's major customers in his territory.

Battery cups continued to be the pottery's major product line, but in less than two years Pickard's sales accounted for a significant portion—possibly as much as one-third—of the pottery's total revenues.[8] *The Wisconsin Tobacco Reporter* carried this notice on November 20, 1891:

"W. A. Pickard, the salesman for the Pauline Pottery, has been in town for a few days this week to replenish his stock of samples.
Mr. Pickard has sold more goods for the pottery this season than all other years put together."

Pauline Pottery occasionally has been likened to Italian Majolica ware, but this is more romanticism than reality. Other than both having a light, earthenware body and a softening of the colors resulting from glaze application, it requires a very active imagination to see a further similarity. It also bore no resemblance to later Pickard china ware.

Although Pauline's forms and decorative themes continued in much the same vein as the ware produced in Chicago, the Edgerton clay was a low-fired clay that produced a chalky-yellow, somewhat friable earthen-ware. A marked difference in the rate of expansion between the bisque forms and the glaze produced a pronounced crazing of the surface. As a result, it is almost impossible to find a piece in mint condition today, and pieces with modest chips, cracks, and under-glaze staining are still considered worth acquiring. Pauline ware had a distinction all its own, and many pieces rank with the better examples of the potter's art. (Fig.3)

*Figure 3. Pauline Pottery 17" high hand-thrown lidded ewer with under glaze decoration. c.1890.*

The Pauline Pottery continued its steady growth for another year and a half. At its height, the pottery employed 25 men[9] and 13 women.[10] But on May 10, 1893, Oscar Jacobus suddenly died of an intestinal constriction, and almost at once, the pottery began to decline. Another financial panic in August exacerbated the pottery's condition, and by the following May it had been re-capitalized under the name of the Edgerton Pottery Company. Pauline Jacobus had no ownership in the new pottery.

Several sources[11] have stated that the advent of dry cell batteries caused the Pauline Pottery to founder, but two facts do not support this: in 1893, battery cups were still required at each subscriber's telephone, and it was not until 1896 that the so-called Common Battery System at telephone companies' central offices came into wide-spread use; dry cells played no part in that conversion. An even more conclusive fact was the successor Edgerton Pottery's report at its annual meeting *two years later* that "about $10,000 worth of porous battery cups had been sold this past year." (Roughly equivalent to $200,000 in today's terms.) This amount was approximately equal to battery cup sales for any prior year. The pottery most probably failed for the simple want of the skillful management that Oscar Jacobus had always provided.

But well before the Pauline Pottery failed, Pickard perceived the potential decline in his own future. His only assets were the customers he had so painstakingly cultivated, and if he had no product to sell, those customers would go to his competitors. So without waiting for the inevitable failure to occur, he made two important decisions: He took out his first classified listing in the 1894 Chicago City Directory under "Manufacturer's Agent" to attract additional lines, and he offered a business proposition to a 28-year-old artist named Mae Johnson.

## The Edgerton Art Studio 1894

Unlike some of the art students that Pauline Jacobus had brought in from other cities, Mae E. Johnson (1866–1936) was a native of Edgerton. The daughter of the town's shoemaker and milliner, she had joined the Pauline decorating staff in September of 1888 in time for the first rush of Christmas orders. She apparently had no formal art training, but as soon as the year-end orders were complete, she went to Chicago for a three-month course at the Art Institute.

The seasonal nature of the art pottery permitted her to take an additional art course in Milwaukee in the spring of 1891. In June of that year, she capitalized on this training by opening a china decorating class in the parlor of the Taylor House, an erstwhile hotel near the pottery. (The building still stands today.) She also found time to decorate pottery of her own, and that fall her work carried off three first prizes and one second prize at the county fair.

Her china decorating classes were of short, or at least intermittent duration, since she continued to work in Pauline's "decorative department." But by February of 1894, the pending demise of the Pauline Pottery was probably obvious to everyone, and Mae Johnson again began teaching china decorating, this time, in her mother's home.

Pickard saw in Mae Johnson's china classes an opportunity to retain what he had built. He proposed to supply her with china blanks and decorating materials, and in return she would supply him with a line of hand-painted china. By May she had gone to Milwaukee for another brief course in china painting, and by the end of that month— coincident with the pottery's recapitalization—she had "...opened up an art studio in the Taylor House...where a line of china decorating will be carried on."[12]

By mid-July Mae Johnson had shipped a line of decorated china to a Waukesha, Wisconsin, dealer, and Pickard's idea seemed an overnight success. But the surprising proportions of this new business were best described in a long article on the evolution of Edgerton's pottery industry in the December 24, 1894, *Wisconsin Tobacco Reporter*:

"...The starting of a pottery established in Edgerton a few years ago, has brought about two other enterprises that began in a small way which in the aggregate do a business that is quite a credit to our town. We refer to the art pottery started by the Sampson Bros.,[13] and the china decorating business conducted by Miss Mae Johnson....In china decorating Miss Johnson has been doing a large business shipping her goods to over 100 customers all over the western states. Some eight or ten hands have been employed the past three months, the last orders being dispatched this week. In this work she has used over

$300 worth of gold alone. The work turned out by her is said to be equal to any to be found on the market...."

The output of "eight or ten hands" painting china for three months would have been substantial. Moreover, in 1894, $300 worth of china decorator's gold packets would also have gilded a great quantity of china. Although Pickard was not given local recognition for his part in Mae Johnson's success, this may have been by agreement, since she sold locally on a direct basis and also through an Edgerton department store.

The relationship between Mae Johnson and Wilder Pickard was quite close in 1894, and on December 28, after their Christmas orders were complete, Mae Johnson traveled to Chicago to attend Pickard's marriage to Minnie Verna Flood.

Pickard probably originated his first trademark in mid-1894 (Mark 1): a 13/32" circle with "EDGERTON" and "HAND PAINTED" reversed out of a red band and "PICKARD" in red across the center. However, this mark was never fired on a piece of china. The marks in both Platt's book and this book were taken from the same copy: a small strip of paper apparently cut from a letterhead.

## *The Flood Home 1895–1897*

In the early 1890s Pickard lived at a boarding house on Dearborn Street, and in 1893, his widowed sister, Anna Atkins, had moved down from Milwaukee to live with him. But after his marriage, Pickard moved back into the Flood family home with his new wife.

From this location, in 1895, he undertook to establish a Chicago version of the Edgerton Art Studio. Whether the long-distance arrangement with Mae Johnson had proved unwieldy or whether the seasonal periods of inactivity prevented her from holding her decorating staff together is open to speculation. But clearly her studio of "eight or ten hands" lasted only one year. Having labored to establish the "Edgerton" name, however, Pickard continued to use the red label in Chicago through 1897. The three known examples of this mark are paper labels. One of the pieces, a jardiniere, is on display in the Pickard, Inc. Museum (Plate 2), another piece is in the author's collection (Plate 1). Both items are signed by the Chicago artist, F. Loba. (Loba worked for Pickard into the 1905–1910 trademark period and then later worked for Stouffer

Studios.) The third piece is in a private collection and is described as an unsigned "squatty" handled pitcher in mauve, decorated with mauve flowers with no resemblance to other Pickard styles.

Although Art Institute students were more plentiful in Chicago than they had been in Edgerton, Pickard could afford a "studio" of no more than a kiln on the third floor of the Flood home. All of his artists were thus "cottage workers" who had to be supplied and directed from outside. No examples of these students' work have been discovered, but given the use of the "Edgerton" paper label, identification would have been lost with the first few washings.

Pickard had to spend much of his time on the road selling, and thus, from the very beginning, the business was a family enterprise. Minnie Pickard's father and brothers contributed their assistance in their spare time, delivering china blanks to the artists' homes, picking up the finished product, carrying the china up to the third floor, firing it, and then carrying it to the basement to pack and ship it.

Business was undoubtedly very cyclical, however. In 1895 and 1896, Minnie Pickard and her mother spent their summers in Marshall, Wisconsin with Pickard's mother; Wilder would pay occasional visits. Summer business was obviously so slow that Minnie's presence in Chicago was not required.

Mae Johnson seems to have assisted Pickard with his Christmas orders in his first year in the Flood home. The December 13, 1895, *Wisconsin Tobacco Reporter* offered this comment:

"Miss Mae Johnson is home from Chicago where she has been for several months employed with a china decorating firm."

Although the firm is not mentioned by name, and even though Pickard did not claim to be a china decorating firm until 1898, the timing for Christmas orders would have been appropriate. If nothing else, it is obvious that she no longer was producing china for Pickard out of an Edgerton studio.

Mae Johnson was probably not a factor in Wilder Pickard's business after 1895, but a few final notes on her might be of interest: After 1894 there is no further mention of her china classes or studio, and by 1896, she was the only china decorator listed in Edgerton. She did continue to decorate for local trade as an individual, and in the fall of 1896, her reputation was such that she was named judge of the china painting exhibit at the Wisconsin State Fair. In that year, she began to spend an increasing amount of time in the company of Elmer Wilt, the son of a Chicago luggage dealer. On October 28, 1898, they were married in a simple ceremony in her mother's home in Edgerton. Pickard did not attend the wedding, possibly because there was no longer any commerce between them, but perhaps also because Minnie Pickard was expecting their first child in December. Subsequent to their wedding, the Wilts took up residence in Chicago where Elmer Wilt eventually became vice president of the family business. No examples of Mae Johnson's work are known to exist, with the possible exceptions of the piece shown in Figure 4, and a poorly executed lemonade pitcher signed "Wilt '06."

*Figure 4. Celery or olive dish signed "M. Johnson" on a T&V Limoges blank.*

Pickard's efforts at earning a living during 1895 and 1896 can only be surmised, for the country was deep in the throes of another depression. The World's Columbian Exposition of 1893 had drawn thousands to Chicago with a promise of a new age of prosperity. But that August, when the fair was at its height, another financial panic sent a devastating shock through the economy. To many, it seemed as though the fair itself was to blame, and as late as 1897, the now four-year-old depression prompted the editor of *The China Decorator* magazine to lament:

> "Everybody who could do so went to the Fair; many spent every dollar they could spare, and more, and others borrowed money for the expenses...and after it was over and good business was expected the great sums of money which were put in circulation seemed to have vanished, and

instead of a great improvement on trade the condition was duller than ever."

Against this background, on April 27, 1897, Pickard wrote to his wife from a hotel in Peoria:

> "...Tell everyone that business is very quiet in the country and that merchants at present are absolutely doing no business at all....."

Following the standard practice of the itinerant "drummer" of those days, he was traveling the railroad routes, "making"[14] every whistle-stop on the Illinois prairies. The professional drummer was easily distinguished from the locals by his city clothes, and his arrival in the smaller towns was often an important event, since he was the source of the latest news. To defray the cost of getting to towns with no rail service, a drummer would often rent a horse and wagon in cooperation with several fellow-drummers. Above all, the drummer was expected to have a good repertoire of jokes, and many a sales call was begun with their recitation. For Pickard, calling on these small towns meant soliciting business from what today would seem very unlikely customers. In the afternoon of the same day his letter continues:

> "...On Train for Pekin - I made a quick snack and got off for the 4.20 train to Pekin. If I don't succeed in interesting the grocery man in Pekin will leave at 7.25 PM for Delavan...."

At this point he was selling an assortment of art goods, including water-color paintings, glassware, and hand-painted china. It is important to note that he still did not regard china as his major line. He claimed "glassware" (he was said to have represented Fostoria) as his line of business in 1897.

Despite the pessimism in his letter, Pickard's business had grown considerably. He now had at least two other "commercial travelers" working for him, and one of them, Frank F. Baggerley, would continue to sell for him for more than twenty years.

At home, Minnie Pickard was very active, running the Chicago end of the business. In this same letter, her husband instructs her to order more stationery, have some water colors framed, evaluate an artist's work, have some art ware photographed, and run a credit check on a Peoria customer (he did make at least one sale that day).

But the poor conditions of which he wrote were about to end. That fall, a record American harvest coincided with a poor harvest in Europe and India, and as grain flowed overseas, gold poured back into the U.S. Treasury in unprecedented amounts. By October of 1897, the depression was over, and Pickard began to build his china-decorating business in earnest.

## The Pickard Home 1898–1903

The timing for Pickard's new focus could not have been more appropriate: *House Beautiful* had just begun publication in Chicago in 1896, offering guidance to the homemaker on interior decoration and the elements of tasteful design. The Chicago Arts and Crafts Society had just been established with such notables as Frank Lloyd Wright included in its membership. And the Art Institute and Hull House were offering classes and lectures in this new wave of arts and crafts.

There were a number of large Chicago wholesale and retail firms that maintained china-decorating departments in the 1890s. Burley & Tyrrell, Pitkin & Brooks, the Western Decorating Works, and the Chicago China Decorating Company all produced hand-painted china, but they tended to concentrate on utilitarian ware, complete dinner settings, and institutional crockery. Independent decorators like the members of the Atlan Ceramic Arts Club produced exquisite decorated china, but the pieces were generally made to order, and the individual artists were neither interested in, nor capable of handling, a volume trade. (In the 1910–1912 period, Pickard paid the Atlan Club a significant compliment by naming one of Edward Donisch's patterns after them: ATLAN ENAMEL.)

His years as a manufacturers' representative had shown Pickard that a middleman's profit in fine cut glass and other goods offered meager satisfaction for his ambitions for the future. But selling for the Pauline Pottery had given him a view of the specialty artware market that the larger firms substantially ignored. His limited activities in hand-painted china had already demonstrated that the real profits were in the "fancy china" portion of the market. Fancy china was the elaborately decorated vases, punch bowls, berry bowls, chargers, nut sets, dresser sets, tea and coffee sets whose first requisite was ornament and which served as a reflection of the owner's taste and social status. The larger firms could have the dinnerware that

was stacked away in pantries and cupboards, Pickard's china would be displayed on sideboards, plate rails, and in glass cases. His success, however, would require a better quality of decoration and closer control over production than he had been able to achieve thus far.

The work of the independent professionals and skillful amateurs notwithstanding, amateur decoration ranging from poor to terrible was plentiful. Pickard's own art students had probably challenged his salesmanship with inferior examples of their own upon occasion. And since the overwhelming majority of china decorators were women, the use of female artists, of whatever level of skill, created a stigma in those times.

As early as 1897 and probably even in 1896, he had begun to replace his art students with male professionals who were willing to work on a cottage labor basis. Only three decorators have thus far been identified with the 1896–1897 period: Loba, whose signature appears on the aforementioned Edgerton-labeled pieces; Edward W. Donath, a young Bavarian immigrant; and Erhardt Seidel, who had come from Germany in 1888, and is said to have started with Pickard about 1896.

These men were typical of the skilled artists among Chicago's huge population of European immigrants. Chicago's original settlers had been families that had moved west from the eastern states, but this original population had been overwhelmed by the great waves of European immigration that began with the Germans and Irish in the 1850s. By the late 1890s, *three-fourths* of Chicago's 1.7 million people were either foreign-born or children of foreign-born parents,[15] and among them were men who had served their apprenticeships in the potteries, china factories, and ateliers of Germany, Poland, Russia, Italy, France, and England. Many of them spoke little or no English and initially were forced to work as laborers; some were very young, but many of them already had families to support. And from among them, Pickard gradually began to form a core of decorators that could produce commercial-quality hand-painted china.

In 1898 the building in which the Floods lived was converted into a nurses' residence, and Pickard and his wife moved half a block away to a home at 316 North LaSalle Street.[16] Pickard then took out his first classified directory listing under "China Decorators" to identify his exclusive concentration on hand-painted china. Although he advertised himself as a china decorator from this date forward, Pickard never did any decorating personally, claiming that he had insufficient skill to connect two dots with a straight line. But this was fortunate, for had he tried to decorate china and simultaneously build a successful business, much of the artistry of the hundreds of decorators whom he eventually employed would never have come to life.

Minnie Pickard, however, did have artistic talent. In addition to raising a family, supervising much of the business detail while her husband was traveling, and keeping the company's books, she somehow also found time to become an accomplished china decorator. She had studied oil painting as a young girl and then had studied china painting just before her marriage, and though none of her earliest work has been identified, her pieces from the 1903–1905 and 1905–1910 periods show a proficient, confident hand. Raised gold paste and violet designs (Plate 398) were among her specialties, but she also did very well with classical fruit and flower themes (Plate 84).

As stated earlier, Pickard's widowed sister, Anna Atkins, had moved down from Milwaukee in 1893. She and her daughter, Myrtle, were teachers and they had boarded with him for several years before his marriage. Anna described herself as a lecturer during that time, but she is missing from the records in 1898 and 1899. This was undoubtedly the period during which she studied art history in France, for by 1900 she had revised her occupation to that of an "Art Lecturer." Also by this date, she and her daughter were boarding with the Pickards and their baby son.

This living arrangement will be viewed as cramped and cumbersome against today's standards, but it was quite usual at the time, and it facilitated Anna's contributions to the success of her brother's business. In an age when itinerant peddlers were almost exclusively men, she proved to be a very effective saleswoman, and much of her time from 1900 onward was spent on the road. More important, however, was her assumption of the studio's art direction. This was a badly needed function that quickly differentiated Pickard from his competitors, giving his china that "Pickard look" which any collector can recognize today. During this time, she also managed to give her brother an informal art education through visits to the Art Institute and Marshall Field's. Seeing art through his sister's eyes not only gave him an appreciation of its intrinsic beauty, but it also

emboldened him to offer untried and even radical designs to his customers and to allow his artists to experiment with departures from their own norms.

The majority of the designs in the 1898–1903 period were responsive to contemporary tastes, however. The public's current penchant for naturalistic fruits and flowers rendered in traditional formats drew on the old-country talents of such artists as Anton Beutlich, Joseph Blaha, and Erhardt Seidel.

Fruit decorations included peaches and pears with a generous pink blush on them (Plate 118), cherries hung in sprays of green leaves, grapes (Plate 205) or red and black raspberries amid variegated autumn leaves, and of course the ubiquitous red currants on their dark maroon background (Plate 16).

Among flower subjects, roses had a particular appeal, and many variations made their appearance. Emil Aulich was considered one of the country's most outstanding china decorators, having operated his own studio in Cincinnati, and then teaching china decorating in New York City. His specialty was roses, and those he executed for Pickard are among his finest (Plate 248). Thomas M. Jelinek (Plate 5) was noted for his life-like blooms emerging from soft backgrounds of leaves and stems. Violets were among the easier flowers to execute and were produced in considerable quantity on a great variety of blanks. But poppies, geraniums, tulips, nasturtiums, lilies, and many less-distinguishable flowers were also popular.

These early designs frequently incorporated a wide gold border embellished with red or black line drawings of the leaves, vines, or blossoms that appeared in the main body of the decoration. Some of the earliest pieces also carried rococo-style scrolls and lattices. The Bohemian love of color was often apparent in blue or lavender highlighting on the gold scroll work and was further emphasized by white paste in the form of decorative dots on flower stamens.

Robert Hessler's poppy design (Plate 18) typified a popular theme and style of the period. Born in Pennsylvania of German parents, Hessler demonstrated considerable creativity and versatility. In his long career with Pickard, he produced many of the studio's best-selling designs.

Many pieces reflected the influence of Art Nouveau, and Hessler's versatility was evident in his nasturtium design (Plate 17) with its narcissistic twining of the vines and broad exposures of leaves and petals.

Two of the most notable designs to appear late in this period were Frederick Lindner's IRIS CONVENTIONAL (Plates 30, 33) and TULIP CONVENTIONAL (Plate 32). They were more stylizations than true conventionalizations, but they were important because they represented a significant departure from naturalism. The public obviously agreed with this new treatment for these designs lasted well into the teens; another version, NEW IRIS CONVENTIONAL (Plates 31, 100), became even more popular. Another dimension of Pickard's subject matter that began in this period and which until recently was little appreciated is that of human, animal, and landscape subjects. Although a number of Pickard's floral artists also produced non-floral work (Gasper, Challinor, Campana, and Seidel to name a few), artists like Aldrich, Edgerton, and Grane seem to have been devoted almost exclusively to such work.

There is every indication that a considerable volume of these subjects was produced; unfortunately very few examples have survived. Tankards and mugs that portrayed monks in various activities, along with Falstaff were the most popular subjects. But chargers, vases, and trays featured such animals as hunting dogs, lions, tigers, moose, and elk. Landscapes, and seascapes that pictured Venice, the Egyptian pyramids, and (later) Dutch canals appeared on vases, mugs, plaques, and plates. Vases picturing Arabs, American Indians, and female subjects were also very popular. Of all these, the female subjects have a special attraction, particularly when they are portrayed in an Art Nouveau style (Plates 23, 60). These rarely found subjects are highly prized by collectors today.

In 1898 Pickard developed his first Chicago trademark, the largest version of the familiar double circle mark (Mark 2). Most firms chose inexpensive rubber stamps or even hand lettering with which to identify their wares. With the exception of a very rare dark brown stamp that was possibly an "out-of-stock" expedient or the original Chicago "start-up" mark (Mark 1.1) and the short-lived 1903 red stamp (Mark 3), this and all succeeding marks through 1922 were paper transfers or decals. It was a small detail, but the decal's uniform size and legibility were an early reflection of Pickard's penchant for quality.

Quality was also evident in the china blanks that Pickard imported. He chose French blanks from the many porcelain factories at Limoges for the majority of his output in these years, possibly through a predilection stemming from his French ancestry, but certainly because of their translucence and delicacy. Although frequent choices included Tressemann & Vogt (T&V), Jean Pouyat (J. P. L.), and Haviland, the majority of the Limoges factories are represented. (Statistics for the year 1900 illustrate America's huge appetite for porcelain: in that year alone, the 35 factories operating in Limoges shipped *18,000 barrels* of decorated and blank porcelain to the United States!)[17] The great variety of Limoges marks on Pickard's china indicates that purchases were probably brokered through an import house from whatever French factory had the most competitive prices at the time. This method also permitted Pickard to offer a very wide variety of blank styles—far wider than any individual French or German competitor. Along with the French blanks, Pickard also purchased some German, Austrian, and Bavarian ware. Some American potteries are also represented in pieces from Syracuse China and two Trenton potteries, Willets Manufacturing Company and the Ceramic Art Company. A 1903 ledger from the latter company lists the studios of Pickard, Fry, Gross, and Sinclaire as customers along with some famous individual decorators of the time: Lycett, Vance-Phillips, Brouwer, Callowhill, and Filkins.[18]

Quality was most apparent in Pickard's generous application of gold. Unlike the thin, brassy golds found on many Japanese imports, Pickard insisted on two coats (and thus two firings) of 24 karat gold. The colors of the various designs were thus set off with a deep, rich gold that imparted warmth and elegance to the finished piece.

Pickard's new home at 316 LaSalle Street was a 25-foot wide, two-family rowhouse which he also listed as his business location through 1902. With his family of five, plus another family of three with two live-in servants occupying the building, there obviously was still no studio space for artists. But Pickard gradually acquired the use of a number of nearby horse barns—none of them larger than today's two-car garage—from which a fragmented studio began to evolve. Although the additional space added capacity and flexibility, much cottage work was undoubtedly still necessary to meet the rapidly growing demand for Pickard's new designs.

But the continuation of the cottage-worker arrangement, while essential, also worked against him, because from among the more entrepreneurial artists, Pickard was involuntarily creating some of his future competition. To function, each artist had to have a studio in his own living quarters, and for most, this was quite literally the kitchen table. Not a few of them also acquired a small kiln which also required no more than a table-top. Connected to a nearby gas fixture with a length of "India rubber" hose, the kiln could be set up or stored in a closet as needed.

The only remaining step to an independent studio was distribution. The majority of artists stopped short of a venture into commercial selling and were content to peddle small quantities of home-fired pieces to friends or a nearby store. But for some, the lure of independence and more income was irresistible.

Before his business was six years old, Pickard saw two of his best artists depart to establish significant competing studios: Edward W. Donath set up his own studio in 1897, and Julius H. Brauer established a studio in 1903. (It actually took Donath two tries: he had a studio in the Chicago Loop initially, but he returned to Pickard in 1903 before permanently establishing a studio in 1905.) Each of these studios in turn, spawned an additional studio. The chart in Appendix A illustrates the evolution of the more prominent Chicago china decorating studios. In addition to this direct competition, almost every year Pickard saw a number of his artists migrate to another studio.

But if Pickard was an incubator for other Chicago studios, the potteries at Trenton, New Jersey, were an incubator for Pickard. Ott & Brewer had been formed in 1865, Willets Manufacturing Company was established in 1879, and Walter Scott Lenox had founded the Ceramic Art Company in 1889 (to be renamed Lenox in 1906). The Trenton potteries had attracted artists and potters for decades to the point that by 1898, with no less than 38 potteries in operation, the city was often referred to as "The Little Staffordshire."

Typical of Pickard's recruits from Trenton was Maxwell Rean Klipphahn. Max Klipphahn had come to America from Dresden, Germany, in 1893. He had been working as a potter in Trenton for two years when in the spring of 1900, at age 33, he moved to Chicago with his wife and two small children to become one of Pickard's most accomplished artists. His move may have been in response to one of Pickard's advertisements in a ceramic journal, but it also may have resulted from "grapevine" information that circulated among immigrant artists in those days.

This bond among china decorators meant that, although they would be strangers to Pickard, they were not necessarily strangers to each other. Among the later arrivals from the Trenton potteries would be Dominick M. Campana (1902), Edward S. Challinor (1903), Joseph C. Beitler (1904), Samuel Heap (1905), and Paul P. Gasper (1905)[19]; it would not end until the arrival of designer John Eustice from Lenox in the 1960s.

As the business expanded, Pickard gradually rented additional nearby horse barns, and one can imagine the constant traffic among them as china was moved about in various stages of completion. Initially, many of the artists chose to live nearby; between 1898 and 1904 there were 17 artists within a 10 block radius of 316 LaSalle. Every year, more artists elected to live farther away, however, and with almost all of them male, cottage labor pick-ups and deliveries were probably abandoned before the turn of the century.

Another, and perhaps more critical aspect of the cottage labor arrangement, was that it was impossible to monitor any of the lesser-talented artists' work-in-process. As a result, some rather poor work became mixed with the very good work. H. C. Dickinson and F. A. Cathanay were short-term artists whose poorly defined flowers and ill-chosen colors did Pickard no credit. These lesser talents notwithstanding, Pickard continued to add accomplished, professional china decorators to his cadre of talent during this period, and some of them would remain with him for the better part of their careers.

*Figure 5. E. Challinor & Co. platter with blue paper transfer of lake and castle.*

Among these artists, the most notable was Edward S. Challinor. Challinor was descended from a family of Staffordshire potters, beginning with his grandfather, Edward, who began making transfer-printed earthenware in 1853 under the name of E. Challinor & Co. (Fig. 5). In 1862 the firm was succeeded by E. & C. Challinor & Co., and in 1891 it became C. Challinor & Co. that operated through 1896.[20]

Edward S. Challinor was born in 1877. He visited the family pottery many times as a youngster and is said to have begun his apprenticeship at age seventeen. He may have served his first two years with the family business until it closed, but it is known that he served an apprenticeship with the Royal Doulton Potteries in Burslem. He also studied at the Newcastle School of Arts in Staffordshire, which was an auxiliary of the South Kensington School of Art in London, but whether this came before or after his work at Doulton is uncertain. He married in 1899, and early in 1903, he left his wife and two-year-old daughter in England to seek employment in America. He intended to live with an uncle and aunt, John and Hannah Challinor, who lived just outside Trenton, New Jersey, in the village of Slackwood. However, upon his arrival, he discovered that his uncle had died so he only worked for a very brief time at the Willets Manufacturing Company. Just one piece from his stay at Willets is known: a vase in a mirror-image peacock design reminiscent of the etched gold and peacock designs he would later produce for Pickard.[21]

By late spring of that year, Challinor had moved to Chicago and was decorating china for Pickard; he apparently saw a good future with the studio, for his wife and daughter crossed the ocean and joined him before the year was out.

Edward Challinor was a very happy, if somewhat reserved man, very patient, and like many of Pickard's artists, his talents were not confined to china decoration. He was an accomplished musician, having been the organist at his Methodist church in England. He had a fine voice and he was a good actor; he took part in the Gilbert and Sullivan operetta performances of the local Opera and Drama Club. Sunday evening musicales in the Challinor home often included other artists.

His arrival coincided with the termination of the 1898–1903 trademark; his signature on items bearing this mark is therefore infrequent. Among the first pieces which Challinor produced for Pickard was a series of bird plates, showing species from his native England (Plates 38–40).

Because of his considerable skill and prolific output, Challinor tends to overshadow other artists. His pieces consistently bring higher prices despite the lesser quality of workmanship that the occasional piece may display. Pickard, Inc. maintains an extremely high level of quality control today, but in those early years Wilder Pickard allowed his artists to give seconds to family or friends, and many of those seconds have survived to appear on today's antique market.

It has been stated that Challinor mixed his own colors, that he never passed the secret on to others, and that the formulas died with him. All of this is undoubtedly true, but it should be understood that all china painters were obliged to mix their own colors. The colors were most commonly available as vials of mineral powders (Fig.6)—as opposed to being squeezed from a tube like oil paints. Most artists had their favorite or secret combinations. However, what was ultimately important was the net result, and Challinor became a master of the china decorating medium, especially in his later pastel-colored scenics.

*Figure 6. China decorating kit sold by D. M. Campana with mineral paint powders and graphite-coated transfer paper. Instruction books and transfer outlines of designs were available from many sources.*

### *Artists active in 1898–1903*

| | |
|---|---|
| Grace M. Aldrich | Farrington |
| Emil Aulich | Grane |
| Joseph C. Beitler | Charles Hahn |
| Anton B. Beutlich | Frank H. Hanisch |
| Walter Bitterly | Robert Hessler |
| Joseph Blaha | Thomas M. Jelinek |
| Julius H. Brauer | Jacob I. Kiefus |
| A. Burton | Maxwell R. Klipphahn |
| Dominick M. Campana | F. Kriesche |
| F. A. Cathanay | Leon |
| Edward S. Challinor | M. Rost LeRoy |
| H. C. Dickinson | Frederick J. Lindner |
| Edward W. Donath | Loba |
| (William O.?) Edgerton | John Loh |

| Mark | Erhardt Seidel |
|------|----------------|
| Zuie McCorkle | Vetter |
| Andrew Motzfeldt | Jeremiah Vokral |
| John Nessy | Albert Wagner |
| Pietrykaski | Arthur J. Weiss |

## The Carriage Barn 1903–1905

By early 1903, the constraints of a scattered work force were substantially reduced as Pickard took full possession of his first studio. The studio was a converted carriage barn that had been built shortly after the 1871 Chicago Fire. It was the largest such building in the area, measuring 33 feet by 64 feet.[22] Records from 1900 show 16 people occupying three apartments in the carriage barn with occupancy continuing for more than another year. None of them were artists or decorators. It is possible that Pickard was able to lease some portion of the building before 1903, nevertheless he does not list this as a business address until late spring of 1903.

This date also coincides with the appearance of his next trademark, the $9/16"$ diameter circle (Mark 4). For a short time, early in 1903, Pickard used a trademark that retained the same wording but omitted the double circles (Mark 3). This was applied as a red rubber stamp, and was probably an interim expedient while the new 1903–1905 decals were being printed. Very few pieces bearing the 1903 mark have been discovered (Plates 40–42, 44–46).

The carriage barn was conveniently located at 98 Whiting Street, only eighty feet south of Pickard's rear gate where a stub of Whiting came to a dead end at Pickard's alley. Whiting has since become a continuation of Walton Street, and neither this stub nor any of the buildings on that block have survived.

Freed from the constraints of pickup and delivery, Pickard began to draw upon artists from all over the city, transportation time now being the concern of the artist, not the studio. This new location allowed the artists some true studio space, and it permitted some economies of scale that were essential to Pickard's growth. Barrels of china could be imported directly from the factories at Limoges, or could qualify for volume discounts from Thayer & Chandler, A. H. Abbott, and the other art supply houses. With room for more kilns, a greater volume of china could be processed. And finally, it permit-ted faster, more efficient handling of the china from barrel to artist to kiln to packing and shipping.

Of all the advantages that the carriage barn provided, the greatest was the accommodation of more kilns. These kilns were larger versions of the gas-fired tabletop models used in home studios. With a number of kilns, the firings could be staggered to adjust to the flow of the artists' production and also allowed simultaneous firings at different temperatures. By contrast, the big porcelain manufacturers had to use large "beehive" kilns accommodating hundreds—and even thousands—of pieces. This great volume and the higher temperatures required days to heat and cool the kiln.

Because he was only firing mineral paint on ready-glazed porcelain, Pickard's kilns ran at lower temperatures and required only hours for their cycles. His workmen had but to open the doors of the muffle kilns and stack wares in place. The kilns were so-called because the flames were separated from the firing chamber by a "muffle" or wall of refractory material. Direct contact with the flames would have ruined the decorations.

In 1903 the country suffered another panic, but this time it was largely confined to financial circles. As a consequence, Pickard saw no more than a mild recession and even this was probably offset by the benefits of his more efficient production. The years at the carriage barn, therefore, were a time of rapid and profitable growth.

His decorations began to take on more individuality in this period, and along with this came a widening variety of styles. Art Nouveau elements appeared in the whiplash curves and borders applied by Loba, Motzfeldt, and Challinor, and his first truly conventionalized pattern appeared. CORNFLOWER CONVENTIONAL (1), attributed to Joseph Yeschek about 1904 (Plate 168), was a great success and was followed very shortly by CORNFLOWER CONVENTIONAL (2) (Plate 166).

Throughout the 1898–1912 period, Pickard often appended the adjective conventional to a pattern name. Conventionalization had been taught at the Art Institute under Louis J. Millet[23] as far back as 1886, and became highly developed in the output of the Atlan Ceramic Arts Club. In this technique, the artist sought to reduce the subject to its most elemental form, short of losing its differentiating characteristics. Pickard's designs, though they often employed the term, rarely warranted the adjective. For example, the initial version of Hessler's MODERN CONVENTIONAL (Plate 173), first appeared in the 1903–1905 period, and although it was very popular, it was neither a conventionalization nor was it modern; it was simply a good ornamental design.

Most designs were stylizations that combined fairly literal depictions in geometric placements. Such patterns as POINSETTIA AND LUSTRE (Plate 367) and EASTER LILY (Plate 184) were introduced in this period. These early stylizations were no less artful or pleasing for want of the conventionalizing technique, however.

As Pickard's designs proliferated and gained in popularity, they also attracted the unwanted attention of some of his competitors. He began to see copies and near-copies of his designs appear with the marks of other studios on them (see Pitkin & Brooks items in Plates 921 and 922). Starting in September of 1904, he attempted to block this practice by filing a series of patents on his artists' designs. Only six patents were issued (see patent section), and Pickard ceased to file by February of 1905. (The attorney whose name appears on the patents, George McCorkle, was Pickard's brother-in-law and a relative of Pickard artist, Zuie McCorkle.)

Patents have little value if they cannot be successfully defended, and in the case of a design patent, it was only necessary to change a few leaves or stems to make it a different design. By this time, Pickard was also in the process of moving into his new Ravenswood studio, and the patent filings may have proved more distraction than they were worth.

A few European china manufacturers also stamped their more popular shapes with their own design patents, so the two patent marks should not be confused; patent marks covering the china itself were applied under glaze and generally in green. Pickard-patented pieces were marked overglaze with a red rubber stamp in the format: DESIGN PAT FEB 28 05 No. 37352.

Although the incidence seems to have been infrequent, Pickard's artists were not entirely innocent of "adapting" the designs of other studios. One of the most popular Pickard designs of all time, AURA ARGENTA LINEAR, bears a strong resemblance to an early Mettlach pattern. The DUTCH DECORATION and ORANGE TREE ENAMEL designs both appeared as sample designs in *Keramic Studio* magazine and were thus intended to be copied directly or reproduced in modified form.

It was customary for china artists to sign their work, and this feature materially adds to the value and interest of the pieces that have survived today. Identification may appear as the last name, a contraction of the last name, a set of initials, or a cartouche of the initials. Some artists eventually Anglicized their names, either by dropping letters or by changing their names outright. For example, Emil J. T. Fischer signed his name "Fish" or "Fisher," Otto Schoner used both "Schoner" and "SHONER," and Falatek became "Falk."

For the most part the signature appears on the face of the piece, often blending in with the design so well that it may take careful study to find it. On handled pieces, the signature is most often found near the handle. Luster paints (paints with an iridescent quality) do not retain signatures as well as normal mineral paints. A strong light at the proper angle may occasionally reveal the vestiges of a signature on what appears to be an unsigned piece.

A few artists like Challinor and Comyn, not only signed the front and back of the piece, but also wrote comments on some of their designs.

A note should also be made here about authenticity. Pickard was very proud of his trademark, and his advertising invariably included his mark together with the words "None genuine without this mark" or "This trademark is on every piece." The mark was occasionally omitted on punch cups or cups or saucers in a coffee set (and breaking up such a set can thus do irreparable damage to their value and authenticity). Marks were also omitted when the *shape* of the china did not accommodate it, as in the case of the jardiniere in Plate 138 and the egg-shaped coffee pot in Plate 45. But an unmarked piece, advertised as Pickard—even though the pattern is identical to Pickard's, and it bears a Pickard artist's signature—should be regarded with the greatest skepticism. Virtually *every* artist—including such top artists as Challinor, Yeschek, Fuchs, and Marker—produced *and signed* unmarked freelance pieces which they sold on the side.

Pickard had no divisions or affiliates. Contrary to the claims of a few dealers, neither the Stouffer Studios nor the White Studios were ever divisions of Pickard. Nor should pieces which bear only the Osborne signature be considered unmarked Pickard. They are products of the Osborne Art Studio. As artists migrated among the many Chicago studios, they took their ideas and styles with them. Although there were some cases of plagiarism, the similarity of their work for other studios should not blur the individuality of those studios.

From the beginning of his career, Pickard's strength had been in selling, and it was his continuing focus on this aspect of the business that kept him well ahead of his competitors. Chicago was the nation's railroad hub, and Pickard's salesmen followed the routes of the major railroads, for this was not only the most efficient means of traveling between sales calls, it was also the most efficient means of shipping the china once the sale had been made. Pickard's strong distribution created a continually expanding demand for more volume and more designs. It also created a need for more artists.

These increases kept a steady pressure on Pickard's physical accommodations. The transfer of materials between the carriage barn and the other smaller barns had to have been a major impediment. He therefore began planning larger quarters almost as soon as he had taken full possession of the carriage barn.

### Artists active in 1903–1905

| | |
|---|---|
| Emil Aulich | F. Kriesche |
| Joseph C. Beitler | Emil Kubasch |
| F. Beulet | George P. Leach |
| Anton B. Beutlich | Walter R. Lemke |
| Edward S. Challinor | Leon |
| Arthur Comyn | M. Rost LeRoy |
| Anthony Coufall | Frederick J. Lindner |
| Edward W. Donath | Loba |
| L. Duran | John Loh |
| Farrington | Henry Marmorstein |
| Emil J. T. Fischer | Harry E. Michel |
| Fox | Andrew Motzfeldt |
| Friedrich | John Nessy |
| Fritz | E. Pfiefer |
| John Fuchs | Minnie Verna Pickard |
| Paul P. Gasper | Otto Podlaha |
| Edward Gibson | C. Pohl |
| Nathan R. Gifford | F. Post |
| Otto W. Goess | Howard B. Reury |
| Grane | Harry Roden |
| Harry R. Griffiths | Max Rost |
| Charles Hahn | A. Roy |
| Samuel Heap | Otto Schoner |
| Robert Hessler | Erhardt Seidel |
| Florence M. James | George Sinclair |
| Thomas M. Jelinek | George W. Stahl |
| Alfred Keates | Harry E. Tolley |
| Jacob I. Kiefus | Rudolph Tomascheko |
| Maxwell R. Klipphahn | Vetter |
| F. H. Koep | Franz Vobornik |

| | |
|---|---|
| Jeremiah Vokral | Arthur J. Weiss |
| Albert H. Wagner | Joseph T. Yeschek |

## *The Ravenswood Studio 1905–1910*

Pickard planned his next move on a grand scale. He decided to build his own studio in the Ravenswood area of what was then the sparsely built far north end of Chicago. The tract that he selected was at 1500 East Ravenswood Park (4853 North Ravenswood Avenue today), just north of Lawrence Avenue and facing the Chicago and Northwestern Railway tracks.

*Photo courtesy H. Poulos.*

*Figure 7. Ravenswood Studios as it appeared in the early 1920s.*

The new building consisted of three floors and a full basement. In the front of the first floor were the business offices, complete with a walk-in safe. Behind the offices were a supply area, shelves of finished goods, and a shipping department. To ensure against contamination and also because of the acids employed, a separate room was provided for the reduction of gold leaf into a number of different gilding formulas. (Reducing gold on the premises saved the mark-up inherent in commercially prepared vials

*Figure 8. Kiln room at Ravenswood Studios c.1907.*

were received and unpacked. Another area allowed for washing, applying the trademark, and storing the china blanks prior to decoration. A large dumbwaiter measuring about five feet square connected the basement with all the floors and facilitated movement of the china throughout the building.

Initially, the studio stood alone on a large plot, but an L-shaped apartment building was added to the south in the next few years, creating a wide, open court. Pickard also built another apartment building a few blocks farther south at Wilson and Ravenswood—the building still bears his name in large bas-relief letters. There has been some speculation that these buildings were erected for the express convenience of the artists, in the fashion of some of the European communes. Records show no more than one or two artists living in either building at any time, however. Pickard also had a strong interest in real estate, and the buildings were simply another investment.

Although the exact month of the start-up at Ravenswood is unknown, there is conclusive evidence that Pickard was operating out of his new building by May of 1905. For the first time, his studio was equipped with a telephone, and also for the first time, he purchased a display ad in the city directory. At the same time, he had also moved his personal residence to the vicinity of the new studio, permitting him to continue to walk to work every day.

and packets. It also enabled Pickard to formulate special blends of the very rich gilding for which he had become famous.) At the rear of the first floor was the kiln room, and next to it was a room reserved for burnishing gold. (Any glass burnishing fibers that were blown onto a palette or settled on china would melt in a subsequent firing and ruin the decoration. Strict isolation and careful cleaning were therefore essential.)

The second and third floors were devoted to studio space. Each artist was given a window along the north or south wall, with the best locations being those with the north light. Each location was U-shaped and included space for a banding wheel (for applying gold bands and stripes), space for a palette (generally a sheet of glass laid flat on the work table), and considerable table space to accommodate the china in its various stages of completion. Some low-temperature ovens were situated in the center of the second floor and were used to accelerate the drying of the painted china prior to firing.

A display room was located in the front of the basement, and it was here that Anna Atkins reviewed new designs prior to their release for production. At the rear of the basement was an area where the barrels of china

*Figure 9. Anna Atkins reviewing china designs in the lower level of the Ravenswood Studios c.1905. (Note large number of plaques and figural pieces.)*

The opening of the new studio also warranted a new trademark—yet a smaller version of the two prior double circle marks (Mark 5). Applied as a brown ¹³⁄₃₂" diameter decal, this is the most commonly found mark today.

Pickard's move farther north did cause some of the carriage barn artists to reconsider the extra time required to get to work. Coincidentally, Jacob H. Stouffer was opening his first china decorating studio on South Lake Park Avenue that same year, and south side artists Joseph Blaha, Samuel Heap, Thomas Jelinek, Jacob Kiefus, and Harry Michel all eventually left Pickard for Stouffer's more convenient location.

But the Ravenswood Studio was not just a larger building with more space and resources, although

of a commercial product? Say you wish to establish a China Painting Studio.... You purchase stock and send to the Art Institute for decorators. This is easy—so far; there are art students a plenty...You pay good wages—that isn't enough. You put a "boss" over him—no, that doesn't work. You experiment a little. You go to Ravenswood and find a quiet spot where nature still lingers about and build there a studio—that helps some. You share your profits with the workers—that helps too. You create an atmosphere of good fellowship through clubs, benefit associations and recreation grounds, put every man and woman on honor to work to the best of his

*Figure 10. Artists and staff of Ravenswood Studio, taken late fall of 1905. Back row: Wilder A. Pickard (48) ———, Mr. Hardwick, Edward S. Challinor (28), ———, ———, William Flood (68), right of center, in light hat, clean shaven, Edward Gibson (22), 5th from the right Joseph T. Yeschek (38), 3rd from the right Maxwell R. Klipphahn (37), 2nd from right Anton B. Beutlich (34). 2nd Row: 3rd from left Robert Hessler (33), Minnie V. Pickard (37) next to him. John Fuchs (37) third from right. Bottom row: Otto Schoner. John Anton "Tony" Coufall second from right.*

Photo courtesy S. Shellenbach.

these had to have constituted a major attraction for the artists. Even more important, was the social environment which Pickard now offered his employees. He described it in part in a 1905 brochure:

### *"Pickard" Is a Synonym of Excellence*

"There is a reason for this—a reason in part artistic and in part sociological. Have you ever thought under what conditions artistic excellence is achieved in the case

or her ability, recognize and award talent, encourage originality and the expression of individuality. Now you have found the secret. Look at the china and see the proof; the finest china ware in the market...."

It will be remembered that the bitter Chicago labor riots at the Pullman Works were only 11 years in the past, and much of the nation's working class still labored under oppressive conditions. By contrast, Pickard seemed determined to provide every social amenity that was within his power to bestow. The emoluments mentioned in his brochure—the profit-sharing, the clubs, the recreation facilities—were no mere advertising puffery. Nor was all this a temporary experiment. In the late teens Gustav Hiecke's son, Herbert, recalls his parents taking him downtown to buy new clothes with his father's profit share, and John Fuch's daughter, Tillie, remembers the Christmas parties at the studio to which all the employees and their families were invited. Though certainly not as idyllic (and as costly) as the Arts and Crafts community at William Morris's Merton Abbey, Pickard probably derived much inspiration from that artistic and social experiment.

Some of his social philosophy may also have been the product of the cottage labor years: his artists had worked well with little supervision in those days, it would seem redundant and unnecessarily expensive to now add a foreman over men and women who had already demonstrated their ability to work independently. (This practice did end later when Joseph Yeschek was made the first shop foreman.)

Typically, a professional china decorator could work at the Ravenswood Studio without any more supervision than the periodic evaluation of his new designs. Once approved, he would fill orders for those designs as they came in from the sales department. If his designs were very popular, he was free to sub-contract his work and collect an over-ride on the orders he could not fill himself. Thus, artists who had fewer orders for their own work would still have steady employment. This practice is evident in the variety of signatures appearing on the same design. Some designs grew substantially in popularity and volume, and a number of artists were hired to do sub-contract work almost exclusively.

During this period, advertising assumed significant proportions. Expensive little brochures with tipped-on color reproductions of various designs were offered to dealers for their clientele. Dealers were offered free advertising copy for their local newspaper, along with cards and catalogs. Pickard was enjoying a good trade in Chicago with Marshall Field's, and the store's seasonal advertisements in the *Chicago Tribune* featured the latest designs. Of most interest was the national advertising which Pickard placed in the *Ladies Home Journal* (see advertisement section for complete listing). For the most part, these ads ran in the early winter and late spring to capitalize on the Christmas and wedding seasons.

Pickard reaped the most from his advertising with some innovative marketing. Promotions included such offers as a free assortment of china for the month of December, after which the shipment would be payable, but any unsold pieces—up to half the assortment—could be returned for credit. Stores could qualify as "exclusive selling agent" for a certain trading area and all responses to advertising from that area were then referred to that agent.

In the spring of 1909 a multi-page catalog of 120 items incorporating several color pages made its appearance (see advertisement section). The variety of designs that were illustrated reflect Pickard's earlier claim of over 1000 designs available through 1000 stores. While most advertising of this period was given to hyperbole, this claim was probably quite accurate, as evidenced today by the continual surfacing of additional designs.

If there was a high period for Pickard's hand-painted china, the 1902–1918 period was certainly that. Which is not to say that there were not numerous outstanding examples on either side of this period. But the sheer volume of diverse designs and the number of top artists employed in these years had no prior or subsequent equivalent. Pickard's advertising in May, 1906 boasted a staff of artists that was, "the largest in America (which) includes about fifty men," and a count of individuals in the 1905 group photo (Fig. 10) does show 49 people. This does not allow for secretaries, clerks, kiln-burners, and stockmen however, and six months later the advertising had backed off to "over forty men."

Regardless of which number was correct, the new studio continued to require more artists, and advertisements in the ceramic journals attracted men from many eastern states. Typical of these artists were John Fuchs and Max Bachmann.

The Fuchs and Bachmann families moved to Chicago early in 1905 from Zanesville, Ohio, where the two men had been employed as decorators at the Roseville Pottery. (So just a few of their pieces bear the 1903–1905 mark.) Bachmann worked for Pickard for about two years and then moved over to the Julius H. Brauer Studio (see biographical details in that section).

Fuchs, however, spent the rest of his career at Pickard. He had been born into a family of 13 children in 1867 in Austria and emigrated to the United States in 1889. Professionally trained in Austria, he worked in New Bedford, Massachusetts, through 1895 as a glass decorator for the Mount Washington Glass Company, just as it was merged into Pairpoint. A brother, Edward, also decorated glass with him in 1892 and 1893. (Arthur Cumming was painting oils and teaching art, and Joseph Yeschek, and Nathan Gifford were decorating glass in New Bedford at this time, and it is possible that Fuchs first made their acquaintance here.) Fuchs obtained his citizenship papers in October of 1895, and then moved on to other decorating jobs in Boston, Philadelphia, and eventually, Zanesville.

Fuchs was both proficient and versatile. He executed fruit and flower subjects (Plate 373) in the formats characteristic of the turn of the century with a free and confident hand. But his distinctive skill and imagination came to the surface when he departed from the norm with stylized and conventionalized interpretations. Using a limited palette and combining floral and geometric themes—often embellished with paste work—he produced some of the best and most popular designs of the period.

Pickard Studios shut down over Christmas, and during this time the artists were expected to produce new designs for the sales department. Fuchs' daughter remembers the Christmas parties given for all the employees, but she also remembers her father working very hard over the holidays to produce new designs. Some of the designs would not be accepted or the design would have to be modified. These experimental pieces would usually be given to friends or family members. As older generations passed away these pieces, which were often signed, made their way into the antique market, hence their Pickard-like appearance without a trademark.

Like other china artists, John Fuchs also produced freelance pieces at home. His wife, Elise, handled these private sales

and developed a number of regular customers. Pickard artist Joseph Yeschek was a good friend and had his own kiln in a little building in the rear of his yard, and Fuchs used this kiln to fire his freelance pieces.

It is not known what income Fuchs derived from the combination of his Pickard and freelance work (artist Otto Podlaha's highest wage in the teens, for example, was $50 per week), but as an orphan, Elise Fuchs had had to make a meal out of one potato, and her resultant frugality enabled them to move into their own house in 1910. Although money was never plentiful—John Fuchs walked to work every day—careful budgeting allowed them to have their clothes *made* for them, rather than having to buy ill-fitting ready-made clothes. Beyond this, there was usually enough money left for John Fuchs' bottle of beer in the evening and an occasional outing for the family at Riverview amusement park.

By 1913 Fuchs' work had begun to show some deterioration. He was developing arthritis, but unbeknown to him and his family, he was also suffering from a brain tumor. (Two later stories attribute the tumor to a blow on the head with a vase wielded by another artist. In one case, it took place in New Bedford as a result of Fuchs' irritating singing or whistling; the other story states that he put oil of lavender in a Pickard artist's pipe with the same result. He was known as a bit of a prankster, so both versions have some merit.) By March, he had to be hospitalized, but his condition continued to worsen over the next months; on August 3, an unsuccessful operation culminated in his death.

After John Fuchs' death, two other china artists roomed with the family for a short while. Paul Nitsche, who worked for Pickard for a number of years, and John H. Schindler, an outstanding china artist from Kalamazoo, did some decorating and experimented with acid-etched china in the Fuchs' home. They used Yeschek's kiln for their firing, but they were

*Figure 11. Yeschek's backyard kiln shed.*

Photo courtesy H. Poulos.

asked to move out when their experiments got out of hand, splattering Mrs. Fuchs' walls with acid or paint.

Like all of Pickard's European artists, John Fuchs came from a male-dominated society, and when he had to associate with women artists, he made it plain that he had little use for them.

Despite this male disdain for women artists, Pickard's social conscience was again evident in his employment of some very talented women. In addition to Minnie Pickard and Zuie McCorkle, there were Florence M. James and Howard Reury's sister-in-law, Bertha L. Moore, and toward the end of the period, Ruth L. Alexander, Nesha Tolpin, and Alfred Keates' very talented daughter, Madeline.

Photo courtesy H. Poulos.

*Figure 12. Florence James with a teapot on a banding wheel in the late teens.*

The most prolific among the women was Florence James. In 1901, at age 16, she had already set up her own china decorating studio in Milwaukee. Her parents were Scots immigrants. Her father was a mold-maker from whom Florence probably derived much of her artistic talent. In late 1904 he passed away, and early in 1905 she moved to Chicago with her widowed mother to become one of the studio's youngest artists, male or female. In the course of her career she demonstrated considerable flexibility in style and subject matter, from naturalistic florals to scenic vellums to simple borders.

Another amenity that Pickard offered his decorators was a library of source books on art and decoration, together with current periodicals and journals of ceramics and china decorating. It was located in the center of the third floor, and an artist could retire there to a comfortable chair to study the latest trends or gain inspiration for a new design.

Animal, portrait, and other figural subjects were popular for most of the 1905–1910 period. William W. Breidel, Arthur J. Weiss, Paul P. Gasper, and Mr. Farrington all produced animals, monks, and similar portraits. Arabian designs and Arabian figural subjects were also very popular: Arthur Comyn produced camel and Egyptian subjects, and Breidel's THE PRAYING MOHAMMEDAN (Plate 52) was featured in color in the 1909 catalog. (The catalog still noted that the artists were "mostly men.")

As this period progressed, the heavily decorated, dark-grounded naturalistic renderings began to wane in favor of other newer styles. Raised gold paste work became quite popular, and experimentation led in many directions; stylized and conventionalized designs proliferated, revealing some hitherto unknown aspects of many artists' creativity.

In addition to all the social benefits that a Pickard artist might enjoy, a few of his artists received one final bit of recognition. CHALLINOR GERANIUM, YESCHEK CURRANTS AND PASTE, GIBSON PANSIES, TOMASCHEKO FLORAL BORDER, and COUFALL GRAPES AND ETCH BORDER were just a few of the patterns that bore their creators' names, and must have contributed substantially to the pride and satisfaction the artists derived from their work. (To the present day, Pickard, Inc. continues this admirable tradition by naming pieces after certain of its employees.)

Although many popular designs were sub-contracted, there was never any mass-production employed at the Pickard Studio. The 1909 catalog reiterated the studio's important philosophies: "Each artist paints his own pieces from start to finish...No decalcomania or print work of any kind is produced...We do not teach china painting."

Gasper's POPPY AND DAISY design was extremely popular and is a good example of the iterations through which a pattern might evolve over the years. Executed with either red or white blossoms, the whiplash gold border was initially embellished with spot-etched, kidney-shaped elements (Plate 368). (This was the version which the Osborne Studio chose to emulate for many years.) By 1910–1912, the gold border carried an intricate, serpentine maze of raised paste. The final version of the border was also produced in 1910–1912 and featured a pen line design of miniature stems, leaves, and poppies (Plate 515).

With the popularity of some designs demanding such volume production that one or more artists in addition to the originator had to execute it, there was always a challenge to maintain uniformity.[25] This was accomplished through either graphite transfer or pouncing. In the former technique, a tracing was made of a master design, the backside of the tracing was then coated with graphite (Fig. 13), and the design was placed on the china blank and retraced, leaving an outline that could be filled in. The graphite would burn off in the kiln.

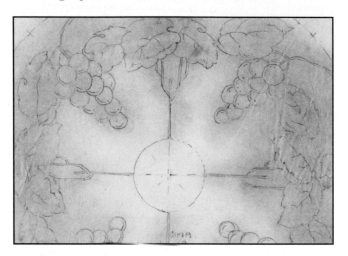

*Figure 13. Tracing of* <u>METALLIC</u> <u>GRAPES</u> *design for application to a plate (every china shape required its own master). Re-tracing it with graphite applied to back transfers the outline of the design.*

In the pounced process, an outline was also traced from a master, but the outline was then pricked with many, many pin holes (Fig. 14). The tracing was then positioned on the china blank, and a "pounce"—a sand-filled cloth or chamois— was used to pat graphite through the pinholes leaving a dotted outline of the design on the china. Both methods assured a faithful reproduction of

*Figure 14. Enlarged view of* <u>AURA</u> <u>ARGENTA</u> <u>LINEAR</u> *tracing showing pinholes.*

the design, and the tracing could be used many times to effect the transfer.

As Pickard's business increased, some unidentified detractors began to circulate a rumor that a portion of the studio's decoration was actually applied as a decal. Discounting the trademark, of course, no transfer decoration was employed until the 1920s. In defense of his claims, Pickard offered a $1000 reward to anyone who could produce a piece of his china that was not strictly hand-painted. That the rumor could be taken seriously was certainly a testimony to the level of quality his artists produced.

Fancy china was still Pickard's primary focus, but he did move successfully into complete dinner settings with a line of monogram ware as early as 1906. The still-novel telephone was used to promote the line in a brochure entitled *Over the Phone*. The brochure told the story of a June bride who had received a set of monogrammed china and featured the "Pickard Monogram Girl" drinking from a monogrammed tea set. Monograms were applied to glazed white china in raised gold paste and were often embellished with turquoise or ruby enamel beads (Plate 143). Monograms cost 25 cents apiece.

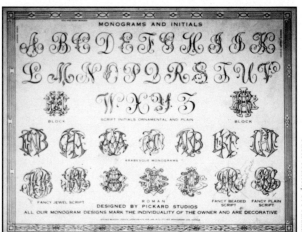

*Figure 15. Examples of monogram styles available from Pickard Studios.*

The skill and labor that went into the painting of a monogram was considerable. It required an extremely steady hand and great accuracy. The surviving samples of Otto Podlaha's studies as an apprentice in Bohemia attest to the skill required to execute these intricate designs (Fig. 16). Monogrammed china remained popular through the late teens.

By 1910 there were commercial china studios in many cities throughout the country. Most of them

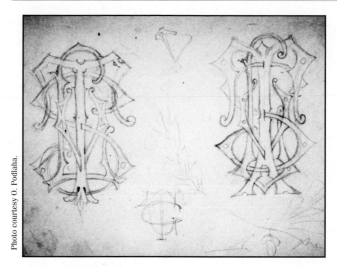

Photo courtesy O. Podlaha.

*Figure 16. Intricate monogram designs executed by Podlaha as an apprenticeship requirement.*

employed but a few artists and only served a local trading area. Many jewelry stores and gift shops set up their own backroom studios, and a few of them produced very high quality work. D'Arcy in Kalamazoo, Michigan, and Wheelock in Rockford, Illinois, were two such studios. Pickard's serious domestic competition was centered in Chicago, however. There were 44 studios listed in the 1910 Chicago City Directory, and among them, Stouffer, Donath, and Brauer were turning out good quality decorated china in considerable volume.

To their output must be added the production of the hand-decorating rooms at the large wholesalers, Pitkin & Brooks and Burley & Company. These wholesalers also imported custom-decorated china, private-labeled for them by various factories at Limoges.

France, Germany, and Japan were all exporting large quantities of decorated china, and much of it was sold through the Chicago mail order houses. Whereas the Japanese factories continued to hand paint their china (albeit on generally inferior blanks), the Germans had long since perfected transfer printing. Despite this, much imported decal-decorated china continued to bear the legend, "hand-painted." This was a stretch of a technicality, taking advantage of some small paste highlights or a simple border that might be hand applied to embellish the decal.

Some of Pickard's retail customers such as Marshall Field's, Wanamaker's, and Bailey, Banks & Biddle also imported custom-decorated and private-labeled china from Europe.

Despite, or perhaps because of this huge competitive traffic in decorated china, Pickard continued to prosper. His competitors' advertising

helped keep the public interest in fine china stimulated, enhancing the market for his product. While the prices on his pieces seem incredibly low in today's light, they were nevertheless the high end of the market: the Marie Vase in Plate 168, for instance, sold for $10.00 in 1909!

From time to time Pickard also purchased the work of other studios' artists for his study, such as the Willets Belleek rose vase by Lebrun (Plate 204). Later, when it had served its purpose, he would simply fire his trademark on the piece and re-sell it. This frugal practice was also followed by the Stouffer studio, and though very infrequent, it can be confusing and misleading for today's collector without a good knowledge of other studios and their artists.

## Artists active in 1905–1910

| | |
|---|---|
| Ruth L. Alexander | F. H. Koep |
| Emil Aulich | F. Kriesche |
| Max L. Bachmann | George P. Leach |
| Anton B. Beutlich | Walter R. Lemke |
| John Blazek | Frederick J. Lindner |
| William W. Breidel | F. Loba |
| Brun | John Loh |
| Edward S. Challinor | Curtis H. Marker |
| Arthur Comyn | Zuie McCorkle |
| Anthony Coufall | Edward P. Mentges |
| Arthur Cumming | Miche |
| Edward F. Donisch | Anton Miller |
| Edward Farrington | Bertha L. Moore |
| | John Nessy |
| Emil J. T. Fischer | Arthur Passony |
| Fox | Petit |
| John Fuchs | Minnie Verna Pickard |
| Paul P. Gasper | Otto Podlaha |
| Edward Gibson | William T. Rawlins |
| Nathan R. Gifford | Noble Ray |
| Otto W. Goess | Howard B. Reury |
| Haag | Anton Richter |
| Frank Haase | Otto Schoner |
| Hardwick (Adolph Heidrich or Walter Hartwig?) | George Sinclair |
| | Harry E. Tolley |
| Hartman | Nesha Tolpin |
| J. Heinz | Rudolph Tomascheko |
| Robert Hessler | Anton Unger |
| Hip | Jeremiah Vokral |
| Florence M. James | Albert H. Wagner |
| Alfred Keates | Frederick Walters |
| Madeline Keates | Phillip Wight |
| Maxwell R. Klipphahn | Frank P. Yeschek |
| Carl F. Koenig | Joseph T. Yeschek |

*Figure 17. Some Pickard artists c.1910. Back row: ——, ——, Anton Beutlich, Robert Hessler. Middle row: Paul Nitsche, ——, ——, Otto Podlaha. Front Row: John Nessy, ——, ——, Anton Richter.*

*Figure 18. Some Pickard artists c.1910. Back row: ——, ——, ——, Max Klipphahn, ——, Antol Schoenig, Emil Tolpin. Middle row: ——, Emil J. T. Fischer, Anton Unger, Frederick Lindner, Paul Gasper. Front row: Joseph Yeschek, Franz Vobornik, Carl Buschbeck, John Fuchs.*

## *Etched Gold 1910–1912*

Early in his china decorating career Pickard's goals had included the manufacture of his own china. The beauty of the more delicate and translucent French blanks which he imported must have tantalized him constantly. Moreover, every piece which bore the Pickard trademark usually bore the blank manufacturer's mark, and that manufacturer invariably sold his own line of decorated china to many of Pickard's same customers. In effect, Pickard was doing some point-of-sale advertising for his competition.

In 1910 Pickard devised a new trademark that would focus his customers exclusively on the Pickard name: a ½" gold square was placed over the blank manufacturer's mark with a ¹³⁄₃₂" red double circle over the gold (Mark 6). (Under certain conditions the mark may occasionally appear black, and Platt erroneously described it as such. However, when held at an oblique angle to the light the red color will be readily discernible.) The red circle also appeared infrequently without the gold square under it, primarily when no blank manufacturer's mark was present. Although this red circle is approximately the same diameter as the 1905–1910 brown circle, the two should not be confused; there was no red mark in the 1905–1910 period.

Pickard continued to advertise in *The Ladies Home Journal* and the *Woman's Home Companion* through 1910. But in 1911 he switched to *The House Beautiful*, and the best and most informative coverage appeared in the October 11 issue. An article extoling the virtues of well-chosen chinaware showed many current designs (see advertising section). A major transition in American taste had begun, and Pickard's current offerings reflected this transition. Elaborate, space-filling designs such as Hessler's MODERN CONVENTIONAL and Gasper's POPPY AND DAISY were still very popular, but some of the patterns illustrated in this article such as Hessler's HYACINTHUS (Plate 464), Donisch's ENAMEL CHRYSANTHEMUM (Plate 460), and Tolpin's ORANGE TREE CONVENTIONAL[26] (Plate 461) illustrated the new trend toward simplicity that would culminate in Art Deco.

Perhaps the most popular of the simpler designs was Florence James' DUTCH DECORATION[27] (Plate 485). Executed on a plain white bisque surface, its few elements could be reproduced quickly. It was so successful that Anton Richter, William Rawlins, and Ruth Alexander also filled

orders for it under their signatures. James developed the PILGRIM DECORATION (Plate 487) in the same style, and Rawlins also executed some of those orders. But the seasonal theme of this second design undoubtedly limited its acceptance and few examples have come to light. A third design in this series was the COLONIAL DECORATION (Plate 484), but it too, is rarely found.

One of Pickard's major achievements in 1911 was his introduction of etched china. Pickard had used some etched borders as far back as 1903 (Plate 129), but they were probably "spot etched" using a commercially available etching paste. This method produced a very shallow etch with a somewhat ragged definition. Before 1911, he had also used china blanks with pre-etched borders, applied in France or Germany by the blank manufacturer. They offered little choice of design, however.

Earlier in 1911, Anna Atkins had suggested that the effect of hammered gold which she had seen on a piece of metal artware made by the Tiffany Studios might be emulated in china. To accomplish this, an acid-etching room was installed in the rear of the second floor of the studio, and Joseph Yeschek's son, Frank, was placed in charge.

*Figure 19. Etching room with Frank Yeschek in protective gloves and apron dipping china in acid bath. Note negative patterns on asphaltum-coated ware.*

The etching process involved the "eating away" of the vitreous glaze on the surface of the china blank using hydrofluoric acid. By sponging and painting the china with an asphaltic "resist," selected portions of the china were protected from the acid and a mottled pattern with a dull finish evolved from the unprotected portions. (Hand sponging was shortly replaced by the use of paper transfers that had been pressed into the asphalt-filled design on an engraved steel master plate.) The strength of the acid and the length of immersion determined how deeply the china would be etched.

Upon removal from the acid bath, the china was rinsed in kerosene, followed by hot baths of soap and a final rinse. The china was then sent to the artists for color decoration, after which it received its first firing. The first coat of gold was then applied and the china was fired a second time. This was followed by a second coat of gold, the application of the trademark (the trademark now became the last step instead of the first), and the final firing. Because of the larger and coarser areas of gold in these patterns, the glass fiber burnishing brush was impractical, and a special burnishing sand was used to bring up the luster of the final coat of gold.

Initial offerings in all-over-gold were ENCRUSTED GOLD and ENCRUSTED GOLD AND SILVER (the silver was actually platinum.) The gold and silver combination was not very popular, but the all-over-gold was destined to last through the ensuing decades and survives today in the form of a best-selling plate in the ROSE AND DAISY pattern. First patterns incorporating the hammered gold effect were ENCRUSTED LINEAR (Plate 453) and BORDURE ANTIQUE (Plate 528). Etched china from this period is readily identified by the coarser encrustation pattern. Subsequent versions of the hammered gold design bear a more uniform, finer-grained etch (Plate 454).

The knowledgeable collector may have noticed that Edward Challinor's name rarely appears in this trademark period. Early in 1910, for reasons unknown today, he abruptly terminated his employment with Pickard, sold many of his household effects, and prepared to return with his family to England. Just as abruptly however, he decided not to return. Instead, he moved to the northwest side of Chicago to live next door to Julius H. Brauer, for whom he then went to work. At that time, Challinor was 33 years old with a wife and two small children; his sudden reversal of plans may have been an accommodation of his young

brothers-in-law, Arthur J. Maylind (21) and Arnold Rhodes (19), who arrived that spring from England and moved in with him. Maylind went to work at the Brauer studio as a clerk and Rhodes, like Challinor, became another of Brauer's artists.

Challinor remained with Brauer for about two years and then moved back near the Pickard studio in the spring of 1912. He worked for Pickard for the rest of his career. It was about the time of Challinor's return that the trademark was changed. A Challinor piece with the 1910–1912 gold square mark is therefore quite rare.

### *Artists active in 1910–1912*

| | |
|---|---|
| Ruth L. Alexander | Frederick J. Lindner |
| Paul B. Anthony | John Loh |
| Edith Arno | Eva E. Maley |
| F. Beulet | Curtis H. Marker |
| Anton B. Beutlich | Edward P. Mentges |
| John Blazek | Anton Miller |
| Buschbeck, Carl | John Nessy |
| Edward S. Challinor | Frank Nittel |
| Arthur Comyn | Arthur Passoni |
| Edward F. Donisch | Minnie Verna Pickard |
| Frank Drzewiecki | Otto Podlaha |
| Edward | William T. Rawlins |
| Emil J. T. Fischer | Anton Richter |
| John Fuchs | S. Richter |
| Paul P. Gasper | Carl Roessler |
| Half | John Thonander |
| Hartman | Harry E. Tolley |
| Ernest V. Hauptmann | Emil E. Tolpin |
| Robert Hessler | Nesha Tolpin |
| Myrtle Hille | Franz Vobornik |
| Ethel R. Honey | Frederick Walters |
| Florence M. James | Phillip Wight |
| Maxwell R. Klipphahn | Frank P. Yeschek |
| Carl F. Koenig | Joseph T. Yeschek |

## War and Transition 1912–1919

Although the years 1912 through 1919 have been treated as a single period, they contain four trademark variations that need some explanation:

The 1910–1912 gold square was frequently too small to hide the blank-maker's mark entirely. In 1912 Pickard substituted a gold maple leaf (Mark 7) for the square, allowing his artists to paint over the maker's mark to suit its size. He continued to apply the red double circle over it. (The first variation, 1912–c.1914.)

In a little over a year a black double circle was substituted for the red. The substitution was not universal however, and the red mark continued to appear occasionally for several years. (The second variation, c.1914–c.1916.)

Pickard was not alone in his practice of covering the blankmaker's mark (when held up to a strong light, the overpainted mark is usually readable); most china decorators who made all-over gold designs followed the same practice. However, the United States Customs Service prohibits the concealment of the country-of-origin marking. According to Pete Pickard, his grandfather received several admonitions to this effect and finally dropped his over-painting practice. The maple leaf then appeared beside the maker's mark. (The third variation, c.1916–c.1918.)

About 1918 it became apparent that the gold maple leaf was unnecessary, and it was dropped. The black double circle (Mark 8) was thus used by itself. (The fourth variation, c.1918–1919.)

Throughout the 1912–1919 period, diameters down to ¼" were applied to salts and other small shapes, but occasionally these smaller marks also appear on much larger pieces. Although the largest black marks for this period are approximately the same diameter as the 1905–1910 brown mark, the two should not be confused; as in the case of the 1910–1912 red circle, there was no black 1905–1910 trademark either. ("Pickard" in a blue hand script has also been sighted on one Challinor vase and may be classified as an additional mark for the 1912–1918 period.)

An additional trademark was used in parallel with the above marks throughout the 1912–1919 period and on through 1925. This was a gold medallion bearing the words, "Pickard Etched China" and was the first trademark actually etched into the china's surface. During this period, it was reserved for etched, gold-bordered dinner services that competed with similar European dinnerware.

In the first two years of this period— 1912–1913—the general business climate was expanding, and it seemed that Pickard's ambition of manufacturing his own china might finally become a reality. Early in 1914 he began negotiations for the purchase of one of the factories in Limoges, France. But the outbreak of war in

*Figure 20. Pickard kiln room in mid teens with <u>ROCOCO</u> <u>SCROLLS</u> and <u>ETCHED</u> <u>BORDER</u> and some vellum scenics laid out.*

Europe that summer, followed by another depression, frustrated his plans; it would be almost 25 more years before he would manufacture his first set of dinnerware.

The economy revived in 1915, and although prosperity extended through the end of the war in 1918, labor and material shortages and price fluctuations were a chronic national problem. For Pickard, his polyglot family of artists was a challenge in itself. Otto Podlaha had made an unsuccessful attempt to form a union, and with tempers strained by the war's tensions, Pickard had to maintain equilibrium among a dozen nationalities; more than one dispute required his good sense of humor to restore order.

On December 18, 1915, Pickard suffered a great loss: Anna Atkins died of typhoid fever. She had contracted the disease while on a sales trip, and one must admire her energy and tenacity, for she was 66 years old by then and still making a yearly circuit. Pickard had leaned heavily on his sister's artistic talents in assessing market changes and evaluating designs as they evolved. Minnie Pickard subsequently took over

*Figure 21. Minnie Verna Pickard.*

the art evaluation, and despite her lack of formal art education, the studio's continuing success was testimony to her natural talent.

As early as 1911 and perhaps several years prior to that, Pickard started publishing a series of booklets promoting his china through social etiquette and menu planning. The title pages state that these booklets were "Compiled and written by the School of Domestic Arts and Science." The school was a bonafide institution, located across Michigan Avenue from the Chicago Art Institute. *Secrets of Correct Table Service* initially bore the imprint of the China Section at Marshall Field's, but Pickard undoubtedly saw the benefit of wider circulation and later editions included imprints of other stores. By 1917 the booklet had become *The Art Of Entertaining* and gave advice on a wide range of social functions, never omitting the importance of selecting china that was appropriate to the occasion. Pattern illustrations in these booklets were also converted into postcards, some of which are shown in the advertising section.

During this period, Pickard communicated with his dealers through an annual publication called *China Chats*. He offered prizes for photographs of outstanding window and counter displays, and he also illustrated some of his new designs for the coming year. In the 1916 edition he writes of expanding business conditions and his high expectations for the year. What is most illuminating, however, was the extent of his distribution by this time: Twin Falls, Idaho; El Paso, Texas; Jackson, Mississippi; Boston, Massachusetts; Bisbee, Arizona; and Norfolk, Virginia, all had jewelry shops, department stores, or specialty stores that actively promoted the sale of Pickard China. The Twin Falls dealer's enthusiasm is worth recounting: he wired the Pickard salesman to meet him in a nearby town at midnight where he spent five hours picking out an assortment of china. He then boarded a 5:30 a.m. train back to Twin Falls. He later wrote Pickard, "...I consider Pickard China one of my best lines. As a line of satisfaction it ranks with sterling...."

Although America did not enter the Great War until 1917, Pickard's supply of French china blanks had been cut off long before that. The situation was further exacerbated by the increase in the number of china decorating studios during these years. In Chicago alone, the number of listed studios rose from 49 in 1912 to 102 by 1916. Some of them were one- or two-person studios, but others, like Julius H. Brauer, J. H. Stouffer, and White's

Art Company, numbered up to 50 decorators. So while the supply of good china dwindled, the nation-wide demand for these blanks spiraled, driving prices ever higher.

Early in 1916, Pickard had notified his dealers that no more European stock was available.[28] By the end of the war the situation had become desperate, and he was purchasing china blanks from whomever had a supply. In a few cases he was forced to buy from local competitor/retailers such as Burley & Company. For the greater part, the cost of operating a large studio dictated Pickard's only option: whatever china was obtainable at wholesale prices was the china he would have to purchase. The only china available in that category was Nippon and Noritake.[29]

As the effects of the war deepened, Pickard struggled to find other sources of revenue, and for a while he even contemplated making hand-wrought silverware. This was not as farfetched as it may sound, for one has only to recall that Chicago was then home to a great many metalsmiths who had set up shop under the inspiration of the Arts and Crafts movement. Silver was in short supply because of the war, however, and it was also considered unpatriotic to purchase such luxuries as china and silver.

The alternative that seemed to hold the most promise, however, was the creation of hand-painted and etched-gold glassware. *Keramic Studio*, a magazine that catered to both the amateur and the professional decorator, was recommending the substitution of glass for china to its readership. Former Pickard artist, Dominick Campana, wrote a series of articles on the technique of glass decorating and glass firing,[30] and within a few short months teachers, kiln-makers, and art supply houses were all extoling the virtues of glass.

Pickard required no additional resources to produce decorated glass, and his artists were certainly capable of handling this medium—some of them had been glass decorators with prior employers. Having sold cut glass in the 1890s, Pickard was familiar with the market, and with more than five years experience in china etching, he probably felt well-prepared to enter the field.

His first glassware included both hand-painted and etched-gold border pieces (Plate 600). Initially, he experienced some difficulty with stemware because the kiln temperature that was needed to fuse the gold, also brought the thin glass to a plastic state resulting in some elliptical and out-of-round pieces.

Campana's articles advised that secondary kiln baffles and the placement of thinner glass in the center of the kiln rendered better results. Pickard probably adopted these remedies because he soon was offering a very complete line of stemware, compotes, perfume bottles, bowls, pitchers, tumblers, and even gold monogrammed glassware.

In addition to etched borders, he offered all-over-gold glassware in the same patterns that had become so popular in his chinaware. "Pickard China" became "Pickard China and Glass" in 1917, but glassware never became a stand-alone line. Everyone, amateur and professional alike, was suddenly producing decorated glass. The pages of *Keramic Studio* were filled with glass-related advertising, and glass, no matter how good, became a glut on the market.

Pickard's hand-painted glass appears not to have lasted more than one selling season (1916 or 1917); only one design, POPPIES, signed by Carl Roessler and marked on the bottom with a hand-painted gold "P" has come to light (Plate 599).

Much of the Pickard etched glassware seen today is heavily worn. Whether the gold was poorly fluxed or whether there was some other shortcoming in the gold formulation can only be speculated, but the etched-gold glass probably did not survive more than a few years (1917–1918). Pickard glassware bore an etched (transparent) ¹³⁄₃₂ double circle with "PICKARD" in the center and "ETCHED GLASS" around the circle.

A side note to Pickard's venture into glassware was Franz X. Parsche's venture into hand-painted china. Parsche Studios had been a top Chicago producer of fine cut glass since 1875. It is interesting to note that each entered the other's field during the teens with equally poor results. The two men were known to have been good friends, however, and Pickard gave Parsche a tall floral vase decorated by M. Rost LeRoy during one of their visits later in life.

The war had a pronounced effect on small studios, and their number declined almost as precipitously as they had risen. The following excerpt from the September 1918 issue of *Keramic Studio* describes the situation well:

"There is little of note being done in the keramic studios in Chicago. Many have given up expensive downtown studios and are working at home, cutting down expenses to a minimum until after the war. Mr.

Campana is spending the summer experimenting on glass in his Chicago studio...."

His excursion into glassware notwithstanding, the last years of the war were probably a very distressing time for Pickard. The Japanese china blanks that he was forced to buy were substantially below European quality, and blemishes and uneven surfaces were commonplace. Added to this, the government's regulation prevented him from over-painting the Japanese marks. The only saving circumstance was that the blemishes could be hidden fairly well under an all-over etched gold design. (Although Pickard returned to European blanks after the war—largely Austrian and German—he continued to use a few of the better-quality Japanese blanks into the 1930s.)

Subsequent to the finer-grained version of ENCRUSTED GOLD, Pickard combined patterns in plain gold with the hammered gold effect; ROCOCO ENCRUSTED, and ENCRUSTED HONEYSUCKLE were representative of this variation. All-over-gold really hit its stride, however, when Challinor produced his first all-over floral design, ROSE AND DAISY (Plate 684.29). This was followed by TRAILING VINE (Plate 684.32), MORNING GLORY (Plate 684.26), GOLD TRACERY (Plate 684.25), SILK MOIRÉ (Plate 684.31), and ARNICA (Plate 684.21). These designs proved immensely popular, and Pickard had Challinor appear in Marshall Field's china department from time to time with a small gold bar in hand to further promote the purity and quality of these designs. SILK MOIRÉ was most often employed as a textured surface for hand-painted subjects, while the other designs

*Photo courtesy S. Shellenbach.*

*Figure 22. The china department on the second floor of Marshall Field's department store. Direct access to the "L" brought large volumes of people past the Pickard display every day.*

were frequently combined with hand-painted panels, medallions, or borders (plates 607, 626, 608). Of all the designs, ROSE AND DAISY was the most popular, and it is the only early design that can still be purchased today.

But if Pickard had been troubled by the plagiarism of his hand-painted designs, the imitations of his ROSE AND DAISY design must have been a great torment. Almost every commercial studio in the country eventually produced a line of all-over gold china, and almost every one of them also included a copy or imitation of ROSE AND DAISY in their line.

In 1912 Pickard introduced a very successful line of vellum scenics. Vases and plates were the most popular shapes, but chargers, bowls, and tea sets were also prevalent. Applied in delicate pastel colors with matte-finish paints, they had a velvet feel that amplified the soft and distant mood that most of the scenes portrayed.

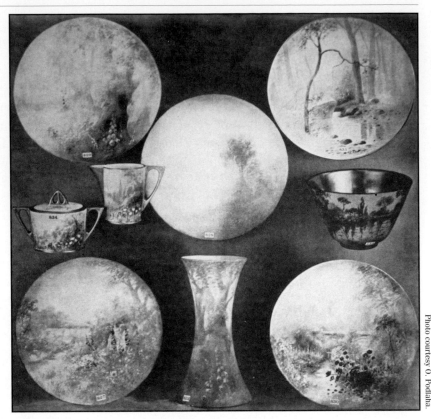

*Photo courtesy O. Podlaha.*

*Figure 24. Keramic Studio illustration of Challinor exhibit entries with* WALLED GARDEN *as second prize award.*

*Photo courtesy S. Shellenbach.*

*Figure 23. Edward Stafford Challinor at work on a set of scenic service plates in the twenties.*

Challinor excelled in this technique, and based on what is seen today, his vellum output was prolific. Many of the scenes he painted were taken from local woodlands, and a few pieces even bore an identification of the location on the back. WILDWOOD (Plate 473), a birch grove setting, was very popular, as were ITALIAN GARDEN and CLASSIC RUINS.

Challinor had begun to develop this technique during his short stay at the Julius H. Brauer Studio. In the fall of 1910, Burley & Company held one of their many china painting competitions at their show room in the Loop, and Challinor carried off a second prize for a vase executed in this style.[31] In 1915 he again entered the Burley Exhibition, held this time at the Chicago Art Institute, with a large collection of vellum scenics: five plates, a vase, a small bowl, and a cream and sugar. The bowl, a gold-lined, deep blue rendering of his WALLED GARDEN earned him another second prize in the "Naturalistic" category.[32] This category placed his work in with the "pretty fruits and flowers" entries, and was certainly an inappropriate classification for the style that he had developed. However, the exhibition's only other category was "Conventionalized" designs, and since all entries had to be placed in one or the other, Challinor seems not to have received the recognition he deserved.

Upon his return to Pickard from his venture with the International Art Studio (see page 264), Curtis Marker also developed a mastery of the vellum format. Mountain, lakeside, and woodland scenes such as HAWTHORNE (Plate 548) were expertly executed, but some of his moonlight scenes were spectacular.

*Figure 25. Curtis Marker applying gold to vellum scenic vase. Note pounces on table to his left.*

Others who produced vellum ware were Ruth Alexander, Marie Bohman, F. Cirnacty, Harriet Corey, J. Göttlich, Florence James, Eva Maley, Anna Seagren, Albert Wagner, and Joseph Yeschek.

The vellum technique did not attract much competition except for the Stouffer and Osborne studios. Stouffer's output was modest (Plate 829) and did not pose a threat to Pickard, but Osborne produced some of his more creditable work in this technique (Plates 760, 762).

By 1918–1919 the market for vellum ware had almost disappeared. Challinor and a few other artists produced some pieces with vellum-style subjects and coloring, while reverting to standard mineral paints. These "glossy scenics" (Plate 540) were not as numerous as the vellums, but they did linger on through the early twenties before they too lost their appeal.

From 1898 and until Pickard moved to Antioch, Illinois, a few designs would occasionally appear that were most un-Pickard-like. Of all these aberrant designs, those of Minnie Luken were probably the least likely to be taken for a piece of Pickard china. They consisted mainly of border decorations with sprays of pale blue forget-me-nots, or pale yellow rosebuds, or a poppy or two (Plate 496)— all the trite amateur subjects that Pickard had deprecated for almost two decades.

Minnie Luken's work was not amateurish, however. She had operated her own studio since 1895, and her renderings were commercial quality. Still, regardless of the quality, one wonders why Pickard ever placed his trademark on these pieces. Perhaps Anna Atkins saw a little of the trend toward simplicity in Minnie Luken's plainer designs and wanted to test the market with them. Perhaps it was just a further instance of Pickard giving another artist an opportunity. Nonetheless, Luken produced china decorations for Pickard for only about a year—1912 or 1913—and then returned to her own studio (see page 268). (Indeed, she may never have worked as a "resident artist" at the Ravenswood Studio inasmuch as she had her own facilities. She may have continued to decorate her ware in her own studio, only bringing them to Ravenswood for the final marking and firing.) Luken pieces with the Pickard mark are quite rare, but in her long career as an independent china decorator, she generated a great quantity of her own chinaware that appears today with considerable frequency.

Service plates (Plate 490) and dinnerware lines were expanded early in the 1912–1919 period, but judging by the photos of dealers' displays from that time, fancy china remained the top attraction. AURA ARGENTA LINEAR and ENCRUSTED LINEAR were very popular and would remain so into the early twenties. Older designs such as IRIS CONVENTIONAL were still represented. Mixed in with these patterns was a new group of unsigned border designs: COLUMBINE, CHIPPENDALE, ADAM BORDER, SHERATON, BLUE FUSCIA[sic], etc. Pickard seemed to be trying to establish a position in the trend toward simplicity, and he brought out a great variety of such patterns (Plates 570–572), describing them in elaborate terms (See items 29 through 52 in Advertising section). It is difficult to imagine a customer or dealer deriving so much from such simple designs, but for the short period of their existence (c.1914–1918), they seem to have been well-accepted.

More than anything else, the simple borders were a harbinger of the decade to come and the artist's declining role in china decoration. Once designed, the pattern required only a good draftsperson to faithfully repeat its few brush strokes. Such "technical" decorators were often women and were paid much lower wages by most commercial studios (ten cents for a bread and butter plate[33]), and Pickard was probably no exception. Whereas such wage scales had been the norm among institutional china wholesalers for several decades, this experiment with simplicity now placed Pickard in competition with commodity chinaware.

The short life of these simple borders also illustrated the struggle between hand decoration and decal decoration. The slight irregularities in line and shape were what had always given the more elaborate hand-painted china its warmth and individuality, but these irregularities were all too prominent in simple symmetrical patterns. And while these designs may have a certain attraction for collectors today, they were a poor match for the flawless decal patterns available on European ware, once the war was over.

Pickard was not lacking in flexibility, however. Almost simultaneous with his digressions into mediocrity with simple borders, Pickard began to experiment with a new group of designs that represented yet another departure. These designs, however, showed a marked advance in sophistication and quality.

For these designs, instead of mineral paints, he chose the Satsuma technique that employed enamels and could be "puddled" in place so as to create slight mounds that added a three-dimensional, tactile quality. The technique required a high degree of skill; enamel consistency was critical, the brush could not touch the ware, and it would tolerate no more than two firings. Any error produced a chipped or blistered product. His earliest and most successful designs in this format were *ENAMELED PEONIES AND PHEASANT* (Plate 505) and ANTIQUE CHINESE ENAMEL (Plate 507), introduced about 1912; OLD FASHIONED FLOWERS (Plate 560) and ORNAMENTAL MOSAIC BORDER were introduced about 1916.

Satsuma-style decoration was not new. It had risen to a high degree of perfection among the members of the Atlan Ceramic Arts Club and had been garnering awards at numerous

*Figure 26. Basement preparation room where bases of china were ground to remove any remaining glaze that would cause the piece to stick to the refractory brick in a kiln. (Frank Yeschek is in foreground.)*

exhibitions for more than a decade. Articles and illustrations in *Keramic Studio* magazine and a number of art supply company instruction booklets gave detailed information on the technique. Although the technique was often executed on porcelain, true Satsuma decoration should only be designated as such when rendered on Satsuma ware. Satsuma pottery had a pale yellow body and a fine crackle glaze and had been developed in Japan in the seventeenth century. These blanks were readily available from the catalogs of a large number of art supply companies who also advertised in the monthly issues of *Keramic Studio*.

primary reason is that Pickard's timing for entry into this market was late. By 1917, when the BOUQUET SATSUMA listing appeared in his pamphlet, *The Art of Entertaining*, Satsuma's popularity had already been in decline for several years.

In addition to the Satsuma style, another group of quality designs in simpler, more modern formats began to make their appearance as early as 1912. DESERTED GARDEN (Plate 552) was very popular and bore the signatures of Max Klipphahn, Curtis Marker, John Nessy, Jerry Vokral, and Joseph Yeschek. Bordered by broad bands of plain, burnished gold, a hand-painted panel depicted a woodland floor strewn with colorful fallen fruit. Substituting roses for fruit, a design in the same format entitled ROSELAND was also introduced in 1912 (Plate 554) and seems to have been the work of Curtis Marker. Although these patterns were generally naturalistic, they no longer incorporated elaborate scrolled and embellished borders, and the blanks themselves were plainer forms.

Figure 27. Third floor decorating room in the late teens. Gustav Hiecke is believed to be second from left.

*Photo courtesy H. Hiecke.*

Many Satsuma blanks were imported from Japan, but many also came from American potteries, such as the Haeger Potteries in nearby Dundee, Illinois.

Beutlich had produced decorated pottery in 1910–1912, and Paul Gasper produced some pottery (Plate 579) early in the 1912–1918 period. Pickard's first designs on actual Satsuma-style pottery blanks began later in that period with Tolpin's charming examples in the form of a vase and lidded box (Plate 582). Beutlich's BOUQUET SATSUMA (Plate 583) was awarded the Gold Medal at the Panama Pacific Exposition in 1915.

Surviving examples of Pickard-decorated pottery are rare. The

*Photo courtesy H. Poulos.*

Figure 28. Second floor decorating room in the late teens. Left to right: Joseph Yeschek, ———, Harriet Corey, ———, Jerry Vokral, John Nessy on end.

Another series of quality designs were developed by Max Klipphahn during this period that, with some variations, maintained their popularity into the early twenties. Like his CHRYSANTHEMUMS, LUSTRE AND MATT RED and similar designs several years earlier, they were stunning conceptions with a very rich appearance. The first design, ANTIQUE ENAMELS (Plate 563), combined an etched gold body with a wide border of enameled flowers on a black background. It appeared in 1912, and was shown at the Chicago Ceramic Arts Association exhibit at the Art Institute.[34] A later design, FRUITS LINEAR (Plate 555), combined a plain gold body and platinum lines with a band of enameled fruits on a black background. The last in this series was probably the design SEVILLE, featured in Pickard's catalog as late as 1931.

It is regrettable that there were so few of these higher quality designs because they assuredly added stature to Pickard's reputation. But this is what differentiated this period from the 1903–1910 period: fewer "name" artists producing fewer designs, but in greater volume, and in a larger selection of shapes.

This period saw more experimentation and more radical changes than any other period in Pickard's history. It saw:

- The decline and retirement of all of the old naturalistic fruit and floral designs.

- The successful introduction and subsequent decline of simpler, cleaner conventionalized designs; of simple, hand-painted border ware; of Satsuma ware, and of hand-painted and etched glassware.

- The introduction of vellum scenic ware and its transition into glossy scenic ware.

- The move away from giftware only, and the introduction of service plates and dinnerware and the expansion of tea and luncheon sets.

Downward pressures on pricing increased steadily, and the war dampened demand for fine china as the purchase of luxury items continued to be viewed as un-patriotic. It was a difficult business climate, but despite this, sales of gold etched china increased steadily, and was probably the determinant in the studio's survival.

By the end of the period Pickard was 61 years old, and his resourcefulness and flexibility had positioned the studio to move into the next decade with a vigorous new focus and a collection of new designs that reflected the post-war spirit of growth and freedom.

### *Artists active in 1912–1919*

| | |
|---|---|
| Ruth L. Alexander | Eva E. Maley |
| Joseph Blaha | Mark |
| B. Boehm | Curtis H. Marker |
| V. Burgner | Anton Miller |
| Edward S. Challinor | John Nessy |
| Harriet L. Corey | Arthur Passony |
| Louis H. Falatek | Otto Podlaha |
| Emil J. T. Fischer | William T. Rawlins |
| John Fuchs | Anton Richter |
| Paul P. Gasper | Carl Roessler |
| J. Göttlich | Anna A. Seagren |
| Louis P. Grumieau | Emil E. Tolpin |
| M. Harp | Franz Vobornik |
| Ernest V. Hauptmann | Jeremiah Vokral |
| Robert Hessler | Albert H. Wagner |
| Gustav H. G. Hiecke | Frederick Walters |
| Florence M. James | Frank P. Yeschek |
| Maxwell Rean Klipphahn | Joseph T. Yeschek |
| Minnie A. Luken | Ziologe |

## Postwar and New Directions 1919–1922

During this period, Pickard departed from the use of his double circle trademark. Very early in this period (c.1918–1919) he apparently tried to differentiate etched and non-etched china with a black decal that bore the words "Pickard Studios Chicago U.S.A." framed in a decorative scroll and topped with an urn (Mark 8.1). It is quite rare and, thus far, has been found on only two patterns CHINESE PHEASANT (Plate 604) and an enameled flower design, (Plate 603).

It was replaced by a similar, slightly larger mark that was applied both as a black decal and a black rubber stamp reading, "PICKARD ETCHED CHINA" (Mark 9). Pickard appears to have given up the differentiation, for mark 9 appears on etched and non-etched china alike. As mentioned previously, the etched gold medallion trademark (Mark 10) continued to be used on dinnerware through this period. It was also selectively applied to luncheon sets.

*Figure 29. Robert Hessler working on <u>ETCHED</u> <u>PANEL</u> <u>AND</u> <u>ROSES</u> with <u>ROCOCO</u> <u>ENCRUSTED</u> <u>IN</u> <u>FOREGROUND</u>.*

After the war, competition in the dinner ware and fancy china markets intensified. There were no tariffs on imported china and cheap labor in Japan and Europe made foreign-decorated china a formidable threat.

From 1919 onward, simpler designs and the greater emphasis on luncheon sets and place settings substantially diminished the number of pieces bearing an artist's signature or initials. Even though there were probably about the same number of individuals employed in decorating china as in prior years, the list of known active artists is therefore much shorter.

Among the new artists of this period were Bessie Nichols, Ingeborg Klein, and Ester Samuelson. Little is known of Bessie Nichols, but Ester Samuelson had come to Chicago from Sweden with

her parents in 1920 at the age of 17. She had no prior art training, but she took lessons at an art store near the Studio that advertised china painting lessons. (Though this store was never identified, Edward Gibson's art supply store was only a few blocks away. He taught china painting there and would have been in a position to recommend promising students to Pickard.)

Samuelson shortly began work at the Ravenswood Studios and was delighted to find that another Swedish girl, Ingeborg Klein, was also a china decorator. Samuelson worked for Pickard into the mid–1930s, but Ingeborg Klein returned to Sweden about 1925. The two young women continued to correspond with each other for the rest of their lives.

Some of Ester Samuelson's reminiscences reveal the changes evolving for the china decorator after the war: Her workbench faced the window so that the light was always in her eyes, the seating was hard, and the work was repetitious and monotonous. "Well, I'm off to paint my Indian Tree," she used to say to her family as she left for work (Plate 637). For all of that, the warmth and family atmosphere that Wilder Pickard had worked so hard to cultivate was still present. In particular, she recalled what a great friend Curtis Marker was to her.

One artist who contributed a high degree of artistry during this period was F. Cirnacty who was a very accomplished portraitist and painter of animals. Pickard had produced lamp bases in prior years, but Cirnacty's vases were particularly appropriate for this use. Pickard's glassware friend, Franz Parsche, did the final drilling and assembly, so some of the lamps bear the marks of both studios.

The vellum scenics of the teens generally covered the entire plate, vase, or charger on which they were painted, and this style had

*Figure 30. Young women decorators working on ORIENTAL BIRD design. Left to right: Ester Samuelson, Ingeborg Klein, and (possibly) Bessie Nichols.*

Figure 31. Franz Vobornik at work on some of the intricately detailed borders that were an essential element of service plates.

our searches have failed to locate any artist by that name. Yet there is no question that a Japanese artist did exist; he does appear in a photograph from this period. Platt describes him as "very talented," and others recall hearing of such an artist whom everyone held in high regard. Using "Messino" as a homonym, our sources suggest that this mysterious artist was very possibly the Japanese artist, Itero N. Matsuo.

largely disappeared by 1920. Nevertheless, smaller, brighter-colored scenics continued to be produced through most of the decade in the form of center medallions on etched, gold-bordered service plates, or on floral-bordered vases, compotes, and bonbons incorporating narrow, etched-gold bands (Plate 638). A large portion of Pickard's output was now what his new trademark said: china that somewhere in its design, incorporated an etched surface. These touches of gold added considerable elegance to the piece, and Challinor, Marker, Yeschek, and Bohman all produced notable work in this style. Other designs took the form of a partial or all-over etch in the SILK MOIRÉ pattern upon which hand-painted flower baskets and some scenics were applied. During this period all-over-platinum was introduced using the same etched patterns as the all-over-gold. Although it continued to be made through the 1925–1930 period, it was not as popular as its gold counterpart and little of it has survived.

There was a Japanese artist employed at the Ravenswood Studio about this time; no designs have been attributed to him, and the author has discovered no pieces bearing his signature or initials. Platt identified him as "Mr. Messino," a very un-Japanese name, but

*Artists active in 1919–1922*
*(Possibly active in italics.)*

| | |
|---|---|
| Isadore Bardos | Ingeborg Klein |
| Anton B. Beutlich | Maxwell R. Klipphahn |
| Edward S. Challinor | Kucia |
| F. Cirnacty | Curtis H. Marker |
| Erbe | *Itero N. Matsuo* |
| Louis H. Falatek | Bessie Nichols |
| Pauline Fuchs | Anton Richter |
| J. C. Gerts | Ester Samuelson |
| J. Göttlich | Franz Vobornik |
| G. Gustav H. Hiecke | Jeremiah Vokral |
| Florence M. James | |

## Toward Simplicity 1922–1925

The 1922–1925 period marked the end of the era of antique hand-painted china as defined in the scope of this book. As stated before, a small amount of hand painting continued into the thirties and beyond, but this was not rendered in the antique style. All-over-gold continued to be a mainstay, and variations that combined small amounts of hand painting, such as the *BUMBLEBEES ON ETCHED HONEYCOMB* (Plate 636) showed real innovation. The old designs were displaced by the growing preference for Art Deco (Plate 643) which had become

Photo courtesy H. Poulos.

the new standard of taste for everything from architecture to furniture, from railway cars to china. Pickard reacted to this trend with new designs and thus insured the studio's survival.

By 1922 Pickard was 65 years old and his three children, William (Bill), Henry Austin (Austin), and Dorothy, were now young adults. He brought his oldest son, Bill, into the Ravenswood Studio to learn the business from the basement up—literally. Bill unpacked barrels of blank china, washed it, committed the names of their various shapes to memory, and performed other basic tasks. Having just completed a year of graduate work at Cambridge University in England, Bill found his father's attempt at bottom-of-the-ladder training demeaning. Pickard shortly compromised and sent Bill out on the road to sell.

From about 1919 through 1925 the "etched coin" trademark (Mark 10) was also applied to pieces that combined an all-over-gold etched pattern with hand-painted borders (Plate 639); it was applied to all china in 1922 through 1925.

### Artists active in 1922–1925

| | |
|---|---|
| Isadore Bardos | Florence M. James |
| Anton B. Beutlich | Ingeborg Klein |
| Marie Bohman | Maxwell R. Klipphahn |
| Edward S. Challinor | Kucia |
| F. Cirnacty | Curtis H. Marker |
| Erbe | Arnold Rhodes |
| Louis H. Falatek | Anton Richter |
| Pauline Fuchs | Ester Samuelson |
| J. C. Gerts | Franz Vobornik |
| J. Göttlich | Joseph T. Yeschek |
| G. Gustav H. Hiecke | |

## Pickard Studios, Inc. 1925–1930

In 1925 the studio was incorporated under the name of "Pickard Studios, Inc.," and the first of the "lion/shield" trademarks was developed (Mark 11). Like the gold coin mark before it, this new mark was also etched into the china with gold fired over it. Platinum was also occasionally used for this mark, but primarily when the piece itself was an all-over-platinum design.

Designs in this period continued to move in the direction of Art Deco. Such hand-painted designs as SEVILLE, FRUITS LINEAR, and some moiré-bordered pastel scenics still required the expert talents of Edward Challinor, Max Klipphahn, Curtis Marker, and Gustav

Hiecke. All-over-gold china ware continued to be very popular and was attracting competition from large and small studios alike (see Yeschek Studios).

Photo courtesy H. Poulos.

*Figure 32. Max Klipphahn at work on a floral design. Note how the mineral paints are applied and fired before the gold is laid on.*

In the fall of 1928, a new trademark was devised that bore no reference to the Pickard Studios. The mark used the same scrolled frame as the 1919–1922 mark, but only the word "Edgerton" appeared in the frame; it was applied as a green rubber stamp that included the legend "Decorated in the U.S.A." (Mark 13). This mark was used for the sale of "seconds" and was in use into the late forties. It was revived again in the sixties but was only used for direct sales.

In 1926 Pickard promoted Edward Challinor to the post of art director, and the new responsibility also included some public relations activities. In April of 1927, a series of advertisements in the *Johnstown* (PA) *Tribune* announced the three-day appearance of Challinor wherein he was to speak on table arrangements. For some of these appearances, he also carried a portable kiln with which he demonstrated the china decorating process.

Just how much travel and promotional work he did is unknown, but certainly no one was better equipped for the job of art director, and Challinor served the business well through the changing climate in the arts until his death in 1952.

In addition to the potential for burns from hydrofluoric acid, the etching process included another hazard that resulted in a great tragedy during this period. On November 13, 1925, Anton Beutlich was in a rear room of the studio, heating a kettle of asphalt-and-turpentine resist which would be used to protect portions of the china from the acid. Flames from the gasoline stove ignited the mixture, and he tried to carry the kettle through a doorway that opened onto a back roof. In doing so, he bumped into the door jamb, splashing the flaming liquid all over himself. Si Simon, who had just started work at the studio, and another artist grabbed fire extinguishers, chased him around the roof, and eventually put out the flames, but Anton Beutlich died in the hospital three days later.

In 1925, Pickard had added his youngest son, Austin, to the business, and placed him under son Bill's direction. Austin proved less of a natural salesman than Bill, but Austin was determined to succeed and pursued this and other facets of the business with dogged determination.

With his sons seemingly positioned to take over the business, Pickard once more returned to his dream of manufacturing his own porcelain. The United States had suffered short depressions in 1921 and in the first half of 1924, but by 1925, the country was again in a prosperous mode. Although England, Germany, and Austria were still in the grip of a post-war depression, France had recovered, and the timing seemed appropriate. In 1926 Pickard sent Bill to France to conduct a search. Having spent some time in Europe during his school years, the prospect of operating a French pottery held some attraction for Bill. Nothing was available however, and he returned empty handed. A year later Bill left the business.

By 1929 Wilder Pickard, now 72 years old, had passed much of the control of the business to Austin, making him executive vice president. That fall Austin married Bernice Davis of Evanston, Illinois, and eventually they had two children, Henry Austin, Jr. ("Pete") and Maria Davis Pickard who would later become the wife of a future Pickard president, Eben C. Morgan. But that fall also brought a calamity to the doorsteps of Pickard Studios that would require all of Wilder and Austin Pickard's resourcefulness to keep the company alive. In October of 1929 the stock market crashed, and the worst depression in the nation's history began.

## Pickard, Inc. The Great Depression 1930–1938

In 1930 the gold etched shield trademark was converted to a rubber stamp (Mark 14). Carefully applied, this mark was as neat and legible as the decals and etched marks that preceded it but was less costly to produce. This small saving was important, for as the Great Depression deepened, manufacturers of luxury items were particularly hard hit.

The most significant cost reduction however, centered around the decorating method itself. Pickard was intensely proud of his "hand-painted" reputation, yet foreign competition, increasing restraints on costs, and the public's preference for simpler, more precise designs made hand painting less and less viable; the simpler designs could not justify a top artist's wage, but they could not satisfy the market if they were not also rendered by a highly experienced hand. This pressure for lower costs and hair-line precision in the designs finally brought decalcomania to Pickard, Inc.

Most of these new designs were taken from original paintings by Challinor. "Hand Decorated" now replaced "Hand Painted" on these pieces; that is, the decals were hand-positioned (very precisely) on the china blanks. Lining and banding, however, remains to this day a hand operation requiring the utmost skill. (Anyone who believes they have a steady hand should try applying a perfect line around a cup lip just once and then consider that every piece of Pickard china has such decoration applied in this manner.)

Many decals could also be purchased as "stock" designs offered by a variety of decal manufacturers. In December of 1931 Pickard began to identify these stock decals with a new trademark: a shield-shaped outline around the word "Ravenswood" (Mark 16). (This should not be confused with H. P. Sinclaire's "Ravenwood" china. See Ravenwood mark at end of Pickard Trademark section.[35]) Unlike the "Edgerton" trademark, the "Ravenswood" mark was often accompanied by an additional "Pickard" stamp. Hand painting did not cease with the appearance of decals however.

There was still a fair market for specialty pieces, and a small market for hand painting continued until its final demise in the early 1950s.

It is not known to what depths Pickard's business declined during this period, but a 1931 sales bulletin gives a glimpse of the times when it identifies its Midwest Representative as Mr. Challinor. If one was to survive, one had to be very flexible and assume a variety of responsibilities. Times were so poor, in fact, that one artist, Albert Bernard Bero, actually commuted to the studio from Tiffin, Ohio, in 1935 and 1936!

In the midst of this impoverished financial climate, Austin Pickard demonstrated some of the leadership and imagination that would characterize his presidency in later years. In 1930 he proposed to his father that, with the acquisition of a foreign pottery now out of the question, they should establish their own laboratory in which to formulate a porcelain which they could then manufacture themselves. Even in good times, this would have been a speculative venture. But with no end to the business decline in sight, the appropriation of capital for basic research in ceramic chemistry must have sounded like the studio's death knell to any outside observer. Nevertheless Wilder Pickard saw the long-term potential in his son's idea and agreed to the investment.

Adolph G. "Si" Simon, Jr. was chosen to work with Austin on the project. Si had learned china decorating from his father who had begun decorating china in Chicago in 1903. Simon, Sr. had operated a successful home studio from 1907 through 1919 and had included glass decorating among his offerings. Si had come to work for Pickard in 1925 and his father joined the studio a few years later.

The laboratory was set up in the rear of the studio's basement where a ramp and large double doors opening onto an alley would facilitate the handling of raw materials. Austin studied government pamphlets on porcelain manufacture, Si studied ceramics at night school, and the two worked in their basement laboratory on the new venture. Wilder Pickard learned of a failed pottery in East Liverpool, Ohio, and dispatched Si to purchase their formulas. Using these formulas as a basis for their many experiments, they succeeded in producing a premium quality porcelain bisque by 1932. By government tests, it proved the equivalent of any English bone china in strength and toughness, but equally important, it could be made in very thin, light, and translucent shapes.

Work on the glaze began next, and Challinor's talents were enlisted to test the compatibility between the many glaze formulations and mineral paints. Hundreds of tiles were decorated for this purpose, and over fifty of them remain today as the facing of a fireplace in the home where Pickard's granddaughter, Sherry Shellenbach, now lives.

*Figure 33. Century of Progress souvenir plate with a paper transfer of the same image (in reverse).*

One event during the depression years that probably helped sustain the studio was the Chicago World's Fair of 1933, "The Century of Progress." Pickard maintained a small exhibit of its own, and produced souvenir plates for this event. These were single-color designs, paper-transferred from steel engravings (Fig. 33), depicting various buildings at the Fair (Plate 671). The plates bore no blank-manufacturers' identification with only the word "Pickard" stamped in gold (Mark 17) on the back. (Si Simon confirmed the fact that these blanks were purchased and were not the product of his and Austin's early experiments.) The fair, it turned out, was doubly helpful, since it was extended into 1934 for an additional season.

Further experimentation on glazes continued, and by 1935, Wilder and Minnie Pickard were presented with the first set of service plates *entirely manufactured* by Pickard Studios, Inc. The magnitude of this accomplishment can hardly be appreciated at this distance in time: the meager quarters, the scarcity of funds, and the small-scale equipment—the kiln in particular was quite small—all of this must have conspired to frustrate progress at every turn. And all of this had to take place in the midst of the struggling, normal business operations.

From the outset of the experiments, it was probably clear that the Ravenswood studio could never accommodate a china manufacturing operation. With its multiple floor levels militating against orderly material flow and the constant passage of steam locomotives spewing ash and cinders just one hundred feet in front of the studio, high manufacturing costs and high product contamination were virtually assured. A search for a contamination-free site began. The search ranged as far as Ohio, but in 1937 a lease was obtained on the former Corona fountain pen factory in Antioch, Illinois, on the Wisconsin border. The new site was about 60 miles northwest of the Ravenswood Studio, and while full-scale china manufacturing commenced in Antioch, the decorating and etching departments continued at the Ravenswood Studio.

The breadth and complexity of this new manufacturing operation required substantial investment in equipment and inventory, and that alone would have strained Pickard's resources. But the transition from a studio of artists and a small kiln room to a full-blown pottery with model-sculpting, mold-making, clay-processing, and a large, high-temperature tunnel kiln required new skills, training, and very adept management that must have challenged the very limits of the transplanted work force. Somehow it all came together, and Wilder Pickard finally saw his ambition realized in 1938 when, after a disappointing first attempt, the company received its first order from Marshall Field & Company for Pickard china, entirely made in Antioch, Illinois. Also in this year, Pickard Studios, Inc. became "Pickard, Inc." A new trademark was devised for the U.S.-made ware to which the pattern number and the pattern name were eventually added (Mark 18). This mark continues in use today.

From time to time the collector may find a piece of Pickard china whereon the trademarks have been defaced by an "X" scored or painted through them (Marks 14.1 and 18.1). During the depression, Pickard augmented its retail revenues by selling some china seconds directly from the studio. The defacement was Austin Pickard's method of identifying these purchases, thus preventing their return to a retailer for an illegal refund.

On May 27, 1939, Wilder Pickard passed away; he was 81 years old. He had established the first commercial studio devoted exclusively to the production of hand-painted specialty china. In so-doing, he had elevated china decoration to a fine art. His studio gave several hundred artists an opportunity to grow and express themselves and achieve individual renown. His studio directly and indirectly contributed to the establishment in Chicago of the largest concentration of china studios in the United States. And finally, he established a pottery which today continues to produce America's most prestigious china.

## Pickard, Inc. Antioch, 1938–Present

Figure 34. Henry Austin Pickard, 1902–1966

Austin Pickard succeeded to the presidency upon his father's death, and he was at once faced with the necessity of raising adequate funding to consolidate his operations. Capital and materials were growing scarce for World War II had broken out on September 1, 1939. Despite these impediments he managed to purchase the Antioch plant along with some adjacent land upon which he built an addition to house the Ravenswood operations. Like the move from the carriage barn, the move to Antioch resulted in the loss of some experienced artists and staff. To ease the transition, a few artists, like Max Klipphahn, commuted on a temporary basis. In mid–1941 the old Ravenswood Studio was finally sold to a candy company, and Pickard, Inc. began exclusive operations out of its new facilities in Antioch.

To maintain its operations through the war, Austin Pickard successfully bid on a Navy contract for gravy boats. These heavy chunks of institutional ware were a far cry from the delicate, sculptured porcelain with which the company had become identified. And while the revenue from the contract was important, the most significant benefit was that as a war materiel contractor, the company qualified for a fuel oil allotment, and it was the oil that fired the kilns and kept the company alive.

After the war, the company returned to full-time production of fine china. Challinor made a last-ditch effort at all-hand-painted china with his beautiful First Edition Floral series of plates (Plate 684). There is no record of how successful this series was, but their artistry ranks with Challinor's very best. Etched gold was still popular in specialty pieces such as candle holders, bon-bons, ashtrays, cigarette boxes, vases, and coffee sets. But the company's major trend in the 1940s was the development of fine dinnerware in more sophisticated patterns and shapes.

This emphasis on dinnerware designs brought the company national recognition in 1955 when its BLUE SKIES pattern earned the Altman Award for American Design. The company's advertising also took on sophistication, appearing in such prestigious magazines as *The New Yorker, House and Garden, House Beautiful,* and *Architectural Digest.*

A new decorating technique was developed in the 1940s. Called "print-and-fill," this technique borrowed from all-over etched gold production, using the transfer of master designs from engraved steel plates.

In the print-and-fill technique, only the outline of the design was engraved on the steel plate, and mineral paint was imprinted on the sheets of transfer paper instead of asphaltic resist. The paper was cut to size and then pressed onto the china blanks, transferring the outline. A preliminary firing made the outline permanent, and the design was then filled in with the appropriate colors. The uniformity which this method produced was essential to the modern designs and was an improvement in time and cost over the pounced or traced methods of design transfer. Austin Pickard could thus advertise this product as hand-painted, and the artist continued to sign his or her name to the design. This technique extended through the 1940s. Challinor's BOTANY series (Plate 681) was one of the more outstanding examples of this technique.

In 1952, after 26 years as art director and almost half a century as a Pickard artist, Edward Stafford Challinor passed away. Today his name is synonymous with antique Pickard, but his contributions in his later years were just as important. His prolific output and his flexibility in producing new designs that embodied the latest trends kept the company in the forefront of fine home appointments.

Not long after Challinor died, Austin Pickard, as his father had done in many instances before him, attracted new talent from an eastern pottery. Unlike the other artists that had followed the same trail to Pickard, John Eustice was neither an immigrant nor an Easterner. Born in 1925 in Rewey, Wisconsin, Eustice had acquired a degree in Art Education from the University of Wisconsin followed by advanced studies at the New York State College of Ceramics at Alfred, New York. He taught ceramics and then went on to design china for Castleton China and Lenox, Inc. He began his association with Pickard on a freelance basis in 1958, and moved to permanent status in 1961. Since he was equally adept at sculpting new shapes or designing new patterns, he contributed an important degree of flexibility to the company. Among John Eustice's more notable contributions, was his development of Pickard's all-time best-selling pattern, BROCADE. Like many of his predecessors, John Eustice is also an accomplished musician, having played the organ professionally most of his career.

In 1956, Austin Pickard suffered a heart attack and his son, Henry A. "Pete" Pickard, Jr. joined the firm to assume some of the burden. Pete was no stranger to the business. He had worked for his father during his college days and for two more years after graduation. He then spent a number of years in sales with a large manufacturing company. This experience, like his grandfather's representation of other manufacturers, helped broaden his perspective, so that he was able to assume full responsibility for sales and product development upon his return to the family business.

But as Pete and his father looked to the future it became evident that strong, professional plant management was essential to the company's continued growth. Fortunately, there was just such talent right in the family. Pete's sister's husband, Eben Morgan, had been working for the Goodyear company after graduation and was also a graduate of that company's manufacturing management training program. Eben Morgan joined Pickard,

Inc. in 1963 as assistant plant manager and within a year became plant manager.

In 1966 Austin Pickard died of a heart attack; he was 64 years old. He had brought the company through some of its most difficult times: depression, porcelain experimentation, the transition from studio to china manufacturer, the constraints of a war-time economy, and of course throughout it all, the constant evolution in china designs.

*Figure 35. Henry Austin ("Pete") Pickard, Jr., President 1966–1994.*

Like his father, Pete Pickard now became president at age 36. The challenges faced by this third generation of Pickards may have been different, but they were no less demanding than those of prior generations. Through the next decades, Pete added focus to the design and marketing of the product, and unlike his father and grandfather, Pete also made contributions to the artistic side of the

business. His CRESCENT design was an immediate success and continues to be a popular choice today.

Eben Morgan, now executive vice-president, continued to build the company from within, enabling the company to keep pace with the growing demand for what had become "America's Finest China." Much new equipment was acquired, including a double-track kiln. New decorating rooms, new offices, and a display room that incorporated a museum were also added.

These efforts have built the company into an internationally recognized producer of premium quality china. Pickard has added many prestigious awards to its laurels, among which have been commissions for the following:

- The Camp David China, specified by First Lady Nancy Reagan.

- A set of china created for Queen Elizabeth II of England.

- The United States Air Force Wing Commander's China.

- A series of service plates for the United States Navy.

- China for the presidential guest house, Blair House, commissioned by Tiffany & Company and designed by Tiffany's Senior Vice President and Design Director.

*Figure 36. "Washington" pattern as a complete service.*

*Figure 37.* <u>BISCAYNE</u>, <u>BALI</u>, *and* <u>MARTINIQUE</u> *patterns used as a combination setting.*

- The china service for Air Force One.

- The official United States Embassy china, used in over 160 embassies around the world for official entertaining.

*Figure 38. Pickard china used at U.S. embassies throughout the world.*

In January of 1994, Pete Pickard retired from the business and Eben Morgan became president. Pete Pickard remains active in a marketing role and continues to make some occasional promotional appearances, assuring continuity of the company's long tradition of quality. Eben Morgan's

wealth of experience will undoubtedly serve the company well as Pickard, Inc. begins its second century of operation.

*Figure 39. Eben C. Morgan, Jr., President 1994–Present.*

Like most American companies today, Pickard must introduce new designs and maintain its market share while laboring under tightening government controls, rising costs, and very aggressive competition from domestic and off-shore competitors. Behind it all, however, there is a strength of tradition that Wilder Pickard originated when he first began his business. As in the early days of the Ravenswood Studio when Gustav Hiecke would take his son to Marshall Field's china department and point to a piece of AURA ARGENTA LINEAR and proudly state, "I made that. There are my initials," this tradition of individual pride still flourishes today. And it derives from the same source as it did in 1905—each of the individuals who strive every day to create the beauty that has graced tens of thousands of American homes is a unique person and an essential contributor to the production of "America's Finest China."

## Pickard Artist Biographies

Various forms of artists' signatures and initials are shown in (parentheses). Trademark dates, shown in [brackets], are ranges for the marks themselves; unless otherwise noted, the artist may have arrived or departed anywhere within that range. Some artists may have departed and then also returned within a range. Finally, though based on extensive observation, the listings for any given artist may be incomplete and additional date ranges may yet be discovered. A few possible names are included in the hope of further identification.

In the following list, many individuals are noted as performing sub-contract art work. For a full explanation of this term, see page 25.

**Aldrich, Grace M.** (Aldrich) [1898–1903] A near-
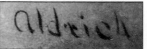
by neighbor of Pickard, she probably worked for Pickard for no more than two years. Among her works were a copy of a monk produced by Richter (not Pickard's Richter) for Affenthaler of Dresden and a diminutive copy (Plate 63) of one of Arthur Weiss' non-Pickard pastoral scenes.

**Alexander, Ruth** (ALEX, R. ALEX) [1905–1910, 1910–1912, 1912–1918] Alexander did much of the sub-contract work on the DUTCH DECORATION

and some of the more popular vellum scenics. Pickard named at least one of her original designs, ALEXANDER ROSES, after her.

**Anthony, Paul B.** (P. Anthony) [1910–1912]

Anthony was born in Georgia in 1892. Anthony was with Pickard in 1911 and perhaps a year or two longer; his work, as exemplified in his BORDURE ANTIQUE, done when he was only 19, was near-perfect. By 1914 he had become an artist for an advertising firm and was made Art Director of that firm in 1916. Much of his later work consisted of book and magazine illustrations.

**Arno, Edith** (Arno. Her signature is occasional-

ly misread as "ARLLO.") [1905–1910, 1910–1912) Her first known commercial china decorating was done at the Stouffer Studios in about 1905–1906 and ranks with the better quality decorations of that time. As a Pickard artist, she did outstanding executions of John Fuchs' designs. Her own work at Pickard was less notable. She ran her own studio in 1910.

**Aulich, Emil** (E. Aulich) [1898–1903,
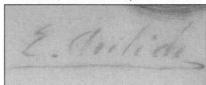
1903–1905, 1905–1910] Born in Berlin, Germany, Aulich first appeared as a glass decorator in New Bedford, Massachusetts, in 1889. His relative, Franz Bertram Aulich had started working for the famous Smith Brothers glass studio in 1883, and upon Emil's arrival, the two men formed their own studio. The enterprise only lasted a year, however, and Emil decorated for others for one more year before moving on. By the time he came to work for Pickard, Emil Aulich had acquired a national reputation as a china decorator. He had operated his own studio in Cincinnati in 1895 and had taught china decorating at the famous Osgood School in New York in 1897–1898. He was known in particular for his roses. Franz Bertram Aulich also came to Chicago, but remained independent as a china artist and teacher (he too, was noted for his roses). Both men were close neighbors of Pickard.

**Bachmann, Max L.** (B., Max, Bachman) [1905–1910] Bachmann was born July 18, 1876, in Nieder Marbach, Saxony, Germany, and received his art training at Munich and Meissen. It is not known when he came to the United States, but by 1904 he was employed as an artist at the Roseville Pottery in Zanesville, Ohio; he married Marie Marguerite Rittenberger on September 3 of that year. While at Roseville, Bachmann became friends with John Fuchs, and in the fall of 1905 the two artists and their families moved to Chicago to work in the newly completed Pickard Studios in Ravenswood. To date, there are no indications that Bachmann stayed at Pickard for more than a few years. See text for more biographical information.

**Bardos, Isadore** (Bardos [and IB at Stouffer])

[1905–1910, 1910–1912, 1912–1918, 1918–1919, 1919–1922] A competent artist who did ENCRUSTED LINEAR and other sub-contract work, he went on to work for Stouffer in the late 1920s where he did some outstanding gold and platinum designs.

**Barges, Edward C.** (Barge, Barges) He lived at the same address as Emil Fischer for seven years but did very little signed work. He also worked for the Brauer Studio in that studio's early years.

**Beitler, Joseph C.** (Beitler, von Beutler)

[1898–1903, 1903–1905] Born in Pennsylvania in 1866, he worked in one of the Trenton potteries just before the turn of the century. He may have come to Chicago as early as 1900, but he was certainly working for Pickard by 1903. He roomed with Otto Goess and originated one of Pickard's few patented designs: No. 37,352. A versatile and accomplished china painter, he left Pickard and opened his own studio in the Chicago Loop in 1907. He sold this studio after a little more than four years and went to work for the Brauer studio where he did some work in the Art Nouveau style (Plate 701). From 1910 through 1912 he also continued to produce work out of a home studio under the pseudonym of "J. C. von Beutler." He eventually turned to woodworking as a profession.

**Bek** See Carl Buschbeck

**Beulet, F.** (F. Beulet) [1903–1905, 1905–1910,

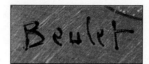

1910–1912] A very skillful artist, Beulet's beautiful execution of the DAHLIA RUBRA design speaks for itself. This signature also appears on Donath studio pieces.

**Beutlich, Anton Berthold** (Beutlich) [1898–1903,

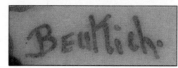

1903–1905, 1905–1910, 1910–1912, 1912–1918, 1918–1919, 1919–1922, 1922–1925. 1925–1930] Anton Berthold Beutlich was born in Stavanger, Norway, on October 10, 1870; he married Dorthea Danielsen of Bergen, Norway, but was later divorced. (Beutlich's ancestry originated in Germany, but the family migrated to Norway in the sixteenth century, hence the un-Norwegian sounding name.) Beutlich and his cousin, Anton Bertram Beutlich, emigrated from Norway to Boston in 1885. A promotion by one of the railroads at that time brought them to Chicago for the incredibly low fare of $1.00 apiece. Anton Bertram Beutlich was a painter and portraitist who maintained a studio in downtown Chicago from 1891 through 1913. Anton Berthold Beutlich was skilled in many styles of china painting, including Satsuma decorations on soft paste pottery. His PEACHES LINEAR shows both the steadiness of his hand and his mastery of subtle shading to best advantage. In 1908 and 1909, he advertised as an independent china decorator working out of his home, but this just seems to have been an experiment with independence; he never actually left Pickard. A very kind and gentle man, he later married Jane Cumming of the Pickard wrapping department. She was the daughter of another Pickard artist, Arthur Cumming. Anton Beutlich died of burns on November 16, 1925. More details are found in the text.

**Bitterly, Walter B.** (Bitterly) [1898–1903] Born in

Illinois in 1882 of Swiss parents, Bitterly lived about a block from Pickard with his artist-brother William and with Pickard artist Emil Aulich. Some of his early work for Pickard was poor, but his later work for Brauer showed significant artistic and technical talent. He probably also worked for Stouffer about 1912. He eventually became a freelance artist in the 1920s.

**Blaha, Joseph** (Blaha) [1898–1903, 1912–1918]

A skillful artist in florals, Blaha was expert at rococo scrolls and paste work that included elaborate, well-executed borders. Currants, gooseberries, and violets were among his frequent subjects. After leaving Pickard, he worked as a freelancer and also for the Stouffer and Osborne studios.

**Blažek, John** (Blazek) [1905–1910, 1910–1912, 1912–1918] Born Jan

Blažek in Austria in 1878 of Bohemian parents, Blažek initially worked at the Royal Porcelain Factory in Prague. From there he went to the Carlsbad porcelain factories and eventually entered the United States in 1905, boarding with artist Ernest Hauptmann for a short while. He did some monogramming for Pickard which of course was unsigned; the few signed examples of his work that are seen today demonstrate good, professional quality composition and brush work.

**(Boeglig, Peter)** [possibly 1898–1903] Swiss china decorator, arrived in United States 1892.

**Boehm, B.** (B. Boehm) [1912–1918] Boehm was an

expert at geometric and small floral designs that included VENETIAN RENAISSANCE.

**Bohman, Marie** (Bohman. Also listed as

Bohmann.) [1922–1925] A one-time member and officer of the Chicago Ceramic Arts Association and the winner of many exhibition awards, this artist's execution of the GOLDEN PHEASANT and VERSAILLES GARDEN designs indicates a well-advanced professional china decorator.

**Brauer, Julius H.** (JB, JBrauer) [1898–1903] See biographical details in text references.

**Breidel, William W.** (Breidel. Some of his signa-

tures can be misread as Brnidnl or other variations.) [1905–1910] Born in Austria in 1875, he arrived in the United States in 1906. Although he executed

some of Frederick Lindner's patterns, his main strength was in scenics and figural work. His PRAYING MOHAMMEDAN was featured in Pickard's 1909 color catalog. By 1910, he had established his own small studio which he carried on for about four years. According to Platt, some marital strife sent him back to Austria or Germany where he was conscripted into the army. He was subsequently killed during the war.

**Brun** (Brun) [1905–1910] Brun may or may not

have been an abbreviation since this name does appear in the old directories; however, none have been identified as artists. Only one floral decorated plate by the artist is known to exist.

**Burgner, V.** (V. Burgner) [1912–1918] Only one example of this unknown person's work has been seen, and it is without doubt, the poorest attempt at art ever to bear the Pickard trademark.

**Burton, A.** (A. Burton) [1898–1903] This artist did good commercial work— strawberry clusters, poinsettias, roses, etc.—first for Pickard, then for Brauer.

**Buschbeck, Carl** (Bek. This signature is some-

times misread as Bok or Beh.) [1910–1912] Buschbeck was born in 1872 in Saxony, Germany, and emigrated to the United States in 1908. He brought his wife, Ella, and his year-old daughter, Truda, over in 1909. He did versions of AURA ARGENTA LINEAR and other stylized and conventionalized designs. By the late 1920s, he had moved to the Stouffer studios.

**Campana, Dominick M.** (Camp) [1898–1903] Born in Venice, Italy, Campana graduated from the School of Fine Arts there before emigrating to the United States. He initially worked as a decorator for the Ceramic Art Company in Trenton, New Jersey, from 1899 through 1901. He worked for Pickard in 1902, and little is known of his work there other than a small tiger plaque in the Platt collection. He opened a studio and art school in the Auditorium Building in 1903. Located in

Chicago's "china painting district," Campana thus made important connections with many Atlan artists as well as ceramic historian, Dr. Edwin Atlee Barber. Campana taught a summer seminar at the Art Institute and became a member of the Chicago Ceramic Arts Association. By 1914 he had gone into the art supply business as the D. M. Campana Art Company. He was a regular advertiser in *Keramic Studio* magazine, and he wrote instruction books on many art subjects. The *Teacher of China Painting* was his most popular text. In 1930 he combined with another firm to form the Maurer-Campana Art Company. (See text for additional information.)

**Cathanay, F. A.** (F. A.Cathanay) [1898–1903] Very few examples of this mediocre artist's work have been found. Cathanay was undoubtedly a short-term decorator for Pickard.

**Challinor, Edward Stafford** (EC, E. Challinor)

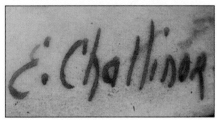

(1877–1952) [1898–1903, 1903, 1903–1905, 1905–1910, 1910–1912, 1912–1918, 1918–1919, 1919–1922, 1922–1925, 1925–1930, 1930–1938. 1938– ] See biographical details in text references.

**Cirnacty, F.** (F. Cirnacty) [1912–1918, 1918–

1919, 1919–1922] Cirnacty probably arrived about 1918. Noted for his portrait and animal rendering skills, Cirnacty also produced outstanding landscape pieces such as THE HIGHLANDS. Many of his vases were sold for lamp bodies. Providing it was professionally drilled, the hole should not detract materially from the value of a vase.

**Comyn, Arthur** (AC, Comyn, A. Comyn. Has been

misread as Cornyn.) [1903–1905, 1905–1910, 1910–1912] A member of a family of French artists, Alphonse, Louie, Julius, and Henri, Arthur was especially noted for his scenics of Egypt, Italy, and Holland. His WILDFLOWERS OF AMERICA series of plates demon-

strated his versatility in naturalistic florals. Most of his work bears some explanatory legend on the reverse side of the piece.

(Cornyn, Arthur) See Arthur Comyn

**Corey, Harriet L.** (HLC, Corey. May be misread as

HLG) [1912–1918] Miss Corey opened a small studio in 1908 which she converted into an art school in 1910. This lasted through 1914 when she joined Pickard Studios. All of her signed work seems to have been scenic vellums. She used both her last name and a rather obtrusive cartouche of her initials for a signature.

**Coufall, John Anton** (AC, [Do not confuse with

Arthur Comyn's initials.], A. Coufall) [1903–1905, 1905–1910] An outstanding producer of punch bowls, pitchers, and trays bearing clusters of luscious, colorful grapes, "Tony" Coufall also created an *ETCHED GOLD ROSE ON MATTE GREEN* design that was very popular. He was considered to be something of a womanizer (note the fashion-plate attire, including spats, in the 1905 photo on page 24). He was working for Stouffer studios by 1922.

**Cumming, Arthur J.** (Cumming, Cummings;

both spellings appear in the records as well as on china, but Cumming is the more frequent.) [1905–1910] Born in England on May 4, 1847, Cumming was a graduate of the Exeter School of Art which was a branch of the South Kensington School of Art in London. He also studied church architecture and civil engineering, and was a pupil of the famous English engraver, Thomas Landseer. He emigrated to the United States in 1872 and worked first for an architectural firm in Philadelphia and then for a firm in Boston. He first appeared in New Bedford, Massachusetts, in 1874 where he was both a superintendent of drawing and an instructor of art in several schools. He was a very accomplished artist and draftsman, and he earned many awards during his residency on the East Coast. There is no indication that he worked for any of the glass com-

panies in New Bedford, but Gifford, Fuchs, and Yeschek were all in residence there during his stay, and he may have made their acquaintance at that time. Cumming's wife, Marie, died in 1904, and he and his eighteen year old daughter, Jane, then moved to Chicago. He cleaned and restored paintings and gave private art instruction and also continued with his own oil painting. He was one of the few artists who took up residence in the apartments that Pickard constructed adjacent to the Ravenswood Studio. He did landscapes and seascapes for Pickard in the 1905–1910 period, but just how much time he spent at Pickard is difficult to assess. His daughter is listed as an art student in the 1910 Census—probably studying with her father. She worked in Pickard's wrapping department, and though no examples have been discovered, she may have done some decorating for Pickard as well; she later married Pickard artist, Anton Beutlich. Arthur J. Cumming died in Chicago on June 20, 1913.

**Dickinson, H. C.** (H. C. Dickinson) [1898–1903] Dickinson was a short-term artist who did passable floral decorations.

**Donath, Edward W.** (Donath) [1894–1897, 1898–1903, 1903–1905] See text for biographical details.

**Donisch, Edward F.** (EFDON) [1905–1910, 1910–1912, 1912–1918] Donisch was an expert artist in enamels. His rendering of Emil Tolpin's ENAMEL CHRYSANTHEMUMS was one of Pickard's best designs in the conventional genre. He also did executions of ATLAN ENAMEL, FLOWERS AND TRACERY, and ANTIQUE CHINESE ENAMELS.

**Drzewiecki, Frank** Worked for Pickard during the 1910–1912 period and is listed in the directories as a painter, but no known examples of his work have been found.

**Duran, L.** (L. Duran) [1903–1905] Duran was a short-term, sub-contract artist who executed Roden's *CROCUS CONVENTIONAL* design.

**Edgerton** (possibly William O.) [1903–1905] Edgerton's known work is limited to a single, well-executed and imaginative figure vase (Plate 23). (Do not confuse his signature with Pickard's Edgerton Studios.)

**Edward** (Edwd) [1910–1912] Edward did sub-contract executions of many of Paul Gasper's designs. His (or her) own designs consisted of nondescript florals.

**EFDON** See Edward F. Donisch

**Erbe** (Erbe) [1919–1922] A short-term artist who executed some of Florence James' designs.

**Falatek, Louis H.** (Falatek. Has been misread as Faladik) [1912–1918, 1918–1919, 1919–1922, 1922–1925] Born in the Hungarian sector of Austria in 1894, he and his mother emigrated to the United States in 1914, just ahead of the hostilities. Falatek did vellum scenics, among which were SPRING BLOSSOMS and some peacock/etched gold border designs. By 1922 he had moved to Rivir Studios. By the early 1930s he had changed his name to Falk; no Pickard pieces are known to bear this new name.

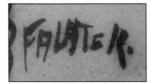

**Falk, Louis H.** See Falatek, Louis H.

**Farrington** (possibly William H.) (Farrington) [1903–1905, 1905–1910] This artist specialized in portrait and animal subjects, and although he spent approximately ten years with Pickard, few of his pieces have survived. PRAYING MOHAMMEDAN, FALSTAFF, *SAINT BERNARD*, and CAPE COD FISHERMAN were some of his most popular designs.

**Fischer, Emil J. T.** (EF, Fisch, Fish, Fisher [Platt refers to him as "John Fisher."]) [1903–1905, 1905–1910, 1910–1912, 1912–1918] Fischer was born in Dresden, Germany, in 1871,

and after completing his art education was said to have worked at the Donath Atelier (or this may have been the porcelain factory of P. Donath). Fischer came directly to Pickard upon his emigration to the United States in 1904. An expert and prolific artist, his CONVOLVULVUS illustrated his deft handling of floral subjects, while VIOLET SUPREME was unquestionably his most beautiful and enduring design.

**Fisher, John** See Fischer, Emil J. T.

(Flood, William F.) Flood is named in the 1905 photograph of Ravenswood Studio personnel and has therefore been assumed by some collectors to have been an artist. William Flood was a retired feed and grain dealer and was Minnie Pickard's father. He and Minnie's brothers had assisted Pickard with many of the non-artistic aspects of the business in the 1890s; at the time of this photograph, he was 68 years old, but he was probably still active in some small capacity.

(Flora) See F. Loba

**Fox** [1903–1905, 1905–1910] This artist's work

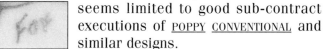

seems limited to good sub-contract executions of POPPY CONVENTIONAL and similar designs.

**Friedrich** (Friedrich) [1903–1905] Friedrich produced good commercial quality work. He has

only been identified with floral subjects.

**Fritz** (Fritz) [1903–1905] Fritz was probably a short-term artist. His (or her) currant design is well-executed.

**Fuchs, John** (JF, Fuchs, J. Fuchs)

[1903–1905, 1905–1910, 1910–1912, 1912–1918] See text for biographical details.

**Fuchs, Pauline** Born in Illinois in 1876 of German parents, Pauline Fuchs began work at the Ravenswood studio as a clerk in 1915. Although she was decorating china by 1920 and stayed with the company through 1940, her signature has yet

to be discovered on any pieces. After Pickard moved to Antioch, she decorated china at Frank Yeschek's Ceramic Artcraft Studios into the late 1940s. She is erroneously listed by Platt as a daughter of John Fuchs—there was no relationship between them.

**Gasper, Paul P.** (PG, Gasper) [1903–1905,

1905–1910, 1910–1912, 1912–1918] Born in Germany in 1864, he learned china decorating in the Royal Bonn Pottery at Bonn-on-the-Rhine. He emigrated to the United States in 1891, and first appeared in Trenton, New Jersey, where he produced some of the delft decorations for the Cook Pottery. In 1901 he moved to Ohio, working as a decorator for the Roseville Pottery in Zanesville. It is possible that he met John Fuchs and Max Bachmann there, for they all worked in Zanesville at the same time and they all came to Pickard in 1905 in time for the opening of the new Ravenswood studio. Gasper did outstanding work in both figures and florals; his FALSTAFF portraits are particularly well rendered. In 1909 he brought out his POPPY AND DAISY design; this was followed by another version of the same design: *WHITE POPPY AND DAISY*. Both designs maintained their popularity into the late teens, which was quite late, considering the strong popular trend toward simpler designs. He lived at the same address as artist Joseph Yeschek for five years and continued his art career into the late 1920s.

**Gerts, J. C.** (Gerts) [1919–1922] Gerts worked

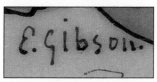

for Pickard for a short time in the early 1920s, probably as a sub-contract artist. ANTIQUE CHINESE ENAMEL is one design upon which this signature occurred.

**Gibson, Edward** (E. Gibson) [1903–1905, 1905–1910] Born in Illinois in 1883 of Swedish parents, Gibson began work for Pickard in 1906 at the age of 23 A very skillful floral artist, he numbered GIBSON PANSIES, the *NARCISSUS DESIGN*, and the *ORCHID DESIGN* among his most popular offerings. In 1910 he left Pickard to become president of the International Art Studio (see page 264). This venture was dissolved after a little over two years, and Gibson then went into business as an art supply dealer and china painting instructor, initially located a few blocks from the Ravenswood studio. He remained in this business into the late 1920s.

**Gifford, Nathan Roswell** (N.R.G., Giff. This artist's 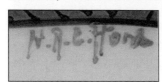 initials easily may be confused with those of Harry R. Griffiths) [1903–1905, 1905–1910] Born in Massachusetts in 1863 of American parents, Gifford first appeared in New Bedford, Massachusetts, in 1887, where he decorated glass for the famous Smith Brothers glass company. While in New Bedford, he may have met Cumming, Fuchs, and Yeschek who all worked there at some time during his residency. In 1894 he married his French-Canadian wife, Octavia, and they eventually had four children. About 1896 the family moved to Pennsylvania and by 1903 they were living in Chicago. Gifford's work at Pickard included both floral and scenic subjects at which he was quite adept. Italian fishing boats, stylized flowers, and corn whiskey jugs were all in his repertoire. His signature disappeared from Pickard pieces about 1910, but he is known to have worked for Stouffer and perhaps others into the late 1920s.

**Goess, Otto W.** (Goess) [1903–1905, 1905–1910]  Born in Germany in 1885, Goess's parents brought him to the United States in 1887. When he joined Pickard in 1904 at age 19, he was one of the studio's youngest, yet best-trained artists. His AUTUMN BLACKBERRIES was one of his earliest designs, and based on the frequency with which it is still seen, was a very successful one. His EGYPTIAN DESIGN, produced after the studio had moved to Ravenswood, was a popular conventionalized design that came in several color combinations. He lived in the same street as Gasper, Challinor, and Yeschek. He left Pickard in 1910 and went into advertising art, later becoming an advertising copywriter and a salesman.

**Göttlich, J.** (J. Göttlich) [1912–1918, 1918–1919, 1919–1922] Göttlich did naturalistic florals as well as many scenic vellum subjects.

**Grane** (Grane. This difficult signature has been  misread as Grahn, Grohn, or Grotin.) [1898–1903, 1903–1905] A very skillful artist, Grane's NUDE WITH RAVEN was one of Pickard's most spectacular offerings in the figural genre. EVENING SPREADS HER MANTLE as well as various monk subjects and a few florals were also part of this very talented artist's repertoire.

**Griffiths, Harry R.** (H.R.G., Griff. This artist's signatures easily may be confused  with those of Nathan Roswell Gifford.) [1903–1905] Griffiths did very good naturalistic fruits and florals, occasional-  ly with some gold "whiplash" embellishments. He later worked for the Stouffer, Brauer, Donath, and France studios; he also worked as a salesman during this time.

**Grumieau, Louis P.** [1912–1918] Born in Belgium in 1872, Grumieau emigrated to the United States in 1899. He began decorating china in Chicago at least as early as 1906 when he lived in the old carriage barn neighborhood. According to Platt, he was the creator of the ANTIQUE CHINESE ENAMELS design, but no Pickard china with his signature has yet been discovered. He operated his own studio briefly in 1913, and one signed plate from this period bears a very simple gold border with blue-banded shields. His wife and two children, Emil and Jack, were also decorators. He was decorating lamp shades by 1922 and eventually went on to work for the Kalita Studios.

**Haag** (Haag) [1905–1910] A short-term artist who did mediocre and nondescript fruits and florals.

**Haase, Frank** (Haase) [1905–1910] Haase paint-  ed simple florals for Pickard as early as 1908. He moved on to do some freelance work for Parsche Studios in the teens and did some very imaginative, well-executed work there.

**Hahn, Charles** (cHahn. The c is often attached to  the H and has been misread as d'John, Cholin, and other variations.) [1898–1903, 1903, 1903–1905] A very versatile artist in florals, he did conservative rose garlands and free-form, brilliantly colored tulips (*TULIP MODERNE*) equally well.

**Half** (Half) [1905–1910] A short-term artist who did mediocre and nondescript florals.

**Hanische, Frank H.** (Platt's Hamische) [c.1905–1910] Hanische was decorating china in Chicago as early as 1902. It is not known how long he worked for Pickard although Platt makes note of him in the wide range of 1905–1919. Inasmuch as he became Parsche Studios' only full-time decorator, he probably departed Pickard by 1912, if not earlier.

**Hardwick** See William S. Hartwig and Adolph J. Heidrich

**Harp, M.** [1912–1918] A short-term artist who did vellum scenics.

**Hartman** (Hart, Hartman) [1910–1912] A very skillful artist who executed Carl Roessler's gold and platinum <u>AURA</u> <u>MOSAIC</u> design.

**Hartwig, William S.** Platt mentions him in her notes as "Walter," and he is listed as a gilder and artist from 1908 through 1922. If he signed his pieces "Hart" as did Hartman, there would be no way currently of differentiating the two. No "Hartwig"-signed pieces have been discovered to date. He may possibly be the "Mr. Hardwick" listed in the 1905 group photograph.

**Hauptmann, Ernest V.** [1910–1912, 1912–1918] A fellow boarder with artist John Blazek, Hauptmann was born in German Bohemia in 1885, and emigrated to the United States in 1906. By 1922 he was operating his own studio on the South Side. Hauptmann and his wife, also a china decorator, were later associates of artist Waclaw Kalita when Kalita opened his own studio.

**Heap, Samuel** (S.H. Heap) [1903–1905] Born in 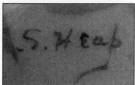 England in 1873, Heap emigrated to the United States in 1896, and worked for one or more of the Trenton, New Jersey, potteries. He came to Chicago in late 1904 or early 1905, and probably did not work for Pickard for more than a year. Despite that short residence, a fair number of his well-painted fruit and floral designs can still be found. A South Side resident, he moved over to the Stouffer studio almost as soon as it opened in 1905 where he continued to produce beautiful work into the 1920s.

(**Heidrich, Adolph J.**) (Heidrich along with Hartwig is another possibility for the "Mr. Hardwick" referred to in Platt's listing. No Pickard china bearing the A. H. or A. Heidrich signature has yet been found, but it is listed here because of that possibility. In all likelihood his work would have been animals and some scenics (and thus rarely found) and would bear the 1903–1905 or the 1905–1910 mark. Some early listings also give "Heidrick.") See text for biographical details.

**Heinz, J.** (J. Heinz) [1905–1910] Capable of good  commercial renderings of fruits and flowers, Heinz subsequently worked for the Donath Studio and also Pitkin & Brooks. While with the latter, he produced a close copy of Pickard's patent number 37,170 <u>CARNATION</u> <u>CONVENTIONAL</u> design.

**Hessler, Robert** (RH, Hess) [1898–1903,  1903–1905, 1905–1910, 1910–1912] Born of German parents in Philadelphia, Pennsylvania, on April 12, 1872, 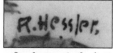 Hessler studied art at the Philadelphia Industrial Art School. He came to Pickard with his new bride about 1902, and his signature thereafter appeared on a long list of top-selling designs: *CYCLAMEN*, <u>MODERN</u> <u>CONVENTIONAL</u>, <u>CARNATION</u> <u>CONVENTIONAL</u>, <u>METALLIC</u> <u>GRAPES</u> <u>AND</u> <u>LEAVES</u>, <u>AURA</u> <u>ARGENTA</u> <u>LINEAR</u>, <u>ENCRUSTED</u> <u>LINEAR</u>, <u>HYACINTHUS</u>, plus many others, including some etched designs. Although skilled in fruit and floral renderings, his great talent was in stylized and conventionalized designs. His daughter, Ginny, remembers him as a quiet man, who made little money but created a happy family. Like

*Figure 40. Robert Hessler when he worked for Frank Yeschek's Ceramic Artcraft Studio.*

located on the near South Side, the Quality Art Studio. In late 1914 or early 1915 he became a china decorator for Pickard. He did his own variation of AURA ARGENTA LINEAR as well as many stylized and geometric border designs. He lived on the South Side and took the "L" train to the studio every day, including a half day on Saturday.

Hiecke, like virtually every other china artist, did much free-lancing at home. His son, Herbert, recalled going down to the Loop on Saturday afternoons with his father to buy china and art supplies. He also recalled being taken to the studio on several occasions and seeing the artists at work at his or her own window. One of the biggest thrills for father and son was to walk through Marshall Field's and see china on display that Gustav Hiecke had decorated. Hiecke worked for Pickard until the studio moved to Antioch. He died on October 11, 1947.

*Figure 41. Gustav Hiecke in the late teens.*

many artists Hessler was not very money-wise, and it was largely through his wife's frugality (only one toy at Christmas for each of three children) that the family was able to save enough to buy their own house. He worked for Pickard until about 1930 and then became a casualty of the Great Depression and was reduced to painting window screens to earn a living. He later decorated for Frank Yeschek's Ceramic Artcraft Studios. He died in Chicago on February 23, 1961.

**Hiecke, Gustav H. G.** (G.H., Hiecke) [1912–1918, 1918–1919, 1919–1922, 1922–1925, 1925–1930, 1930–1938] Gustav Heinrich Gregor Hiecke was born on July 15, 1869, in Bohemia and received his art education in Meissen, Germany.

He came to Chicago in August of 1896, bringing with him his widowed mother, Theresa, and his piano. He married on November 1, 1902, and had three children. Initially, he made his living as a music teacher, but by 1911 he was decorating for a small firm

**Hille, Myrtle** (M. Hille) [1910–1912] A short-term artist whose only known rendering, the FORGET-ME-NOT pattern, was nevertheless very well executed.

**Hip** (Hip) [1905–1910] This artist was probably very short-term, and the name is undoubtedly an abbreviation. Workmanship was nevertheless excellent as evidenced in the *DAISIES IN GOLD PASTE ON GREEN LUSTRE* design.

**Honey, Ethel R.** (Hon) [1910–1912] A short-term artist who also worked for the Stouffer Studios. Technically accomplished, her work included renderings of DAHLIA RUBRA.

**James, Florence M.** (FJames) [1903–1905, 1905–1910, 1910–1912, 1912–1918, 1918–1919, 1919–1922] James arrived in very early

1905 and probably worked a little later than 1922, but no marks have been found to confirm this. She did many naturalistic floral designs: Easter lilies, poppies, lilies-of-the-valley, and daisies. Her most popular design was the DUTCH DECORATION, followed by two variations: the *COLONIAL DECORATION* and the *PILGRIM DECORATION*. In addition to these she did some scenic vellums and some renderings of ROSABELLE. In the 1919–1922 period she produced the very attractive *WATER LILIES AND ENCRUSTED GOLD* design. See text for further biographical details.

**Jelinek, Thomas M.** (TMJ, Jelinek) [1898–1903, 1903–1905] Born in Austria/Bohemia in 1877, Jelinek emigrated to the United States in 1885. Jelinek's style was largely naturalistic. He was very adept at roses and his early designs were very colorful. He went to work at the Stouffer studio about 1905 and stayed there through 1922. Simultaneously he ran

his own small studio in 1914–1915. By 1928 he was decorating lamp shades for the Rembrandt Lamp Company.

**Johnson, Mae E.** [1894–1898] Biographical details are found in the text.

**Kalita, Waclaw** A. (1891–1971) [1930–1938] Few Pickard items bear his signature because of his late appearance at Pickard (early 1930s through late 1930s) when most china was unsigned, and also because of his specialization in gold border design. Biographical details are found in the text.

**Keates, Alfred** (Keates) [1903–1905, 1905–1910]

Platt states that Keates was Curtis Marker's maternal grandfather; this does not seem very likely inasmuch as, at the time of their joint establishment of the International Art Studios, Keates was 49 years old and Marker was 28 years old. Keates did a few naturalistic scenics, but he tended to concentrate on florals: poppies, apple blossoms, and orchids. Generally conservative in his compositions, they were occasionally stylized, but nothing of his can be described as conventionalized. More biographical details are found in the text.

**Keates, Madeline** (M. Keates) [1905–1910] Born

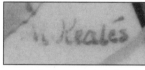

in England in 1892, she emigrated to the United States with her family in 1902. Her father, Alfred, gave her expert training, for she was producing outstanding floral designs for Pickard by the time she was 18 (1910). She probably left Pickard at the same time that her father left to pursue his independent ventures; none of her work subsequent to that time has been discovered.

**Kiefus, Jacob I.** (JK, JKiefus) [1898–1903, 1903, 1903–1905] Jacob Kiefus

was born in the Polish sector of Austria in 1874; he emigrated to the United States in 1898. Kiefus started work in Chicago as a finisher, but was at work for Pickard by late 1902 or early 1903. Although never termed a "top" Pickard artist, he was certainly expert in his stylized arrangements of florals. His earliest work showed a very even hand with gold scrolling, and he was capable of developing very soft moods in his fruit compositions. A South Side resident, he went to work for

Stouffer as soon as Stouffer opened his studio in 1905. He lived or boarded with Jacob Stouffer and his family for almost five years, producing some outstanding stylized florals for him. Upon Stouffer's death in 1912, Kiefus became the firm's corporate secretary and held that post through 1917. By 1924, he had left Stouffer and gone into retail or wholesale china sales. He died about 1927.

**Klein, Ingeborg** (K, Klein) [1919–1922, 1922–1925,

1925–1930] A Swedish immigrant who started work in her early twenties at Pickard in 1920 or 1921, she was a close companion of artist Ester Samuelson. Her work seems

confined to sub-contract executions of ORIENTAL BIRD, INDIAN TREE, and a fruit basket design. She went back to Sweden about 1926 or 1927 and never returned.

(Kline) This name appears in Platt's list, but no such signature has been discovered; it is probably a corruption of Klein.

**Klipphahn, Maxwell Rean** (Rean, [sometimes

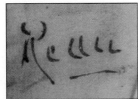

misread as Reau] Klipp, M.K.) [1898–1903, 1903, 1903–1905, 1905–1910, 1910–1912, 1912–1918, 1918–1919, 1919–1922, 1922–1925, 1925–1930, 1930–1938] One of Pickard's best and most prolific artists, Klipphahn did fruits and flowers in naturalistic, stylized, and conventionalized formats equally well. A very imaginative artist, his designs included REAN MUMS; CHRYSANTHE-MUMS, LUSTRE AND MATTE RED; *CARNA-TIONS, LUSTRE AND MATTE GREEN*; FRUITS LINEAR; AND SEVILLE. Curious-

ly, the popularity of Klipphahn's

work did not keep him continuously employed at Pickard. His ambition constantly seemed to pull him into independent ventures. In 1915, he opened his own studio just four blocks east of the Ravenswood Studio; he maintained this studio into 1917. As one artist observed, "He was always leaving, but Pickard was always talking him into coming back." Despite his absences, his signature is found with every Chicago trademark, from his

arrival in 1900 through the last one used at the Ravenswood studio. Most of his work was signed "Rean"; very few pieces were signed "Klipp" while he was working for Pickard. A number of "M.K." pieces are to be found, but as Waclaw Kalita's son, Zenon, observed, these pieces were his "off" days and are generally inferior to the balance of his work. See text for more biographical details.

**Koenig, Carl F.** (CK, Koenig. Koenig's initials are

sometimes erroneously read as AC, Arthur Comyn.) [1905–1910, 1910–1912] Koenig was born on March 30, 1881 in Arnstadt, Thuringen, Germany,

where he became an apprentice at age 14. He arrived in the United States in 1905, and it is believed that he came directly to Chicago. He did naturalistic fruits and flowers as well as *BLUEBELLS CONVENTIONAL*. His signature is most frequently found on CORNFLOWER CONVENTIONAL pieces. See additional details under Koenig Studios.

**Koep, F. H.** (F. H. Koep) [1903–1905, 1905–1910]

Koep did sub-contract renderings of Lindner's TULIP CONVENTIONAL. METALLIC GRAPES most often bears this signature.

**Kriesche, F.** (possibly Frederick) (F.K., Kries, Kriesche. Occasionally

misread as Krivsyie, Krietschs, or Kriesuie.) [1898–1903, 1903–1905, 1905–1910] Kriesche did careful, beautifully colored work that included many florals such as *NASTURTIUM CONVENTIONAL* and a variety of violet patterns. His *CARP POND* portraying a fish in golden currents illustrates his skill at its best.

**Kubasch, Emil** (Kubasch) [1903–1905] Little of his work is known inasmuch

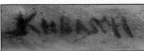

as he seems to have been devoted exclusively to figural subjects. His ARROW MAKER is a copy of a postcard from that period, while his *MOOR WITH TIGER*, and CATTLE BY A HIGHLAND LAKE are unusually large pieces.

**Kucia** (Kucia) [1919–1922] Probably a short term, sub-contract artist who executed *CHINESE PEACOCKS* and similar designs.

**Leach, George P.** (Leach) [1903–1905, 1905–1910] Born in Ire-

land in 1879, his parents brought him to the United States that same year. While working for Pickard he roomed with artists Nobel Ray and George Sinclair. Leach produced some unique effects in his compositions. His <u>POND</u> <u>LILY</u> was featured in Pickard's 1909 catalog. In 1911 he moved to the South Side and went to work for Jacob Stouffer. He then went to work for the short-lived Rogers-Martini studio. By 1915 he had opened his own studio which he operated into the mid-twenties.

**(Lebrun)** [1903–1905] Although this artist's name

appears on a Pickard-marked piece, Lebrun was an East Coast artist, and was never employed by Pickard. (See text for further information.)

**Lemke, Walter R.** (W. Lemke) [1903–1905, 1905–1910] Born in Wisconsin in 1886, Lemke was decorating china for Pickard when he was only 21. Colorful compositions of tulips and nasturtiums were among his designs. By 1914 he had become a machinist.

**Leon** (Leon. Platt states that this artist used his

first name as a signature, however there were many artists in Chicago with Leon as a last name and though proper identification has yet to by established, the first name theory seems very improbable.) [1898–1903, 1903–1905] Leon's work was primarily fruits and flowers in traditional, naturalistic formats and included gooseberries, currants, apple blossoms, and apple clusters among his subjects. His signature also appears on china produced by the D'Arcy Studio in Kalamazoo, Michigan.

**LeRoy, M. Rost** (LeRoy, M. Rost LeRoy. Often misread as DeRoy; it should not be confused with Max Rost.)

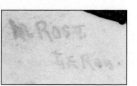

[1898–1903, 1903, 1903–1905] LeRoy was possibly a relative of artist Max Rost since they both worked for Pickard and then for Donath at about the same time. LeRoy was a prolific producer of a wide variety of traditional subjects that included cherry sprays, strawberry sprays, apple blossoms, gooseberries, and an occasional bird. His compositions with dark backgrounds and embellished gold borders with raised paste were some of Pickard's best in this style. LeRoy went to the Donath studio about 1906.

**Lindner, Frederick J.** (Lind, F. Lind. This signature is occasion-

ally misread as Ling.) [1898–1903, 1903, 1903–1905, 1905–1910, 1910–1912] Lindner was a native of Dresden, Germany, where he received his training in the porcelain decorating studios of Richard Klemm. Born in 1866, he emigrated to the United States in 1898, and settled initially in Pennsylvania where he met and married his wife, Emily. He came to Pickard in 1903. He was a masterful artist who produced many of Pickard's finest designs, Lindner skillfully adapted them to a wide variety of china shapes. Among his designs were <u>IRIS</u> <u>CONVENTIONAL</u>, <u>NEW</u> <u>IRIS</u> <u>CONVENTIONAL</u>, *IRIS LINEAR*, <u>TULIP</u> <u>CONVENTIONAL</u>, <u>ARABIAN</u>, <u>NEW</u> <u>ARABIAN</u>, and <u>YELLOW</u> <u>CHERRIES</u> <u>AND</u> <u>MATT</u> <u>GREEN</u>. He also did a considerable quantitiy of Pickard's very ornate monogrammed china.

**Loba, F.** (F. Loba. Misread by Platt as Flora)

[1894–1897, 1898–1903, 1903–1905, 1905–1910] Despite his (or her) long association with Pickard this artist remains an enigma. The signature appears on two examples from Pickard's Edgerton Studio period. Loba's style in roses is unmistakable; other work included renderings of Fred Walters' white poppy design. Loba went on to work for Stouffer.

**Loh, John** (Loh. Sometimes misread as initials.) [1898–1903, 1903–1905, 1905–1910, 1910–1912] Loh's work was mostly focused on poppies; in fact, he

signed himself "Poppy John" in a letter to Frank Yeschek. His tenure with Pickard probably spanned about ten or twelve years.

**Luken, Minnie A.** (Luken) [1912–1918] A Pickard

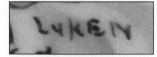

artist for a year or less, biographical details are found in the text.

**Maley, Eva E.** (Maley) [1910–1912, 1912–1918]

Maley did some sub-contract work, primarily in scenic vellums such as ITALIAN GARDEN. Her rendering of the *RED-HAIRED SYLPH* was unusual in itself, but also because Pickard had largely dropped figural pieces by that time. ·

**Mark** (Mark) [1893–1903, 1912–1918] This signa-

ture was not an abbreviation for that of Curtis Marker; it differs substantially from Marker's, moreover, the first example of it pre-dates Marker's arrival by quite a few years. The span of years separating the trademark periods in which it occurs is also noteworthy. The three pieces of this artist's work that have been examined are nondescript depictions of violets, cherries, and roses in a naturalistic style.

**Marker, Curtis H.** (Marker) [1905–1910, 1910–1912, 1912–1918, 1918–1919, 1919–1922, 1922–1925, 1925–1930]

Born in Ohio of Ohio-born parents in 1882, Marker lived with artist Howard Reury upon his arrival at Pickard in 1908. After just two years he joined with Gibson and Keates to form the International Art Studios. The attempt was unsuccessful, and he returned to Pickard and worked as a decorator into the late 1920s. From the very beginning, he produced premium-quality work. His CALLA LILY was painted when he was only 26 and displays superb talent in color and design. In the realm of scenic vellums, his ITALIAN GARDEN, YOSEMITE FALLS, WILDWOOD, and HAWTHORNE placed him in the same league as Challinor. Dark, moonlit scenics were one of his specialties. His representations of fruits and flowers are nowhere better displayed than in his DESERTED GARDEN and ROSELAND designs.

**Marmorstein, Henry** (Marmorstein) [1903–1905]

See text for biographical details.

(Matsuo, Itero N.) See text for details.

**McCorkle, Zuie** (Z.M., Z. Mac, Z. Mack, Zuie Mac.

The Z may occasionally resemble an L.) [1905–1910] Born in Illinois in 1868, Miss McCorkle was a relative of Pickard's attorney and brother-in-law, George McCorkle. She first appeared in Chicago in 1898, working as an artist on the South Side. By 1907, she had moved north to Hermitage Avenue in the same neighborhood with Alfred Keates and Joseph Yeschek. She worked for Pickard Studios through 1910, after which she left and became an osteopath. Her work seems confined to well-executed florals in stylized and Art Nouveau patterns.

**Mentges, Edward P.** (MGS, Menges, E. Mentges)

[1905–1910, 1910–1912] Born in Cincinnati, Ohio, of a French father and German mother in 1870, Mentges married an Ohio girl ten years his junior. Mentges' soft rendering of white and pink poppies was a very popular design, but nothing else is known of his work at Pickard, for whom he probably worked for only three years. He opened his own studio in 1914 which he operated through 1920. He continued decorating china for others into the late twenties. His wife was also a china decorator.

(Messino) See Matsuo, Itero N.

**Miche** (Do not confuse with Michel; may be misread

as Mighe) [1905–1910] A very accomplished floral artist who decorated for White's Art Company after 1913.

**Michel, Harry E.** (H.E.M., Michel) [1898–1903,

1903–1905] Born in Pennsylvania in 1881 of Pennsylvania-born parents, Michel was an accomplished artist from the time his work first appeared. Violets, tulips, and nasturtiums were some of the subjects of his many stylized designs. His *REGENCY WATER LILIES* show him at his very best. Michel moved to the Stouffer studio as soon as it opened in 1905 and remained there through the late twenties.

**Miller, Anton** (Mill, Miller) [1905–1910,  1910–1912, 1912–1918] Born in Germany in 1884, Miller emigrated to the United States in 1907. A near neighbor of artist Howard Reury, Miller did the very unique and charming CELTIC DECORATION consisting of a harp and shamrocks on green lustre ground framed in a gold ribbon; he also did renderings of AURA ARGENTA LINEAR and SPRING BLOSSOMS. By 1922, he had moved to the Rivir Studios and from there he went to the J. H. Stouffer Company where he did a number of fine gold and platinum designs.

**Monti, H. A.** [possibly 1919–1922 and 1922–1925] Described by Platt as an expert bander, he listed himself as a china decorator. He is listed here in the eventuality that he may have done some work in addition to banding.

**Moore, Bertha L.** (B.M., Moore) [1905–1910]  Born in Pennsylvania of English parents in 1878, Miss Moore was the sister-in-law of artist Howard Reury with whom she lodged. She produced several 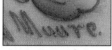 good-quality violet designs, but she probably was with Pickard no more than three years.

**Motzfeldt, Andrew** (Motzfeldt signed vertically)  [1898–1903, 1903, 1903–1905] It is unclear whether Motzfeldt was the son of an engraver or was himself originally an engraver. His work at Pickard, while occasionally rather crude, spanned an interesting and broad range of decoration, going from conservative, naturalistic florals to fish, birds, and very colorful florals with gold whiplash embellishments. Like a number of other Pickard artists, he was a member of the Chicago Ceramic Arts Association and the National League of Mineral Painters; he showed two decorated pieces in their May, 1906, exhibit at the Art Institute. He lived with his widowed mother and later became a designer at another unspecified company.

**Mullen** See Walters, Frederick

**Neitsche, Paul** See Nitsche, Paul R.

**Nessy, John** (JN, Nessy, JNessy) [1898–1903,  1903–1905, 1905–1910, 1910–1912, 1912–1918] Born in Prague, Bohemia, in 1855, Nessy emigrated to the United States in 1895. Nessy did good commercial designs of fruits, flowers, and nuts in mostly naturalistic styles. He did renderings of DESERTED GARDEN and similar designs, but his FRUIT PANELS were his most outstanding original work and went through several variations. Always a South Side resident, Nessy moved to the suburb of Cicero and to the Stouffer studio by 1922.

**Nichols, Bessie** (Nichols) [1919–1922] Miss  Nichols was a subcontract artist who did renderings of the ORIENTAL BIRD design.

**Nitsche, Paul R.** (Nitshe) Nitsche was born in Germany in 1875, and emigrated to the United States in 1908. Nitsche, along with Kalamazoo artist John H. Schindler, roomed with the Fuchs family after John Fuchs died in 1913. Free-lance naturalistic floral plates from his short stay with the family are extant, but nothing of his work at Pickard has been identified. He is known to have lived in the vicinity of the Ravenswood Studio from 1914 through 1928, working for himself about 1920, then decorating for Yeschek, Inc. in the late 1920s.

*Figure 42. Frank Nittel when he worked for Frank Yeschek's Ceramic Artcraft Studio.*

**Nittel, Frank** (F. Nittel) [1910–1912] Born in Austria in 1870, Nittel and his wife, Sophie, emigrated to the United States in 1908. Nittel was a technically accomplished artist whose gold and platinum variant of HYACINTHUS, *AURA ARGENTA HYACINTHUS*, was quite striking. Although his signature is rarely seen, he probably worked for Pickard for about five years. He later decorated for Frank Yeschek's Ceramic Artcraft Studio.

**Passony, Arthur** (AP, APassony, Passony, Passoni. Listed as "Passoni" from 1908 through 1917, he had changed to "Passony" by 1928. Both spellings appear on china ware.) [1905–1910, 1910–1912, 1912–1918] Born Arturo Passoni in Italy, he studied at the Milan Academy of Breta with continuing studies under Pompeo Coppini where he acquired particular skills in Florentine decoration. Passony's most outstanding works were CALLA LILIES, FLORENTINE, and the rarely seen *CARNATION AND PLATINUM*; he also executed versions of AURA ARGENTA LINEAR and the SCOTCH design. He operated his own art studio from 1914 through 1916, but returned to Pickard in 1918–1919 (or he may have operated this studio in parallel with his work at Pickard). He went to work for the Chicago Photoprint Company in the 1920s.

**Petit** (possibly Ellsworth.) (Petit) [1905–1910] Only one example of Petit's work is known: a bowl with cherry spray and spider web. The workmanship is of moderate quality.

**Pfiefer, E.** (possibly Earl P.) (E. Pfiefer) [1903–1905] Only one example of Pfiefer's work is known: a plate with currants on maroon ground. The workmanship is acceptable commercial quality.

**Pickard, Minnie Verna** (M.P.) [1903–1905, 1905–1910, 1910–1912] Minnie Pickard undoubtedly produced decorated china under earlier trademarks, but none have yet come to light. Born Victoria Verna Flood in Illinois in April of 1868 of English parents, she

spent her early years as a teacher. Her father and brothers were occupied at various times in the feed and grain business. See text for additional biographical information.

**Pietrykaski** (Pietrykaski) [1898–1903] Only one example of Pietrykaski's work is known: a small, ornate sugar bowl with well-executed violets.

**Podlaha, Otto** (OP, Podl, Podlaha) [1903–1905, 1905–1910, 1910–1912, 1912–1918] Podlaha was born on September, 21, 1878, in Meisterdorf, Bohemia (about 30 kilometers north of Prague). After studying art and design at the Fachschule, he spent a number of years on his journeyman's tour, working at various studios for a year or two at a time; samples of his work from this time show a broad proficiency in ornamental design, floral art, and portraiture. He served in the Austrian army for a while and then emigrated to the United States on June 6, 1904. Unlike many Pickard artists who initially went to work in an East Coast studio, Podlaha, whose sponsor was his uncle, Franz X. Parsche, came directly to Chicago where he did

Photo courtesy O. Podlaha.

*Figure 43. Otto Podlaha at about the time he arrived at Ravenswood.*

layouts of glass designs in his uncle's famous studio. He did some work for Pickard as early as 1905 while Pickard was still in the carriage barn, but he did not "officially" move from Parsche to Pickard until 1908. His early work for Pickard included currants, roses, and a variety of other floral subjects. A good portion of his later work seemed to concentrate on the AURA ARGENTA LINEAR design. He left Pickard about 1917, and married Helene Von Selow in 1918. The records show him working for the Osborne Art Studio by 1922, and in 1925 his only child, Otto, was born. He returned to Parsche as a china decorator, but the Great Depression was a very difficult time; Podlaha was without work for four years. He found work with the Stouffer Studio in 1934–35 where he produced Stouffer's best-selling GOLDEN ORCHID design (Plate 843). His last employment was with the Kalita Studios in 1949–1953 where his wife also did some non-decorative work. Otto Podlaha died in 1957 at the age of 79.

**Pohl, C.** (C. Pohl) [1903–1905] Nothing is known of Pohl, other than the few pieces that bear his rather prominent signature. Of these, the very striking Art Nouveau vase patterned after a painting by Mucha speaks well for him.

**Post, F.** (F. Post Possibly Francis Post who decorated for one or more Trenton, New Jersey, potteries.) [1903–1905] Only one example of Post's work is known: a well-decorated vase with narcissus on green ground.

**Rawlins, William T.** (W. Rawlins) [1905–1910, 1910–1912, 1912–1918] Rawlins did executions of the DUTCH DECORATION and the *PILGRIM DECORATION* but his signature is most often seen on vellum and glossy scenics.

**Ray, Noble** (N. Ray. Do not confuse with A. Roy) [1905–1910] Ray boarded with artists George Leach and George Sinclair for a short time. Delicate violets on lustre ground, irises, and poppies were among his specialties. He also

worked for Pitkin & Brooks where he did an outstanding variation of POPPY CONVENTIONAL on a green-black ground.

**Rean** See Klipphahn, Maxwell Rean.

**Reury, Howard B.** (HR, Reury. Platt erroneously gives "Henry" as a first name.) [1903–1905, 1905–1910, 1910–1912] Reury was born in New York of New York-born parents in 1870. His earliest work included a charming design, *CLOVER GARDEN*, that closely paralleled Yeschek's *CARNATION GARDEN*. He did some executions of MODERN CONVENTIONAL, but for the most part, his work was exclusively floral, including some very large and colorful vases. He opened his own studio in the teens and also worked for the Wight Studios.

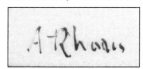

**Rhodes, Arnold** (A. Rhodes) [1922–1925 1930–1938] Born in England in 1891, Rhodes emigrated to the United States in 1909. Rhodes moved in with his brother-in-law, Edward Challinor, and they all went to work at the Julius Brauer studio. He moved successively to Osborne, Pickard, Tolpin, and then back to Pickard. He worked at Stouffer and finally retired to freelance in suburban Downers Grove where he also did cottage work for Ceramic Artcraft Studios. His early work at Brauer included some conventionalized designs. By the time he was at Pickard, he was doing simple border designs such as ROSE BASKET as well as a variety of scenics. He freelanced some outstanding scenic service plates for the Philadelphia firm of Bailey, Banks & Biddle, but his skill is best shown in his *MOUNTAIN STAG* vase which was painted in the 1930s.

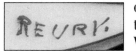

**Richter, Anton** (A.R., A. Richter.) [1905–1910, 1910–1912, 1912–1918, 1918–1919, 1919–1922] Richter initially studied at the art schools of Mlada Boleslav, Bohemia, and then took additional studies in Dresden and Paris. He operated his own studio in Dresden for 20 years and in 1891 earned a first prize at Dresden's Keramische Ausstellung. He earned additional honors at the Art Manufacturers Exhibition in 1896. Richter was one of

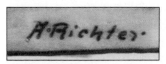

Pickard's best and most prolific artists. His signature appears on many bestsellers including MODERN CONVENTIONAL, DAHLIA RUBRA, AURA ARGENTA LINEAR, DUTCH DECORATION, and CAMPANULA. He also painted service plates and simpler designs such as ROSE BASKET.

**Richter, S.** (S. Richter. Possibly Sophia)

[1910–1912] Probably a relative of Anton Richter, this signature appears on well-executed pieces of AURA ARGENTA LINEAR and GOLDEN CLOVER.

**Roden, Harry** (Roden) [1903–1905] Only one pat-

tern has thus far been associated with Roden: his very colorful and popular *CROCUS CONVENTIONAL*. He appears to have worked for Pickard in 1903 and 1904 after which he disappeared.

**Roessler, Carl** (C. Rosl, Rosler, C. Roesl, Ross)

[1910–1912, 1912 1918] Roessler was expert in a variety of styles. He did versions of ENCRUSTED LINEAR and *SATSUMA PEONIES AND CHINESE BIRDS*, but the one design attributed directly to him was his stunning composition in black, gold, and platinum, AURA MOSAIC. He also did the only known hand-painted Pickard glassware pattern, called simply, POPPIES. He later moved on to the Stouffer studios.

**Rosler** See Roessler, Carl.

**Ross** See Roessler, Carl.

**Rost, Max** (Rost. Do not confuse with M. Rost LeRoy) [1903–1905] Born in Germany in 1869, Rost emigrated to the United States in 1892. He worked for Pickard for a short time where he did a design named GINKHO [sic] LEAF and also a rococo border design. Only a few pieces of his work have been discovered. Most of his career was with the Donath studio. See text for additional biographical details.

**Roy, A.** (A. Roy. Do not confuse with N. Ray) [1903–1905] A careful, meticulous style characterized Roy's colorful, realistic

renderings of currants, cherries, and blossoming foliage. He was probably with Pickard no more than two years.

**Samuelson, Ester** (S—N, Samuelson) [1919–1922,

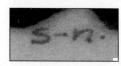

1922–1925, 1925–1930, 1930–1938] A skillful and meticulous artist, Samuelson was mainly associated with the INDIAN TREE, *ORIENTAL BIRD*, and *FRUIT BASKET* designs. See text for biographical details.

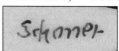

**Schoenig, Antol** (Also listed as Antal and Andrew) No example of this artist's work has yet been found. He appears in a photograph with Emil Tolpin (who arrived at Pickard about 1909) and John Fuchs (who died in 1913), so one may derive a rough approximation of the time of his employment at Pickard.

**Schoner, Otto** (O.S., Schoner, Shoner)

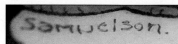

[1903–1905, 1905–1910] Born in the Schwartzwald in Germany, he arrived at Pickard in 1901 (no signed pieces from the 1898–1903 period have yet been seen) and was said to have been the brother-in-law of artist Max Klipphahn[36].

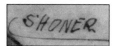

Schoner produced a number of Pickard's most popular designs. Beautifully shaded clusters of oranges or peaches against dark foliage, with bold borders embellished with scrolls and lattices characterized his early work. His later work became more stylized and his *TWIN TULIPS* and EASTER LILY were stunning additions to Pickard's offerings. He does not seem to have produced much beyond 1910, although he continued to

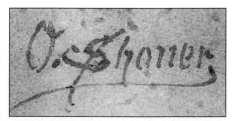

be listed as a decorator until his death in 1916.

**Seagren, Anna A.** (Seagren) [1912–1918] Originally a partner in the

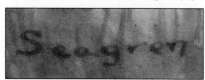

studio of Seagren & Carlson, this artist did scenic vellum designs for a short period of time, probably 1917–1918.

**Seidel, Erhardt** (Seidel) [1898–1903, 1903–1905]
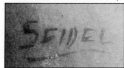
Seidel's talents were very broad and included figural work, fruits, and flowers. Each of these subjects was treated with a richness of color and depth that lent an air of opulence to his pieces. See text for biographical details.

**Shoner** See Schoner, Otto

**Simon, Adolph G., Jr.** (1925–1958) "Si" Simon learned china decorating from his father while working in his father's studio after school. He did some banding for Pickard in his first years there, but he quickly moved into the production side of the business when experimentation on china manufacturing began. After his retirement, he still contributed to the Antioch operation on a consulting basis. He moved to California and passed away in 1993. See text for other details.

**Simon, Adolph G., Sr.** (1940–) No signed pieces by Simon have been found, and coming to Pickard as late as he did, it is not probable that he decorated many pieces that accommodated a signature. He was born in Germany where he learned his craft; he also earned many awards for his work there. He ran his own studio in Chicago from about 1903 through 1917. In 1911 the studio included Rudolph Schweikert under the name of Simon & Schweikert. He eventually moved to California, but his family convinced him to return to Illinois (and Antioch) when threats of Japanese shelling of the West Coast became a concern during World War II.

**Sinclair, George** (Sinclair) [1903–1905, 1905–1910] Sinclair did good commercial, naturalistic florals. He boarded with artists Noble Ray and George Leach for a short time.

**Stahl, George W.** (Stahl) [1903–1905,

1905–1910] Born in Pennsylvania in 1882, Stahl moved to Chicago with his wife and infant son in 1903. After about a year at Pickard, he moved successively to the Donath, Brauer, and Robert W. France studios. He may also have worked at the Wight Studios for a short time. Stahl produced good naturalistic fruit and flower designs embellished with gold scrolls and lattices. He occasionally employed the striking German technique of heavily outlining his flowers.

**Steiner, August W.** Platt lists Steiner as a Pickard artist, but none of his work has yet been identified. He is listed as a decorator in the city directories from 1911 through 1917. From 1924 through 1928 he operated his own studio which he then sold to Frank Yeschek.

**(Steininger, Emil)** [possibly 1905–1910, 1910–1912] A bohemian china decorator who lived next door to Jelinek. Included here only as a possibility.

**Thonander, John** (1910–1912) The son of a

woodworker and cabinetmaker, little is known of this artist's work. He operated his own studio in 1910 out of which one floral/scenic vase of very good quality has come to light. No other examples of his work at any studio are known. He may have operated his studio contemporaneously with his Pickard employment. Platt's notes indicate that he also served as a Pickard shipping clerk for a time. By 1922 he had moved to the newly formed Rivir Studios where he worked as a department manager. Thonander's brother, Oscar, is said to have acted as Pickard's attorney for a time.

**Tolley, Harry E.** (H.T., H. Tolley) [1903–1905,

1905–1910, 1910–1912] Born in England in 1866, Tolley's parents brought him to the United States in 1870. He worked initially in Pennsylvania before coming to Chicago and Pickard. Tolley's work ranged from naturalistic to stylized to conventionalized floral subjects, and it was almost always top quality. He did versions of ORANGE TREE CONVENTIONAL and CORNFLOWER CONVENTIONAL, plus his own POINSETTIA AND LUSTRE and *POPPIES LINEAR*.

**Tolpin, Emil E.** (Tol, E. Tolpin) [1910–1912,

1912–1918] Emil Tolpin was born in 1889 in Riga, Russia (Latvia), and studied art both there and at the Imperial Art School in Odessa. He worked at the Kusnetzov Pottery and Studios before emigrating to the United States in 1909 or 1910; his wife, Sony, arrived in 1911. Coming directly to Pickard, Tolpin was a

very versatile and highly skilled artist. He did sub-contract renderings of FRUITS LINEAR, ANTIQUE ENAMELS, and ANTIQUE CHINESE ENAMELS. His own work included ENAMEL CHRYSANTHEMUMS, OLD FASHIONED FLOWERS, VENETIAN RENAISSANCE, and the *RUSSIAN DESIGN*. By 1920 he had opened the Tolpin Studios (see page 299). Additional biographical information is found in the text.

**Tolpin, Nesha** (N. Tolpin) [1905–1910,  1910–1912] Born in Russia in 1888, she emigrated to the United States in 1907. Of all the Pickard artists, Nesha Tolpin exhibited one of the most meticulous hands. Because of her precision, Pickard probably enlisted her talent for much of his monogram work, hence little of her signed work is seen. See text for further biographical details.

**Tomascheko, Rudolph** (Tomas) [1903–1905,  1905–1910] Intricate, precise borders characterized Tomascheko's very original work which included TOMASCHEKO FLORAL BORDER and *TOMASCHEKO POPPY BORDER*. He also did sub-contract renderings of CARNATION CONVENTIONAL and TULIP CONVENTIONAL.

**Unger, Anton** (Unger) [1905–1910] Born in Germany in 1868, Unger emigrated to the United States in 1892. Listed as a china decorator in 1910, he continued in this profession through 1928, but how much of this was with Pickard is unknown. Aside from a well-executed violet decoration, none of his signed work has been discovered.

**Vetter** (Vetter) [1898–1903, 1903–1905] Most  of this artist's output was probably sub-contract work. Only a few pieces decorated with currants on a maroon ground have been discovered.

**Vobornik, Franz** (FV, F. Vobor, Vobornik) 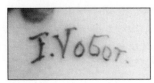 [1903–1905, 1905–1910, 1910–1912, 1912–1918, 1918–1919, 1919–1922, 1922–1925] Born Frederick Woornik in Bohemia,

he studied art at Mlada Boleslav. He spent a number of years at Le Rosey Studios in the Rue de la Paix in Paris. His work spanned naturalistic florals, some excellent raised gold paste, scenic vellums, and medallions on etched all-over-gold. He also executed versions of AURA ARGENTA LINEAR, ROSE BASKET, and CLASSIC RUINS.

**Vokral, Jeremiah** (Vokral) [1898–1903,  1903–1905, 1905–1910, 1910–1912, 1912–1918, 1918–1919, 1919–1922] Said to have been the protégé of John Nessy, "Jerry" Vokral was born in Prague, Bohemia. He attended the Prague Industrial Art School and also served apprenticeships at both the Rudolph Fritsche and Thein decorating shops. His long tenure at Pickard included many variations of his specialty, nuts and autumn leaves. He also did naturalistic currants and grapes, scenic vellums, medallions on all-over-gold, and executions of DESERTED GARDEN.

**Wagner, Albert H.** (Wag, Wagner) [1903–1905,  1905–1910, 1910–1912, 1912–1918] Wagner did a great many stylized floral designs that included daisies, poppies, violets, and lilies. He did scenic vellum executions of WILDWOOD and the *MOORISH DESIGN*. Although his signature has not yet been found beyond 1919, it is probable that he worked at the Ravenswood studio until about 1930.

**Walters, Frederick** (FW, Walt, Walter, FWalt, FWalter.  Misread as Mullen and other variations.) [1903–1905, 1905–1910, 1910–1912, 1912–1918] Born in Austria in 1861, Walters and his wife emigrated to the United States in 1886. They lived in Massachusetts until about the turn of the century and then came to Chicago. Although he is listed in the city directories and the United States Census as Frederick Walter, he clearly signs himself as Walters in a congratulatory note to Frank Yeschek. Walters specialized in florals that included poppies, lilies, tulips, and apple blossoms. A number of his designs were characterized by a very soft treatment of his subject.

**Weiss, Arthur J.** (A. Weiss) [1903–1905] Weiss

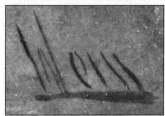

made his living as a portraitist specializing in copy work. He did this both before and after he worked for Pickard. He was Pickard's finest portraitist, and his brief stay at Pickard included extremely well-rendered monks, Arabs, animals, and pastoral scenics.

**Weissflog, Gustav** (Gust, Weiss. Do not confuse

with Arthur J. Weiss; the signatures and trademark ranges are quite different.) [1925–1930, 1930–1938] Born in Dresden, Germany, in 1886, Weissflog and his wife, Maria, emigrated to the United States in 1906. Weissflog originally worked at the Stouffer and the Mathurin Studios. After his years with Pickard—probably 1925 through 1940—he decorated for the Kalita Studio. Much of Pickard's production during that period did not accommodate signatures, but his signature does appear on the CHINESE PEACOCK design.

**Wight, Phillip** (Wight) [1905–1910, 1910–1912] Wight produced good commercial floral designs. He tended to be conservative and naturalistic with only a

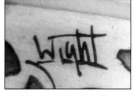

few digressions into stylized designs. See Wight Studios for biographical information.

**Yeschek, Frank P.** (F.Yeschek) [1905–1910,

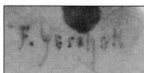

1910–1912, 1912–1918, 1918–1919, 1919–1922, 1922–1925, 1925–1930] Born in Eleonorenhain, Austria/Bohemia, on April 2, 1891, his mother emigrated with him to the United States when he was six months old. The son of artist Joseph Yeschek, he acquired much of his father's skill in decorating. He was probably the youngest employee the Ravenswood studio ever had, beginning his employment with Pickard when he was just 14 years old. Executions of YESCHEK CURRANTS IN GOLD and VIOLET SUPREME constituted some of his work. He was made foreman of the acid-etching department (which went into operation in 1911), and his artistic output was thus limited thereafter. He formed his own studio in 1928. See text for more biographical details.

**Yeschek, Joseph T.** (JY, Yeschek) [1903–1905,

1905–1910, 1910–1912, 1912–1918, 1918–1919, 1919–1922, 1922–1925] Born Josef Jezek in Güntersdorf, Austria/Bohemia, on February 7, 1866, Joseph Yeschek was the son of a textile designer and served glass decorating apprenticeships in a number of cities. On July 22, 1889, he married Marie Kuplent, and their first child died in infancy. In 1890, while Marie was still pregnant with their second child, Yeschek abruptly emigrated to the United States to avoid conscription into the army; his wife followed him when the baby, Frank, was six months old. He settled initially in New Bedford, Massachusetts, where he decorated for the Mount Washington Glass Company (merged into Pairpoint in 1894). Yeschek's uncle, Frank Guba was also a glass decorator and had come to New York in 1884. In April of 1891 Guba moved to New Bedford in time to sponsor Joseph Yeschek's immigration that same year. Guba eventually became Pairpoint's most famous artist. Three more children were born to Joseph and Marie Yeschek in New Bedford. In 1898 Yeschek became a United States citizen. He then moved to Philadelphia where he was later recruited by Pickard; he arrived in Chicago in 1903. Yeschek was a superb artist. He painted naturalistic, stylized, and conventionalized subjects equally well and with great imagination and originality. Two of his earliest designs, *CARNATION GARDEN* and *TULIP GARDEN* were followed by YESCHEK CURRANTS AND PASTE, three versions of CORNFLOWER CONVENTIONAL, LILY ORNATUM, TRIPLE TULIP (YELLOW & WHITE), and TRIPLE TULIP (YELLOW & RED). Joseph Yeschek moved to northern Wisconsin in the early twenties; he died there on October 13, 1927.

**Ziologe** (Ziologe) [1912–1918] Probably a short-term, sub-contract artist. A well-defined signature on an ANTIQUE CHINESE ENAMEL design as all that is known of this artist.

*Miscellaneous unknown names and initials:*

| | |
|---|---|
| HH (Possibly | oe |
| Hans Hansen), | Sciu |
| or IH or HI | AR |
| HEN | WR |
| JHR | H |
| GRT | ML or LM |

# *Pickard Artists with Multiple Studio Affiliations*

*Note: Order of studio affiliation in many cases is "best guess."*

| ARTIST | STUDIO A | STUDIO B | STUDIO C | STUDIO D | STUDIO E | STUDIO F |
|---|---|---|---|---|---|---|
| Arno, Edith | Arno | Stouffer | Pitkin & Brooks | Pickard | | |
| Aulich, Emil | Smith Bros., MA | Aulich, OH | Osgood-NY | Pickard | | |
| Bachmann, Max L. | Roseville, OH | Pickard | Brauer | Koenig | Pioneer | |
| Bardos, Isadore | Brauer | Pickard | Stouffer | | | |
| Beitler, Joseph C. | Trenton pottery | Pickard | Beitler | Brauer | | |
| Beulet, F. | Pickard | Donath | | | | |
| Bitterly, Walter K. | Pickard | Brauer | Stouffer | Bitterly | | |
| Blaha, Joseph | Pickard | Stouffer | Osborne | | | |
| Brauer, Julius H. | Pickard | Brauer | | | | |
| Breidel, Wm. W. | Pickard | Breidel | | | | |
| Burton, A. | Pickard | Brauer | | | | |
| Buschbeck, Carl | Pickard | Stouffer | | | | |
| Campana, D.M. | CAC-Trenton | Pickard | Campana | Campana Art | | |
| Challinor, Edward | Willets-Trenton | Pickard | Brauer | Pickard | | |
| Corey, Harriet L. | Corey | Pickard | | | | |
| Coufall, Anthony | Pickard | Stouffer | | | | |
| Donath, E. W. | Pickard | Donath | Pickard | Pitkin & Brooks | Donath | |
| Falatek, Louis H. | Pickard | Rivir | | | | |
| Fuchs, Pauline | Pickard | Yeschek-CAC | | | | |
| Gasper, Paul P. | Cook-Trenton | Roseville -OH | Pickard | | | |
| Gibson, Edward | Pickard | Int'l Art | Art Store | | | |
| Gifford, Nathan R. | Pickard | Stouffer | | | | |
| Griffiths, Harry R. | Pickard | Brauer | France | Stouffer | Donath | |
| Grumieau, Louis P. | Grumieau | Pickard | Yeschek, Inc. | Kalita | | |
| Haase, Frank | Pickard | Parsche | | | | |
| Hahn, Charles | Pickard | White | | | | |
| Hanische | Pickard | Parsche | | | | |
| Heap, Samuel | Trenton pottery | Pickard | Stouffer | | | |
| Heidrich, Adolph J. | Trenton pottery | Pickard-? | Donath | Heidrich | | |
| Heinz, J. | Pitkin& Brooks | Pickard | Donath | | | |
| Hessler, Robert | Pickard | Yeschek-CAC | | | | |
| Jelinek, Thomas M. | Pickard | Stouffer | | | | |
| Kalita, Waclaw | Osborne | Stouffer | Tolpin | Pickard | Kalita | Pickard |
| Keates, Alfred | Pickard | Intl Art | White's | Keates | | |
| Kittler, Joseph R. | Stouffer | Donath | Kittler | | | |
| Klipphahn, Max R. | Trenton pottery | Pickard | Kalita | | | |
| Koenig, Carl F. | Pickard | Brauer | Donath | Koenig | Yeschek-CAC | |
| Leach, George P. | Pickard | Stouffer | Rogers-Martini | Leach | | |
| Leon | Pickard | D'Arcy's - MI | | | | |
| LeRoy, M. Rost. | Pickard | Donath | | | | |
| Loba, F. | Pickard | Stouffer | | | | |
| Luken, Minnie A. | Luken | Pickard | Luken Art Std. | | | |
| Marker, Curtis | Pickard | Intl. Art Std. | Pickard | | | |

## Pickard Artists with Multiple Studio Affiliations

*– continued –*

| ARTIST | STUDIO A | STUDIO B | STUDIO C | STUDIO D | STUDIO E | STUDIO F |
|---|---|---|---|---|---|---|
| Mentges, Edward | Pickard | Mentges | | | | |
| Miche | Pickard | White's | | | | |
| Michel, Harry E. | Pickard | Stouffer | | | | |
| Miller, Anton | D'Arcy's - MI | Pickard | Stouffer | | | |
| Nessy, John | Pickard | Stouffer | | | | |
| Nittel, Frank | Pickard | Yeschek-CAC | | | | |
| Podlaha, Otto | Pickard | Osborne | Parsche | Stouffer | Kalita | |
| Ray, Noble | Pickard | Pitkin & Brooks | | | | |
| Reury, Howard B. | Pickard | Pitkin & Brooks | Wight | | | |
| Rhodes, Arnold | Brauer | Pickard | Osborne | Tolpin | Stouffer | Yeschek-CAC |
| Rost, Max | Donath | Pickard | Donath | Rost | | |
| Seidel, Erhardt | Pickard. | Marmorstein | White's | Seidel - WA | | |
| Stahl, George W. | Pickard | Donath | Brauer | France | | |
| Thonander, John | Pickard | Thonander | Rivir | | | |
| Tolpin, Emil | Pickard | Tolpin | Tolpin Art Stds | | | |
| Tolpin, Nesha | Pickard | Rivir | | | | |
| Weissflog, Gustav | Stouffer | Mathurin | Pickard | Kalita | | |
| Wight, Phillip | Pickard | Wight | | | | |
| Yeschek, Frank | Pickard | Yeschek, Inc. | Yeschek-CAC | | | |
| Yeschek, Joseph | Mt. Wash/Pairpoint | Pickard | Yeschek, Inc | | | |

## Pickard Trademarks

*Mark 1. 1894–1897, ¹³⁄₃₂" dia. red paper label used in Edgerton, Wisconsin, in 1894, and in Chicago in 1895–1897. Extremely rare.*

*Mark 3. 1903, ⁹⁄₁₆" dia. red stamp. An interim mark during the expansion into the carriage barn studio. Infrequently found.*

*Mark 1.1. c.1898–c.1903, ⁷⁄₁₆" dia. dark brown stamp. Possibly an "out-of-stock" expedient or the original Chicago startup mark. Very rare.*

*Mark 4. 1903–1905, ⁹⁄₁₆" dia. light brown to very dark reddish brown decal. Used at the carriage barn studio.*

*Mark 2. 1898–1903, ⅝" dia. maroon to pale brown decal. Used at LaSalle Street studio.*

*Mark 5. 1905–1910, ¹³⁄₃₂" dia. brown decal. The first mark used at the Ravenswood studio.*

Mark 6. 1910–1912, ¹³⁄₃₂" dia. red decal over gold square. Also used without gold square when underside of piece is all gold or platinum or when no blank mark is present. Do not confuse with Mark 5.

Mark 12. 1925–1930, small etched gold or platinum escutcheon used on smaller items.

Mark 7. 1912–c.1918, ¹³⁄₃₂" dia. red (early) or black (later) decal over gold maple leaf. Covers blank mark (early) or beside blank mark (later). Other dias.: ¼", ²¹⁄₆₄", ⅜", and ²⁵⁄₆₄".

Mark 13. 1928–1938, green or gold stamp. Registered July 24, 1947, first used in late 1928. Used only on seconds.

Mark 8. c.1918–1919, ²⁵⁄₆₄" dia. black decal only. Do not confuse with Mark 5.

Mark 14. 1930–1938, gold stamp.

Mark 8.1. c.1918–c.1919, ¹¹⁄₁₆" wide black decal used on a small number of pieces at end of World War I. Infrequently found.

Mark 14.1. 1930–1938, X-painted trademarks were a means of identifying factory-vended seconds.

Mark 9. 1919–1922, ¹¹⁄₁₆" wide black decal, also hand stamp. Used on both etched and non-etched china.

Mark 15. 1930–1938, small gold decal escutcheon used on salts and other small pieces.

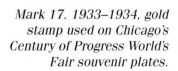

Mark 10. 1912–1922, 1922–1925, ¹⁹⁄₃₂" dia. etched gold coin. Used 1912–1922 for etched dinnerware, 1922–1925 for all china.

Mark 11. 1925–1930, etched gold or platinum coat of arms. The first registered trademark of Pickard Studios, Inc. First used September 1, 1925.

Mark 16. 1931–c.1938, blue stamp. First used on December 15, 1931, it was applied to stock decal items.

Mark 17. 1933–1934, gold stamp used on Chicago's Century of Progress World's Fair souvenir plates.

*Mark 18. 1938–present, gold stamp, first used in 1938. *A registered trademark of Pickard, Inc.*

*Mark 18.1 1938–present. Scored trademarks were a means of identifying factory-vended seconds.*

*Mark 19. 1938–c.1949, Edgerton gold stamp. Same as mark 13, but indicating U.S.A. manufacture. Revived in the 1960s for factory sales.*

*Mark 20. 1916 or 1917, ¼"h. Hand painted in gold. Used on hand-painted glass only.*

*Mark 21. 1917–1918, ¹³⁄₃₂" dia. Clear etch into glass. Used on etched glass only.*

*H.P. Sinclaire, 1900–c.1914, ½"h., black or red decal. Erroneously attributed to Pickard, it was the mark of H.P. Sinclaire Glass Co. See endnote no. 34.*

*Edgerton P.C., c.1898–c.1902. (Also may include artist's initials such as M.I.A., F.C., etc.) This mark also has been erroneously attributed to Pickard. It was the mark of a local group of Edgerton artists, some of whom were associated with the Pauline Pottery.*

## Pickard Patents

Only six design patents have been ascribed to Pickard. Costly to originate and costlier still to defend, they were easily altered and circumvented by competitors.

DESIGN.

No. 37,332.
PATENTED FEB. 7, 1905.

W. A. PICKARD.
PLATE OR DISH.
APPLICATION FILED DEC. 30, 1904.

Witnesses.
Frederick C. Becker
C.H. Eich.

Inventor
Wilbur A. Pickard
per
George A. McCulla
Attorney.

DESIGN.

No. 37,337.
PATENTED FEB. 14, 1905.

W. A. PICKARD.
PLATE OR DISH.
APPLICATION FILED JAN. 19, 1905.

Witnesses.
Ida Fleischmann
Benjamin Wolf

Wilbur A. Pickard
Inventor
per
George A. McCulla
Attorney

DESIGN.

No. 37,338.
PATENTED FEB. 14, 1905.

W. A. PICKARD.
PLATE OR DISH.
APPLICATION FILED JAN. 19, 1905.

Witnesses.
Ida Fleischmann
Benjamin Wolf

Wilbur A. Pickard
Inventor
per George A. McCulla
Attorney

DESIGN.

No. 37,352.
PATENTED FEB. 28, 1905.

W. A. PICKARD.
PLATE OR DISH.
APPLICATION FILED FEB. 2, 1905.

Witnesses.
C.H. Eich.
Ida Fleischmann.

Inventor
Wilbur A. Pickard
per George A. McCulla
Attorney

74

## *Pickard Advertising*

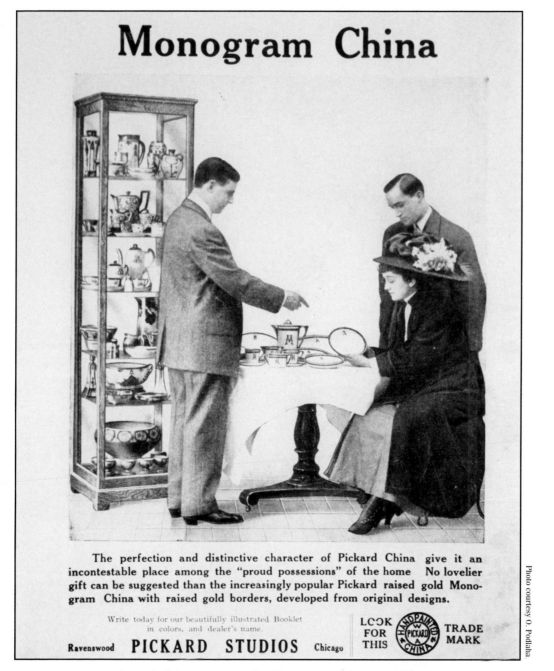

*Item 1. Advertisement for Monogram china, c.1908.*

*Item 2. Catalog page, c.1908–1909.*

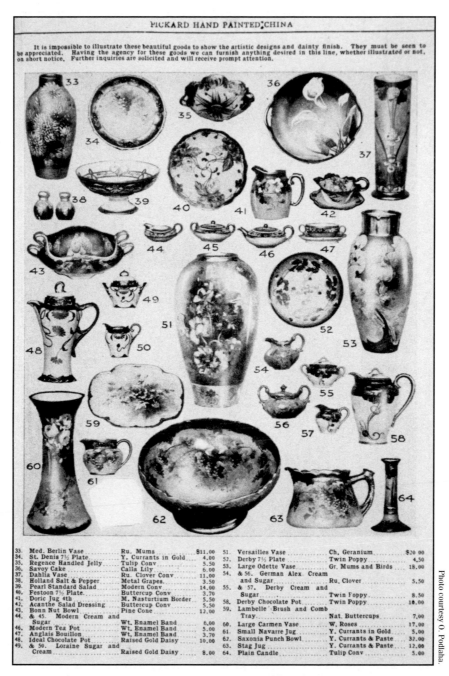

*Item 3. Catalog page, c.1908–1909.*

PICKARD HAND PAINTED CHINA

It is impossible to illustrate these beautiful goods to show the artistic designs and dainty finish. They must be seen to be appreciated. Having the agency for these goods we can furnish anything desired in this line, whether illustrated or not, on short notice. Further inquiries are solicited and will receive prompt attention.

| | | | | |
|---|---|---|---|---|
| 1. | Small Columbia Vase | Ru. Lily Conv. | $ 5.50 |
| 2. | Savoy Cake | Tulip Conv. | 7.00 |
| 3. | Pearl Olive | Y. Crab Apple | 3.20 |
| 4. | Large Juno Vase | Poppy and Black | 9.00 |
| 5. | Med. Gypsy Rose Bowl | New Iris Conv. | 8.50 |
| 6. | Small Tankard | Metal Grapes | 12.00 |
| 7. | Alice Tea | Gib. Pansies | 3.50 |
| 8. | Alex. Cream and Sugar | Rean Mums | 7.00 |
| 9. | Large Basel Jug | Carnation Conv. | 6.00 |
| 10. | Victoria Tea | Butterfly | 4.50 |
| 11. | Modern Tankard | Ginkho Leaf | 21.00 |
| 12. | Beaufort, 7½ inch Plate | Y. Crab Apple | 4.00 |
| 13. | Tall Stein | Metal Grapes | 7.00 |
| 14. | Decanter | Metal Grapes | 7.50 |
| 15. | Roma Jug | Ch. Geraniums, DK | 11.00 |
| 16. | Doric Jug, Small | Iris Conv. | 3.50 |
| 17. | Pompeian Vase | Poppy and Black | 14.00 |
| 18. | Century Handled Salad | Poinsetta and Luster | 18.00 |
| 19. | Odette Cream and Sugar | Poppy and Luster | 8.50 |
| 20. | Royal Nut Bowl | Hazelnuts | 8.00 |

Photo courtesy O. Podlaha.

*Item 4. Catalog page, c.1908–1909.*

Item 5. Catalog page, c.1908–1909.

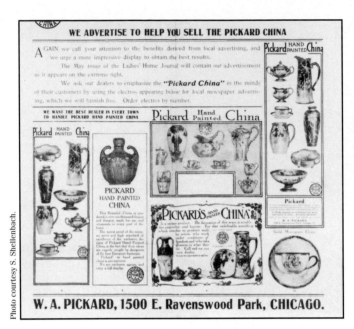

*Item 6. Series of "electros" available for dealer advertising.*

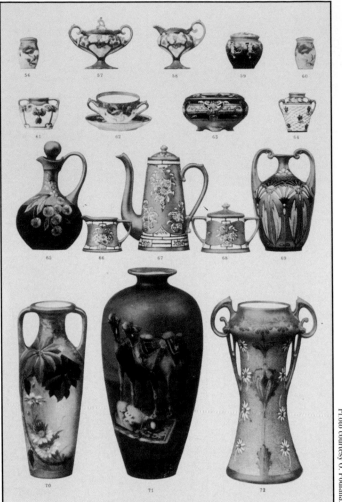

*Item 8. Color catalog page, c.1909.*
POPPY IRIDESCENT..... 56, 60, 62
WHITE MORNING GLORIES..... 57, 58
MODERN CONVENTIONAL..... 63
YELLOW CHERRIES AND MATTE GREEN..... 65
FLOWERS AND GOLD..... 66, 67, 68
CORNFLOWER CONVENTIONAL (1)..... 69
POINSETTIAS AND MARGUERITES..... 70
PRAYING MOHAMMEDAN..... 71
DAISIES IN GOLD PASTE ON GREEN LUSTRE..... 72

*Item 7. Color catalog page, c.1909.*
FLORA GOLD AND WHITE..... 39
YELLOW CHERRIES AND MATTE GREEN..... 40
POPPY IRIDESCENT..... 41, 42
DAISIES IN GOLD PASTE ON GREEN LUSTRE..... 43
ROSA EMERALDUS..... 44
CARNATION AND BLACK..... 47
AURA ARGENTA LINEAR..... 48, 50
PURPLE GRAPES AND MATTE GREEN..... 49
MOORISH DESIGN.....51
CORNFLOWER CONVENTIONAL (2)..... 52

*Item 9. Interior page of color catalog, c.1909.*

Item 10. Interior page of color catalog, c.1909.

Photo courtesy O. Podlaha.

*Item 11. Ladies Home Journal Advertisement, May 1906.*

Pickard China

*Item 13. Ladies Home Journal Advertisement, May 1907.*

*Item 12. Ladies Home Journal Advertisement, November 1906.*

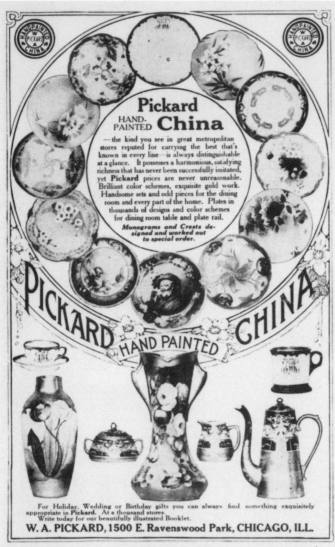

Item 14. Ladies Home Journal Advertisement, November 1907.

Item 15. Ladies Home Journal Advertisement, May 1908.

# Pickard China

### Pickard Hand Painted China

In comparison with all Hand-Painted Chinas, Pickard's shows remarkable individuality in design of decoration and shape of china.

Pickard is hand-painted by professional artists of both Foreign and American reputations, who attain great brilliancy in the color harmony of Pickard China.

As a suggestion for an appropriate wedding, birthday or anniversary gift—pieces of Pickard Hand-Painted China are most acceptable, principally because they are genuine, useful and beautiful.

In exclusive department stores, jewelers' and art establishments you will find among Pickard's selections stunning things for decorative purposes.

For the dining-room service you will be interested in unordinary luncheon, berry and chocolate sets, cream and sugars, salads, tankards, etc.

Consider Pickard Hand-Painted China for your Gift Presentations — also for your own.

Our little brochure, "Over the Phone," will tell you more about Pickard's. We will enjoy receiving your request.

This seal on every piece

### W. A. Pickard
1500 East Ravenswood Park
Ravenswood
**Chicago Illinois**

*Item 16. Ladies Home Journal Advertisement, June 1908.*

*Item 17. Ladies Home Journal Advertisement,*
*October 1908.*

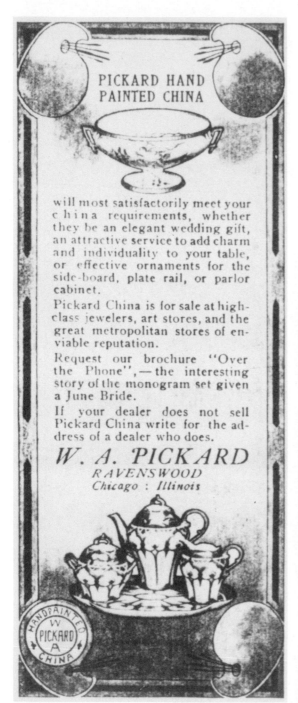

*Item 18. Ladies Home Journal Advertisement, November 1908.*

*Item 19. Ladies Home Journal Advertisement, April 1909.*

*Item 20. Ladies Home Journal Advertisement, May 1909.*

*Item 21. Ladies Home Journal Advertisement, June 1909.*

*Item 22. Ladies Home Journal Advertisement, October 1909.*

*Item 23. Ladies Home Journal Advertisement, November 1909.*

*Item 24. Ladies Home Journal Advertisement, June 1910.*

**FOR WEDDINGS**

If you would present a gift of rare beauty, let us suggest

## Pickard China

The infinite pains taken to perfect even the minutest detail of this China — painted by highly trained professional Artist Crafts-men, give it exclusive individuality.

Special Decorations, Monograms and Initials in both raised gold and etched gold, etc., to order.

Write for beautifully illustrated Booklet and name of your nearest Pickard Dealer.

**PICKARD STUDIOS**

Ravenswood                    CHICAGO

*Item 25. Ladies Home Journal Advertisement, May 1911 and Woman's Home Companion.*

Item 26. Ladies Home Journal Advertisement, November 1910.

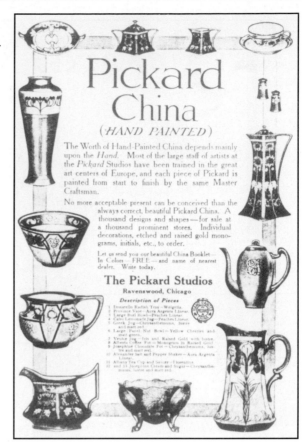

Item 27. The House Beautiful advertisement and reprint, October 1911.

Item 28. The House Beautiful advertisement and reprint, October 1911.

# Pickard China

### Pink Enamel Flowers

The most interesting of the recent enamel designs is the so-called "pink enamel flower." Clusters of flowers forming an ornamental design are set below a gold band and upon two parallel gold lines. Each of these clusters has for its center a delicate enameled flower which possesses the color-beauty of palest pink coral. This flower is surrounded by enameled green leaves and smaller flowers of different hues. Alternating with this group are smaller similar groups.

From about 1911 through 1918, Pickard furnished his dealers with postcards for distribution to their customers. The cards described in considerable detail some of his more popular patterns. All cards courtesy S. Shellenbach.

*Item 29.*

*Item 30.*

# Pickard China

### The Sheraton

Sheraton, a little younger than Chippendale, started with that artist's motifs, but later worked out original effects of his own. In his work often appears a beautiful lyre-form combined with flowers. This form has been chosen as the central motif in the new Sheraton design for the decoration of china. The central or lyre group alternates with a smaller decoration, which consists of a single rose-colored flower with leaves. These groups are placed below a gold border, and are held together by parallel encircling lines of gold. In the central group the lyre is inverted and worked in gold, while the drooping scrolls on either side are painted a soft green which, with the rose-colored flowers, form a charming color combination.

# Pickard China

### Walled Garden

This shows a garden surrounded by high stone walls, of which the view pictured is from the outside. Glimpses are had of feathery green tops of trees within. The weathered walls are beautiful, with their thick curtain of grey-green ivy vines and leaves, while the vigorous rose tree from within throws great sprays of brilliant roses over the wall, where they gaily swing in every breeze. The design is painted on a delicate semi-glaze or vellum background, which, while perfectly smooth to the touch, has an effect of great depth and softness.

*Item 31.*

## Pickard China

### *Lakes of Killarney*

*Item 32.*

Three views of the famous Lakes of Killarney have been painted against the beautiful vellum-like background which has become a specialty in the Pickard Studios. This wonderful trio of mountain lakes, so celebrated in song and story, is surrounded by purple topped heights on the sides of which appear the extraordinary foliage effects for which Killarney is renowned; the light green of the arbutus trees mingles with the dark green of holly; the blue green of the yew; the purple of heather; the brown of gorse; etc. Numerous small islands dot the lakes, and show the same exquisite wooded effects. The "Sweet Innesfallen" of Moore is perhaps the best known of these islands. The three selected scenes show calm lakes with richly colored mountain backgrounds. In the foregrounds are quiet wooded shores where magnificent oak and beech trees stand prominently forth, while the miniature islets appear like emerald jewels on the surface of the waters.

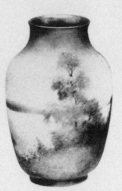

## Pickard China

### *Etched Panel and Roses*

*Item 33.*

Each panel is covered, with the exception of the edges, with a rich fine gold etching. The effect is of gold panels surrounded by a white border. These white border surfaces are ornamented by narrow gold lines, terminated with small groups of tiny pink roses which add the needed touch of delicate color. The tops of the upright gold panels are beautifully shaped to simulate the neck and shoulders of a graceful vase, from which rise curving plume-like scrolls of gold.

## Pickard China

### *Rococo Scrolls and Etched Border*

*Item 34.*

A cheerful, rich decoration, in which broad leaf-like scrolls form the basis of the design. From the scrolls drops a slender loop, from which swings free a group of two diminutive pink roses with sprays of tiny forget-me-nots. The flowers are arranged in an entirely straight line in contrast to the curves of the gold scrolls above. The scrolls and flowers form a group, which, repeated at regular intervals, produces a delightful border decoration. This is further enriched by encircling bands of brilliant gold etching.

# Pickard China

## The Broken Fret

The Broken Fret, consisting of a succession of small lines bent at right or oblique angles, is a decoration which had its origin with primitive man and its use seems to have been almost universal. It is found, with some variations of arrangement, in the early works of Asia and Europe, as well as among native races of America. The Navajoes of our western country still use this motive in the ornamentation of their pottery and famous blankets. The present version of the decoration shows the lines of the fret painted in dark green or bright red against a lighter background. The band so formed is ornamented with many touches of gold. The design, while simple, is pleasing and very effective.

The Broken Fret, when worked out in the red color scheme, is especially attractive for breakfast and porch sets.

*Item 35.*

# Pickard China

*Item 36.*

**PANEL DRESDEN AND RAISED GOLD** consists of an arrangement of roses and grape vines fitted to the decoration of panels.

The panels are divided by heavy gold bands. On the central panels clusters of brightly hued roses with narrow rose sprays extending above and below form a brilliant decoration of the Dresden style. On the side panels are massive undulating raised gold grape vines with leaves, grape clusters with tendrils also worked out in high raised gold. This elaborate gold work gives great distinction to this dashing high toned composition.

# Pickard China

## Plain Etched Gold

The Plain Etched Gold is an attractive, new, all-over gold encrustation. In this design the etching is exceedingly fine and small, but it is as distinct as it is fine. The surfaces of the pieces are charmingly brilliant with a texture more beautiful than that of cloth of gold.

*Item 37.*

*Item 38.*

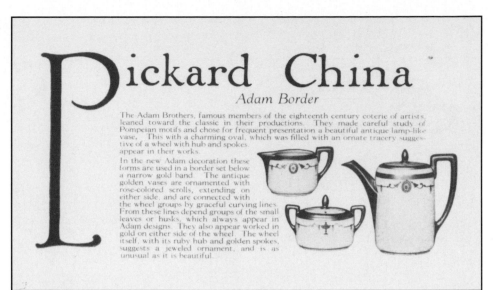

# Pickard China
## *Adam Border*

The Adam Brothers, famous members of the eighteenth century coterie of artists, leaned toward the classic in their productions. They made careful study of Pompeian motifs and chose for frequent presentation a beautiful antique lamp-like vase. This with a charming oval, which was filled with an ornate tracery suggestive of a wheel with hub and spokes, appear in their works.

In the new Adam decoration these forms are used in a border set below a narrow gold band. The antique golden vases are ornamented with rose-colored scrolls, extending on either side, and are connected with the wheel groups by graceful curving lines. From these lines depend groups of the small leaves or husks, which always appear in Adam designs. They also appear worked in gold on either side of the wheel. The wheel itself, with its ruby hub and golden spokes, suggests a jeweled ornament, and is as unusual as it is beautiful.

# Pickard China
## *Wildwood Decoration*

This decoration possesses unusual features. The china is so treated that it acquires a vellum like surface, which is covered with tints and shadings of greenish grey and violet. Against this background are shown groups of birch trees raising their silvery mottled trunks and feathery foliage to the sky. At the base of the trees are woodsy growths of shrubs. In the foreground are small clumps of wild rose bushes covered with little pink blossoms.

*Item 39.*

# Pickard China
## *Chippendale*

An interesting adaptation or china painting of the motifs of the great "Chippendale." This epoch-making furniture designer and decorator made lavish use of leaves combined with the form of the letter "C," a play on the first letter of the artist's name. The Chippendale china design shows a center formed by these letters which have a leafy outline and are worked in gold. They are so arranged that they form a medallion with an open center. In the center of this medallion appears a delicately tinted leaf with its base adorned with gold scrolls, which also have a "C" center. The alternating or smaller decorative groups show also "C" forms, with the gold letters arranged back to back. The leaves themselves, wherever they appear in the decoration, are toned in delicate pinks and translucent greens forming a most dainty and attractive color combination.

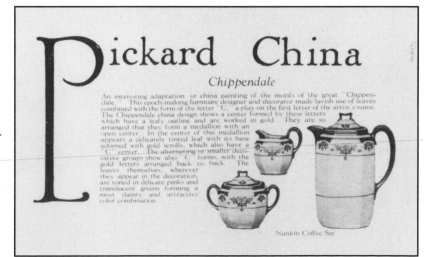

Nankin Coffee Set

*Item 40.*

*Item 41.*

## Pickard China

### *Adam*

THE Adam decoration is an adaptation of three of the characteristic Adam motives — the vase-like Pompeian lamp, the elegant handled urn and the small leaves or husks. The design is in rich raised gold upon a delicate bluish, green or ivory background. The lamp and urn motives, used alternately, are connected by festoons of leaves, giving a rythmic effect which adds to the charm of the design. The Adam is peculiarly appropriate for service and dinner plates and for numerous odd pieces.

Robert Adam was a British architect and designer of the 18th century. His "period" designs are increasingly popular.

## Pickard China

### *Dutch Decoration*

ON these quaint shapes a band decoration, in panels, illustrates some of the characteristic features of the Dutch land — the winding canal-like streams with their tiny green islands and their low green shores adorned with tiny windmills, and groups of dull pink tulips. On the center panel is a Dutch maiden in peasant costume. The china itself is a bisque ware, having a firm vitrified body with a soft vellum-like surface.

*Item 42.*

*Item 43.*

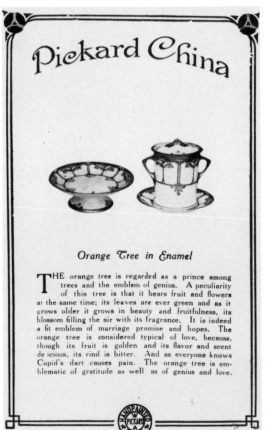

## Pickard China

### *Orange Tree in Enamel*

THE orange tree is regarded as a prince among trees and the emblem of genius. A peculiarity of this tree is that it bears fruit and flowers at the same time; its leaves are ever green and as it grows older it grows in beauty and fruitfulness, its blossom filling the air with its fragrance. It is indeed a fit emblem of marriage promise and hopes. The orange tree is considered typical of love, because, though its fruit is golden and its flavor and scent delicious, its rind is bitter. And as everyone knows Cupid's dart causes pain. The orange tree is emblematic of gratitude as well as of genius and love.

## Pickard China

### *Bordure Antique*

THIS is a design of encrusted gold which is relieved by a rich border or band of a deep royal blue. On this band at regular intervals appear quaint, conventionalized bird forms the beautiful flowing lines of which, distinctly marked, remind one of old cloisonne or mosaic. The intense blue of this border against the gorgeous background of the encrusted gold, produces a striking yet pleasing and harmonious contrast.

*Item 44.*

*Item 45.*

## Pickard China

### Encrusted Linear

AN elegant design showing the beautiful encrusted gold surface, which is an invention of the Pickard Studios. This gold surface is adorned by a band of a delicate olive green color around the top of the design. This band, in its turn, is edged top and bottom by very narrow bands of a lustrous purplish blue. In this composite band are set at regular distances apart, roundals, from the lower parts of which linear bands extend to the bottom of the design.

## Pickard China

#### *Convolvulus*

GROUPS of these roadside white flowers are set in an irregular wide gold band. Their raised gold stems with a fuss of tiny gold leaves and tendrils, extend to the bottom of the design. Green stems outline the gold border, then turning downward, parallel the raised gold stems, then encircle the base of the piece. The background is deep ivory which gives the entire decoration a charming softness.

*Item 46.*

*Item 47.*

*Pickard China*

### Antique Chinese Enamel

*Developed from the study of famous ancient pieces in the Louvre Collection*

THE work is done entirely in enamels after the Chinese method. The design is arranged in panels, the center panel showing a conventionalized peony and plum blossom motive done in the rich coloring characteristic of Chinese art. On another panel is shown the famous flower and stork design and around this some of the symbols of honor so generally used by the Chinese. These symbols indicated the profession or character of the man to whom the decorated pieces were to be presented.

## Pickard China

### Encrusted Honeysuckle

THE Encrusted Honeysuckle is one of the most attractive of the all-over gold decorations from the Pickard Studios. It shows the encrusted surface which resembles hammered gold, and to this is added a wide border in a bold and beautiful design taken from a famous old Greek motive known as the "Honeysuckle." This design, however, is so strictly conventionalized that it shows little resemblance to the flower of that name. The Honeysuckle border stands out in strong relief from the plain encrusted surface of the pieces and, though embodying an old idea, through its treatment takes on an original and striking character.

*Item 48.*

Item 49.

*Pickard*        *China*

## Violet Supreme

THE "Violet Supreme" decoration shows an original and successful treatment of an old and much used motive. Usually it has been portrayed in simple natural sprays, or in one of the simpler conventional forms. In the present instance however, the violet has become the center of an elaborate and rich semi-conventional design in which the violets are gathered into clusters and set in an elegant wide gold band. The flowers are true to nature, but they have golden stems, which extend to a small central disk of gold, surrounded by violets. Between these clusters are small violets in the gold band, which are worked in silver touched with gold. Altogether the "Violet Supreme" shows the climax of beautiful effect in depicting this favorite flower.

## Pickard China

*Pastel Rose and Silver*

THIS most attractive new design employs the rose motif (flowers, stems and leaves) in an elaborate border of pure, high-relief silver, worked out entirely by hand. Below the border is a raised silver lattice. Dainty pinkish roses peep out from behind the lattice and extend in beautiful sprays to the bottom of the piece. The combination of raised silver and delicate color on the white china is exquisite.

Item 50.

Item 51.

*Pickard China*

## The Idealistic

IN the Pickard Studios some naturalistic work was always done and is still being done alongside the later conventional forms; and at the present time, there has been produced what may be called an idealized form of naturalistic work. A series of pieces have been painted in soft very pale grey tones, in which sprays of pale pink poppies or primroses seem to sink into the delicate backgrounds giving the effect of underglaze painting.

## Pickard China

*Campanula*
*(Little Bell)*

THIS is a very rich and pleasing decoration. The salient features are groups of bell-shaped flowers in blue, against a band of gold. The calyx and stems of the flowers are raised gold against a mellow ivory background. Between the flower groups are heads of wheat in raised gold, and above, in the gold border, are rose pink buds. This design makes an admirable decoration for breakfast sets as well as for ornamental pieces.

Item 52.

## *Pickard Plates*

With a few exceptions, items are shown chronologically by trademark time period; however, within those time periods, they are in no chronological order.

- The same pattern name was occasionally used on different designs (such as CARNATION CONVENTIONAL).
- Many patterns were called by more than one name and are so-noted in the Pickard Pattern Index. The author's use of one alternative over another should not be considered anything but an arbitrary choice.
- Pickard's own pattern names are UNDERLINED SMALL CAPITALS.
- Author-applied names are in *ITALICIZED SMALL CAPITALS*.
- Names of china shapes in *ITALICISED UPPERCASE* are actual shape designations employed by W. A. Pickard.
- Values given assume prime condition. Value ranges may be derived from dealer asking prices, actual prices paid, or prices realized at auction.

Plate 2. Jardiniere on separate footed pedestal, 9¾"h. Rose cluster on green ground. Signed: Loba (Loba, F.). TM date: 1894–1898. Blank: AK D, France. Value: $2,500.00–2,800.00.

Plate 3. Single-service breakfast set on 12¼" x 16" tray. Narrow gold border embellished with black chain and hearts, red enamel centers, pale yellow ground. (unsigned). TM date: c.1898–c.1903 (TM no. 1.1). Blank: none. Value: $350.00–450.00.

Plate 1. Large CARMEN vase, 14"h. Purple and white mums on blue/green ground, wide embellished gold borders. Signed: LOBA (Loba, F.). TM date: 1894–1898. Blank: D&Co., France. Value: $2,300.00–2,600.00.

Plate 4. Plate, 8"d. TULIP MODERNE. Signed: cHahn (Hahn, Charles). TM date: 1898–1903. Blank: T&V rectangle, Limoges, France. Value: $140.00–165.00.

Plate 5. Dish, scalloped, 7¼"d. Naturalistic orange and red roses on green ground. Signed: T. M. Jelinek (Jelinek, Thomas M.). TM date: 1898–1903. Blank: Limoges, France. Value: $125.00–160.00.

Plate 6. Pitcher, 5"h. Strawberry clusters on maroon band with strawberry blossoms. Signed: Michel (Michel, Harry E.). TM date: 1898–1903. Blank: J.P.L., France. Value: $335.00–395.00.

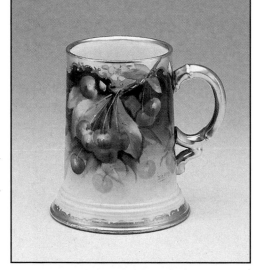

Plate 7. Mug, 5¼"h. Cherry spray on blue ground, paste scrolls. Signed: LeRoy (LeRoy, M. Rost). TM date: 1898–1903. Blank: J.P.L., France. Value: $300.00–425.00.

Plate 8. MALMAISON plate, scalloped rim, 9"d. Blackberries on variegated leaves. Signed: JNessy (Nessy, John). TM date: 1898–1903. Blank: crown crossed scepters, R.C. Bavaria, Malmaison. Value: $110.00–185.00.

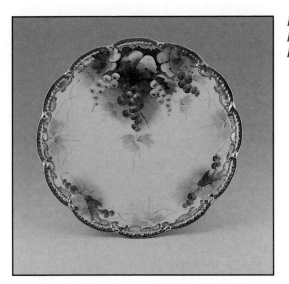

*Plate 9. Plate, CENTURY, 8½"d. Red and green grape cluster. Signed: Blaha (Blaha, Joseph). TM date: 1898–1903. Blank: Century Patd Feb 26 1901 T&V Limoges, France. Value: $120.00–150.00.*

*Plate 10. Bonbon, scalloped rim, pierced handles, 5½"d. Violet spray on green ground, gold rim embellished with colored violets. Signed: MARK (Mark). TM date: 1898–1903. Blank: J.P.L., France. Value: $70.00–90.00.*

*Plate 11. MALMAISON bowl, scalloped rim, 10½"d., ROSE FESTOONS. (unsigned). TM date: 1898–1903. Blank: RC crossed scepters, Malmaison. Value: $225.00–275.00.*

*Plate 12. Lidded jam jar with under plate, 5"h. Pink apple blossom spray. Signed: Leon (Leon). TM date: 1898–1903. Blank: crown crossed scepters, RC Bavaria. Value: $425.00–475.00.*

*Plate 14. Cup and saucer, CROCUS CONVENTIONAL. Signed: Roden (Roden, Harry). TM date: 1898–1903. Blank: D.&Co. France. Value: $125.00–185.00. Rose bowl, 3½"h, CROCUS CONVENTIONAL. (unsigned). TM date: 1898–1903. Blank: crown shields, Vienna, Austria. Value: $145.00–225.00.*

Plate 15. (rear) Plate, cake, perforated handles, 10½"d., CRO-
CUS CONVENTIONAL. Signed: L. Duran (Duran, L.). TM date:
1903–1905. Blank: D.&Co., France. Value: $135.00–175.00.
(front) Cream (1903–1905) and lidded sugar (1898–1903),
CROCUS CONVENTIONAL. (unsigned). TM date: 1898–1903.
Blank: none. Value: $145.00–195.00.

Plate 16. Desert bowl, fancy-edged, 7"d., CURRANTS AND
AUTUMN LEAVES WITH ROCOCO GOLD BORDER. Signed:
J.VOKRAL (Vokral, Jeremiah). TM date: 1898–1903.
Blank: J.P.L., France. Value: $95.00–125.00.

Plate 17. Plate, scalloped, 8⅝"d., NASTURTIUM CONVENTIONAL.
Signed: R.H. RH (twice) (Hessler, Robert). TM date:
1898–1903. Blank: A.K.D, France. Value: $150.00–175.00.

Plate 18. Cup and saucer. Poppies on cream ground,
embellished gold border. Signed: R. Hessler, (Hessler,
Robert). TM date: 1898–1903. Blank: R.C. Louis Seize
Bavaria green mark. Value: $125.00–150.00.

*Plate 19. GALOIS jug, 7½"h., <u>POPPY</u>. Signed: Loh (Loh, John). TM date: 1898–1903. Blank: J.P.L., France. Value: $325.00–375.00.*

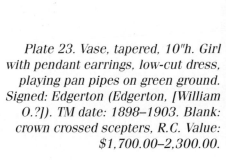

*Plate 20. Plate, 8¾"d. Three groups of three red raspberries with tendrils on gold border. Signed: Bitterly (Bitterly, Walter K.). TM date: 1898–1903. Blank: Haviland, France. Value: $75.00–90.00.*

*Plate 21. Vase, 8"h. St. Bernard dog on brown/yellow ground. Signed: Farrington (Farrington). TM date: 1898–1903. Blank: none. Value: $800.00–1,000.00.*

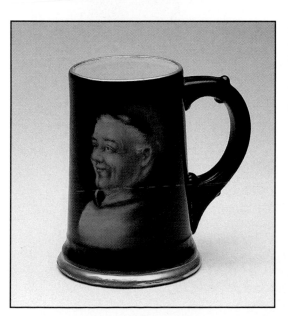

*Plate 22. Mug, 6"h. Smiling monk with green skull cap. Signed: Grane (Grane). TM date: 1898–1903. Blank: scrolls, W.G.&Co., France. Value: $375.00–450.00.*

*Plate 23. Vase, tapered, 10"h. Girl with pendant earrings, low-cut dress, playing pan pipes on green ground. Signed: Edgerton (Edgerton, [William O.?]). TM date: 1898–1903. Blank: crown crossed scepters, R.C. Value: $1,700.00–2,300.00.*

Plate 24. Toasting goblet, 11¼"h., CHEVALIER. (unsigned). TM date: 1898–1903. Blank: Belleek serpent, Willets. Value: $750.00–900.00.

Plate 25. Vase, 9½"h., EVENING SPREADS HER MANTLE. Signed: Grane (Grane). TM date: 1898–1903. Blank: none. Value: $2,300.00–2,600.00.

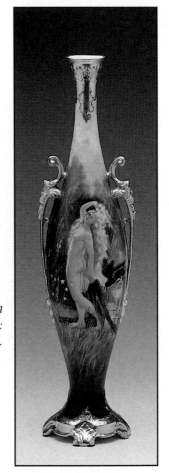

Plate 26. Vase, footed, very slim, open elaborate handles, 19¾"h. Nude female with long blonde hair and raven in woods, gilt handles. Signed: Grane (Grane). TM date: 1898–1903. Blank: none. Value: $3,400.00–4,200.00.

Plate 27. (left) Plate, 9¾"d., PERSIAN DECORATION. Signed: Lind (Lindner, Frederick J.). TM date: 1905–1910. Blank: Haviland, France. Value: $135.00–185.00. (right) Plate, 8½"d., PERSIAN DECORATION. Signed: JBrauer (Brauer, Julius H.). TM date: 1898–1903. Blank: T&V rectangle, Limoges, France. Value: $125.00–150.00.

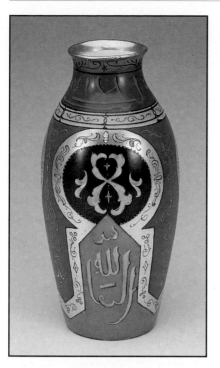

*Plate 28. Vase, oval with flared neck, 8¾"h., <u>ARABIAN</u>. Signed: JBrauer (Brauer, Julius H.). TM date: 1898–1903. Blank: crown crossed scepters R.C. Value: $195.00–295.00.*

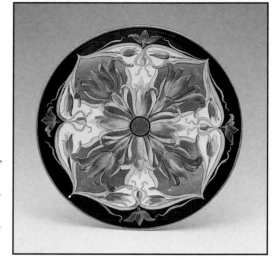

*Plate 29. Plate, 8½"d. Tiger lilies on brown border. (unsigned). TM date: 1898–1903. Blank: J.P.L., France. Value: $125.00–195.00.*

*Plate 30. Candlesticks, pair, 8¾"h., <u>IRIS</u> <u>CONVENTIONAL</u>. Signed: Lind (Lindner, Frederick J.). TM date: 1898–1903. Blank: Limoges scroll W.G.&Co., France. Value: $450.00–525.00.*

*Plate 32. FESTOON plate, 8½"d., <u>TULIP</u> <u>CONVENTIONAL</u>. Signed: Lind (Lindner, Frederick J.). TM date: 1898–1903. Blank: Limoges, France. Value: $175.00–195.00.*

*Plate 31. GALOIS jug, 7½"h., <u>NEW</u> <u>IRIS</u> <u>CONVENTIONAL</u>. (unsigned). TM date: 1898–1903. Blank: J.P.L., France. Value: $450.00–575.00.*

Plate 33. Vase, pedestalled, 10"h., IRIS CONVENTIONAL. Signed: Lind (Lindner, Frederick J.). TM date: 1898–1903. Blank: MR on JL brackets, France (Gibus and Redon). Value: $275.00–350.00.

Plate 34. Lidded teapot, 6" h. with animal-headed spout, lidded sugar and creamer, all on footed bases, ROSE GARLAND ROCOCO. (unsigned). TM date: 1898–1903. Blank: crown embellished staff, Germany. Value: $475.00–575.00.

Plate 35. Cup and saucer. Yellow and pink rose clusters on yellow ground. Black outlined gold border. Signed: Blaha (Blaha, Joseph). TM date: 1898–1903. Blank: J.P.L., France. Value: $125.00–150.00.

Plate 36. Shallow bowl, 8¾"d. Pink, yellow, and red roses with blue ground above and cream ground below. Rococo gold rim. (unsigned). TM date: 1898–1903. Blank: Limoges, France. Value: $95.00–115.00.

Plate 37. Sugar bowl, small, footed, 6½"l. Violet spray on yellow and green ground. Signed: Pietrykaski (Pietrykaski). TM date: 1898–1903. Blank: Century Patd Feb 26 1901 T&V, Limoges, France. Value: $85.00–110.00.

Plate 38. Plate, scalloped edged, 9½"d., CAPERCAILZIE. Signed: EChallinor (Challinor, Edward S.). TM date: 1898–1903. Blank: Limoges, France. Value: $225.00–250.00.

Plate 39. Plate, scalloped rim, 9¼"d., PHEASANT. Signed: E.Challinor (Challinor, Edward S.). TM date: 1898–1903. Blank: Limoges, France. Value: $225.00–250.00.

Plate 40. Plate, 9¼"d., PLOVER. Signed: E.Challinor (Challinor, Edward S.). TM date: 1903. Blank: Limoges, France. Value: $225.00–250.00.

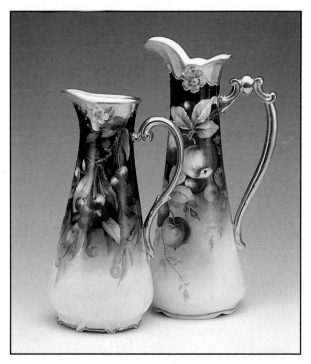

Plate 41. (left) Ewer, 10¾"h. Cherry spray on blue ground with blossoms in gold bordcr. Signed: LeRoy (LeRoy, M. Rost). TM date: 1903. Blank: T&V rectangle, Limoges, France, CENTURY PATd Feb 26, 1901. Value: $450.00–695.00. (right) Claret jug, 13"h. Apple cluster on green ground with blossoms on gold border. Signed: Leon (Leon). TM date: 1903–1905. Blank: none. Value: $595.00–800.00.

Plate 42. Small pitcher, 4"h. Poppies on green ground. Signed: Cathanay (Cathanay, F. A.). TM date: 1903. Blank: T&V rectangle, Limoges, France. Value: $140.00–175.00.

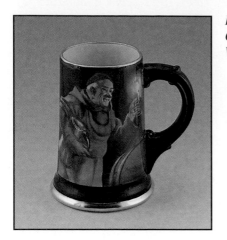

*Plate 43. Mug, 6"h. Monk with tankard and candle. Signed: Aldrich (Aldrich, Grace M.). TM date: 1898–1903. Blank: Limoges scroll, W.G.&Co., France. Value: $250.00–350.00.*

*Plate 44. Plate, rimmed, slight scallop, 8½"d. Red raspberry spray, rococo gold border on Prussian blue rim. Signed: JKiefus (Kiefus, Jacob). TM date: 1903. Blank: J.P.L., France. Value: $135.00–175.00.*

*Plate 45. Lidded, footed, egg-shaped coffee, 6 footed demi-tasses, 6 saucers, IRIS CONVENTIONAL. Signed: F.Lind (Lindner, Frederick J.). TM date: 1903. Blank: Limoges scroll, W.G.&Co., France. Value: $950.00–1,100.00.*

*Plate 46. Plate, 8½"d. Pale orange/pink poppies on cream ground. Signed: Challinor (Challinor, Edward S.). TM date: 1903. Blank: Haviland, France. Value: $125.00–175.00.*

*Plate 47. Plate, 8½"d. Art nouveau pastel floral. Signed: E. Challinor (Challinor, Edward S.). TM date: 1903–1905. Blank: Haviland, France. Value: $180.00–210.00.*

*Plate 48. Charger with perforated handles, 10¼"d., YESCHEK RASPBERRIES. Signed: Yeschek (Yeschek, Joseph T.). TM date: 1903–1905. Blank: J.P.L., France. Value: $225.00–295.00.*

*Plate 49. Cream and lidded sugar with double ring handles, 5"d., YESCHEK RASPBERRIES. Signed: Yeschek (Yeschek, Joseph T.). TM date: 1903–1905. Blank: GDA, France. Value: $165.00–210.00.*

*Plate 50. (left) Bowl, scalloped-edged, 7¼"d., CROCUS CONVENTIONAL. Signed: Roden (Roden, Harry). TM date: 1903–1905. Blank: Limoges. Value: $135.00–165.00. (right) Bowl, 5½"d., CROCUS CONVENTIONAL. (unsigned). TM date: 1903–1905. Blank: Haviland, France. Value: $185.00–225.00.*

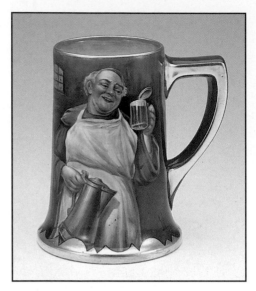

*Plate 51. Mug, 6"h. Smiling monk in apron with tankard and stein. Signed: Weiss ( Weiss, Arthur J. ). TM date: 1903–1905. Blank: scrolls, W.G.&Co., France. Value: $525.00–625.00.*

*Plate 52. Vase, tapered, narrow neck, 13½"h., <u>PRAYING MOHAMMEDAN</u>. Signed: Farrington (Farrington). TM date: 1903–1905. Blank: crown crossed scepters, RC Bavaria. Value: $1,800.00–2,500.00.*

*Plate 53. Large round tray, 16"d. Hunting dogs at point in green meadow. Signed: Farrington (Farrington). TM date: 1903–1905. Blank: T&V rectangle, Limoges, France. Value: $2,300.00–2,800.00.*

*Plate 54. Plaque, 15½"l., MOOR WITH TIGER. Signed: KUBASH (Kubasch, Emil). TM date: 1903–1905. Blank: circle, Limoges (incomplete). Value: $800.00–1,300.00.*

*Plate 55. Toasting goblet, 11¼"h. Bearded Arab with ear ring. (unsigned). TM date: 1903–1905. Blank: Belleek serpent, Willets. Value: $850.00–1,100.00.*

*Plate 56. Vase, 9½"h., LION. Signed: Weiss (Weiss, Arthur J.). TM date: 1903–1905. Blank: none. Value: $1,500.00–2,000.00.*

*Plate 57. Plaque, 15⅜"l., CATTLE BY A HIGHLAND LAKE. Signed: KUBASCH (Kubasch, Emil). TM date: 1903–1905. Blank: circle Limoges star, France (Legrand). Value: $1,200.00–1,800.00.*

*Plate 58. Vase, 7½"h., HENRY VI AS A CHILD. (unsigned). TM date: 1903–1905. Blank: none. Value: $1,900.00–2,600.00.*

*Plate 59. Vase, 7"h., PATRICIAN WOMAN. (unsigned). TM date: 1903–1905. Blank: none. Value: $1,900.00–2,600.00.*

*Plate 60. Vase, 9½"h. Medallion on white: Two women with upswept hair before seascape. (unsigned). TM date: 1903–1905. Blank: palette CAC Belleek. Value: $2,800.00–3,200.00.*

*Plate 61. Vase, open handled, 16"h. Art nouveau lady with gold hair, grape cluster on green ground. Signed: C. Pohl (Pohl, C.). TM date: 1903–1905. Blank: scrolls, W.G.&Co., Limoges, France. Value: $2,800.00–3,200.00.*

*Plate 62. Vase, three-handled, 5¼"h. Barn-yard fowl in flowered grass. (unsigned). TM date: 1903–1905. Blank: Haviland, France. Value: $800.00–1,200.00.*

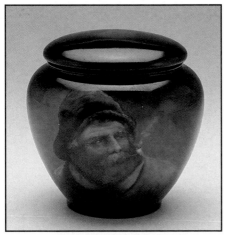

*Plate 63. Vase, bud, 6"h. Pastoral setting with cow. Signed: Aldrich (Aldrich, Grace M.). TM date: 1903–1905. Blank: none. Value: $650.00–850.00.*

*Plate 64. Mug, 6"h. Monk in maroon robe with tankard. Signed: Weiss (Weiss, Arthur J.). TM date: 1903–1905. Blank: scrolls, W.G.&Co., France. Value: $450.00–550.00.*

*Plate 67. Humidor, 5"h., CAPE COD FISHERMAN. Signed: Farrington (Farrington). TM date: 1903–1905. Blank: GDA, France. Value: $1,500.00–2,100.00.*

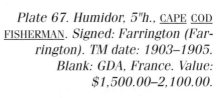

*Plate 65. Stein, 7"h., ARROW MAKER. Signed: Kubasch (Kubasch, Emil). TM date: 1903–1905. Blank: none. Value: $850.00–1,200.00.*

*Plate 66. Vase, tubular, 12"h., JAPANESE WOMAN WITH COMB. (unsigned). TM date: 1903–1905. Blank: Belleek serpent, Willets. Value: $1,600.00–2,100.00.*

*Plate 68. Vase, 10"h., THE CITADEL. Signed: Weiss (Weiss, Arthur J.). TM date: 1903–1905. Blank: crown crossed scepters, R.C. Bavaria. Value: $3,500.00–4,000.00.*

*Plate 69. Vase, Aladdin lamp style, 8½"h. Carp in gold-current water, blue/green ground. Signed: F.Kriesche (Kriesche, F.). TM date: 1903–1905. Blank: none. Value: $250.00–300.00.*

*Plate 70. Vase, 7½"h. Italian fishing boats. Signed: N.R.Gifford (Gifford, Nathan R.). TM date: 1903–1905. Blank: none. Value: $450.00–575.00.*

*Plate 71. Large nappy, 7"d., CARP POOL. Signed: MOTZFELDT (Motzfeldt, Andrew). TM date: 1903–1905. Blank: bird banner, Limoges, France. Value: $140.00–185.00.*

*Plate 72. Low vase, Aladdin lamp style, 7½"h. Sea gull on blue ground. Signed: Motzfeldt (Motzfeldt, Andrew). TM date: 1903–1905. Blank: none. Value: $200.00–250.00.*

*Plate 73. Plate, embossed, scalloped edge, 8½"d. Red and yellow nasturtiums on green leaves, gold-embellished yellow rim. (Unusual rim treatment for Pickard.) (unsigned). TM date: 1903–1905. Blank: AK D, France. Value: $85.00–125.00.*

111

*Plate 76. Cache or ferner, 7"h., <u>POND</u> <u>LILY</u>. Signed: Leach (Leach, George P.). TM date: 1903–1905. Blank: Limoges, France. Value each: $395.00–450.00.*

*Plate 74. Lidded claret, 11½"h., MORNING GLORY TRELLIS. Signed: Stahl (Stahl, George W.). TM date: 1903–1905. Blank: GDA, France. Value: $425.00–475.00.*

*Plate 77. Lidded teapot, lidded sugar, creamer, ornate handles and rims, JELINEK ROSES. Signed: TMJelinek (Jelinek, Thomas M.). TM date: 1903–1905. Blank: J.P.L., France. Value: $450.00–550.00.*

*Plate 78. Plate, 9¼"d. Roses on gold border. Signed: Leach (Leach, George P.). TM date: 1903–1905. Blank: Haviland, France. Value: $125.00–165.00.*

*Plate 75. ST. DENIS vase, 8"h. Red-orange tulip arched over white tulip gold lining on cream. Signed: W. LEMKE (Lemke, Walter R.). TM date: 1903–1905. Blank: none. Value: $250.00–300.00.*

*Plate 79. (left) Bowl, scalloped rim, 10½"d., AUTUMN BLACKBERRIES AND GOLD PASTE. Signed: O.Goess (Goess, Otto W.). TM date: 1905–1910. Blank: none. Value: $225.00–285.00. (right) VENICE jug, 10½"h. Signed: O.Goess (Goess, Otto W.). TM date: 1903–1905. Blank: T&V rectangle, Limoges, France. Value: $495.00–575.00.*

Plate 80. Bowl, scalloped rim, pierced handles, 10"d., PURPLE GRAPES AND ETCHED GOLD BORDER. Signed: Coufall (Coufall, John Anton). TM date: 1903–1905. Blank: none. Value: $325.00–450.00.

Plate 81. (rear) Platter, 12¼" Pale orange and purple grapes, grapevine etched into gold border. Signed: Coufall (Coufall, John Anton). TM date: 1905–1910. Blank: T&V rectangle, Limoges, France. Value: $225.00–275.00. (front) ROMA jug (lemonade pitcher with scalloped rim), 6"h. Signed: A.COUFALL (Coufall, John Anton). TM date: 1903–1905. Blank: crown Vienna shields, Austria. Value: $375.00–475.00.

Plate 82. MALMAISON plate, scalloped edge, 9"d. Currants on maroon ground, autumn leaves, yellow center, gold border. Signed: E. Pfiefer (Pfiefer, E.). TM date: 1903–1905. Blank: crown crossed scepters, R.C. Malmaison Bavaria. Value: $115.00–130.00.

Plate 83. Large ALEXANDER Jug, 9"d. Design patent 37,352 CHERRY LATTICE. Signed: Beitler (Beitler, Joseph C.). TM date: 1903–1905. Blank: T&V, Limoges, France. Value: $425.00–575.00.

Plate 84. Plate, 8¼"d. Cherry spray, variegated leaves, inner rococo gold border, cream ground. Signed: MP (Pickard, Minnie Verna). TM date: 1903–1905. Blank: CA, France. Value: $185.00–200.00.

Plate 85. Pitcher, 8"h. Grape cluster on yellow and maroon grounds. Signed: SEIDEL (Seidel, Erhardt). TM date: 1903–1905. Blank: AK D, France. Value: $350.00–425.00.

Plate 86. Tray, lion-spouted teapot, cream and sugar, 11"l., EGYPTIAN PAPYRUS AND LUSTRE. Signed: Lind (Lindner, Frederick J.). TM date: 1903–1905. Blank: T&V rectangle, Limoges, France. Value: $850.00–1,200.00.

Plate 87. (rear) Plate, scalloped rim, 8½"d., GIBSON PANSIES. Signed: E. Gibson (Gibson, Edward). TM date: 1903–1905. Blank: Limoges, France. Value: $150.00–175.00. (front) Hatpin/ring holder, 4½"h. Signed: CM or MC (unknown). TM date: 1903–1905. Blank: none. Value: $245.00–285.00.

Plate 88. Tray with footed, egg-shaped lidded teapot, lidded sugar, and creamer, 11"w., HESSLER VIOLET BOUQUET. Signed: RH (Hessler, Robert). TM date: 1903–1905. Blank: MR on JL brackets, France (Gibus and Redon). Value: $795.00–895.00.

Plate 89. Coffee pot, cream and sugar, CARNATION CONVENTIONAL. Signed: Tomas (Tomascheko, Rudolph). TM date: 1903–1905. Blank: T&V rectangle, Limoges, France. Value: $400.00–475.00.

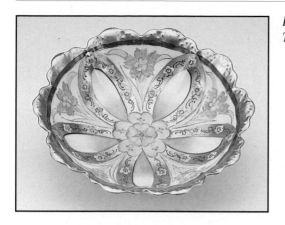

Plate 90. Candy dish, 6"d., 37,170 CARNATION CONVENTIONAL. (unsigned). TM date: 1903–1905. Blank: Haviland. Value: $100.00–135.00.

Plate 91. (rear) MALMAISON plate, fancy-edged, 8"d., 37,170 CARNATION CONVENTIONAL. Signed: RH (Hessler, Robert). TM date: 1903–1905. Blank: R.C. Malmaison Bavaria. Value: $155.00–195.00. (front) LARGE BASEL jug, 5"h. Signed: AB (unknown). TM date: 1903–1905. Blank: Limoges, France on banners over bird. Value: $375.00–450.00.

Plate 92. DORIQUE jug, wide mouthed, 7"h., IRIS CONVENTIONAL. Signed: Lind (Lindner, Frederick J.). TM date: 1898–1903. Blank: T&V rectangle, Limoges, France. Incised: DORIQUE Patd JUNE 3d 84 5½. Value: $325.00–400.00.

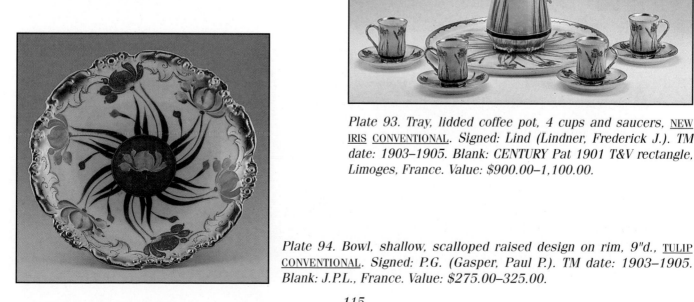

Plate 93. Tray, lidded coffee pot, 4 cups and saucers, NEW IRIS CONVENTIONAL. Signed: Lind (Lindner, Frederick J.). TM date: 1903–1905. Blank: CENTURY Pat 1901 T&V rectangle, Limoges, France. Value: $900.00–1,100.00.

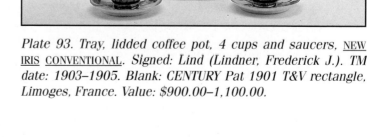

Plate 94. Bowl, shallow, scalloped raised design on rim, 9"d., TULIP CONVENTIONAL. Signed: P.G. (Gasper, Paul P.). TM date: 1903–1905. Blank: J.P.L., France. Value: $275.00–325.00.

Plate 95. Lidded sugar and creamer, <u>TULIP</u> <u>CONVENTIONAL</u>. Signed: Tomasch (Tomascheko, Rudolph). TM date: 1903–1905. Blank: Haviland, France. Value: $250.00–275.00.

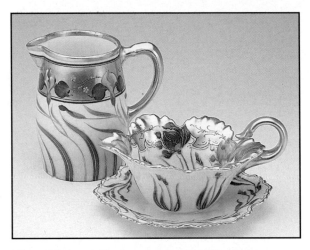

Plate 97. (rear) Pitcher, small milk, 5"h., <u>NEW</u> <u>IRIS</u> <u>CON-VENTIONAL</u>. (unsigned). TM date: 1903–1905. Blank: GDA, France. Value: $200.00–245.00. (front) Leaf mayonnaise with attached underplate, open handle, deeply scalloped, 6¾"l., <u>TULIP</u> <u>CONVENTIONAL</u>. Signed: Koep (Koep, F. H.). TM date: 1903–1905. Blank: T&V rectangle, Limoges, France. Value: $225.00–295.00.

Plate 96. Bowl, regency with wishbone handles, 7½"d., <u>TULIP</u> <u>CONVENTIONAL</u>. Signed: Koep. (Koep, F. H.). TM date: 1903–1905. Blank: T&V rectangle, France. Value: $215.00–265.00.

Plate 98. Shaving mug, 3½"h., <u>NEW</u> <u>IRIS</u> <u>CONVEN-TIONAL</u>. Signed: Lind (Lindner, Frederick J.). TM date: 1903–1905. Blank: T&V rectangle, Limoges, France. Value: $425.00–475.00.

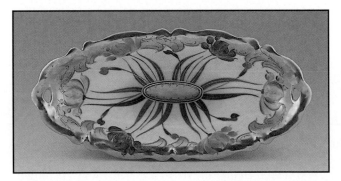

Plate 99. Celery Dish, 13"l., <u>TULIP</u> <u>CONVENTIONAL</u>. (unsigned). TM date: 1903–1905. Blank: none. Value: $175.00–200.00.

Plate 100. Chocolate set: Tray, pot, cream and sugar, 4 cups and saucers, <u>NEW</u> <u>IRIS</u> <u>CONVENTIONAL</u>. Signed: Lind (Lindner, Frederick J.). TM date: 1903–1905. Blank: GDA, France. Value: $1,700.00–1,800.00.

Plate 101. Oval dish, art nouveau style, 9"l., *VOBORNIK CHRYSAN-THEMUMS.* Signed: Vobornik. (Vobornik, Franz). TM date: 1903–1905. Blank: D&Co., France. Value: $135.00–160.00.

Plate 102. Pitcher, small, 5¼"h., REAN PINK MUMS. Signed: Rean (Klipphahn, Maxwell Rean). TM date: 1903–1905. Blank: bird & banner, Limoges, France. Value: $225.00–275.00.

Plate 103. Bowl, 10"d. Cherry sprays with leaves and blossoms, gold border, yellow ground. Signed: Friedrich (Friedrich). TM date: 1903–1905. Blank: France BM de M Limoges. Value: $175.00–200.00.

Plate 104. (left) Mug, 6"h. Cherry spray, gold border with lattices. Signed: J C Beitler (Beitler, Joseph C.). TM date: 1903–1905. Blank: Limoges scroll, W.G.&Co., France. Value: $265.00–325.00. (right) Mug, 6"h. Grape clusters, autumn leaves, etched gold grape and vine border. Signed: SEIDEL (Seidel, Erhardt). TM date: 1903–1905. Blank: Limoges scroll, W.G.&Co., France. Value: $275.00–350.00.

Plate 105. Side plate, scalloped rim, 6¼"d. Apple cluster, olive green ground, three pink blossoms on scalloped border. Signed: Leon (Leon). TM date: 1903–1905. Blank: Limoges, France. Value: $70.00–85.00.

*Plate 106. (left) Bonbon, boat-shaped, footed, with scalloped edges, 5¾"l. Currants, autumn leaves, maroon ground, interior decorated. Signed: Leon (Leon). TM date: 1903–1905. Blank: crown Vienna shields Austria. Value: $110.00–135.00. (right) Small oval mug, 3½"h. Currants on maroon ground. Signed: Vetter (Vetter). TM date: 1903–1905. Blank: T&V rectangle, Limoges, France. Value: $150.00–185.00.*

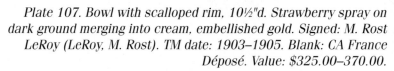

*Plate 107. Bowl with scalloped rim, 10½"d. Strawberry spray on dark ground merging into cream, embellished gold. Signed: M. Rost LeRoy (LeRoy, M. Rost). TM date: 1903–1905. Blank: CA France Déposé. Value: $325.00–370.00.*

*Plate 108. Bowl, scalloped edges, tabbed handles, 9½"d. Bright red currant spray, white-pink blossoms, variegated ground. Signed: A. Roy (Roy, A.). TM date: 1903–1905. Blank: Century Patd Feb 26th 1901 T&V rectangle, Limoges, France. Value: $185.00–225.00.*

*Plate 109. ALEXANDER jug and matching plate, 8¾"d., CHERRY BRANCH. (unsigned). TM date: 1903–1905. Blank: T&V rectangle, Limoges, France (jug), Haviland, France (plate). Value: (jug) $325.00–395.00; (plate) $125.00–150.00.*

*Plate 110. Charger, 12½"d., PLUM BRANCH. Signed: Rean (Klipphahn, Maxwell Rean). TM date: 1903–1905. Blank: CA France. Value:*

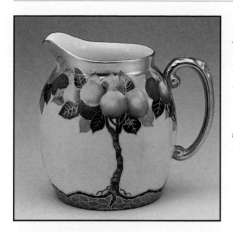

Plate 111. DORIQUE jug, 7¾"h., ORANGE TREE PANELS. Signed: N.R.Gifford (Gifford, Nathan R.). TM date: 1903–1905. Blank: T&V rectangle, Limoges, France. Value: $325.00–395.00.

Plate 112. Charger, 12½"d. Cherry spray. Signed: Rean (Klipphahn, Maxwell Rean). TM date: 1903–1905. Blank: GDA, France. Value: $350.00–425.00.

Plate 113. Plate, 8¾"d. Yellow poppy cluster. Signed: Seidel (Seidel, Erhart). TM date: 1903–1905. Blank: Haviland, France. Value: $150.00–195.00.

Plate 114. Plate, 9"d., ORANGES AND ROCOCO GOLD PASTE. Signed: Schoner (Schoner, Otto). TM date: 1903–1905. Blank: J.P.L., France. Value: $225.00–275.00.

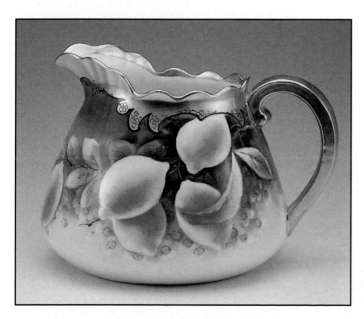

Plate 115. Pitcher, 6¾"h., SCHONER LEMONS. Signed: Schoner (Schoner, Otto). TM date: 1903–1905. Blank: crown shield, Vienna, Austria. Value: $395.00–525.00.

*Plate 116. Plate, scalloped-edge, 9"d., NATURALISTIC PEACHES. Signed: SEIDEL (Seidel, Erhardt). TM date: 1903–1905. Blank: Limoges, France. Value: $145.00–195.00.*

*Plate 117. Lemonade jug, 8"h. Peaches on green leaf ground. Signed: S. Heap (Heap, Samuel). TM date: 1903–1905. Blank: palette, circle, CAC, Belleek. Value: $345.00–395.00.*

*Plate 118. (left) Scalloped MALMAISON plate, 9"d. Peach spray on brown ground with embellished gold border. Signed: O. Shoner (Schoner, Otto). TM date: 1903–1905. Blank: crown, scepters, R.C. Malmaison Bavaria. Value: $135.00–185.00. (right) Mug, 6"h. Signed: Shoner (Schoner, Otto). TM date: 1903–1905. Blank: Limoges wreath, W.G.&Co., France. Value: $260.00–310.00.*

*Plate 119. Plate with scalloped rim, 8"d. Deep red peaches on green leaf spray, blossoms, ornate gold border. Signed: JKiefus (Kiefus, Jacob). TM date: 1903–1905. Blank: scrolls, W.G.&Co., France. Value: $125.00–185.00.*

*Plate 120. Plate, scalloped edges, 9"d., ANTIQUE DAY LILIES. Signed: LeRoy (LeRoy, M. Rost). TM date: 1903–1905. Blank: Limoges scroll, W.G.&Co., France. Value: $160.00–195.00.*

*Plate 121. Plate, 8½"d. Roses with embellished gold nouveau streamers. Signed: LOBA (Loba, F.). TM date: 1903–1905. Blank: T&V rectangle, Limoges, France. Value: $140.00–185.00.*

*Plate 124. Plate, 8¾" d., GOOSEBERRY CONVENTIONAL. Signed: F. Walter (Walters, Frederick). TM date: 1903–1905. Blank: Haviland, France. Value: $145.00–185.00.*

*Plate 122. Mug, 5½"h., REAN PEARS. Signed: Rean (Klipphahn, Maxwell Rean). TM date: 1903–1905. Blank: J.P.L., France. Value: $225.00–350.00.*

*Plate 125. ALEXANDER lidded sugar and creamer, CHERRIES AND GOLD. Signed: H.Tolley (Tolley, Harry E.). TM date: 1903–1905. Blank: T&V rectangle, Limoges, France. Value: $165.00–195.00.*

*Plate 123. Charger, 13"d., REAN PEARS. Signed: Rean (Klipphahn, Maxwell Rean). TM date: 1903–1905. Blank: J.P.L., France. Value: $400.00–595.00.*

*Plate 126. Side plate, scalloped, perforated, 6¼"d., NASTURTIUM CONVENTIONAL. Signed: F.K (Kriesche, F.). TM date: 1903–1905. Blank: crown R.C. crossed scepters LION D'OR Bavaria. Value: $85.00–100.00.*

Plate 127. (rear) Side dish, scalloped rim, 7"d., 37,322 RASPBERRY NOUVEAU. Signed: E Challinor (Challinor, Edward S.). TM date: 1903–1905. Blank: Limoges, France. Value: $100.00–125.00. (front) SECESSION cream and lidded sugar. Signed: EChallinor (Challinor, Edward S.). TM date: 1903–1905. Blank: crown, crossed scepters, R.C. SECESSION Bavaria. Value: $275.00–350.00.

Plate 128. Scalloped-footed MALMAISON bowl with scalloped rim, 10"d. Red raspberry sprays, autumn leaves on gold border. Signed: JN (Nessy, John). TM date: 1903–1905. Blank: crown crossed scepters, R.C. Malmaison Bavaria. Value: $235.00–285.00.

Plate 129. Berry set, 10"d., ring-footed bowl with 12 berry dishes, RASPBERRIES AND ETCHED GOLD. Signed: Coufall (Coufall, John Anton). TM date: 1903–1905. Blank: J.P.L., France. Value: $650.00–775.00.

Plate 130. (left) Candy dish, oblong, 7"l, CRAB APPLE BLOSSOMS. Signed: Leach (Leach, George P.). TM date: 1903–1905. Blank: Haviland, France. Value: $75.00–100.00. (rear) Cake plate with perforated handles, 10"d. Signed: Leach (Leach, George P.). TM date: 1903–1905. Blank: J.P.L., France. Value: $130.00–185.00. (right) Bowl, small shallow, scalloped edge, 7¼"d. Signed: LEON (Leon). TM date: 1898–1903. Blank: Limoges, France. Value: $100.00–125.00.

Plate 131. Lidded teapot, cream and sugar, ornate blank 8½"d., CRAB APPLE BLOSSOMS. Signed: Leach (Leach, George P.). TM date: 1903–1905. Blank: Century Patd Feb 26th 1901, T&V rectangle, Limoges, France. Value: $375.00–450.00.

Plate 134. GALOIS jug, 7½"h., ARABIAN. (unsigned). TM date: 1903–1905. Blank: J.P.L., France. Value: $450.00–575.00.

Plate 132. Cup and saucer. Spray of pink and maroon roses on dark green ground; gold rim with rust and white outlining. Signed: V (Vobornik, Franz). TM date: 1903–1905. Blank: Haviland, France. Value: $125.00–150.00.

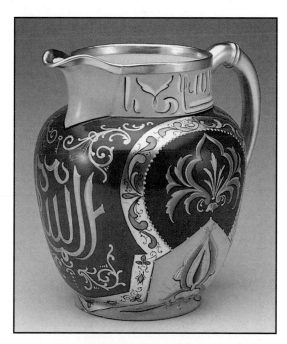

Plate 135. Pitcher with bamboo-style handle, 7¾"h., ARABIAN. (unsigned). TM date: 1903–1905. Blank: AK D, France. Value: $375.00–450.00.

Plate 133. Lidded sugar and creamer, 5"l., ROSE BOWER. Signed: Leon (Leon). TM date: 1903–1905. Blank: GDA, France. Value: $175.00–225.00.

Plate 136. Punch bowl with scalloped rim and 12 RAN-SON punch cups (Haviland France), 13½"d., <u>ARABIAN</u>. (unsigned). TM date: 1903–1905. Blank: T&V rectangle, Limoges, France Déposé. Value: $3,500.00–4,800.00.

Plate 137. Medium CARMEN vase, 9¼"h., REAN PINK MUMS. Signed: Rean (Klipphahn, Maxwell Rean). TM date: 1903–1905. Blank: D.&Co., France. Value: $595.00–525.00.

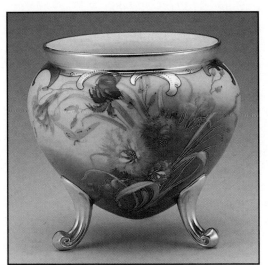

Plate 138. Jardiniere, three legged 6¾"d., CARNATION GARDEN. Signed: Yeschek (Yeschek, Joseph T.). TM date: (1903–1905 range; unmarked due to shape.) Blank: none. Value: $600.00–750.00.

Plate 139. Vase, 12"h., TULIP GARDEN. Signed: Yeschek (Yeschek, Joseph T.). TM date: 1903–1905. Blank: none. Value: $650.00–775.00.

Plate 140. VENICE jug, 10½"h., CARNATION GARDEN. Signed: Yeschek (Yeschek, Joseph T.). TM date: 1903–1905. Blank: T&V rectangle, Limoges, France. Value: $700.00–850.00.

Plate 141. CENTURY salad bowl, scalloped rim, scalloped pedestal, upswept open handles, 10¼"d., POINSETTIA AND LUSTER. Signed: N.R.Gifford (Gifford, Nathan Roswell). TM date: 1903–1905. Blank: CENTURY PATd FEB 26th, 1901, T&V rectangle, Limoges, France. Value: $625.00–725.00.

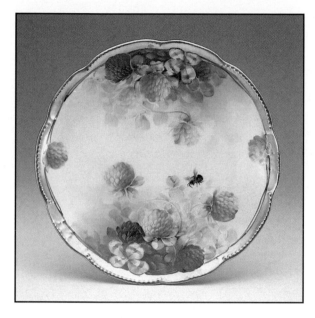

Plate 142. Plate, 8¾"d., CLOVER BLOSSOMS AND HONEY BEE. Signed: Reury (Reury, Howard B.). TM date: 1903–1905. Blank: AK D, France. Value: $100.00–175.00.

Plate 143. Plate, 8¾"d. Monogram AEH with blue paste points, gold paste border. (unsigned). TM date: 1903–1905. Blank: Haviland, France. Value: $75.00–100.00.

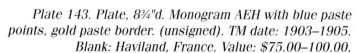

Plate 144. Pinched vase, 5½"h., BUTTERFLY. (unsigned). TM date: 1903–1905. Blank: none. Value: $300.00–375.00.

Plate 145. Plate, 8¼"d., <u>BUTTERFLY</u>. (unsigned). TM date: 1903–1905. Blank: Limoges, France. Value: $225.00–260.00.

Plate 146. Cup and saucer. White poppy on green ground. Signed: cHahn (Hahn, Charles). TM date: 1903–1905. Blank: crown crossed scepters, RC Bavaria. Value: $50.00–125.00.

Plate 147. (rear) Nappy, 7"d., <u>TOMASCHEKO</u> <u>FLORAL</u> <u>BORDER</u>. Signed: Tomash (Tomascheko, Rudolph). TM date: 1903–1905. Blank: J&C crossed clovers Louise Bavaria. Value: $100.00–125.00. (front) Covered dish with underplate, 5¾"d. Signed: HH or IH or HI. TM date: 1905–1910. Blank: D.&Co. France. Value: $155.00–215.00.

Plate 149. Plate, 8¾"d. Violet medallion with Greek key border. Signed: JNessy (Nessy, John). TM date: 1903–1905. Blank: Haviland, France. Value: $95.00–125.00.

Plate 148. Cup and saucer. BLACKBERRY CONVENTIONAL. Signed: Fisch (Fischer, Emil J. T.). TM date: 1903–1905. Blank: T&V rectangle, Limoges, France. Value: $100.00–145.00.

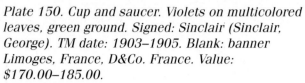

Plate 150. Cup and saucer. Violets on multicolored leaves, green ground. Signed: Sinclair (Sinclair, George). TM date: 1903–1905. Blank: banner Limoges, France, D&Co. France. Value: $170.00–185.00.

Plate 151. Plate, scalloped rim, 8"d. Pink, yellow, and red currants on spray of green leaves, embellished gold rim. Signed: GPLeach (Leach, George P.). TM date: 1903–1905. Blank: France BM de M Limoges. Value: $65.00–95.00.

Plate 152. Small pitcher, 4½"h. Nasturtiums with embellished gold whiplash. Signed: Hessler (Hessler, Robert). TM date: 1903–1905. Blank: T&V rectangle, Limoges, France, Patd 6–3–1884. Value: $180.00–225.00.

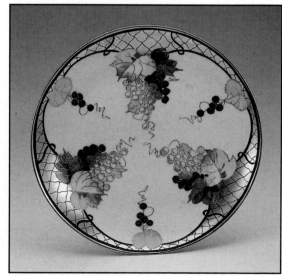

Plate 153. Plate, 8¾"d. Three grape clusters pendent on gold border. Signed: Challinor (Challinor, Edward S.). TM date: 1903–1905. Blank: BMdeM, France. Value: $135.00–150.00.

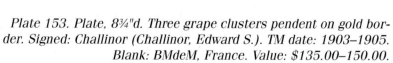

Plate 154. Bonbon, scalloped edges, 7"d., SUMMER MEADOW. Signed: H. Reury (Reury, Howard B.). TM date: 1903–1905. Blank: Limoges, France. Value: $55.00–85.00.

Plate 157. Cruet, 6½"h. CYCLAMEN. (unsigned). TM date: 1903–1905. Blank: T&V rectangle, Limoges, France Déposé. Value: $300.00–400.00.

Plate 155. Demitasse and saucer, GIFFORD SHOOTING STARS. Signed: N.R.Gifford (Gifford, Nathan R.). TM date: 1903–1905. Blank: crown crossed scepters, R.C. Bavaria. Value: $145.00–165.00.

Plate 158. (left) Plate, scalloped edge, 8½"d., CYCLAMEN. Signed: RH (Hessler, Robert). TM date: 1903–1905. Blank: crown R.C. Bavaria. Value: $185.00–235.00. (right) Demi-tasse and saucer. Signed: RH (Hessler, Robert). TM date: 1903–1905. Blank: Limoges scroll, W.G.&Co., France. Value: $165.00–185.00.

Plate 156. Cream and lidded sugar, double ring handles, GIFFORD SHOOTING STARS. Signed: N.R. Gifford (Gifford, Nathan R.). TM date: 1903–1905. Blank: GDA, France. Value: $175.00–225.00.

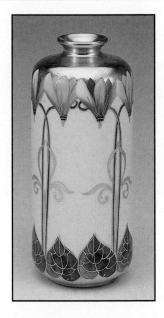

*Plate 159. Vase, cylindrical, narrow mouth, 6½"d., CYCLAMEN. Signed: oe (unknown). TM date: 1903–1905. Blank: none. Value: $165.00–225.00.*

*Plate 160. TOURAINE chamber stick, 4¾"d., CYCLAMEN. (unsigned). TM date: 1903–1905. Blank: Déposé Touraine T&V rectangle, Limoges, France. Value: $195.00–245.00.*

*Plate 161. (rear) Cream and sugar, CYCLAMEN. Signed: RH (Hessler, Robert). TM date: 1903–1905. Blank: T&V, Limoges, France. Value: $140.00–175.00. (front) Cup and saucer, (unsigned). TM date: 1903–1905. Blank: banner, Limoges, France bird. Value: $125.00–155.00.*

*Plate 162. Whiskey jug, stoppered, 7"h. Ears of corn on green ground. Signed: N.R.Gifford (Gifford, Nathan R.). TM date: 1903–1905. Blank: D&Co., France. Value: $225.00–350.00.*

*Plate 163. Vase, 7"h, CHALLINOR HOLLYHOCKS. Signed: Challinor (Challinor, Edward S.). TM date: 1903–1905. Blank: none. Value: $400.00–550.00.*

*Plate 164. Vase, tapered, narrow-mouthed, 7"h., POINSETTIA AND LUSTER. Signed: H. Tolley (Tolley, Harry E.). TM date: 1903–1905. Blank: none. Value: $275.00–350.00.*

Plate 165. Vase, 13½"h. Deep red irises on maroon ground. Signed: E.Challinor (Challinor, Edward S.). TM date: 1903–1905. Blank: PL Limoges, France. Value: $350.00–475.00.

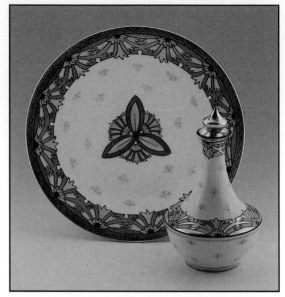

Plate 166. (rear) Plate, 8½"d., CORNFLOWER CONVENTIONAL (2). (unsigned). TM date: 1903–1905. Blank: Limoges, France. Value: $145.00–175.00. (front) Bottle, cologne, stoppered, 6"h. Signed: Yeschek (Yeschek, Joseph T.). TM date: 1903–1905. Blank: Limoges. Value: $200.00–265.00.

Plate 167. (rear) Plate, 8½"d., CORNFLOWER CONVENTIONAL (1) pink. (unsigned). TM date: 1903–1905. Blank: CA, France. Value: $165.00–225.00. (front) Large JUNO vase, 8½"h., CORNFLOWER CONVENTIONAL (1). (unsigned). TM date: 1903–1905. Blank: none. Value: $300.00–500.00.

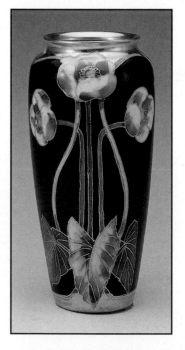

Plate 169. Vase, 7½"h., BULL-HEAD LILIES. Signed: N.R.Gifford (Gifford, Nathan R.). TM date: 1903–1905. Blank: crown crossed scepters, R.C. Bavaria. Value: $325.00–395.00.

Plate 168. MARIE vase, 5½"h., CORNFLOWER CONVENTIONAL (1). (unsigned). TM date: 1903–1905. Blank: 358 incised. Value: $225.00–285.00.

Plate 170. Plate, scalloped edges, 8½"d. Red and pink rose on green leaves, cream ground. Signed: Stahl (Stahl, George W.). TM date: 1903–1905. Blank: MR JL Limoges, France. Value: $135.00–150.00.

Plate 171. Vase, 9"h., REURY LILY CONVENTIONAL. Signed: H.Reury (Reury, Howard B.). TM date: 1903–1905. Blank: crown, R.C. Bavaria. Value: $425.00–575.00.

Plate 172. Footed nut bowl with deeply scalloped rim, 9½"d. Beige fruit on dark vari-colored ground. Signed: LeRoy (LeRoy, M. Rost). TM date: 1903–1905. Blank: miniature crown, scepter, H Germany. Value: $350.00–395.00.

Plate 174. Plate, scalloped rim, 8¾"d., APPLE BLOSSOM BOWER. Signed: LeRoy (LeRoy, M. Rost). TM date: 1903–1905. Blank: Haviland, France. Value: $165.00–195.00.

Plate 173. ALICE lidded sugar and creamer, MODERN CONVENTIONAL (Earliest version of this pattern, note white handles.) (unsigned). TM date: 1903–1905. Blank: crown design SILESIA Alice. Value: $235.00–275.00.

Plate 175. Chop plate, 12½"d., *37,323 AUTUMN BORDER.* Signed: EF (Fischer, Emil J. T.). TM date: 1903–1905. Blank: CA, France. Value: $225.00–295.00.

Plate 176. Small vase, 7"h. Daisies on russet and green ground. Signed: Ths. Jelinek (Jelinek, Thomas). TM date: 1903–1905. Blank: none. Value: $160.00–225.00.

Plate 177. Plate, 9"d., HAZELNUT CONVENTIONAL. (unsigned). TM date: 1903–1905. Blank: J.P.L., France. Value: $135.00–165.00.

Plate 178. (rear) CLAIRE plate, 8½"d., <u>HAZELNUTS</u>. Signed: Marmorstein (Marmorstein, Henry). TM date: 1903–1905. Blank: crown crossed scepters, R.C. Claire, Bavaria. Value: $125.00–165.00. (front) ROYAL NUT BOWL, (footed with convoluted edges) 8½"d. (unsigned). TM date: 1903–1905. Blank: 35. Value: $200.00–245.00.

Plate 179. Large fluted MONTRAUX bowl, 10¾"d., <u>HAZELNUTS</u>. (unsigned). TM date: 1903–1905. Blank: Montraux crown crossed scepters, RC, Bavaria. Value: $375.00–475.00.

Plate 180. Plate, 8½"d., AUTUMN BORDER. Signed: Fisher (Fischer, Emil J. T.). TM date: 1903–1905. Blank: CA, France. Value: $135.00–165.00.

Plate 181. Vase, 13"h., GINKHO [sic] LEAF. Signed: M. Rost (Rost, Max). TM date: 1903–1905. Blank: bird and banner, Limoges, France. Value: $900.00–1,400.00.

Plate 183. (left) Plate, 8½"d., EASTER LILY. Signed: Fisher (Fischer, Emil J. T.). TM date: 1903–1905. Blank: Haviland, France. Value: $185.00–215.00. (right) Syrup, 6"h. Signed: O. S. (Schoner, Otto). TM date: 1903–1905. Blank: none. Value: $200.00–250.00.

Plate 182. Mug, with full-length handle, 4½"h., GINKHO [sic] LEAF. (unsigned). TM date: 1903–1905. Blank: J.P.L., France. Value: $295.00–375.00.

Plate 184. (rear) Tray, dresser, 11"l., EASTER LILY. Signed: Schoner (Schoner, Otto). TM date: 1905–1910. Blank: Limoges. Value: $190.00–225.00. (left) Hair receiver, 4¼"d. (unsigned). TM date: 1905–1910. Blank: A.K. D, France. Value: $100.00–135.00. (right) Bowl, small, scalloped edge, 7½"d. Signed: SCHONER (Schoner, Otto). TM date: 1903–1905. Blank: Limoges, France. Value: $120.00–145.00.

Plate 185. Cup and saucer. Red and blue raspberry clusters on gold vines, yellow center. Signed: Beutlich (Beutlich, Anton B.). TM date: 1903–1905. Blank: crown over VB. Value: $110.00–135.00.

Plate 186. Plate, festoon, 8¾"d. Violets on cream ground radiating from peach blush center, gold rim. Signed: Wagner (Wagner, Albert H.). TM date: 1903–1905. Blank: AK D, France. Value: $160.00–185.00.

Plate 187. Cream and open sugar bowl. Violet with two leaves stemmed into russet base. Signed: H.R.G. (Griffiths, Harry R.), TM date: 1903–1905. Blank: J.P.L., France. Value: $245.00–285.00.

Plate 188. Side plate, 6"d., HESSLER VIOLET BOUQUET. Signed: RH (Hessler, Robert). TM date: 1903–1905. Blank: T&V rectangle, Limoges, France. Value: $10.00–20.00.

Plate 189. Art Nouveau bonbon with scalloped rim, 9"l. Violets on airbrushed green ground. Signed: JNESSY (Nessy, John). TM date: 1903–1905. Blank: none. Value: $165.00–210.00.

Plate 190. (left) MALMAISON plate, deep scalloped with raised edge nodules, 9"d., REGENCY WATER LILIES. Signed: H.E.M. (Michel, Harry E.). TM date: 1903–1905. Blank: crown crossed scepters, RC Malmaison, Bavaria. Value: $225.00–295.00. (right) Small DORIQUE jug, 5"h. Signed: H.E.M. (Michel, Harry E.). TM date: 1903–1905. Blank: Dorique, Pat June 3d, 84. Value: $210.00–260.00.

Plate 191. Bowl, shallow, ornate scalloped rim, 9½"d., GIBSON NARCISSUS. Signed: E. Gibson (Gibson, Edward). TM date: 1903–1905. Blank: J.P.L., France. Value: $185.00–250.00.

Plate 192. Fluted vase with scalloped, flared mouth, 8½"h. White water lilies with yellow centers on deep green and russet ground, gold base border with lilies and lily pads. Signed: Leach (Leach, George P.). TM date: 1903–1905. Blank: J.P.L., France. Value: $185.00–265.00.

Plate 193. Plate, 8⅝"d. Strawberries on embellished gold rim. Signed: JFuchs (Fuchs, John). TM date: 1903–1905. Blank: bird and banner, Limoges, France. Value: $140.00–175.00.

Plate 194. Dish, scalloped edges, 7½"d., MICHEL TULIPS CONVENTIONAL. Signed: H.E.M. (Michel, Harry E.). TM date: 1903–1905. Blank: Limoges, France. Value: $160.00–185.00.

*Plate 195. Candy dish, tab handles, 5½"d. Pansies, three stems radiating from center, cream ground, gold rim. Signed: H.E.M. (Michel, Harry E.). TM date: 1903–1905. Blank: T&V Limoges, France. Value: $95.00–125.00.*

*Plate 196. Chocolate pot, 6¼"h. CHALLINOR NASTURTIUMS. Signed: E. Challinor (Challinor, Edward S.). TM date: 1903–1905. Blank: crossed clovers, J&C Louise. Value: $495.00–595.00.*

*Plate 197. Lidded condiment, 3¼"d. Cluster of three red raspberries on green and brown leaves on white ground. Signed: W.R. (W.R.). TM date: 1903–1905. Blank: none. Value: $95.00–125.00.*

*Plate 198. Bowl, 6½"d. Roses overpainted with gold whiplashes. Signed: MOTZFELDT (Motzfeldt, Andrew). TM date: 1903–1905. Blank: none. Value: $70.00–95.00.*

*Plate 199. (left) Vase, 13¼"h., POPPIES IN GOLD. Signed: Gasper (Gasper, Paul P.). TM date: 1905–1910. Blank. J.P.L., France. Value: $425.00–550.00. (right) Jug, 6½"h. Signed: P.G. (Gasper, Paul P.). TM date: 1905–1910. Blank: Belleek palette, Lenox. Value: $325.00–495.00.*

Plate 200. (rear) Pitcher, 8"h., <u>POPPY</u> <u>AND</u> <u>BLACK</u>. (unsigned). TM date: 1903–1905. Blank: A.K. de France. Value: $395.00–600.00. (front) Pair of goblets, 6"h. Signed: Loh (Loh, John). TM date: 1903–1905. Blank: Belleek serpent, Willets. Value: $200.00–250.00.

Plate 201. Lidded humidor, 6¼"h., <u>POPPY</u> <u>AND</u> <u>BLACK</u>. Signed: Loh (Loh, John). TM date: 1903–1905. Blank: J.P.L., France. Value: $600.00–750.00.

Plate 202. (left) Charger, 13"d., LEON POPPIES. Signed: Leon (Leon). TM date: 1903–1905. Blank: J.P.L., France. Value: $295.00–395.00. (right) Pitcher, dragon-handled, 11¼"h. Signed: Leon (Leon). TM date: 1903–1905. Blank: J.P.L., France. Value: $495.00–595.00.

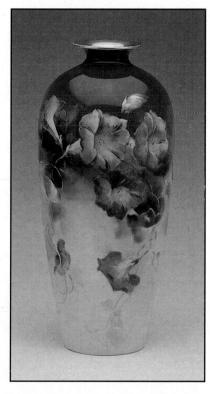

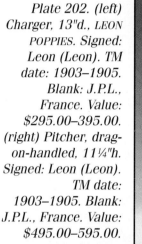

Plate 203. Vase, 10¾"h., JELINEK MORNING GLORIES. Signed: T.M.Jelinek (Jelinek, Thomas M.). TM date: 1903–1905. Blank: Belleek serpent, Willets. Value: $495.00–625.00.

Plate 204. Vase, wide-mouthed, 13½"h. Rose spray on green ground into yellow ochre ground. Signed: Lebrun (Lebrun). TM date: 1903–1905. Blank: Belleek serpent, Willets. Value: $595.00–750.00.

Plate 205. *Tankard and four mugs, 15"h.,* SEIDEL PURPLE GRAPES. *Signed: Seidel (Seidel, Erhardt). TM date: 1898–1903. Blank: Limoges scroll, W.G.&Co., France. Value: $2,600.00–2,900.00.*

Plate 206. *(left) Scalloped rim and scalloped foot MALMAI-SON bowl, 10"d.,* CARNATION CONVENTIONAL. *Signed: RH (Hessler, Robert). TM date: 1903–1905. Blank: crown crossed scepters, R.C. Malmaison, Bavaria. Value: $165.00–215.00. (right) Deeply fluted bowl on three loop feet, 7¼"d. Design Patent 37,170* CARNATION CONVENTIONAL. *(unsigned). TM date: 1903–1905. Blank: D.&Co., France. Value: $225.00–295.00.*

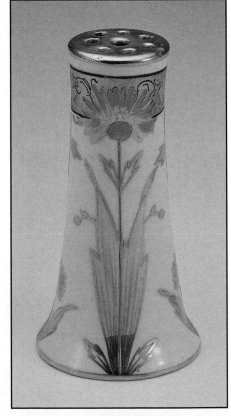

Plate 207. *Plate, 8¾"d.,* WIGHT TULIPS. *Signed: Wight (Wight, Phillip). TM date: 1905–1910. Blank: Haviland, France. Value: $100.00–145.00.*

Plate 209. *Hatpin holder, 4¾"h.,* MARIGOLDS. *Signed: Walter (Walters, Frederick). TM date: 1905–1910. Blank: PL Limoges, France. Value: $275.00–325.00.*

Plate 208. *Plate, 8½"d. Decorated gold border with three pink daisy sprays. Signed: Tolley (Tolley, Harry E.). TM date: 1905–1910. Blank: Haviland, France. Value: $100.00–135.00.*

*Plate 210. Plate, 8¾"d., <u>MARIGOLDS</u>. Signed: F W. (Walters, Frederick). TM date: 1905–1910. Blank: Haviland, France. Value: $125.00–155.00.*

*Plate 211. Salt and pepper, 3¼"h., <u>MARIGOLDS</u>. Signed: Schoner (Schoner, Otto). TM date: 1905–1910. Blank: none. Value: $110.00–145.00.*

*Plate 212. GALOIS jug, 7"d., <u>NEW</u> <u>ARABIAN</u>. Signed: LIND (Lindner, Frederick J.). TM date: 1905–1910. Blank: J.P.L., France. Value: $325.00–395.00.*

*Plate 213. REGENCE dish, handled, 7"d., ORCHIDS AND GOLD PASTE. Signed: fuchs (Fuchs, John). TM date: 1905–1910. Blank: none. Value: $135.00–165.00.*

*Plate 214. (rear) Plate, 8¾"d. Four sets of pink orchids on embellished gold border. Signed: Keates (Keates, Alfred). TM date: 1905–1910. Blank: Haviland, France. Value: $130.00–150.00. (front) Dish, small, shallow, 6"d. Three lavender and purple orchids radiused to center, embellished gold border. Signed: E. Gibson (Gibson, Edward). TM date: 1905–1910. Blank: CA, France Déposé. Value: $100.00–145.00.*

Plate 215. Bowl, deep, square, fluted corners, 9"d., CARNATION AND RAISED GOLD. Signed: Fisher (Fischer, Emil J. T.). TM date: 1905–1910. Blank: Limoges scroll, W.G.&Co., France. Value: $350.00–425.00.

Plate 216. (left) Vase, tubular, 8½"h., CARNATION AND RAISED GOLD. (UNSIGNED). TM date: 1905–1910. Blank: none. Value: $185.00–225.00. (right) Dish, small vegetable, 5"d. Signed: Rean (Klipphahn, Maxwell Rean). TM date: 1905–1910. Blank: none. Value: $75.00–95.00.

Plate 217. Lemonade jug, 7"d., CARNATION AND RAISED GOLD. Signed: Fisher (Fischer, Emil J. T.). TM date: 1905–1910. Blank: Belleek serpent, Willets. Value: $350.00–475.00.

Plate 218. Cup and saucer, CARNATION AND RAISED GOLD. Signed: Fisher (Fischer, Emil J.T.). TM date: 1905–1910. Blank: crown crossed scepters, Rosenthal Bavaria. Value: $155.00–185.00.

Plate 219. Plate, 8½"d., CARNATION AND RAISED GOLD. Signed: Fisher (Fischer, Emil J.T.). TM date: 1905–1910. Blank: Haviland, France. Value: $185.00–225.00.

Plate 220. Pitcher with bamboo style handle, 8½"h., <u>POND</u> <u>LILY</u>. Signed: Leach (Leach, George P.). TM date: 1905–1910. Blank: AK D, France. Value: $525.00–645.00.

Plate 221. (left) Bowl with scalloped rim, 9¾"d., <u>PINK</u> <u>WEIGELAS</u>. Signed: Edwd (Edward). TM date: 1910–1912. Blank: overpainted. Value: $175.00–210.00. (right) Small milk pitcher, 4¾"h., <u>GREEN</u> <u>WEIGELAS</u>. Signed: Edwd (Edward). TM date: 1905–1910. Blank: T&V rectangle, Limoges, France. Value: $195.00–225.00.

Plate 222. Platter, 10" x 14", CORNFLOWER AND ROYAL BLUE. Signed: YESCHEK (Yeschek, Joseph T.). TM date: 1905–1910. Blank: J.P.L., France. Patd 5-12-08. Value: $225.00–260.00.

Plate 224. Dresser set: 8" x 12" tray, covered powder, hair receiver, pin tray, hairpin holder, hat pin holder, <u>CORNFLOWER</u> <u>CONVENTIONAL</u> (2). Signed: Yeschek (Yeschek, Joseph T.). TM date: 1905–1910. Blank: none. Value: $575.00–625.00.

Plate 223. (rear) Bonbon, scalloped rim, perforated handle, 6½"d., <u>CORNFLOWER</u> <u>CONVENTIONAL</u> (2). Signed: CK (Koenig, Carl F.). TM date: 1905–1910. Blank: Haviland, France. Value: $145.00–165.00. (front) Bouillon cup and saucer, 3⅜"d. Signed: CK (Koenig, Carl F.). TM date: 1905–1910. Blank: crown crossed scepters, R.C. Bavaria. Value: $125.00–165.00.

Plate 225. (rear) DONATELLO perforated handle bonbon, 7"l., <u>BLUEBELLS</u>. Signed: Loh (Loh, John). TM date: 1905–1910. Blank: crown crossed scepters, Rosenthal Donatello Bavaria. Value: $120.00–145.00. (left) ELITE candy dish, 6½"d. Signed: CK (Koenig, Carl F.). TM date: 1905–1910. Blank: Elite L, France. Value: $120.00–145.00. (right) Demi-tasse and saucer. Signed: CK (Koenig, Carl F.). TM date: 1905–1910. Blank: T&V rectangle, Limoges, France. Value: $100.00–135.00.

Plate 226. Tray, coffee pot, four cups and saucers, <u>CORNFLOWER</u> <u>CONVENTIONAL</u> *(2)*. Signed: CK (Koenig, Carl F.). TM date: 1905–1910. Blank: crown scepter, Rosenthal. Value: $725.00–875.00.

Plate 227. COPENHAGEN sugar, creamer, *TOMASCHEKO EDELWEISS BORDER*. (unsigned). TM date: 1905–1910. Blank: D.&Co., France. Value: $100.00–175.00.

Plate 228. Ball-footed condiment with underplate, 6"d., *TOMASCHEKO POPPY BORDER*. (unsigned). TM date: 1905–1910. Blank: Haviland, France (underplate), T&V rectangle, Limoges, France (bowl). Value: $120.00–145.00.

Plate 229. (rear) Cream and sugar, low profile, TOMASCHEKO POPPY BORDER. (unsigned). TM date: 1905–1910. Blank: Limoges P P. Value: $185.00–235.00. (front) Tray, pin, 5¼"d. (unsigned). TM date: 1905–1910. Blank: La Seynie Limoges P.P., France. Value: $80.00–110.00.

Plate 230. Mustard, lidded with captive underplate, 5"l., TOMASCHEKO POPPY BORDER. (unsigned). TM date: 1905–1910. Blank: Haviland, France. Value: $135.00–165.00.

Plate 231. Plate, 8½"d. Green/red apple spray on embellished gold border. Signed: Bardos (Bardos, Isadore). TM date: 1905–1910. Blank: CA, France. Value: $110.00–125.00.

Plate 232. Large BURL bowl, 7¾"d., PEACHES LINEAR. Signed: Beutlich (Beutlich, Anton B.). TM date: 1905–1910. Blank: Favorite Bavaria. Value: $175.00–240.00.

Plate 233. CHARLOTTE square, curved edge bowl, 8"d., FISHER PANSIES AND RAISED GOLD. Signed: Fisher (Fischer, Emil J. T.). TM date: 1905–1910. Blank: Charlotte circle JHR Bavaria, also Favorite. Value: $185.00–275.00.

Plate 234. (rear) Plate with scrolled edges, 8½"h., BLOSSOM TIME. (unsigned). TM date: 1905–1910. Blank: PATd JAN, 23rd, 1906 J.P.L., France. Value: $145.00–165.00. (front) Lidded syrup with underplate, 5"h. Signed: M.Keates (Keates, Madeline). TM date: 1905–1910. Blank: D&Co., France. Value: $350.00–425.00.

Plate 235. (rear) Tankard, 14¾"h., TULIP IN LUSTRE. Signed: Fisher (Fischer, Emil J. T.). TM date: 1905–1910. Blank: scrolls W.G.&Co. Limoges, France. Value: $600.00–750.00. (front) Mug, 5¼"h. Signed: Bek (Buschbeck, Carl). TM date: 1910–1912. Blank: J.P.L., France. Value: $225.00–275.00.

Plate 237. Dresser set: 11" tray, pin tray, hair pin holder, jewelry box, YELLOW ROSE. Signed: O.Goess (Goess, Otto W.). TM date: 1905–1910. Blank: Limoges 3 stars France. Value: $395.00–550.00.

Plate 236. (rear) Plate, 8½"d., TULIP IN LUSTRE. Signed: Fisher (Fischer, Emil J. T.). TM date: 1910–1912. Blank: Favorite Bavaria. Value: $145.00–195.00. (front) Muffineer, 5"h. Signed: Yeschek (Yeschek, Joseph T.). TM date: 1905–1910. Blank: Bavaria. Value: $185.00–235.00.

Plate 238. Leaf Mayonnaise set, 6½"l., TRUMPET FLOWERS AND TRELLIS. Signed: Z.M. (McCorkle, Zuie). TM date: 1905–1910. Blank: Haviland, France. Value: $225.00–250.00.

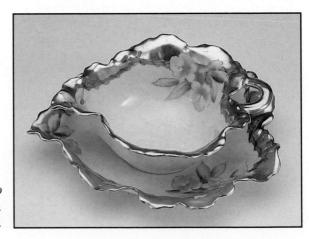

*Plate 239. Cake plate, 10½"d., TRUMPET FLOWERS AND TRELLIS. Signed: Moore (Moore, Bertha L.). TM date: 1905–1910. Blank: D&Co., France. Value: $100.00–150.00.*

*Plate 240. Cake plate, perforated handles, 11¾"d. Oranges and blossoms against brown leaf ground with embellished gold border. Signed: Schoner (Schoner, Otto). TM date: 1905–1910. Blank: France BM de M Limoges. Value: $350.00–395.00.*

*Plate 241. Milk pitcher, 6½"h., GIBSON IRIS. Signed: E.Gibson (Gibson, Edward). TM date: 1905–1910. Blank: 2 banners & bird Limoges, France. Value: $250.00–325.00.*

*Plate 242. Milk pitcher, 6"h., IRIS AND RAISED GOLD WITH LUSTRE. Signed: Arno (Arno, Edith). TM date: 1905–1910. Blank: none. Value: $185.00–265.00.*

*Plate 243. Bowl, scalloped, footed, 11"d., IRIS AND RAISED GOLD WITH LUSTRE. (unsigned). TM date: 1905–1910. Blank: T&V rectangle, Limoges, France. Value: $525.00–650.00.*

Plate 244. Handled pitcher, 11"d., IRIS AND RAISED GOLD WITH LUSTRE. Signed: Arno (Arno, Edith). TM date: 1905–1910. Blank: none. Value: $475.00–575.00.

Plate 245. Fluted bowl, loop-footed 7½"d., RED AND GOLD POINSETTIAS AND LUSTRE. Signed: H. Tolley (Tolley, Harry E.). TM date: 1905–1910. Blank: D&Co., France. Value: $225.00–275.00.

Plate 246. Salt and pepper, 3¼"h. Lily pads on gold border. Signed: Schoner (Schoner, Otto). TM date: 1905–1910. Blank: none. Value: $75.00–100.00.

Plate 247. Nut set, scalloped. 5½"d. White blossoms on green leaves, green wash on white and gold. Signed: O. Goess (Goess, Otto W.). TM date: 1905–1910. Blank: none. Value: $350.00–450.00.

Plate 248. Plate, 8½"d. White, yellow, and pink roses on green leaf spray. Signed: E. Aulich (Aulich, Emil). TM date: 1905–1910. Blank: Haviland, France. Value: $250.00–300.00.

Plate 249. Lidded coffee pot, 8½"d., ALICE cream and lidded sugar, SPRINGTIME. Signed: WAGNER (Wagner, Albert H.). TM date: 1905–1910. Blank: crown design Silesia Alice. Value: $295.00–395.00.

Plate 250. Vase, five-footed cylindrical with perforated top, 9½"h. Three white/pink crab apple blossoms on green ground, long stems. Signed: Marker (Marker, Curtis H.). TM date: 1905–1910. Blank: none. Value: $250.00–295.00.

Plate 251. Vase, 13¾"h., DAISIES IN GOLD PASTE ON GREEN LUSTRE. Signed: Hip (Hip). TM date: 1905–1910. Blank: none. Value: $500.00–695.00.

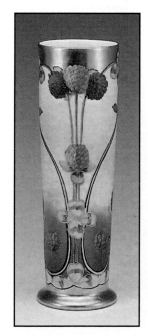

Plate 253. DAHLIA vase, 12"h., CLOVER CONVENTIONAL. Signed: Reury (Reury, Howard B.). TM date: 1905–1910. Blank: T&V rectangle, Limoges, France. Value: $295.00–495.00.

Plate 252. Bowl, 9¼"d. Pastel grape bunch. Signed: Beutlich (Beutlich, Anton B.). TM date: 1905–1910. Blank: crown crossed scepters, R G Bavaria. Value: $195.00–240.00.

Plate 254. REGENCE bowl, scalloped rim with handles, 10¼"d. <u>TULIP</u> <u>CONVENTIONAL</u>. Signed: Tomash (Tomascheko, Rudolph). TM date: 1905–1910. Blank: 2610 43. Value: $500.00–625.00.

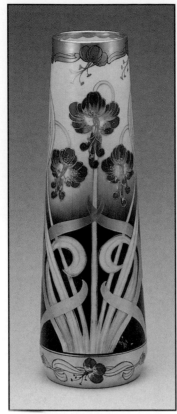

Plate 255. Vase, 12"h., FLORA GEO-METRICA. Signed: Kriesche (Kri-esche, F). TM date: 1905–1910. Blank: none. Value: $395.00–500.00.

Plate 256. Leaf dish with raised veining, perforated handle, 9½"l. Purple/russet grape clusters, leaf-embellished rim, gold outlines. Signed: Beutlich (Beutlich, Anton B.). TM date: 1905–1910. Blank: GDA, France. Value: $140.00–175.00.

Plate 257. Pitcher, 7"h. Blackberries with variegated leaves. Signed: Fuchs (Fuchs, John). TM date: 1905–1910. Blank: none. Value: $295.00–450.00.

Plate 258. Plate, 8½"d., REAN PLUMS. Signed: Rean (Klipphahn, Maxwell Rean). TM date: 1905–1910. Blank: Haviland, France. Value: $155.00–195.00.

*Plate 259. Tankard, 11"h., <u>PINE CONE</u>. Signed: Rean (Klipphahn, Maxwell Rean). TM date: 1905–1910. Blank: J.P.L., France. Value: $350.00–450.00.*

*Plate 260. Footed punch bowl and 12 RANSON punch cups, <u>COUFALL GRAPES AND ETCH BORDER</u>. Signed: Coufall (Coufall, John Anton). TM date: 1905–1910. Blank: T&V rectangle, Limoges, France. Value: $2,100.00–2,450.00.*

*Plate 261. Vase, 11"h., <u>CALLA LILY</u>. Signed: Marker (Marker, Curtis H.). TM date: 1905–1910. Blank: none. Value: $425.00–550.00.*

*Plate 262. Plate, 9"d., <u>CALLA LILY</u>. Signed: MARKER (Marker, Curtis H.). TM date: 1905–1910. Blank: Haviland, France. Value: $195.00–275.00.*

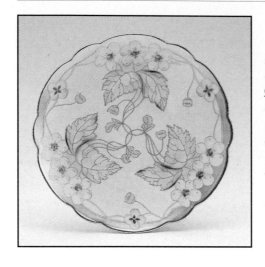

*Plate 263. Plate, 8½"d., <u>BUTTERCUP CONVENTIONAL</u>. Signed: Beutlich (Beutlich, Anton B.). TM date: 1905–1910. Blank: none. Value: $165.00–185.00.*

*Plate 264. Deep bowl with scalloped rim, 9"d., YELLOW IRIS CONVENTIONAL. Signed: Beutlich (Beutlich, Anton B.). TM date: 1905–1910. Blank: C.&G. wreath Royal Austria. Value: $160.00–225.00.*

*Plate 265. Bud vase, 3¾"h., <u>BUTTERCUP CONVENTIONAL</u>. Signed: Beutlich. (Beutlich, Anton B.). TM date: 1905–1910. Blank: GDA, France. Value: $55.00–85.00.*

*Plate 266. Hat-pin/ring tray, 4½"h., <u>BUTTERCUP CONVENTIONAL</u>. Signed: Beutlich (Beutlich, Anton B.). TM date: 1905–1910. Blank: none. Value: $350.00–450.00.*

*Plate 267. Plate, 8¾"d. Spray of small white flowers against green leaves and green/cream ground. Signed: MICHE (Miche). TM date: 1905–1910. Blank: Haviland, France. Value: $110.00–135.00.*

Plate 268. Plate, scalloped rim, 8¼"d. Red raspberry spray amid green leaves and white blossoms. Signed: Challinor (Challinor, Edward S.). TM date: 1905–1910. Blank: none. Value: $75.00–90.00.

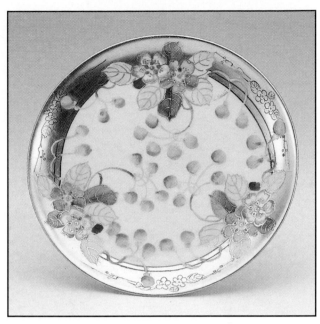

Plate 269. Plate, desert, 6"d. Cherry blossoms with cherry sprays in border, embellished gold rim. Signed: M.Keates (Keates, Madeline). TM date: 1905–1910. Blank: Haviland, France. Value: $30.00–40.00.

Plate 270. Side plate, 6"d. Yellow, orange, pink, and red nasturtiums in two clusters on embellished gold border. Signed: W LEMKE (Lemke, Walter R.). TM date: 1905–1910. Blank: crown crossed scepters, Rosenthal, Bavaria. Value: $25.00–30.00.

Plate 271. Underplate with serving bowl, 10½"d., YESCHEK STRAWBERRIES IN GOLD. Signed: Yeschek (Yeschek, Joseph T.). TM date: 1905–1910. Blank: GDA, France (underplate), rectangle Porcelain A Feu GDA, France (bowl). Value: $625.00–695.00.

Plate 272. CRYSANTHEME *perforated handle leaf dish with six leaf cups, 10½"d.,* NUT HARVEST. *Signed: Vokral (Vokral, Jeremiah). TM date: 1905–1910. Blank: crown R.C. crossed scepters, Crysantheme, Bavaria. Value: $265.00–325.00.*

Plate 273. *Plate, 8¾"d. Red, yellow, and white chrysanthemums on russet/blue ground. Signed: Brun (Brun). TM date: 1905–1910. Blank: Limoges, France. Value: $60.00–85.00.*

Plate 274. *Plate, scalloped rim, 8½"d. Pink cascade of flowers and green leaves, green branches, on pink/cream ground. Signed: F. James (James, Florence). TM date: 1905–1910. Blank: none. Value: $140.00–170.00.*

Plate 275. *Plate with scalloped rim, 8¾"d. Deep red naturalistic flowers with green leaves. Signed: Z. Mack (McCorkle, Zuie). TM date: 1905–1910. Blank: crown crossed scepters, R.C. Bavaria. Value: $30.00–45.00.*

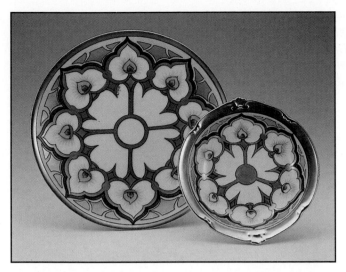

Plate 277. Vichyssoise bowl and underplate, 7¼"d., MOORISH DESIGN. Signed: O.G. (Goess, Otto). TM date: 1905–1910. Blank: T&V rectangle, Limoges, France. Value: $175.00–220.00.

Plate 276. (left) Plate, 8½"d., MOORISH DESIGN. Signed: WAGNER (Wagner, Albert H.). TM date: 1905–1910. Blank: shield Thomas Sevres Bavaria. Value: $160.00–210.00. (right) Shallow bonbon dish with sculpted rim, 6"d. Signed: RH (Hessler, Robert). TM date: 1905–1910. Blank: D.&Co., France. Value: $100.00–130.00.

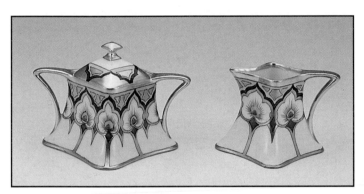

Plate 278. JOSEPHINE creamer and lidded sugar, MOORISH DESIGN. Signed: RH (Hessler, Robert). TM date: 1905–1910. Blank: Limoges, France. Value: $275.00–375.00.

Plate 280. (rear) Candlesticks, handled, 7¼"h., VIOLETS AND LUSTRE. Signed: Ray (Ray, Noble). TM date: 1905–1910. Blank: Limoges scroll W.G.&Co., France. Value: $300.00–375.00. (front) Bowl with flared base, 5½"d. Signed: RAY (Ray, Noble). TM date: 1905–1910. Blank: Haviland, France. Value: $275.00–325.00.

Plate 279. Teapot, cream, and sugar, MOORISH DESIGN. Signed: Hessler (Hessler, Robert). TM date: 1905–1910. Blank: D.&Co., France. Value: $450.00–550.00.

Plate 281. (left) Plate, 8¾"d., GIFFORD POPPIES. Signed: NGifford (Gifford, Nathan R.). TM date: 1905–1910. Blank: Haviland, France. Value: $150.00–185.00. (right) Milk pitcher, 6"h. Signed: Giff (Gifford, Nathan R.). TM date: 1905–1910. Blank: none. Value: $185.00–225.00.

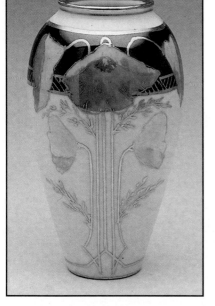

Plate 282. ST. DENIS vase, 6½"h., GIFFORD POPPIES. Signed: N. Gifford (Gifford, Nathan R.). TM date: 1905–1910. Blank: none. Value: $300.00–375.00.

Plate 283. Plate, 8¾"d., POND LILY AND LUSTRE. Signed: Leach (Leach, George P.). TM date: 1905–1910. Blank: Haviland, France. Value: $110.00–145.00.

Plate 284. Vase, 9"h., EASTER LILY. Signed: Schoner (Schoner, Otto). TM date: 1905–1910. Blank: D&Co., France. Value: $190.00–225.00.

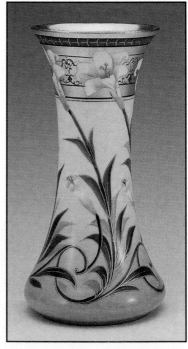

Plate 285. CRYSANTHEME bonbon, deeply scalloped, with perforated handle, 8"d., EASTER LILY. Signed: Fisher (Fischer, Emil J. T.). TM date: 1905–1910. Blank: crown crossed scepters, R.C. Crysantheme, Bavaria. Value: $185.00–225.00.

Plate 286. Bowl, 10¼"d., TWIN TULIP. Signed: F. Wall (Walters, Frederick). TM date: 1905–1910. Blank: Haviland, France. Value: $350.00–425.00.

Plate 287. (rear) Bowl, scalloped, 7½"d., TWIN TULIP. Signed: Schoner (Schoner, Otto). TM date: 1905–1910. Blank: Rosenthal, Bavaria. Value: $225.00–295.00. (front) Punch cups. Signed: Schoner (Schoner, Otto). TM date: 1905–1910. Blank: none. Value: $100.00–135.00.

Plate 288. RANSON pitcher, scalloped edges, 9"h., TWIN TULIP. Signed: SHONER (Schoner, Otto). TM date: 1905–1910. Blank: Haviland, France. Value: $695.00–795.00.

Plate 289. (right) Tapered, narrow-mouthed, vase, 8"h., TWIN TULIP. Signed: Schoner (Schoner, Otto). TM date: 1905–1910. Blank: 1698. Value: $225.00–325.00. (left) Plate, scalloped edged, 8¾"d. Signed: CMarker (Marker, Curtis H.). TM date: 1905–1910. Blank: France BM de M Limoges. Value: $150.00–225.00.

Plate 290. Regency bowl with wish-bone handles, 7½"d., TWIN TULIP. Signed: SHONER (Schoner, Otto). TM date: 1905–1910. Blank: T&V rectangle, Limoges, France. Value: $225.00–265.00.

*Plate 291. Vase, 6¾"h. Three tulips on gold border. Signed: W. Lemke (Lemke, Walter R.). TM date: 1905–1910. Blank: none. Value: $160.00–225.00.*

*Plate 292. Plate, 8½"d. Orange and magenta tulips on embellished gold panel, beaded rim. Signed: Breidel (Breidel, William V.). TM date: 1905–1910. Blank: Haviland, France. Value: $150.00–195.00.*

*Plate 293. Small bowl, 4½"d. Red and blue conventionalized flowers. (unsigned). TM date: 1905–1910. Blank: Belleek serpent, Willets. Value: $150.00–250.00.*

*Plate 294. Bonbon boat, 6¾"l., HONEYSUCKLE DESIGN. Signed: A.Passoni (Passony, Arthur). TM date: 1905–1910. Blank: Favorite Bavaria. Value: $165.00–195.00.*

*Plate 295. Cream and sugar, BLACK AND ORANGE CONVENTIONAL. (unsigned). TM date: 1905–1910. Blank: D.&Co., France. Value: $135.00–195.00.*

*Plate 296. Mug, 6¾"h., B.P.O.E. Signed: Coufall (Coufall, John Anton). TM date: 1905–1910. Blank: none. Value: $200.00–225.00.*

*Plate 297. Lemonade pitcher, (Regence-style), 8"h., LILY PALMATE. Signed: SHONER (Schoner, Otto). TM date: 1905–1910. Blank: Haviland. Value: $395.00–475.00.*

*Plate 298. CENTURY bowl, 10½"d., LILY PALMATE. Signed: SHONER (Schoner, Otto). TM date: 1905–1910. Blank: Century Patd Feb, 26th, 1901, large T&V rectangle, Limoges, France. Value: $275.00–350.00.*

*Plate 299. Liquor set, AUTUMN GRAPES AND MATTE GREEN. Signed: Lind (Lindner, Frederick J.). TM date: 1905–1910. Blank: Vienna, Austria. Value: $375.00–425.00.*

*Plate 300. Tankard, 10¾"h., HOPS IN LUSTRE AND MATTE GREEN. Signed: Lind (Lindner, Frederick J.). TM date: 1905–1910. Blank: T&V rectangle, Limoges, France. Value: $375.00–450.00.*

*Plate 301. (rear) Plate, 8½"d., <u>YELLOW CHERRIES AND MATTE GREEN</u>. Signed: Breidel (Breidel, William W.). TM date: 1905–1910. Blank: Haviland, France. Value: $160.00–185.00. (front) Vase 6½"h. Signed: Lind (Lindner, Frederick J.). TM date: 1905–1910. Blank: none. Value: $250.00–325.00.*

Plate 302. Toasting goblet, 11¼"h., HOPS IN LUSTRE AND MATTE GREEN. Signed: Lind (Lindner, Frederick J.). TM date: 1905–1910. Blank: Belleek serpent, Willets. Value: $450.00–575.00.

Plate 303. Tray with stoppered decanter and six cups, 11½"d., ROSA EMERALDUS. Signed: Coufall (Coufall, Anthony). TM date: 1905–1910. Blank: T&V rectangle, Limoges, France. Value: $725.00–850.00.

Plate 304. EGYPTIAN vase, 7"h., ROSA EMERALDUS. Signed: Coufall (Coufall, John Anton). TM date: 1905–1910. Blank: none. Value: $200.00–275.00.

Plate 305. Pitcher, 6"h., CRAB APPLES IN GOLD ON MATTE GREEN. Signed: Coufall (Coufall, John Anton). TM date: 1905–1910. Blank: none. Value: $275.00–350.00.

Plate 306. Coffee set: tray, creamer, lidded sugar, and lidded coffee, ROSA EMERALDUS. Signed: Coufall (Coufall, John Anton). TM date: 1905–1910. Blank: T&V Limoges. Value: $1,200.00–1,400.00.

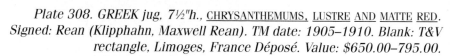

Plate 307. JOSEPHINE cream and sugar, 3¼"h., <u>CHRYSAN-THEMUMS</u>, <u>LUSTRE</u> <u>AND</u> <u>MATTE</u> <u>RED</u>. Signed: Rean (Klipphahn, Maxwell Rean). TM date: 1905–1910. Blank: Limoges, France. Value: $395.00–495.00.

Plate 308. GREEK jug, 7½"h., <u>CHRYSANTHEMUMS</u>, <u>LUSTRE</u> <u>AND</u> <u>MATTE</u> <u>RED</u>. Signed: Rean (Klipphahn, Maxwell Rean). TM date: 1905–1910. Blank: T&V rectangle, Limoges, France Déposé. Value: $650.00–795.00.

Plate 309. OMNIUM punch bowl with ten cups, 14"d., <u>CHRYSANTHEMUMS</u>, <u>LUSTRE</u> <u>AND</u> <u>MATTE</u> <u>RED</u>. Signed: Rean (Klipphahn, Maxwell Rean). TM date: 1905–1910. Blank: T&V rectangle, Limoges, France. Value: $3,300.00–3,600.00.

Plate 310. Oval vase with upswept open handles, 11½"h., CHRYSANTHEMUMS, LUSTRE AND GOLD. Signed: Rean (Klipphahn, Maxwell Rean). TM date: 1905–1910. Blank: none. Value: $750.00–850.00.

Plate 311. (rear) Mug, 6"h., RED AND BLUE PARAKEETS ON MATTE GREEN. Signed: Lind (Lindner, Frederick J.). TM date: 1905–1910. Blank: scrolls W.G.&Co., France. Value: $275.00–350.00. (front) Powder box, 6½"d. Signed: Lind (Lindner, Frederick J.). TM date: 1905–1910. Blank: 3 stars Limoges, France. Value: $275.00–325.00.

Plate 312. Large vase, 14½"h. Two tigers on cliff side. Signed: Breidel (Breidel, William W.). TM date: 1905–1910. Blank: palette L Belleek. Value: $2,900.00–3,300.00.

Plate 313. Plate, 9¼"d., ON THE NILE AT BENI HASSEN - EGYPT - 1909. Signed: A. Comyn (Comyn, Arthur). TM date: 1905–1910. Blank: Haviland, France. Value: $400.00–475.00.

Plate 314. Plate, 10¼"d., TORCELLO CANAL AND CHURCH. Signed: AC, Arthur Comyn (Comyn, Arthur). TM date: 1905–1910. Blank: Haviland, France. Value: $325.00–375.00.

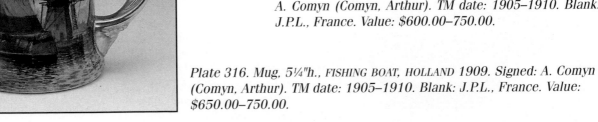

Plate 315. (rear) Plate, scalloped rim, 8½"d., SAILBOATS IN VENICE HARBOR. Signed: N. Roswell Gifford ( Gifford, Nathan R. ). TM date: 1905–1910. Blank: crown scepters, Rosenthal Bavaria. Value: $225.00–275.00. (front) Mug with spiral floral handle, 5"h., VENICE. Signed: A. Comyn (Comyn, Arthur). TM date: 1905–1910. Blank: J.P.L., France. Value: $600.00–750.00.

Plate 316. Mug, 5¼"h., FISHING BOAT, HOLLAND 1909. Signed: A. Comyn (Comyn, Arthur). TM date: 1905–1910. Blank: J.P.L., France. Value: $650.00–750.00.

*Plate 317. Plate, 10"d.,* <u>SANTA</u> <u>MARIA</u> <u>DELLA</u> <u>SALUTE</u>. *Signed: AC (Comyn, Arthur). TM date: 1905–1910. Blank: Haviland, France. Value: $475.00–550.00.*

*Plate 318. Mug, 7"h.,* <u>FALSTAFF</u>. *Signed: P.Gasper (Gasper, Paul P.). TM date: 1905–1910. Blank: none. Value: $475.00–625.00.*

*Plate 319. Vase, 7¾"h., CAMELS AT OASIS. Signed: A. Comyn (Comyn, Arthur). TM date: 1905–1910. Blank: Rosenthal Bavaria. Value: $695.00–1,000.00.*

*Plate 320. Tankard, 14"h. Monk pceling turnip. Signed: Gasper (Gasper, Paul P.). TM date: 1905–1910. Blank: scrolls, W.G.&Co. Limoges, France. Value: $800.00–1,200.00.*

*Plate 321. Plate, 8¾"d., DUTCH WINDMILL. Signed: A. Cumming (Cumming, Arthur J.). TM date: 1905–1910. Blank: Haviland, France. Value: $300.00–395.00.*

*Plate 322. Tea tile, 6"h., OLD DUTCH MILL. Signed: Cummings (Cumming, Arthur J.). TM date: 1905–1910. Blank: GDA, France. Value: $250.00–325.00.*

*Plate 323. Plate, 9"d., THE SEASONS. Signed: A. Comyn (Comyn, Arthur). TM date: 1905–1910. Blank: Haviland, France. Value: $135.00–175.00.*

*Plate 326. SEVRES Plate, 8½"d., SCILLA CAMPANULA. Signed: Comyn, AC (Comyn, Arthur). TM date: 1905–1910. Blank: shield, Thomas Sevres, Bavaria. Value: $145.00–175.00.*

*Plate 324. Teapot with upswept handle, 7½"h. Single pink flower on gold border with green and blue leaves, white ground. Signed: Wight (Wight, Phillip). TM date: 1905–1910. Blank: T&V rectangle, Limoges, France Déposé. Value: $85.00–110.00.*

*Plate 327. Plate, 8½"d., WILDFLOWERS OF AMERICA: VIOLETS. Signed: Comyn, AC (Comyn, Arthur). TM date: 1905–1910. Blank: Rosenthal crown, Bavaria. Value: $145.00–195.00.*

*Plate 325. Bowl, 9"d. Sea shells with spider web. Signed: Kriesche (Kriesche, F.). TM date: 1905–1910. Blank: none. Value: $150.00–200.00.*

*Plate 328. Plate, 7½"d., WHITE DAY LILIES. Signed: FJames (James, Florence M.). TM date: 1905–1910. Blank: crossed clovers, J&C Bavaria. Value: $75.00–110.00.*

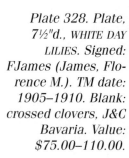

Plate 329. Vase, 9"h. White lily sprays on embellished gold border, pale green ground. Signed: F. Walter (Walters, Frederick). TM date: 1905–1910. Blank: Rosenthal (crown) Bavaria. Value: $375.00–450.00.

Plate 330. Plate, 8¼"d. Red and white pansies on green leaf ground. Signed: Marker (Marker, Curtis H.). TM date: 1905–1910. Blank: none. Value: $50.00–65.00.

Plate 331. Vase, narrow, 8"h., SALSIFY. Signed: LEACH (Leach, George P.). TM date: 1905–1910. Blank: none. Value: $175.00–325.00.

Plate 332. Bowl, scalloped rim, 7¼"d. Green apple cluster. Signed: Beutlich (Beutlich, Anton B.). TM date: 1905–1910. Blank: CA, France Déposé. Value: $95.00–145.00.

Plate 333. ALEXANDER sugar or cracker jar, 6½"d., AMARYLLIS AND ETCHED GOLD. Signed: Beutlich (Beutlich, Anton B.). TM date: 1905–1910. Blank: shield, Weimar Germany. Value: $325.00–495.00.

Plate 334. Deep bowl with rimmed base, 10"d., AMARYLLIS AND ETCHED GOLD. Signed: Beutlich (Beutlich, Anton B.). TM date: 1905–1910. Blank: Limoges 3 stars France. Value: $375.00–450.00.

*Plate 335. Plate, scalloped, 8½"d. Yellow blossoms on green spray, embellished gold rim. Signed: Keates (Keates, Alfred). TM date: 1905–1910. Blank: Rosenthal crown, crossed scepters Bavaria. Value: $120.00–140.00.*

*Plate 336. Plate, 8½"d., <u>ENAMEL GRAPES AND LEAVES</u>. (unsigned). TM date: 1905–1910. Blank: Haviland, France. Value: $170.00–210.00.*

*Plate 337. Lidded sugar and creamer, 4½"h., <u>ENAMEL GRAPES AND LEAVES</u>. (unsigned). TM date: 1905–1910. Blank: Germany. Value: $180.00–225.00.*

*Plate 338. Lidded teapot, lidded creamer, sugar, low-profile, HARVEST IN RAISED GOLD AND WHITE. Signed: AR (unknown). TM date: 1905–1910. Blank: Limoges scroll, W.G.&Co., France. Value: $275.00–350.00.*

*Plate 339. Lidded syrup with underplate, 5½"h., VIOLET NOUVEAU. Signed: COUFALL (Coufall, John Anton). TM date: 1905–1910. Blank: D&Co., France. Value: $250.00–295.00.*

*Plate 340. Tureen, 8"d., HARVEST IN RAISED GOLD AND WHITE. Signed: AR (unknown). TM date: 1905–1910. Blank: T&V rectangle, Limoges, France. Value: $110.00–165.00.*

*Plate 344. Cream and sugar, CARNATION AND PLATINUM. Signed: AP, Passony (Passony, Arthur). TM date: 1905–1910. Blank: none. Value: $300.00–350.00.*

*Plate 341. Syrup pitcher and underplate, 5"h., <u>CELTIC DECORATION</u>. Signed: Mill (Miller, Anton). TM date: 1905–1910. Blank: D&Co., France. Value: $325.00–375.00.*

*Plate 343. Lidded syrup with underplate, 6"h., FLORA GOLD AND WHITE. Signed: FV (Vobornik, Franz). TM date: 1905–1910. Blank: none. Value: $225.00–265.00.*

*Plate 342. (left and right) Lidded sugar and creamer, JEWELED FLORA IN RAISED GOLD. Signed: H. (H.). TM date: 1905–1910. Blank: D.&Co., France. Value: $275.00–325.00. (center) Salt and pepper. (unsigned). TM date: 1910–1912. Blank: none. Value: $110.00–125.00.*

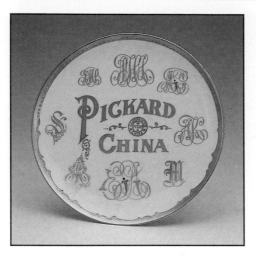

*Plate 345. Plate, 8⅝"d. Monogram sample plate. (unsigned). TM date: 1905–1910. Blank: Haviland, France. Value: $300.00–495.00.*

*Plate 346. Lidded IDEAL chocolate pot, 12"h., 4 demitasse and saucers, <u>RAISED</u> <u>GOLD</u> <u>DAISY</u>. (unsigned). TM date: 1905–1910. Blank: J.P.L. France, Limoges scrolls, W.G.&Co., France. Value: $450.00–595.00.*

*Plate 347. Large ALEXANDER jug, 8"d., <u>AURA</u> <u>ARGENTA</u> <u>LINEAR</u>. Signed: Hessler. (Hessler, Robert). TM date: 1905–1910. Blank: T&V rectangle, Limoges, France. Value: $425.00–595.00.*

*Plate 349. (left) Lidded syrup with underplate, 5"h., <u>AURA</u> <u>ARGENTA</u> <u>LINEAR</u>. Signed: O.P. (Podlaha, Otto). TM date: 1905–1910. Blank: D&Co., France. Value: $295.00–375.00. (right) Relish dish, handled, three-sectioned, 8"d. Signed: A. Richter (Richter, Anton). TM date: 1912–1918. Blank: none. Value: $165.00–195.00.*

*Plate 348. (left) Tall pitcher, wide-mouthed, 6½"h., <u>AURA</u> <u>ARGENTA</u> <u>LINEAR</u>. Signed: Bek (Buschbeck, Carl). TM date: 1910–1912. Blank: none. Value: $225.00–275.00. (right) Muffineer, 4½"h. Signed: Richter. (Richter, Anton). TM date: 1905–1910. Blank: Bavaria. Value: $185.00–225.00.*

Plate 350. Tray, coffee pot, 6 cups and saucers, creamer and sugar, <u>AURA</u> <u>ARGENTA</u> <u>LINEAR</u>. Signed: Podlaha (Podlaha, Otto). TM date: 1905–1910. Blank: D.&Co. France. Value: $2,000.00–2,500.00.

Plate 351. (left) Bowl, rectangular, 7"d., <u>AURA</u> <u>ARGENTA</u> <u>LINEAR</u>. (unsigned). TM date: 1912–1914. Blank: scrolls W.G.&Co., Limoges, France. Value: $180.00–250.00. (center) Plate, 8½"d. Signed: OP (Podlaha, Otto). TM date: 1905–1910. Blank: shield, Thomas Sevres Bavaria. Value: $160.00–225.00. (right) Pitcher, 8"h. Signed: Podlaha (Podlaha, Otto). TM date: 1905–1910. Blank: J.P.L., France Patented May 12, 1908. Value: $350.00–450.00.

Plate 352. Vase, 10¼"h., *ARROW ROOT ON GREEN LUSTRE*. Signed: N.R.Gifford (Gifford, Nathan R.). TM date: 1905–1910. Blank: none. Value: $200.00–275.00.

Plate 353. (left) Serving bowl, straight-sided, 8¼"d. Currant spray, wide gold, red berry and green leaf embellished border. Signed: Heinz (Heinz, J.). TM date: 1905–1910. Blank: rounded rectangle Porcelaines A Feu G.D.A. Limoges black. Value: $125.00–150.00. (right) Small *NAVARRE* jug, 4"h., <u>YESCHEK</u> <u>CURRANTS</u> <u>IN</u> <u>GOLD</u>. Signed: F.Yeschek (Yeschek, Frank P.). TM date: 1905–1910. Blank: D&Co., France. Value: $125.00–155.00.

Plate 354. Bouillon cup and saucer, 5½"d. Formal garlands between gold pendants, stippled, sawtooth border. Signed: N. tolpin (Tolpin, Nesha). TM date: 1905–1910. Blank: T&V rectangle, Limoges, France. Value: $120.00–155.00.

Plate 355. Cream soup bowl with wishbone handles, ORANGE TREE CONVENTIONAL. Signed: M.L. or L.M.. TM date: 1905–1910. Blank: Favorite Bavaria. Value: $120.00–145.00.

Plate 356. Oval platter with perforated handles, 14¾"l. Individual orange/red poppy sprays on cream ground, embellished gold border. Signed: F.V. (Vobornik, Franz). TM date: 1905–1910. Blank: GDA, France. Value: $165.00–195.00.

Plate 357. (left) Charger, perforated handles, 12"d., AUTUMN ARBOR. Signed: Breidel (Breidel, William W.). TM date: 1905–1910. Blank: GDA, France. Value: $175.00–225.00. (right) Lidded coffee pot, 8"h. Signed: CF (Koenig, Carl F.). TM date: 1905–1910. Blank: crown Vienna crests Austria. Value: $175.00–225.00.

Plate 358. Bowl, scalloped rim, footed, 10½"d., THISTLES IN PASTE. Signed: Fisher (Fischer, Emil J. T.). TM date: 1905–1910. Blank: crossed clovers, J&C (no country). Value: $250.00–365.00.

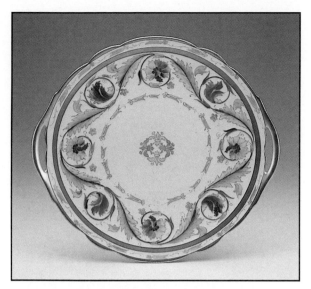

Plate 362. Vase, 8"h. Pink apple blossoms on black ground with gold leaves on green lustre border. Signed: Rean (Klipphahn, Maxwell Rean). TM date: 1905–1910. Blank: none. Value: $250.00–300.00.

Plate 359. Cake plate, 9¾"d., <u>FLORENTINE</u>. Signed: JB. TM date: 1905–1910. Blank: D.&Co., France. Value: $140.00–200.00.

Plate 360. Whiskey jug, stoppered, 6"h., <u>MODERN</u> <u>CONVENTIONAL</u>. Signed: Hessler (Hessler, Robert). TM date: 1905–1910. Blank: T&V rectangle, Limoges, France. Value: $300.00–400.00.

Plate 363. (left) Boat dish, scalloped, handles, 9"l., <u>CALLA LILIES</u>. Signed: AP (Passony, Arthur). TM date: 1905–1910. Blank: Elite K France. Value: $200.00–260.00. (right) Demi-tasse and saucer. Signed: AP (Passony, Arthur). TM date: 1905–1910. Blank: none. Value: $175.00–195.00.

Plate 361. After dinner coffee set: 11"d. tray, lidded coffee pot, lidded sugar, creamer, 4 demitasse and saucers, <u>MODERN</u> <u>CONVENTIONAL</u>. Signed: Hessler (Hessler, Robert). TM date: 1905–1910. Blank: T&V rectangle, Limoges, France. Value: $895.00–1,050.00.

Plate 364. Serving bowl with underplate, 10½"d., <u>CALLA</u> <u>LILIES</u>. Signed: AP (Passony, Arthur). TM date: 1905–1910. Blank: GDA, France, rectangle Porcelains A Feu GDA, France. Value: $175.00–260.00.

Plate 365. (left) Salt and pepper, 4"h., <u>CALLA</u> <u>LILIES</u>. Signed: Beulet (Beulet, F.). TM date: 1910–1912. Blank: none. Value: $125.00–155.00. (right) Vase, narrow, slight handles, 7"h. Signed: AP (Passony, Arthur). TM date: 1905–1910. Blank: none. Value: $225.00–295.00.

Plate 366. After dinner coffee pot, <u>CALLA</u> <u>LILIES</u>. Signed: A. P. (Passony, Arthur). TM date: 1905–1910. Blank: Limoges. Value: $250.00–325.00. (right) Cup and saucer. Signed: Passony (Passony, Arthur). TM date: 1905–1910. Blank: T&V rectangle, Limoges, France. Value: $175.00–195.00.

Plate 368. Humidor, lidded, 5"h., <u>POPPY</u> <u>AND</u> <u>DAISY</u>. Signed: Gasper (Gasper, Paul P.). TM date: 1905–1910. Blank: GDA, France. Value: $900.00–1,250.00.

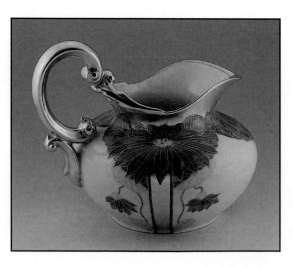

Plate 367. ALEXANDER jug, 8"d., <u>POINSETTIA</u> <u>AND</u> <u>LUSTRE</u>. Signed: H.Tolley (Tolley, Harry E.). TM date: 1905–1910. Blank: T&V rectangle, Limoges, France. Value: $375.00–495.00.

Plate 370. Small milk pitcher, 6"h., POPPY AND DAISY. Signed: Shoner (Schoner, Otto). TM date: 1905–1910. Blank: none. Value: $250.00–365.00.

Plate 369. (left) Plate, 8½"d., POPPY AND DAISY. Signed: GASPER (Gasper, Paul P.). TM date: 1910–1912. Blank: Haviland, France. Value: $145.00–175.00. (right) Vase, tapered, 8"h. Signed: Gasper (Gasper, Paul P.). TM date: 1905–1910. Blank: none. Value: $225.00–275.00.

Plate 372. Demi-tasse set, POPPY IRIDESCENT. Signed: Fuchs. (Fuchs, John). TM date: 1905–1910. Blank: Limoges scroll, W.G.&Co., France Value each: $135.00–175.00.

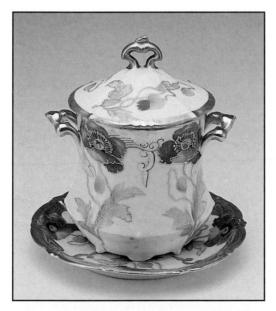

Plate 371. Lidded jam jar with underplate, 6½"h., POPPY CONVENTIONAL. Signed: Fox (Fox). TM date: 1905–1910. Blank: none. Value: $325.00–450.00.

Plate 373. (left) Pitcher with fluted sides, 7"h., FUCHS POP-PIES. Signed: Fuchs (Fuchs, John). TM date: 1905–1910. Blank: none. Value: $325.00–395.00. (right) Mug, 5½"h., TWIN POPPY. Signed: Fuchs (Fuchs, John). TM date: 1905–1910. Blank: J.P.L., France. Value: $225.00–295.00.

Plate 374. Basket-style bonbon, 7½"l., <u>TWIN</u> <u>POPPY</u>. Signed: Loh (Loh, John). TM date: 1905–1910. Blank: T&V rectangle, Limoges, France. Value: $175.00–225.00.

Plate 375. Hatpin holder, 5"d. Red poppy on cream ground, gold decorated border. Signed: Loh (Loh, John). TM date: 1905–1910. Blank: Rosenthal. Value: $275.00–350.00.

Plate 376. (left) Plate, scalloped rim, 9"d., POPPY CONVENTIONAL AND BLACK. Signed: Loba (Loba, F.). TM date: 1905–1910. Blank: Limoges BMdeM France. Value: $125.00–145.00. (right) Pitcher, 7"h. Signed: Loh (Loh, John). TM date: 1905–1910. Blank: D.&Co., France. Value: $300.00–395.00.

Plate 378. Mug, 5"h. Red raspberry cluster on maroon. Signed: E. Challinor (Challinor, Edward S.). TM date: 1905–1910. Blank: J.P.L., France. Value: $250.00–395.00.

Plate 377. Small milk jug, 4¾"h., CARNATION AND BLACK. Signed: Loh (Loh, John). TM date: 1905–1910. Blank: T&V rectangle, Limoges, France. Value: $275.00–325.00.

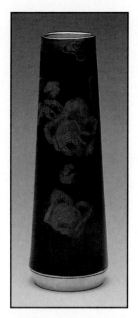

Plate 380. Mug, 5¾"h.
Cherry spray on
maroon ground.
Signed: EChallinor
(Challinor, Edward S.).
TM date: 1905–1910.
Blank: scrolls
W.G.&Co. Limoges,
France. Value:
$325.00–475.00.

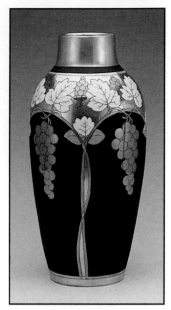

Plate 381. Vase, 13½"h., LUSTRE GRAPES AND LEAVES.
Signed: Hessler (Hessler, Robert). TM date: 1905–1910.
Blank: none. Value: $475.00–625.00.

Plate 379. Vase,
narrow, 11½"h. Red
roses on deep red
ground, embellished
gold border. Signed:
Challinor (Challinor,
Edward S.). TM
date: 1905–1910.
Blank: none. Value:
$350.00–475.00.

Plate 382. (left) Plate, 9"d.
Triad of purple grapes, grape
leaves in gold border. Signed:
Hess. (Hessler, Robert). TM
date: 1905–1910. Blank:
Favorite Bavaria. Value:
$165.00–195.00. (right) Sher-
bet cups, 4"d., METALLIC
GRAPES. Signed: RH (Hessler,
Robert). TM date: 1905–1910.
Blank: Haviland, France. Value
each: $125.00–150.00.

Plate 384. Large
COLUMBIA vase, 9"h.,
LUSTRE GRAPES AND
LEAVES. Signed: Hessler
(Hessler, Robert). TM
date: 1905–1910.
Blank: crown scepters,
Rosenthal, Bavaria.
Value:
$275.00–350.00.

Plate 383. Cream and sugar, hollow finial, LUSTRE
GRAPES AND LEAVES. Signed: Hess (Hessler, Robert). TM
date: 1905–1910. Blank: Limoges CMC France. Value:
$300.00–400.00.

Plate 385. Goblet, 5¾"h., AUTUMN CURRANTS. Signed: Vokral (Vokral, Jeremiah). TM date: 1905–1910. Blank: Belleek serpent, Willets. Value: $295.00–365.00.

Plate 386. Hair receiver, powder box, hat pin holder, pin box, AUTUMN CURRANTS. Signed: Vokral (Vokral, Jeremiah). TM date: 1905–1910. Blank: GDA, France. Value: $550.00–650.00.

Plate 387. Lemonade jug, wide-mouthed, 7"h., AUTUMN CURRANTS. Signed: O. Goess (Goess, Otto W.), TM date: 1905–1910. Blank: Limoges 3 stars, France. Value: $250.00–300.00.

Plate 390. Vase, 10"h., CHALLINOR NASTUR-TIUMS. Signed: Challinor (Challinor, Edward S.). TM date: 1905–1910. Blank: crown Vienna, Austria. Value: $425.00–475.00.

Plate 388. Charger, 12¼"d. Poppies on etched border. Signed: FWAlt (Walters, Frederick). TM date: 1905–1910. Blank: CA, France. Value: $260.00–300.00.

Plate 389. Vase, 7¼"h. Twin poppies on gold border. Signed: P.G. (Gasper, Paul P.). TM date: 1905–1910. Blank: none. Value: $275.00–350.00.

*Plate 391. Vase, tapered with flared top, 8"h. Narcissus on dark green foliage. Signed: F Post. (Post, F.). TM date: 1903–1905. Blank: 3660 impressed. Value: $225.00–295.00.*

*Plate 392. (left) Small BURL bowl, 5"d., EGYPTIAN DESIGN. Signed: Goess (Goess, Otto W.). TM date: 1905–1910. Blank: Elite France. Value: $175.00–250.00. (right) Handled boat dish, 8"l. Signed: Goess (Goess, Otto W.). TM date: 1905–1910. Blank: Elite, France. Value: $195.00–260.00.*

*Plate 393. Plate, 8½"d. Four lavender and yellow poppy groups radiating from center, gold border with white ground. Signed: N. R. Gifford (Gifford, Nathan R.). TM date: 1905–1910. Blank: Haviland, France. Value: $135.00–150.00.*

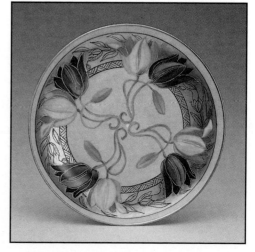

*Plate 394. Platter, handled, 14"l. Pale branch of purple and pink chrysanthemums. Signed: Blazek (Blazek, John). TM date: 1905–1910. Blank: GDA, France. Value: $175.00–255.00.*

*Plate 395. Plate, 8¾"d., GIFFORD TULIPS. Signed: Gifford (Gifford, Nathan R.). TM date: 1905–1910. Blank: Haviland, France. Value: $165.00–195.00.*

Plate 396. Plate, 8½"d. Three violet clusters radiating from center, decorated gold rim. Signed: R. Alex. (Alexander, Ruth L.). TM date: 1905–1910. Blank: Haviland, France. Value: $35.00–55.00.

Plate 397. (left) Lidded hairpin holder, 3¼"d. Violets on multicolored leaves on pale green wash. Signed: Sinclair (Sinclair, George). TM date: 1905–1910. Blank: none. Value: $110.00–145.00. (right) Hatpin holder, 5"h. Violet spray on yellow-green ground, gold top. Signed: B.M. (Moore, Bertha L.). TM date: 1905–1910. Blank: Rosenthal cross-on-heart Sebrauchsmusterschutz. Value: $225.00–275.00.

Plate 398. Relish dish, oval, 7"l. Violets on green ground, embellished gold border. Signed: MP (Pickard, Minnie Verna). TM date: 1905–1910. Blank: miter, sashes Hohenzollern, Germany. Value: $100.00–125.00.

Plate 399. (rear) LION D'OR bonbon, 6"d. Five violets radiused out of gold/green leaf center, embellished gold border. Signed: Kriesche (Kriesche, F.). TM date: 1905–1910. Blank: crown, crossed scepters, R.C. Bavaria. Value: $90.00–115.00. (front) Pin tray, heart-shaped, 5¼"l. Three violets on green leaves over pale cream/peach ground. Signed: Kriesche (Kriesche, F.). TM date: 1905–1910. Blank: T&V rectangle, Limoges, France. Value: $110.00–140.00.

Plate 400. *Candy dish, Art Nouveau, 7"d. Violet clusters on cream ground with white daisies, wide gold banding. Signed: M.P. (Pickard, Minnie Verna). TM date: 1905–1910. Blank: crossed shamrocks, J&C Louise Bavaria. Value: $120.00–145.00.*

Plate 401. *ALEXANDER cracker jar, 7"d., PINK TWIN POPPY. Signed: Gifford (Gifford, Nathan Roswell). TM date: 1905–1910. Blank: shield Weimar, Germany. Value: $375.00–465.00.*

Plate 403. *Demi-tasse and saucer, PINK TWIN POPPY. Signed: E Menges (Mentges, Edward P.). TM date: 1905–1910. Blank: J.P.L., France/T&V rectangle Limoges, France. Value: $125.00–165.00.*

Plate 402. *(left) Charger, 12¼"d., PINK TWIN POPPY. Signed: Menges (Mentges, Edward P.). TM date: 1905–1910. Blank: AC, France. Value: $375.00–495.00. (right) Berry bowl, three-legged with underplate, 7"d. Signed: MGS (Mentges, Edward P.). TM date: 1905–1910. Blank: T&V rectangle, Limoges, France. Value: $425.00–550.00.*

Plate 404. *Small milk pitcher with bamboo-style handle, 6" h., PINK TWIN POPPY. Signed: Gifford (Gifford, Nathan Roswell). TM date: 1905–1910. Blank: crown Royal diamond C Coleston, England. Value: $210.00–245.00.*

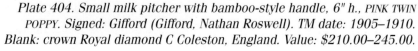

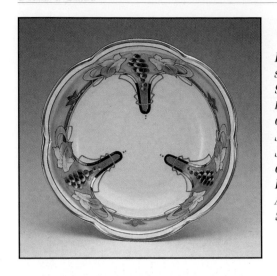

*Plate 405. Bowl, scalloped rim, 9½"d., GRAPES IN PLATINUM AND GOLD. Signed: JNessy (Nessy, John). TM date:1905–1910. Blank: circle JHR Alice. Value: $185.00–250.00.*

*Plate 406. Cup and saucer, NAVAJO. Signed: HH (unknown). TM date: 1905–1910. Blank: scrolls W.G.&Co., France. Value: $140.00–175.00.*

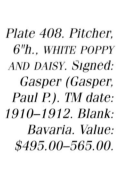

*Plate 408. Pitcher, 6"h., WHITE POPPY AND DAISY. Signed: Gasper (Gasper, Paul P.). TM date: 1910–1912. Blank: Bavaria. Value: $495.00–565.00.*

*Plate 407. Plate, 8½"d., REAN CARNATIONS AND GOLD. Signed: Rean (Klipphahn, Maxwell Rean). TM date: 1905–1910. Blank: Haviland, France. Value: $175.00–200.00.*

*Plate 409. Lidded teapot, lidded sugar, creamer. POPPY AND DAISY. Signed: Edwrd (Edward). TM date: 1910–1912. Blank: Limoges star-Limoges, France. Value: $285.00–350.00.*

*Plate 410. Vase, gothic-handled, narrow-mouthed, 9½"h., POPPY AND DAISY. Signed: Gasper (Gasper, Paul P.). TM date: 1910–1912. Blank: none. Value: $295.00–350.00.*

*Plate 411. Large pitcher, 8"h. Russet grape clusters on russet ground. Signed: Vokral (Vokral, Jeremiah). TM date: 1910–1912. Blank: overpainted. Value: $275.00–375.00.*

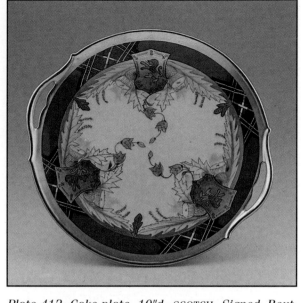

*Plate 412. Cake plate, 10"d., SCOTCH. Signed: Beutlich (Beutlich, Anton B.). TM date: 1910–1912. Blank: overpainted. Value: $225.00–300.00.*

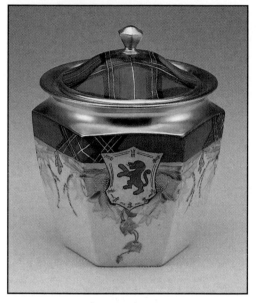

*Plate 413. Humidor, 7¼"h., SCOTCH. Signed: Beutlich (Beutlich, Anton B.). TM date: 1910–1912. Blank: D.&Co., France. Value: $475.00–595.00.*

*Plate 414. Plate, 8¾"d., SCOTCH. Signed: APASSONY (Passony, Arthur). TM date: 1910–1912. Blank: Favorite Bavaria. Value: $125.00–150.00.*

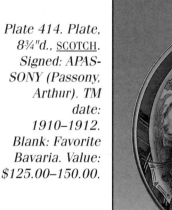

*Plate 415. Cup and saucer, IRIS LINEAR. Signed: Lind (Lindner, Frederick J.). TM date: 1910–1912. Blank: none. Value: $180.00–215.00.*

Plate 416. (rear) Plate, 8½"d., <u>LILUM</u> <u>ORNATUM</u>. Signed: Yeschek *(Yeschek, Joseph T.). TM date: 1910–1912. Blank: Favorite Bavaria. Value: $165.00–225.00. (front) Cream and sugar. Signed: Yeschek (Yeschek, Joseph T.). TM date: 1910–1912. Blank: none. Value: $245.00–295.00.*

Plate 417. Syrup pitcher and underplate, 6"h., <u>LILUM</u> <u>ORNATUM</u>. Signed: Yeschek (Yeschek, Joseph T.). TM date: 1910–1912. Blank: France. Value: $275.00–350.00.

Plate 418. Bowl, ring foot, 8¼"d., <u>DAISY</u> <u>MULTI-FLORA</u>. Signed: Fisher (Fischer, Emil J. T.). TM date: 1910–1912. Blank: Favorite Bavaria. Value: $185.00–225.00.

Plate 419. Cake plate with open handles, 10"d., <u>TRIPLE</u> <u>TULIP</u> (<u>YELLOW</u> & <u>WHITE</u>). Signed: Yeschek (Yeschek, Joseph P.). TM date: 1910–1912. Blank: none. Value: $250.00–325.00.

Plate 420. Oval bowl, perforated handles, 8½"d., *RUSSIAN DESIGN. Signed: E. Tolpin (Tolpin, Emil E.). TM date: 1910–1912. Blank: O.&E.G. wreath ROYAL Austria. Value: $235.00–285.00.*

Plate 421. Plate, 8¾"d., *FLORA POLYCHROME*. Signed: *Tolley (Tolley, Harry E.)*. TM date: 1910–1912. Blank: Favorite Bavaria. Value: $135.00–165.00.

Plate 422. Cake plate with perforated handles, 10"d., VIOLETS IN PANEL. Signed: S. TM date: 1910–1912. Blank: D.&Co., France. Value: $135.00–185.00.

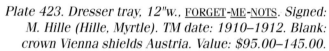

Plate 423. Dresser tray, 12"w., FORGET-ME-NOTS. Signed: M. Hille (Hille, Myrtle). TM date: 1910–1912. Blank: crown Vienna shields Austria. Value: $95.00–145.00.

Plate 424. Condensed milk holder and under-plate, TULIP IN LUSTRE. Signed: Bek (Buschbeck, Carl). TM date: 1910–1912. Blank: Favorite Bavaria. Value: $265.00–325.00.

Plate 425. Coffee pot, creamer, and sugar, square, AURA ARGENTA LINEAR. Signed: S. Richter (Richter, S.). TM date: 1910–1912. Blank: none. Value: $395.00–495.00.

Plate 426. Octagonal dish/ attached open handles, 6"d., WATER LILY CONVENTIONAL. Signed: Fuchs (Fuchs, John). TM date: 1910–1912. Blank: Noritake. Value: $175.00–195.00.

Plate 427. Vase, 10¼"h., WATER LILY CONVENTIONAL. Signed: Fuchs (Fuchs, John). TM date: 1910–1912. Blank: none. Value: $375.00–450.00.

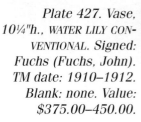

Plate 428. ALEXANDER jug, large, 10"d., FLORA LINEAR. Signed: Arno (Arno, Edith). TM date: 1910–1912. Blank: none. Value: $525.00–675.00.

Plate 429. Plate, 8⅜"d. Three white lilies on gold border on white. Gold linear stems to center. Signed. F. Walt. (Walters, Frederick). TM date: 1910–1912. Blank: 3101. Value: $140.00–185.00.

Plate 430. Pitcher, 6¾"h., DAHLIA AND RAISED GOLD WITH LUSTRE. Signed: Arno (Arno, Edith). TM date: 1910–1912. Blank: overpainted. Value: $325.00–495.00.

Plate 431. Vase, 13¼"h., PASTEL ROSE AND SILVER. (unsigned). TM date: 1910–1912. Blank: PL Limoges, France. Value: $450.00–575.00.

Plate 432. (rear) Charger with perforated handles, 11"d., FLORA PRIMAVERA. Signed: Walt (Walters, Frederick). TM date: 1910–1912. Blank: T&V rectangle, France. Value: $185.00–225.00. (front) Bonbon, open-handle, nouveau shape, 7"l. Signed: Walt (Walters, Frederick). TM date: 1912–1918. Blank: Limoges, Limoges in star France Emile Coiffe. Value: $110.00–125.00.

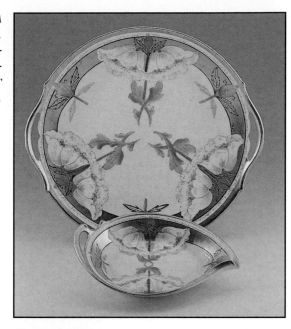

Plate 433. Vase, five-footed cylindrical with perforated top, 10"h. Lily on gray/gold ground, obverse: same design in incised gold. (unsigned). TM date: 1910–1912. Blank: none. Value: $120.00–185.00.

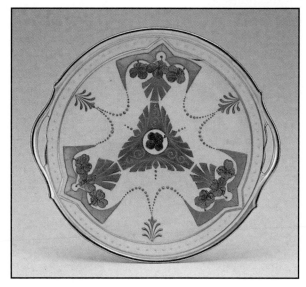

Plate 434. Cake plate, 11"d. SILVER PANSY. (unsigned). TM date: 1910–1912. Blank: T&V rectangle, Limoges, France. Value: $200.00–240.00.

Plate 435. Vase, wishbone handles, 8½"h., CHEROKEE ROSE. Signed: WALT (Walters, Frederick). TM date: 1910–1912. Blank: overpainted. Value: $325.00–450.00.

Plate 436. Plate, 8½"d., WILDFLOWERS OF AMERICA: DAISIES, BUTTERCUPS, FORGET-ME-NOTS. Signed: A. Comyn (Comyn, Arthur). TM date: 1910–1912. Blank: Favorite Bavaria. Value: $125.00–160.00.

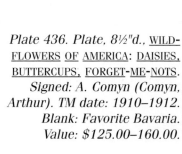

183

Plate 437. Plate, 8½"d., <u>WILDFLOWERS</u> <u>OF</u> <u>AMERICA</u>: <u>FIELD</u> <u>POPPIES</u>, <u>FOR-GET</u>-<u>ME</u>-<u>NOTS</u>-<u>WHEAT</u>. *Signed: A. Comyn (Comyn, Arthur). TM date: 1910–1912. Blank: Favorite Bavaria. Value: $135.00–165.00.*

Plate 438. Charger, two perforated handles, 11"d., TWIN LILIES. *Signed: Walter (Walters, Frederick). TM date: 1910–1912. Blank: circle JHR Bavaria Favorite. Value: $180.00–245.00.*

Plate 439. Mug, 5"h., POINSETTIA CONVENTIONAL. *Signed: Tolley (Tolley, Harry E.). TM date: 1910–1912. Blank: none. Value: $225.00–275.00.*

Plate 440. Cup and saucer, POPPIES LINEAR. *Signed: Tolley (Tolley, Harry E.). TM date: 1910–1912. Blank: Limoges. Value: $120.00–145.00.*

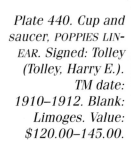

Plate 441. (rear) Shallow, pedestalled bowl, 9"d., <u>PEACHES</u> <u>LINEAR</u>. *Signed: Beutlich (Beutlich, Anton B.). TM date: 1910–1912. Blank: overpainted. Value: $180.00–225.00. (front) Bowl, 7½"d. Signed: Beutlich (Beutlich, Anton B.). TM date: 1905–1910. Blank: France Déposé. Value: $120.00–165.00.*

*Plate 442. Footed condiment bowl, 5"d., <u>CHEROKEE</u> <u>ROSE</u> <u>BOR-</u><u>DER</u>. Signed: Sciu (unknown). TM date: 1910–1912. Blank: T&V rectangle, France overstamped. Value: $75.00–100.00.*

*Plate 443. Small COLO-NIAL vase, 5¼"h., <u>GOLDEN</u> <u>CLOVER</u>. Signed: S Richt. (Richter, S.). TM date: 1910–1912. Blank: Austria. Value: $145.00–175.00.*

*Plate 444. Vase, tapered 8"h., GRAPES IN PANEL. Signed: Lind (Lindner, Frederick J.). TM date: 1910–1912. Blank: none. Value: $285.00–360.00.*

*Plate 445. Vase, tapered with nar-row mouth, 6¼"h., CHRYSANTHEMUMS, LUSTRE, AND MATTE PEACH. Signed: Rean (Klipphahn, Maxwell Rean). TM date: 1910–1912. Blank: none. Value: $225.00–295.00.*

*Plate 446. Bowl, 9"d., CARNATIONS, LUSTRE, AND MATTE GREEN. Signed: Rean (Klipphahn, Maxwell Rean). TM date: 1910–1912. Blank: Favorite Bavaria. Value: $380.00–475.00.*

*Plate 447. (center) Lidded chocolate pot, lidded sugar, and creamer, CARNATIONS, LUSTRE, AND MATTE GREEN. Signed: Rean (Klipphahn, Maxwell Rean). TM date: 1910–1912. Blank: star wreath, RS Germany. Germany red. Value: $495.00–595.00. (right and left) Candlesticks, square base, 8½"h. Signed: Rean (Klipphahn, Maxwell Rean). TM date: 1910–1912. Blank: overpainted. Value: $225.00–300.00.*

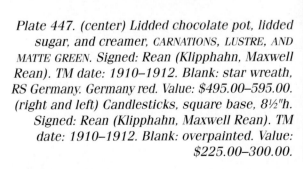

*Plate 448. Vase, 13"h., <u>AURA</u> <u>MOSAIC</u>. Signed: ROSL (Roessler, Carl). TM date: 1910–1912. Blank: overpainted. Value: $600.00–725.00.*

*Plate 449. CORINTHIAN punch bowl, 10½"h x 10"d., <u>AURA</u> <u>MOSAIC</u>. Signed: C.Rosl. (Roessler, Carl). TM date: 1910–1912. Blank: overpainted. Value: $2,200.00–2,600.00.*

*Plate 451. Shaving mug, 3½"h., <u>AURA</u> <u>MOSAIC</u>. Signed: Hartman (Hartman). TM date: 1910–1912. Blank: overpainted. Value: $275.00–395.00.*

*Plate 450. Creamer and lidded sugar, <u>AURA</u> <u>MOSAIC</u>. Signed: C. Rosl (Roessler, Carl). TM date: 1910–1912. Blank: overpainted. Value: $325.00–375.00.*

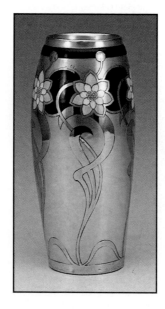

*Plate 452. Reverse-tapered vase, 8"h., <u>AURA</u> <u>MOSAIC</u>. Signed: C. Rosl. (Roessler, Carl). TM date: 1910–1912. Blank: overpainted. Value: $245.00–290.00.*

*Plate 453. Bowl and six sherbets, 9"d., <u>ENCRUSTED</u> <u>LINEAR</u>. Signed: Hess (Hessler, Robert). TM date: 1910–1912. Blank: none. Value: $575.00–675.00.*

Plate 454. Hexagonal lemonade jug, 7½"d., ENCRUST-ED LINEAR. (unsigned). TM date: 1910–1912. Blank: overpainted. Value: $425.00–495.00.

Plate 455. (rear) Plates, 8½"d., DAHLIA RUBRA. Signed: Beulet (Beulet, F.). TM date: 1910–1912. Blank: Favorite Bavaria. Value each: $200.00–245.00. (front) ODETTE demi-tasse pot, creamer and sugar. Signed: A. Richter (Richter, Anton). TM date: 1910–1912. Blank: none. Value: $595.00–695.00.

Plate 456. TROJAN vase, 17⅜"h., DAHLIA RUBRA. Signed: A. Richter (Richter, Anton). TM date: 1910–1912. Blank: none. Value: $1,300.00–1,800.00.

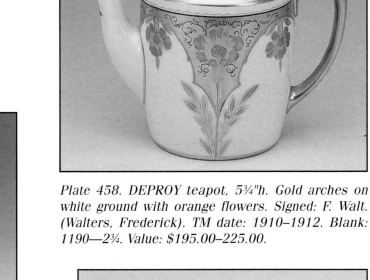

Plate 458. DEPROY teapot, 5¾"h. Gold arches on white ground with orange flowers. Signed: F. Walt. (Walters, Frederick). TM date: 1910–1912. Blank: 1190—2¾. Value: $195.00–225.00.

Plate 457. Small vase, 6"h. All over gold encrusted with blue/orange enamel flowers and pendants. (unsigned). TM date: 1910–1912. Blank: crown, H.&Co. Selb Bavaria. Value: $160.00–190.00.

Plate 459. Demi-tasse and saucer. Two white blossoms, green leaves in three groups, green wash, on gold border. Signed: FJames (James, Florence M.). TM date: 1910–1912. Blank: T&V rectangle, Limoges, France. Value: $140.00–160.00.

Plate 460. Plate with perforated handles, 10¾"d., <u>ENAMEL CHRYSANTHEMUMS</u>. Signed: Efdon (Donisch, Edward F.). TM date: 1910–1912. Blank: T&V rounded rectangle, France. Value: $175.00–235.00.

Plate 461. Cup and saucer, <u>ORANGE TREE CONVENTIONAL</u>. Signed: E.Tolpin (Tolpin, Emil E.). TM date: 1910–1912. Blank: Limoges scroll W.G.&Co., France. Value: $100.00–125.00.

Plate 462. Pitcher, 8¼"h., BLUEBELLS ON GOLD. (unsigned). TM date: 1910–1912. Blank: overpainted. Value: $400.00–550.00.

Plate 463. Bowl, 9¾"d., <u>PINK WEIGELAS</u>. Signed: Edward (Edward). TM date: 1910–1912. Blank: overpainted. Value: $225.00–275.00.

Plate 464. Pitcher, hexagonal, 10"h., <u>HYACINTHUS</u>. Signed: Hessler (Hessler, Robert). TM date: 1910–1912. Blank: none. Value: $500.00–650.00.

*Plate 465. Vase, straight taper, square sided, footed 12"h., HYACINTHUS. Signed: Hess (Hessler, Robert). TM date: 1910–1912. Blank: crossed hammers and crown, Austria. Value: $225.00–285.00.*

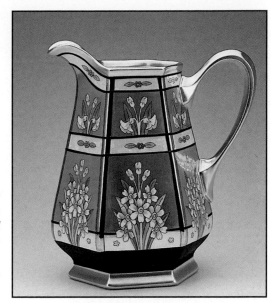

*Plate 466. Pitcher, hexagonal, 10"h., AURA ARGENTA HYACINTHUS. Signed: F. Nittel (Nittel, Frank). TM date: 1910–1912. Blank: B.&Co., France. Value: $500.00–700.00.*

*Plate 467. Plate, 8¾"d., PEONY CONVENTIONAL. Signed: YESCHEK (Yeschek, Joseph T.). TM date: 1910–1912. Blank: Favorite, Bavaria. Value: $180.00–235.00.*

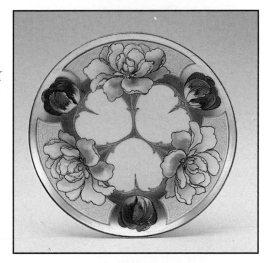

*Plate 468. Bowl, 10"d., POINSETTIA PENDANT. Signed: JNESSY (Nessy, John). TM date: 1910–1912. Blank: overpainted. Value: $225.00–275.00.*

*Plate 469. Charger, 13"d. Six red-orange flowers on wide gold border with blue scallops on white. Signed: Wight (Wight, Phillip). TM date: 1910–1912. Blank: Limoges, Limoges in star France. Value: $100.00–135.00.*

*Plate 470. GOTHAM vase, 7½". Vellum: MIDNIGHT. Signed: E. Challinor (Challinor, Edward S.). TM date: 1912–1918. Blank: crown crossed hammers, Austria Gotham. Value: $495.00–600.00.*

*Plate 472. (left) Plate, 8¾"d. Vellum: FLORIDA MOONLIGHT. Signed: Marker (Marker, Curtis H.). TM date: 1912–1918. Blank: UNO IT Favorite Bavaria. Value: $225.00–275.00. (right) Plate, 8½"d. Signed: H.L.Corey (Corey, Harriet L.). TM date: 1912–1918. Blank: shield Thomas Bavaria. Value: $150.00–185.00. (Note different renderings of same subject.)*

*Plate 471. Rectangular vase, 6"h. Vellum: lavender woodland scenic with lake. Signed: E. Challinor (Challinor, Edward Stafford). TM date: 1912–1918. Blank: none. Value: $250.00–345.00.*

*Plate 474. Plate, 8¼"d. Vellum: AUTUMN STREAM. Signed: E.Challinor (Challinor, Edward S.). TM date: 1912–1918. Blank: crossed clover, J&C Bavaria. Value: $175.00–275.00.*

*Plate 473. (left) Nut dish, 4½"l. Vellum: red foliage beside lake. Signed: E.Challinor (Challinor, Edward S.). TM date: 1912–1918. Blank: Burley & Co., Chicago Made In Germany. Value: $145.00–185.00. (right) Vase, footed, with perforated handles, 6"h. Vellum: WILDWOOD. Signed: E. Challinor (Challinor, Edward S.). TM date: 1912–1918. Blank: Noritake Nippon. Value: $275.00–375.00.*

*Plate 475. DAHLIA VASE, 12"h. Vellum: EVERGLADES. Signed: E. Challinor (Challinor, Edward S.). TM date: 1912–1918. Blank: T&V rectangle, Limoges, France. Value: $525.00–800.00.*

*Plate 476. (rear) Plate, 8¾"d. Vellum: WILDWOOD. Signed: Marker (Marker, Curtis H.). TM date: 1912–1918. Blank: Favorite Bavaria. Value: $195.00–245.00. (front) Cylindrical vase with bulbous base, 5¾"d. Signed: Marker (Marker, Curtis H.). TM date: 1912–1918. Blank: none. Value: $175.00–225.00.*

*Plate 477. Charger, 13½"d. Vellum: AUTUMN BIRCHES. Signed: E. Challinor (Challinor, Edward S.). TM date: 1912–1918. Blank: none. Value: $350.00–425.00.*

*Plate 478. Plate, 8¾"d. Vellum: pale gooseberries and green leaves. Signed: EChallinor (Challinor, Edward S.). TM date: 1912–1918. Blank: Favorite Bavaria. Value: $100.00–160.00.*

*Plate 479. Plate, 8½"d. Glossy pastel pink and white poppy cluster. Signed: EChallinor (Challinor, Edward S.). TM date: 1912–1918. Blank: Favorite Bavaria. Value: $175.00–225.00.*

Plate 480. Plate, 8¾"d. Vellum: pink and white hollyhocks on tall stems, pale lavender ground. Signed: E. Challinor (Challinor, Edward S.). TM date: 1912–1918. Blank: Favorite Bavaria. Value: $180.00–260.00.

Plate 481. Vase, 10½"h. Red haired sylph in diaphanous veil, butterflies. Signed: E. Maley (Maley, Eva E.). TM date: 1912–1918. Blank: overpainted. Value: $700.00–900.00.

Plate 482. Plate, dinner, 9"d., BORDURE CHINOISE. Signed: A. Richter (Richter, Anton). TM date: 1912–1918. Blank: Rosenthal crown & scepters Selb-Bavaria overpainted. Value: $65.00–95.00.

Plate 483. Plate, 8½"d. Vellum: Border of oriental women. Signed: FJames (James, Florence M.). TM date: 1912–1918. Blank: JHR Hutchenreuther, Bavaria. Value: $250.00–275.00.

Plate 484. Pitcher, milk 6"h., COLONIAL DECORATION. Signed: FJames (James, Florence M.). TM date: 1912–1918. Blank: none. Value: $225.00–350.00.

Plate 485. Lidded teapot, lidded creamer, sugar, salt and pepper, 4 cups, plate, 4 side plates, DUTCH DECORATION. Signed: FJames (James, Florence M.). TM date: 1912–1918. Blank: B&Co, France. Value: $650.00–750.00. Tea tile, (under teapot) hexagonal, 6"d. Signed: A. Richter (Richter, Anton). TM date: 1912–1918. Blank: none. Value: $125.00–145.00.

*Plate 486. (left) Milk pitcher, 6½"h., <u>DUTCH</u> <u>DECORATION</u>. Signed: A. Richter (Richter, Anton). TM date: 1912–1918. Blank: Burley & Co., Chicago; Made In Germany. Value: $100.00–125.00. (right) Pitcher, small with perforated handle, 6"h. Signed: F. James (James, Florence M.). TM date: 1912–1918. Blank: O.&E.G. wreath Royal Austria. Value: $125.00–145.00.*

*Plate 487. Lidded sugar, 4¾"d., PILGRIM DECORATION. Signed: W. Rawlins (Rawlins, William T.). TM date: 1912–1918. Blank: B.&Co., France. Value: $225.00–340.00.*

*Plate 488. SUSIE jewel box and pin tray. Border of alternating gold and black panels with flower sprays on white. (unsigned). TM date: 1912–1918. Blank: T&V Limoges, France. Value (set): $150.00–195.00.*

*Plate 489. Lidded serving bowl with underplate, 12"d., BORDER PRIMAVERA. Signed: APassoni (Passony, Arthur). TM date: 1912–1918. Blank: J.P.L., France (bowl), T&V rectangle, Limoges, France (underplate). Value: $330.00–425.00.*

Plate 490. Service plate, 8¾"d. Decal floral and gold scroll border with radii to center. (unsigned). TM date: 1912–1918. Blank: UNO IT Favorite Bavaria overpainted. Value: $85.00–110.00.

Plate 491. DONATELLO radish tray with upswept open handles, 7"d., VENETIAN RENAISSANCE. Signed: Passoni (Passony, Arthur). TM date: 1912–1918. Blank: crown crossed scepters, Rosenthal R.C. Bavaria Donatello. Value: $110.00–125.00.

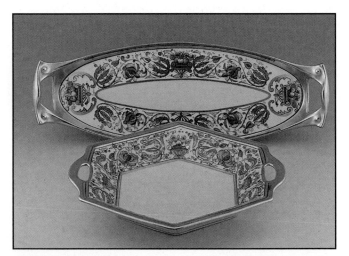

Plate 492. (rear) Bread plate, raised perforated handles, 14"l., VENETIAN RENAISSANCE. Signed: Boehm (Boehm, B.). TM date: 1912–1918. Blank: crown scepters, R.C. Bavaria overpainted. Value: $100.00–135.00. (front) Dish, hexagonal with perforated handles, 10"d. Signed: Tolpin (Tolpin, Emil E.). TM date: 1912–1918. Blank: Imperial crown PSL. Value: $120.00–145.00.

Plate 493. Plate, desert, 8"d. White blossom spray on green leaves on pale lavender border. Signed: Mark (Mark). TM date: 1912–1918. Blank: Favorite Bavaria. Value: $35.00–45.00.

*Plate 494. Plate, 8¾"d. Cluster of violets on pale lavender border. Signed: (unintelligible). TM date: 1912–1918. Blank: circle JHR Hutschenreuther Selb Bavaria. Value: $45.00–65.00.*

*Plate 495. Pedestalled compote, 9"d. Rose medallion and rose garlands on white. Signed: R.Alex (Alexander, Ruth L.). TM date: 1918–1919. Blank: Haviland, France. Value: $175.00–275.00.*

*Plate 497. Plate, 8¾"d. Green apples, pink blush on light green ground. Signed: Gasper (Gasper, Paul P.). TM date: 1918–1919. Blank: UNO IT Favorite Bavaria. Value: $125.00–165.00.*

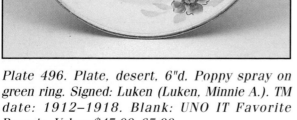

*Plate 496. Plate, desert, 6"d. Poppy spray on green ring. Signed: Luken (Luken, Minnie A.). TM date: 1912–1918. Blank: UNO IT Favorite Bavaria. Value: $45.00–65.00.*

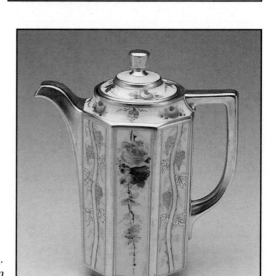

*Plate 498. CARMEN coffee pot, 7"h., <u>PANEL</u> <u>DRESDEN</u> <u>AND</u> <u>RAISED</u> <u>GOLD</u>. Signed: B. Boehm (Boehm, B.). TM date: 1912–1918. Blank: Carmen crown H&Co. Selb Bavaria. Value: $300.00–340.00.*

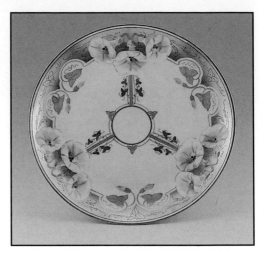

Plate 499. Nappy, handled, 7"d. White flowers with two white blossoms, gold paste stems, green leaves, radiused to center. Signed: A. Richter (Richter, Anton). TM date: 1912–1918. Blank: Royal crown Bavaria. Value: $120.00–145.00.

Plate 500. Plate, 8¾"d., <u>CONVOLVULVUS</u>. Signed: Fisher (Fischer, Emil J. T.). TM date: 1912–1918. Blank: Favorite Bavaria. Value: $140.00–165.00.

Plate 501. DONATELLO radish tray, 7"d., <u>CAMPANULA</u>. Signed: A. Richter (Richter, Anton). TM date: 1912–1918. Blank: GDA, France. Value: $120.00–145.00.

Plate 502. Pitcher, 7⅝"h., <u>CAMPANULA</u>. Signed: A. Richter (Richter, Anton). TM date: 1912–1918. Blank: M-Z eagle. Value: $250.00–350.00.

Plate 503. Vase with open handles, 12¾"h., <u>CAMPANULA</u>. Signed: A. Richter (Richter, Anton). TM date: 1912–1918. Blank: T&V rectangle, Limoges, France. Value: $725.00–845.00.

*Plate 504. (rear) Vase, oval with handles, 7"h., <u>CONVOLVULUS</u>. (unsigned). TM date: 1912–1918. Blank: (1372 incised). Value: $250.00–325.00. (front) Bowl, handled, 6½"d. Signed: fisher (Fischer, Emil J. T.). TM date: 1912–1918. Blank: (incised JF). Value: $225.00–260.00.*

*Plate 505. Plate, 8¾"d., ENAMELED PEONIES AND PHEASANT. (unsigned). TM date: 1910–1912. Blank: Haviland, France. Value: $185.00–225.00.*

*Plate 506. Demi-tasse pot, creamer and sugar, 10¾"h., <u>ANTIQUE</u> <u>CHINESE</u> <u>ENAMELS</u>. Signed: Tolpin (Tolpin, Emil E.). TM date: 1912–1918. Value: $550.00–695.00.*

*Plate 507. Four-handled square vase, 9½"h., <u>ANTIQUE</u> <u>CHINESE</u> <u>ENAMEL</u>. Signed: E. Tolpin (Tolpin, Emil E.). TM date: 1912–1918. Blank: (6089 incised). Value: $395.00–450.00.*

*Plate 508. Vase, 11"h., ENAMELED PEONIES AND PHEASANT. (UNSIGNED). TM date: 1912–1918. Blank: over-painted. Value: $425.00–575.00.*

*Plate 509. Milk pitcher, wide-mouthed, 6"h., <u>TRIPLE</u> <u>TULIP</u> (<u>YELLOW</u> & <u>WHITE</u>). Signed: Yeschek (Yeschek, Joseph T.). TM date: 1912–1918. Blank: Bavaria. Value: $350.00–395.00.*

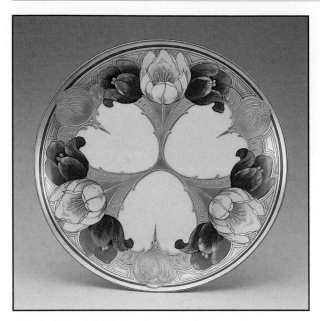

Plate 510. Plate, 8½"d., <u>TRIPLE</u> <u>TULIP</u> (<u>YELLOW</u> & <u>RED</u>) *Signed: Yeschek (Yeschek, Joseph T.). TM date: 1912–1918. Blank: Favorite Bavaria. Value: $195.00–245.00.*

Plate 511. Coffee cup and saucer, WHITE POPPY AND DAISY. Signed: Falatek. (Falatek, Louis H.). TM date: 1912–1918. Blank: none. Value: $140.00–160.00.

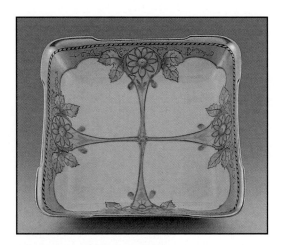

Plate 512. Square bowl, 8⅝"w., DAISY CONVENTIONAL. Signed: Fuchs (Fuchs, John). TM date: 1912–1918. Blank: none. Value: $195.00–245.00.

Plate 513. Plate, 8¾"d., <u>GOLDEN</u> <u>CLOVER</u>. Signed: Vobor (Vobornik, Franz). TM date: 1912–1918. Blank: Favorite Bavaria. Value: $115.00–165.00.

Plate 514. Plate, 9"d., POPPY AND SERPENTINE PASTE. Signed: Gasper (Gasper, Paul P.). TM date: 1912–1918. Blank: UNO IT Favorite Bavaria. Value: $195.00–250.00.

Plate 515. (left) Bowl, shallow, perforated handles, 7½"d., WHITE POPPY AND DAISY. Signed: Gasper (Gasper, Paul P.). TM date: 1912–1918. Blank: GDA, France. Value: $200.00–265.00. (right) Pitcher, wide mouth, 7¼"h. Signed: Gasper (Gasper, Paul P.). TM date: 1912–1918. Blank: MZ crown double eagles, Austria. Value: $425.00–550.00.

Plate 516. Mustard boat with cover, and spoon, 5"d., WHITE POPPY AND DAISY. Signed: Gasper. (Gasper, Paul P.). TM date: 1912–1918. Blank: overpainted. Value: $225.00–275.00.

Plate 517. (left) REGENCE jelly, wishbone handles, 7½"d., WHITE POPPY AND DAISY. Signed: Gasper (Gasper, Paul P.). TM date: 1912–1918. Blank: T&V rectangle, Limoges, France. Value: $185.00–225.00. (right) Vase with straight, high-rise handles, 9½"h. Signed: Gasper (Gasper, Paul P.). TM date: 1912–1918. Blank: overpainted. Value: $375.00–450.00.

Plate 518. Large pitcher, hexed major perimeter, 7½"h., LILIUM ORNATUM. Signed: Yeschek (Yeschek, Joseph T.). TM date: 1910–1912. Blank: none. Value: $475.00–595.00.

Plate 519. Footed compote, 6¼"d., <u>LILIUM</u> <u>ORNATUM</u>. Signed: Yeschek (Yeschek, Joseph P.). TM date: 1912–1918. Blank: none. Value: $225.00–295.00.

Plate 520. Pitcher, scalloped rim, fluted sides, 6½"h., WATER LILY CONVENTIONAL. Signed: Fuchs (Fuchs, John). TM date: 1910–1912. Blank: 1087/2. Value: $375.00–495.00.

Plate 521. (left) Plate, 8¾"d., WHITE VIOLETS LINEAR. Signed: Beutlich (Beutlich, Anton B.). TM date: 1910–1912. Blank: Favorite Bavaria. Value: $95.00–115.00. (right) Pitcher, 8"h. (unsigned). TM date: 1910–1912. Blank: Bavaria. Value: $160.00–195.00.

Plate 523. Bowl, handled, 6¼"d., <u>VIOLET</u> <u>SUPREME</u>. Signed: Fish (Fischer, Emil J. T.). TM date: 1912–1918. Blank: Haviland, France. Value: $210.00–245.00.

Plate 522. Creamer and lidded sugar, <u>VIOLET</u> <u>SUPREME</u>. Signed: Fisher (Fischer, Emil J. T.). TM date: 1912–1918. Blank: none. Value: $375.00–425.00.

*Plate 524. Lemonade jug, hexagonal, 7"h., <u>VIOLET</u> <u>SUPREME</u>. Signed: Fish (Fischer, Emil J. T.). TM date: 1912–1918. Blank: B&Co, France. Value: $550.00–675.00.*

*Plate 525. Bowl, large, 10"d., <u>VIOLET</u> <u>SUPREME</u>. Signed: Fisher (Fischer, Emil J. T.). TM date: 1910–1912. Blank: none. Value: $300.00–425.00.*

*Plate 526. CORINTHIAN punch bowl, 10½"d., <u>ENCRUSTED</u> <u>HONEY-SUCKLE</u>. (unsigned). TM date: 1910–1912. Blank: overpainted. Value: $600.00–895.00.*

*Plate 527. Bowl, 6"d., <u>BORDURE</u> <u>ANTIQUE</u>. (unsigned). TM date: 1912–1918. Blank: M&Z Austria. Value: $275.00–350.00.*

*Plate 528. Vase, wide-mouthed, 7½"h., <u>BORDURE</u> <u>ANTIQUE</u>. Signed: P. Anthony '12 (Anthony, Paul B.). TM date: 1910–1912. Blank: crown crossed scepters, Rosenthal Selb-Bavaria. Value: $325.00–395.00.*

*Plate 529. Lidded milk pitcher, 7"h., <u>ENCRUSTED</u> <u>HONEY-SUCKLE</u>. (unsigned). TM date: 1912–1918. Blank: Noritake. Value: $150.00–185.00.*

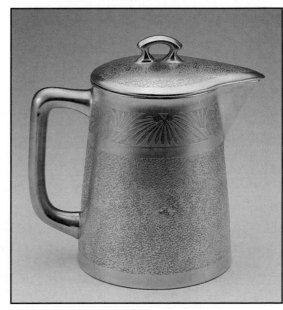

*Plate 530. Vase, 6½"h., ENCRUSTED LINEAR. (unsigned). TM date: 1912–1918. Blank: none. Value: $275.00–350.00.*

*Plate 531. Coffee pot, cream and sugar, 10½"h., ENCRUSTED LINEAR. Signed: Hessler (Hessler, Robert). TM date: 1910–1912. Blank: obscure. Value: $450.00–600.00.*

*Plate 533. Bowl on pedestal with handles, 6"d., AURA MOSAIC. Signed: Hartman. (Hartman). TM date: 1910–1912. Blank: none. Value: $275.00–395.00.*

*Plate 532. (rear) Muffineer, 5"h., CALLA LILIES. Signed: Beulet (Beulet, F.). TM date: 1910–1912. Blank: none. Value: $250.00–295.00. (front) Dish, covered, handled, with underplate, 6"d. Signed: Beulet (Beulet, F.). TM date: 1910–1912. Blank: none. Value: $300.00–425.00.*

*Plate 534. Coffee set, round-contour, AURA MOSAIC. Signed: C. Rosl. (Roessler, Carl). TM date: 1910–1912. Blank: overpainted. Value: $450.00–575.00.*

Plate 535. CENTURY salad bowl, 10¼"d., FLORA PRIMAVERA. Signed: Walt (Walters, Frederick). TM date: 1912–1918. Blank: Century Patd Feb. 26, 1901, large rectangle T&V, Limoges, France. Value: $325.00–425.00.

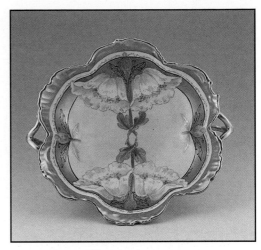

Plate 536. Wishbone-handled regency bowl, 7½"d., FLORA PRIMAVERA. Signed: FWalt (Walters, Frederick). TM date: 1910–1912. Blank: T&V rectangle, France. Value: $185.00–235.00.

Plate 537. Nouveau style mayonnaise, underplate, and ladle, 7½"l. Two white blossoms, green leaves, green wash, on gold border. Signed: FJames (James, Florence). TM date: 1910–1912. Blank: Limoges star with Limoges in points France. Value: $250.00–295.00.

Plate 538. (left) Muffineer, 5½"h., VIOLET BORDER. Signed: Wag. (Wagner, Albert H.). TM date: 1912–1918. Blank: overpainted. Value: $165.00–185.00. (right) Candy dish on three ball feet, 4¾"d. Signed: Wag. (Wagner, Albert H.). TM date: 1912–1918. Blank: T&V Limoges, France. Value: $65.00–95.00.

Plate 539. Cylindrical vase, footed square base, flared mouth, 11½"h., TWIN LILIES. Signed: Walt. (Walters, Frederick). TM date: 1910–1912. Blank: overpainted. Value: $360.00–425.00.

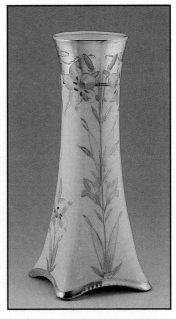
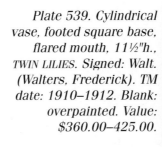

Plate 540. Cake plate, perforated handles, 9½"d. Glossy scenic, autumn birches with lake in background. Signed: EChallinor (Challinor, Edward S.). TM date: 1918–1919. Blank: Made In Japan. Value: $350.00–450.00.

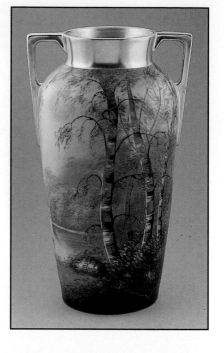

Plate 541. Vase 12"h. Vellum: BIRCHES. Signed: Marker (Marker, Curtis H.). TM date: 1918–1919. Blank: crown H&Co. Selb Bavaria. Value: $600.00–895.00.

Plate 543. Bonbon, handled, 6"d. Vellum: SOUVENIR OF FLORIDA. Signed: Vokral (Vokral, Jeremiah). TM date: 1918–1919. Blank: Made in Japan. Value: $95.00–145.00.

Plate 542. Cake plate, open handles, 10"d. Vellum: ENCHANTED FOREST. Signed: Marker (Marker, Curtis H.). TM date: 1918–1919. Blank: Made In Japan. Value: $325.00–395.00.

Plate 544. Charger, 12½"d. Vellum: HILLSIDE EDEN PARK. Signed: E. Challinor (Challinor, Edward S.). TM date: 1918–1919. Blank: star wreath, RS, Tillowitz Silesia. Value: $500.00–700.00.

Plate 545. Vase, 9½"h. Vellum: FLORIDA LAGOON. Signed: Marker (Marker, Curtis H.). TM date: 1918–1919. Blank: crown, H.&Co. Selb Bavaria. Value: $600.00–895.00.

*Plate 546. Cake plate, 10½"d. Vellum: <u>WALLED GARDEN</u>. Signed: Challinor (Challinor, Edward S.). TM date: 1918–1919. Blank: Noritake Nippon. Value: $375.00–475.00.*

*Plate 547. OMAR sandwich plate, perforated handles, 11¼"d. Vellum: <u>TWILIGHT</u>. Signed: E Challinor (Challinor, Edward S.). TM date: 1918–1919. Blank: Made In Japan. Value: $300.00–395.00.*

*Plate 548. Small ALICE celery, 10¼"l. Vellum: <u>HAWTHORNE</u>. Signed: Marker (Marker, Curtis H.). TM date: 1918–1919. Blank: none. Value: $235.00–285.00.*

*Plate 550. Lidded condensed milk jar and underplate, 4½"h., <u>DESERTED GARDEN</u>. Signed: Marker (Marker, Curtis H.). TM date: 1912–1918. Blank: overpainted. Value: $325.00–375.00.*

*Plate 549. Claret jug, tray, and six tumblers, 8½"h., <u>DESERTED GARDEN</u>. Signed: Marker, Curtis H. (Marker). TM date: 1912–1918. Blank: none. Value: $1,800.00–2,200.00.*

*Plate 551. Vase, 19½"h.,* DESERTED GARDEN. *Signed: Vokral (Vokral, Jeremiah). TM date: 1912–1918. Blank: overpainted. Value: $1,800.00–2,500.00.*

*Plate 552. Cone-shaped punch bowl, 9¼"h. x 12½"d. Signed: Yeschek (Yeschek, Joseph T.). 12 punch cups,* DESERTED GARDEN. *Signed Vokral (Vokral, Jeremiah). TM date: 1912–1918. Blank: overpainted. Value: $3,600.00–4,200.00.*

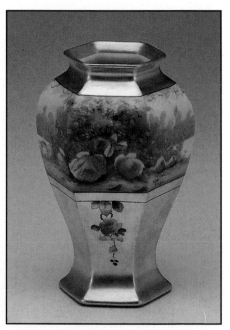

*Plate 554. Vase, hexagonal, 7"h.,* ROSELAND. *Signed: Marker (Marker, Curtis H.). TM date: 1912–1918. Blank: B.&Co., France. Value: $425.00–500.00.*

*Plate 553. Handled fruit bowl, 9"d.,* DESERTED GARDEN. *Signed: Vokral (Vokral, Jeremiah). TM date: 1912–1918. Blank: overpainted. Value: $375.00–425.00.*

*Plate 555. (rear) Elanor [sic] bread tray, 14½"l.,* FRUITS LINEAR. *Signed: Rean (Klipphahn, Maxwell Rean). TM date: 1912–1918. Blank: Noritake Nippon. Value: $165.00–195.00. (front)* LESLIE *tea set with four cups and saucers. Signed: Rean (Klipphahn, Maxwell Rean). TM date: 1912–1918. Blank: Noritake Nippon. Value: $495.00–550.00.*

Plate 556. Compote, circular base, pierced handles, 9½"d., ENCRUSTED FRUIT. Signed: Rean (Klipphahn, Maxwell Rean). TM date: 1912–1918. Blank: none. Value: $255.00–295.00.

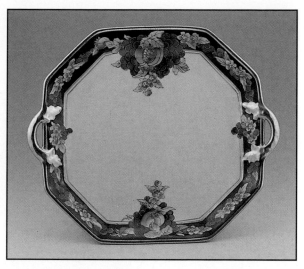

Plate 557. Chop plate, 9½"d., PURPLE GRAPES AND POMEGRANATES. Signed: Rean (Klipphahn, Maxwell Rean). TM date: 1918–1919. Blank: none. Value: $175.00–250.00.

Plate 558. Bonbon, oval, open handled, 8"l. Fruit bowl in center of encrusted gold border. Signed: M.K. (Klipphahn, Maxwell Rean). TM date: 1912–1918. Blank: overpainted. Value: $65.00–95.00.

Plate 559. Vase, 7¾"h., PHEASANT ON BLACK AND GOLD ENCRUSTED. Signed: Challinor (Challinor, Edward S.). TM date: 1912–1918. Blank: paper label covered. Value: $500.00–650.00.

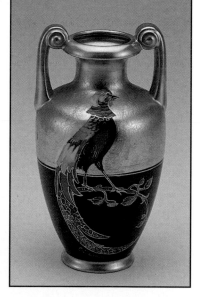

Plate 560. Vase, 7½"h., OLD FASHIONED FLOWERS. Signed: Tolpin (Tolpin, Emil E.). TM date: 1912–1918. Blank: none. Value: $350.00–425.00.

Plate 558.1. ALMA covered jug, 9"h., ASTORS [sic] BLUE ENCRUSTED. (unsigned). TM date: 1912–1918. Blank: overpainted. Value: $210.00–295.00.

Plate 561. Vase, 9"h., <u>DESERTED</u> <u>GARDEN</u>. *Signed: Vokral (Vokral, Jeremiah). TM date: 1912–1918. Blank: crown crossed scepters, Rosenthal Selb Bavaria. Value: $285.00–350.00.*

*Plate 562. Compote, quatrefoil, 9¼"d., <u>FRUIT</u> <u>PANELS</u>. Signed: J. Nessy (Nessy, John). TM date: 1912–1918. Blank: none. Value: $375.00–450.00.*

*Plate 563. Demi-tasse and saucer, <u>ANTIQUE</u> <u>ENAMELS</u>. Signed: Tol (Tolpin, Emil E.). TM date: 1912–1918. Blank: Limoges scroll, W.G.&Co., France. Value: $110.00–135.00.*

*Plate 564. Vase, 8½"h, <u>FRUITS</u> <u>LINEAR</u>. Signed: Tolpin. (Tolpin, Emil E.). TM date: 1912–1918. Blank: Noritake Nippon. Value: $375.00–425.00.*

*Plate 565. Plate, 8¼"d, <small>GRAPE ARBOR</small>. Signed: J. Gottlich (Gottlich, J.). TM date: 1912–1918. Blank: Hutschenreuther JH Selb Bavaria. Value: $95.00–125.00.*

*Plate 566. Lidded teapot, lidded sugar, creamer, <u>AURA</u> <u>ARGENTA</u> <u>LINEAR</u>. Signed: Hiecke (Hiecke, Gustav H. G.). TM date: 1912–1918. Blank: B&Co, France. Value: $300.00–375.00.*

Plate 567. Deep bowl with open handles, 7½"d., AURA ARGENTA LINEAR. Signed: Hiecke (Hiecke, Gustav H. G.). TM date: 1912–1918. Blank: B.&Co. Limoges, France. Value: $225.00–260.00.

Plate 568. Nut set: bowl and six dishes, seven different nut designs on brown ground. Signed: Vokral (Vokral, Jeremiah). TM date: 1914–1916. Blank: crown wreath, RS, Germany. Value: $275.00–325.00.

Plate 569. Vase, 15½"h., PASTEL ROSES. Signed: EChallinor (Challinor, Edward S.). TM date: 1914–1916. Blank: scrolls, W.G.&Co. Limoges, France. Value: $785.00–900.00.

Plate 570. (left) Desert plate, 6½"d., RUSSIAN FLOWERS. (unsigned). TM date: 1912–1918. Blank: none. Value: $20.00–28.00. (left center) Plate, desert, 8"d. Simple border, four purple bell flowers, pink leaves beneath gold leaves. (unsigned). TM date: 1912–1918. Blank: Hutschenreuther oval lion LHS Selb Bavaria. Value: $15.00–20.00. (right center) Desert plate, 8"d. Simple border: reversed gold scrolls with pink leaves, wide gold border, white ground. (unsigned). TM date: 1918–1919. Blank: Hutschenreuther lion Selb Bavaria. Value: $45.00–55.00. (right) Desert plate, 6½"d. Simple border: Blue bell, gold pendent leaf, green side-leaves. (unsigned). TM date: 1912–1918. Blank: JHR Hutchenreuther Selb Bavaria. Value: $20.00–25.00. (rear center) Footed bonbon with open handles, 5½"l. Simple border: lavender morning glory, red posy on gold band on white. (unsigned). TM date: 1918–1919. Blank: Made In Japan. Value: $65.00–95.00. (center) Salt and pepper, 2"h., SHAMROCK. (unsigned). TM date: 1912–1918. Blank: Bavaria. Value: $30.00–38.00. (front) Nappy, oval, raised perforated handles, 8½"d. Simple border: yellow flower, blue fleurets, gold and green pendants. (unsigned). TM date: 1912–1918. Blank: Noritake Nippon. Value: $35.00–45.00.

Plate 572. (left) Desert plate, 6"d. Simple border with red-orange tulip, green leaves. (unsigned). TM date: 1912–1918. Blank: Favorite Bavaria. Value: $20.00–25.00. (left center) Plate, desert, 8"d. Simple border, three fleur-de-lys, pink and lavender flower garland. (unsigned). TM date: 1912–1918. Blank: circle JR Hutchenreuther. Value: $25.00–35.00. (right center) Desert plate, 8"d. Simple border: pink border rose on gold scrolls on wide gold border on white. (unsigned). TM date: 1912–1918. Blank: Hutschenreuther lion Selb Bavaria. Value: $45.00–60.00. (right) Desert plate, 6"d. Simple border: three small pale blossoms on twined stem border. (unsigned). TM date: 1912–1918. Blank: Favorite Bavaria. Value: $12.00–18.00. (left front) Dish, candy, handled, 5"d., LOUIS XIV. (unsigned). TM date: 1912–1918. Blank: T&V rectangle, Limoges, France. Value: $35.00–45.00. (center) Creamer, cereal. Simple border: gold scroll with pink roses pendent on gold band, white ground. (unsigned). TM date: 1912–1918. Blank: crown lion Austria or Bavaria. Value: $45.00–55.00. (right front) Nappy, perforated handles, 7"d. Simple border: rose buds in gold frame, gold pendants. (unsigned). TM date: 1912–1918. Blank: Noritake Nippon. Value: $30.00–40.00.

Plate 571. (left) Bouillon cup with wishbone handles and saucer, 6¼"d. Simple border: pale blue overlapping rectangles. (unsigned). TM date: 1912–1918. Blank: UNO IT Favorite Bavaria. Value: $45.00–65.00. (left center) Shallow bowl, 8½"d. Simple border: eight lavender balls on spindles, rose arbor, etched rim. (unsigned). TM date: 1912–1918. Blank: J&C crossed clovers, Bavaria. Value: $25.00–35.00. (right center) Tea tile, round, 6½"d., ROSE BASKET. (unsigned). TM date: 1912–1918. Blank: H&Co. Selb Bavaria crown. Value: $40.00–55.00. (right) Desert plate, 6"d. Simple border: small red rose in gold harp. (unsigned). TM date: 1912–1918. Blank: UNO IT Favorite Bavraria. Value: $12.00–18.00. (rear) Salt and pepper, 2"h., ROSE BASKET. (unsigned). TM date: 1912–1918. Blank: Bavaria. Value: $35.00–45.00. (front center) Boat-shaped butter pat dish, 3"l. Simple border: floral sprays between blue stripes on white ground. (unsigned). TM date: 1912–1918. Blank: none. Value: $25.00–35.00. (front right) Nappy, single multi-perforated handle, 7"d., THE SHERATON. (unsigned). TM date: 1912–1918. Blank: Royal Bayreuth shield T, Bavaria. Value: $40.00–55.00.

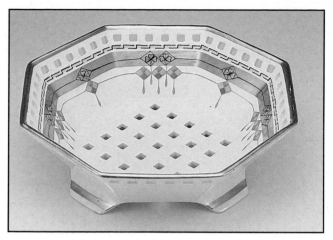

Plate 573. Footed, hexagonal strawberry bowl with square drain holes, 8½"d., SHAMROCK. (unsigned). TM date: 1912–1918. Blank: none. Value: $125.00–140.00.

Plate 574. Muffineer, tapered sides, 4¾"h. Simple border: blue bell, gold pendent leaf, green side-leaves. (unsigned). TM date: 1912–1918. Blank: overpainted. Value: $45.00–65.00.

Plate 575. Mustard, lidded with captive underplate, 5"l. Geometric gold/green border with red flower on white ground. (unsigned). TM date: 1912–1918. Blank: overpainted. Value: $95.00–135.00.

Plate 576. Cheese dip bowl with attached underplate, 9"d. Simple border: four purple bell flowers, pink leaves beneath gold leaves. (unsigned). TM date: 1918–1919. Blank: Noritake Nippon. Value: $65.00–85.00.

Plate 577. Lidded coffee pot, lidded creamer, and sugar. Satsuma-style flower border above beige with gold linears. (unsigned). TM date: 1918–1919. Blank: star RS wreath, Germany. Value: $375.00–475.00.

*Plate 578. Bowl, Satsuma body, 6½"d. Interior band of flowers with floral enameled medallion. Signed: TOLPIN (Tolpin, Emil E.). TM date: 1912–1918. Blank: overpainted. Value: $175.00–250.00.*

*Plate 579. Vase, soft paste, 8½"h. Fruit medallion. Signed: Gasper (Gasper, Paul P.). TM date: 1912–1918. Blank: none. Value: $250.00–350.00.*

*Plate 580. Vase, soft paste, 6"h. ANTIQUE ENAMELS. Signed: Tolley (Tolley, Harry E.). TM date: 1912–1918. Blank: none. Value: $250.00–300.00.*

*Plate 582. (left) Vase, soft paste, 6"h., ENAMELED FLORAL MEDALLION. Signed: Tolpin (Tolpin, Emil E.). TM date: 1912–1918. Blank: none. Value: $295.00–350.00. (right) Footed circular box, soft paste, 5¾"d. Signed: Tolpin (Tolpin, Emil E.). TM date: 1912–1918. Blank: none. Value: $265.00–350.00.*

*Plate 581. Bowl, Satsuma body, 7"d., ANTIQUE ENAMELS. Signed: TOLPIN (Tolpin, Emil E.). TM date: 1912–1918. Blank: overpainted. Value: $175.00–225.00.*

*Plate 583. Lidded, footed box, soft paste, 5"d., BOUQUET SATSUMA. Signed: Beutlich (Beutlich, Anton B). TM date: 1918–1919. Blank: none. Value: $225.00–250.00.*

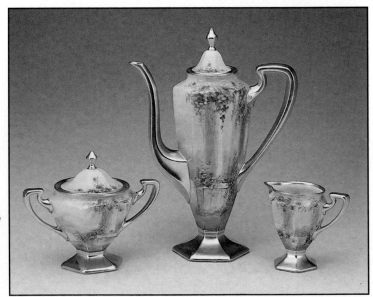

*Plate 584. Lidded COLONIAL coffee pot, lidded sugar, and creamer, 10½"h., ITALIAN GARDEN. Signed: Yeschek (Yeschek, Joseph T.). TM date: 1912–1918. Blank: overpainted. Value: $725.00–825.00.*

*Plate 585. Hexagonal pitcher, 8"h. Glossy scenic: CASTLE MERE. Signed: Rawlins (Rawlins, William T.). TM date: 1912–1918. Blank: Limoges, France. Value: $295.00–495.00.*

*Plate 586. Vase, 10"h. Vellum: WISCONSIN DELLS. Signed: E.Challinor (Challinor, Edward S.). TM date: 1912–1918. Blank: none. Value: $350.00–425.00.*

*Plate 587. Vase with perforated handles, 7¼"h. Vellum: lakeside forest. Signed: Challinor (Challinor, Edward S.). TM date: 1912–1918. Blank: none. Value: $450.00–550.00.*

*Plate 589. (left) Plate, 8"d. Vellum: mountain landscape. Signed: Marker (Marker, Curtis H.). TM date: 1918–1919. Blank: lion Hutschenreuther LHS Selb Bavaria. Value: $145.00–225.00. (right) Plate, 8"d. YOSEMITE FALLS. Signed: Marker (Marker, Curtis H.). TM date: 1912–1918. Blank: circle Hutschenreuther LHS Selb Bavaria. Value: $145.00–225.00.*

*Plate 588. Tall hex vase, 11½"h. Vellum: WILDWOOD. Signed: E.Challinor (Challinor, Edward S.). TM date: 1912–1918. Blank: overpainted. Value: $600.00–900.00.*

Plate 590. Vase, 8"h. Vellum: woodland scene. Signed: Challinor (Challinor, Edward S.). TM date: 1912–1918. Blank: crown Vienna shields Austria. Value: $325.00–475.00.

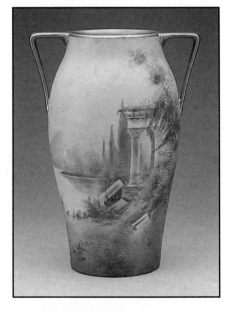

Plate 592. Plate, 8¼"d. Vellum: pines with lake and mountains. Signed: Seagren (Seagren, Anna A.). TM date: 1912–1918. Blank: circle JHR Hutchenreuther Selb Bavaria. Value: $145.00–185.00.

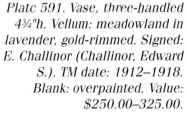

Platc 591. Vase, three-handled 4¾"h. Vellum: meadowland in lavender, gold-rimmed. Signed: E. Challinor (Challinor, Edward S.). TM date: 1912–1918. Blank: overpainted. Value: $250.00–325.00.

Plate 594. Vase, open handles, 13"h. Vellum: CLASSIC RUINS. Signed: F.Vobor. (Vobornik, Franz). TM date: 1912–1918. Blank: T&V rectangle, Limoges, France. Value: $625.00–925.00.

Plate 593. Vase, 7"h. Vellum: birches beside mountain lake. Signed: Challinor (Challinor, Edward S.). TM date: 1918–1919. Blank: circle P.S.A.A. Bavaria. Value: $325.00–375.00. Vase, 7"h. Vellum: YOSEMITE FALLS. Signed: Marker (Marker, Curtis H.). TM date: 1912–1918. Blank: diamond OHIO. Value: $275.00–325.00.

Plate 595. Plate with slight handles, 10½"d. Vellum: WALLED GARDEN. Signed: Maley (Maley, Eva E.). TM date: 1912–1918. Blank: none. Value: $75.00–100.00.

Plate 596. (left) Vase, 8½"h. Vellum: FLORI-DA MOONLIGHT. Signed: Marker (Marker, Curtis H.). TM date: 1912–1918. Blank: crossed hammers, Austria. Value: $375.00–425.00. (right) Vase with open handles, 8¼"h. Vellum: CLASSIC RUINS BY MOONLIGHT. Signed: Challinor (Challinor, Edward S.). TM date: 1912–1918. Blank: Noritake Nippon. Value: $375.00–425.00.

Plate 597. Vase, 9"h. Vellum: FLORIDA MOONLIGHT. Signed: H.L.C. (Corey, Harriet L.). TM date: 1912–1918. Blank: overpainted. Value: $350.00–550.00.

Plate 599. Glass compote, 5"h., POPPIES. Signed: Ross (Roessler, Carl). TM date: 1916–1917. Blank: none. Value: $125.00–195.00.

Plate 598. Glass cream and sugar, star base FLORAL SCROLL. (unsigned). TM date: 1917. Blank: 7011 scratched on sugar, 7010 on creamer. Value: $85.00–100.00.

Plate 600. Sherbet/champagne glasses, two each, 4⅜"h. (unsigned). TM date: 1917–1918. Blank: none. Value each set: $50.00–75.00.

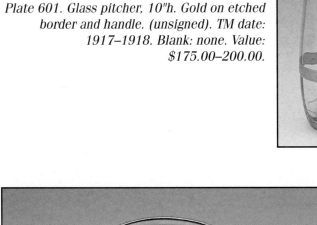

Plate 601. Glass pitcher, 10"h. Gold on etched border and handle. (unsigned). TM date: 1917–1918. Blank: none. Value: $175.00–200.00.

Plate 602. Perfume bottle, 4¾"h. Gold gilding on etched band and stopper. (unsigned). TM date: 1917–1918. Blank: none. Value: $225.00–300.00.

Plate 603. Condiment dish with perforated handles, 4¾"d. Bouquet of diverse enameled flowers in center with four small floral clusters on rim. (unsigned). TM date: 1918–1919 (Mark 8.1). Blank: Noritake Nippon. Value: $55.00–85.00.

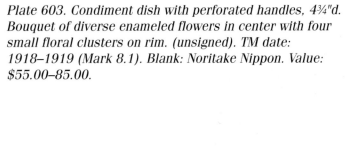

Plate 604. (left) Small, open-handled bonbon, 6"d., CHI-NESE PHEASANT. (unsigned). TM date: 1918–1919 (Mark 8.1). Blank: Noritake Nippon. Value: $85.00–125.00. (right) Lidded sauce cup with underplate, 4"h. (unsigned). TM date: 1918–1919 (Mark 8.1). Blank: Noritake Nippon. Value: $145.00–195.00.

*Plate 605. Lemonade pitcher, 6½"h., CHINESE PHEASANT. (unsigned). TM date: 1918–1919 (Mark 8.1). Blank: Hutschenreuther Selb ellipse lion LHS Bavaria. Value: $200.00–265.00.*

*Plate 606. Cake plate with perforated handles, 10"d. Vellum: TWILIGHT. Signed: Marker (Marker, Curtis H.). TM date: 1918–1919. Blank: B.&Co. Limoges, France. Value: $225.00–275.00.*

*Plate 608. TUSCAN vase, 10"h., DUCHESS OF DEVONSHIRE. Signed: F. Cirnac (Cirnacty, F.). TM date: 1919–1922. Blank: none. Value: $850.00–1,050.00.*

*Plate 607. Vase, 10¼"h. Woman with water jug. Signed: F. Cirnacty (Cirnacty, F.). TM date: 1919–1922. Blank: none. Value: $1,200.00–1,500.00.*

*Plate 609. (rear) Pair candlesticks, 8"h., TRACERY AND BLUE LUSTRE. (unsigned). TM date: 1919–1922. Blank: none. Value: $200.00–250.00. (front) Bowl, 6"d. (unsigned). TM date: 1919–1922. Blank: none. Value: $120.00–140.00.*

Plate 610. Coffee pot, cream and sugar, ETCHED GOLD PEA-COCK ON BLUE. (unsigned). TM date: 1919–1922. Blank: none. Value: $375.00–475.00.

Plate 613. Ball-footed condiment bowl with ladle, 5½"d., BUTTERFLIES AND ETCHED GOLD. Signed: A. Richter (Richter, Anton). TM date: 1919–1922. Blank: none. Value: $195.00–225.00.

Plate 611. Bonbon. Value: $135–$165.00. Cup and saucer. Value: $125.00–145.00. Plate. Value: $130.00–150.00. Oval celery tray, TRACERY AND BLUE LUSTRE. (unsigned). TM date: 1919–1922. Blank: None. Value: $125.00–165.00.

Plate 614. Shallow bonbon with fan-perforated handles, 7¼"w., ROSE AND DAISY AOG. (unsigned). TM date: 1919–1922. Blank: star wreath, RS, Tillowitz Silesia. Value: $65.00–85.00.

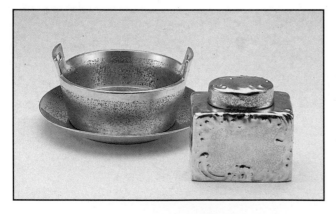

Plate 612. (left) Three-piece gold butter tub, 5½"d. (unsigned). TM date: 1919–1922. Blank: Z.&S.Co. Bavaria. Value: $115.00–140.00. (right) Lidded tea caddy, 3½"h. Plain gold. (unsigned). TM date: 1919–1922. Blank: scroll W.G.&Co., France. Value: $125.00–160.00.

*Plate 615. Lidded coffee, lidded sugar, creamer. AOG encrusted with medallion of fruit bowl, top white border with pink floral. Signed: Vokral (Vokral, Jeremiah). TM date: 1919–1922. Blank: none. Value: $275.00–350.00.*

*Plate 616. COLONIAL lidded coffee, lidded sugar and creamer. 10½"h., ENCRUSTED LINEAR, ROSE AND DAISY AOG. (unsigned). TM date: 1919–1922. Blank: B.&Co. Limoges, France. Value: $425.00–550.00.*

*Plate 617. Lidded sugar and creamer, WATERLILIES AND ENCRUSTED GOLD. Signed: FJames, FJ (James, Florence M.). TM date: 1919–1922. Blank: none. Value: $165.00–195.00.*

*Plate 618. Plates, set of eight, 11"d. Garden scenes with gold daisies over cobalt border. Signed: E.Challinor (Challinor, Edward S.). TM date: 1919–1922. Blank: crown crossed scepters, Rosenthal Selb Bavaria. Value (set): $2,200.00–2,800.00.*

*Plate 619. Vase, 6¾"h., HUM-MING BIRD AND GOLD. (unsigned). TM date: 1919–1922. Blank: none. Value: $125.00–160.00.*

*Plate 620. Cake plate, open handles, 11"d. Gold daisies over blue border with glossy garden scenic in center. Signed: Challinor (Challinor, Edward S.). TM date: 1919–1922. Blank: Hutschenreuther Selb Bavaria LHS. Value: $225.00–275.00.*

*Plate 621. Pedestalled bowl, open handles, 10"d., <u>BLUE</u> <u>ROSE</u> <u>AND</u> <u>DAISY</u>. (unsigned). TM date: 1919–1922. Blank: Noritake Nippon. Value: $180.00–240.00.*

*Plate 622. (left) Footed bowl, <u>ROSE</u> <u>AND</u> <u>DAISY</u> <u>AOP</u>. (unsigned). TM date: 1919–1922. Blank: RS, Tillowitz Silesia. Value: $135.00–165.00. Bonbon, <u>ROSE</u> <u>AND</u> <u>DAISY</u> <u>AOP</u>. (unsigned). TM date: 1925–1930. Blank: overpainted. Value: $75.00–95.00.*

*Plate 623. (rear) Lidded syrup, <u>ORIENTAL</u> <u>BIRD</u>. Signed: Nichols (Nichols, Bessie). TM date: 1919–1922. Value: $145.00–195.00. (front) Bonbon, 5½"d. TM date: 1919–1922. Blank: star, RS wreath, Tillowitz Silesia. Value: $95.00–125.00.*

Plate 624. (rear) Plate, 8"d., ZINNIAS AND BLUE ON ENCRUST-ED GOLD. Signed: Erbe (Erbe). TM date: 1919–1922. Blank: Hutschenreuther Selb lion LHS Bavaria. Value: $45.00–55.00. (front) Plate, 8"d. Signed: James (James, Florence M.). TM date: 1919–1922. Blank: Hutschen-reuther Selb lion LHS Bavaria. Value: $45.00–55.00.

Plate 625. Cache pot with reticulated top rim and captive ring handles, 11"h., <u>ROSE</u> <u>BASKET</u> / <u>TRAILING</u> <u>VINE</u> <u>AOG</u>. Signed: F. Vobor (Vobornik, Franz). TM date: 1919–1922. Blank: B.&Co. France. Value: $325.00–395.00.

Plate 626. Footed quatrefoil bowl, 9¼"d., <u>GOLDEN PHEASANT</u>. Signed: EChallinor (Challinor, Edward S.). TM date: 1919–1922. Blank: none. Value: $425.00–485.00.

Plate 628. Pitch-er, 8¼"h., <u>GOLDEN PHEASANT</u>. Signed: E. Challi-nor (Challinor, Edward Stafford). TM date: 1919–1922. Blank: B.&Co. France. Value: $495.00–595.00.

Plate 627. Charger, 12½"d., <u>GOLDEN</u> <u>PHEASANT</u>. Signed: Challinor (Challinor, Edward S.). TM date: 1919–1922. Blank: none. Value: $400.00–475.00.

*Plate 629. Vase, 8¾"h.,* THE HIGHLANDS. *Signed: FC (Cirnacty, F.). TM date: 1919–1922. Blank: none. Value: $375.00–450.00.*

*Plate 630. Plate, 8⅜"d.,* PEACOCK. *Signed: E. Challinor (Challinor, Edward S.). TM date: 1919–1922. Blank: Thomas Bavaria. Value: $295.00–375.00.*

*Plate 631. Amphora-shaped vase with open handles, 8½"h.,* PEACOCK. *Signed: FALATEK (Falatek, Louis H.). TM date: 1919–1922. Blank: none. Value: $550.00–695.00.*

*Plate 632. Vase, 8½"h., PEACOCK ON GOLD AND BLACK. Signed: Marker (Marker, Curtis H.). TM date: 1925–1930. Blank: crown TK Czechoslovakia. Value: $395.00–525.00*

*Plate 633. (rear) Small bonbon with single perforated handle, 5"d.,* FRUIT BASKET. *Signed: SAMUELSON (Samuelson, Ester). TM date: 1919–1922. Blank: none. Value: $30.00–45.00. (front) Cream and lidded sugar. Signed: K (Klein, Ingeborg). TM date: 1919–1922. Blank: star wreath, RS, Tillowitz Silesia. Value: $90.00–125.00.*

Plate 635. Center piece bowl and two candlesticks. Gold scroll with flowers. (unsigned). TM date: 1922–1925. Blank: none. Value: $375.00–425.00.

Plate 634. Sauce bowl, ladle, and underplate, MORNING GLORY AOG. (unsigned). TM date: 1922–1925. Blank: overpainted. Value: $175.00–195.00.

Plate 636. Solid-handled bonbon, 6"w x 7"l., BUMBLEBEES ON ETCHED HONEYCOMB. (unsigned). TM date: 1922–1925. Blank: overpainted. Value: $175.00–235.00.

Plate 638. (rear) Compote, footed, 8¾"d., ITALIAN GARDEN. Signed: Yeschek (Yeschek, Joseph T.). TM date: 1922–1925. Blank: none. Value: $200.00–250.00. (front) Bonbon, handled, 5"d., VERSAILLES GARDEN. Signed: BOHMAN (Bohman, Marie). TM date: 1922–1925. Blank: none. Value: $100.00–145.00.

Plate 637. (rear) Plate, 8½"d., INDIAN TREE. Signed: Klein (Klein, Ingeborg). TM date: 1925–1930. Blank: Thomas shield Bavaria. Value: $125.00–155.00. (front) Lidded teapot, lidded sugar, creamer. Signed: Samuelson (Samuelson, Ester). TM date: 1925–1930. Blank: crown Wreath Union T Made In Czecho-Slovakia. Value: $275.00–325.00.

Plate 639. Vase, PHEASANT MEDALLION ON WHITE. Signed: E. Challinor (Challinor, Edward S.). TM date: 1922–1925. Blank: T&V rectangle, Limoges, France. Value: $395.00–595.00.

Plate 640. Cake plate, 10"d., GOLDEN PHEASANT. Signed: E.Challinor (Challinor, Edward S.). TM date: 1922–1925. Blank: T&V rectangle, Limoges, France. Value: $350.00–425.00.

Plate 641. Vase, 8"h. Rose Medallion on MORNING GLORY AOG. Signed: C. Marker (Marker, Curtis H.). TM date: 1922–1925. Blank: overpainted. Value: $250.00–350.00.

Plate 642. Small pedestalled bonbon, 6"d. Rose medallion on MORNING GLORY AOG. Signed: Marker (Marker, Curtis H.). TM date: 1922–1925. Blank: none. Value: $225.00–275.00.

Plate 643. Vase, 9¾"h., CHROMA DECO AND PLANETS AOG. (unsigned). TM date: 1925–1930. Blank: crown H.&Co. Selb Bavaria Heinrich & Co. Value: $375.00–450.00.

Plate 644. Service plates (3), 10¾"d. Scenics with gold scrolling over border. Signed: C.Marker (Marker, Curtis H.). TM date: 1925–1930. Blank: crown H.&Co. Selb Bavaria Heinrich & Co. Value each: $300.00–400.00.

*Plate 645. Small dish with perforated handles, 6¾"d,* <u>ENCRUSTED</u> <u>AOG</u> *with black border of flower sprays. Signed: Rean (Klipphahn, Maxwell Rean). TM date: 1925–1930. Blank: none. Value: $85.00–110.00.*

*Plate 646. AIDA cup and saucer,* <u>ENCRUSTED</u> <u>HONEYSUCKLE</u>. *(unsigned). TM date: 1925–1930. Blank: crown crossed scepters, Rosenthal Selb-Bavaria Aida. Value: $100.00–145.00.*

*Plate 647. (rear) Bonbon, square, 4"w., AOG DAISY. (unsigned). TM date: 1925–1930. Blank: Tillowitz Silesia. Value: $40.00–55.00. (front) VICTORIA cup and saucer,* <u>ROSE</u> <u>AND</u> <u>DAISY</u> <u>AOG</u>. *(unsigned). TM date: 1925–1930. Blank: PMR eagle Bavaria. Value: $35.00–50.00.*

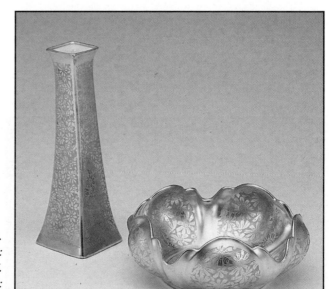

*Plate 648. (left) Bud vase, 6"h.,* <u>ROSE</u> <u>AND</u> <u>DAISY</u> <u>AOG</u>. *(unsigned). TM date: 1925–1930. Blank: none. Value: $95.00–125.00. (right) Bonbon, tulip bowl, 5"d., AOG DAISY. (unsigned). TM date: 1925–1930. Blank: none. Value: $85.00–100.00.*

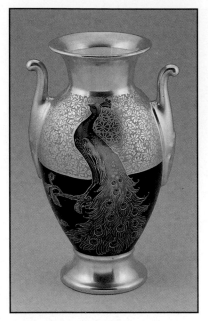

*Plate 651. Vase, 10"h., <u>CHI-NESE</u> <u>PEACOCK</u>. Signed: Weiss (Weissflog, Gustav). TM date: 1925–1930. Blank: H.&Co., Selb Bavaria. Value: $675.00–750.00,*

*Plate 649. Vase, 8"h. Peacock on <u>ROSE</u> <u>AND</u> <u>DAISY</u> <u>AOG</u>. Signed: Marker (Marker, Curtis H.). TM date: 1925–1930. Blank: shield, Thomas Bavaria. Value: $550.00–800.00.*

*Plate 650. Vase, square on ball feet, 6"h. Vellum: wooded road. Signed: Marker (Marker, Curtis H.). TM date: 1925–1930. Blank: Epiag crossed hammers, Czechoslovakia. Value: $325.00–500.00.*

*Plate 652. ISOLDE cream and lidded sugar, ETCHED PEACOCK AND GOLD TRACERY OVER GREEN. (unsigned). TM date: 1925–1930. Blank: Modell von Ph. Rosenthal crown Selb-Bavaria Isolde. Value: $85.00–100.00.*

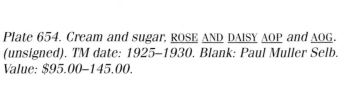

*Plate 653. Bonbon, perforated handle, 7"d. Platinum rose and daisy with gold border. (unsigned). TM date: 1925–1930. Blank: over-painted. Value: $125.00–150.00.*

*Plate 654. Cream and sugar, <u>ROSE</u> <u>AND</u> <u>DAISY</u> <u>AOP</u> and <u>AOG</u>. (unsigned). TM date: 1925–1930. Blank: Paul Muller Selb. Value: $95.00–145.00.*

Plate 655. Tulip-shaped bonbon, 6"d, <u>ROSE</u> <u>AND</u> <u>DAISY</u> <u>AOG</u> and <u>AOP</u>. (unsigned). TM date: 1925–1930. Blank: star wreath, RS, Germany. Value: $120.00–145.00.

Plate 656. Open-handled compote, 8"d. Etched peacock in center medallion, pea green border with <u>GOLD</u> <u>TRACERY</u>, <u>ROSE</u> <u>AND</u> <u>DAISY</u> exterior etch. (unsigned). TM date: 1925–1930. Blank: none. Value: $200.00–245.00.

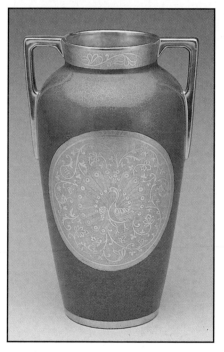

Plate 657. Vase, square-handled, 9½"h., *ETCHED PEACOCK AND GOLD TRACERY OVER GREEN.* (unsigned). TM date: 1925–1930. Blank: crown H&Co., Selb Bavaria. Value: $300.00–365.00.

Plate 658. Small ring-footed bowl with scalloped rim, 6½"d., *PLANETS AOG* with mint green inner bowl scattered with stars. (unsigned). TM date: 1925–1930. Blank: none. Value: $65.00–90.00.

Plate 659. Art Nouveau-style two-compartment handled bonbon, 7½"d., <u>ROSE</u> <u>AND</u> <u>DAISY</u> <u>AOG</u>. (unsigned). TM date: 1925–1930. Blank: none. Value: $45.00–95.00.

*Plate 660. Service plate, 11"d. Vellum scenic in center of pea-green border with gold overpaint. Signed: Marker (Marker, Curtis H.). TM date: 1925–1930. Blank: crown H&Co. Selb Bavaria Heinrich & Co. Value: $250.00–350.00.*

*Plate 662. Two piece (assembled) compote with reticulated rim, 6"d., <u>ROSE</u> <u>AND</u> <u>DAISY</u> <u>AOG</u>. (unsigned). TM date: 1925–1930. Blank: none. Value: $110.00–145.00.*

*Plate 661. Footed bonbon with scalloped rim and upswept, perforated handles, 6"w., <u>ROSE</u> <u>AND</u> <u>DAISY</u> <u>AOG</u> interior and mint green exterior. (unsigned). TM date: 1925–1930. Blank: none. Value: $85.00–110.00.*

*Plate 663. (rear) Lidded coffee, lidded sugar, and creamer. Gold etched daisy and scroll, <u>SILK</u> <u>MOIRÉ</u> <u>AOG</u>, maroon base. (unsigned). TM date: 1925–1930. Blank: star wreath, RS, Germany. Value: $275.00–350.00. (front) Demi-tasse and saucer, 2 sets. (unsigned). TM date: 1925–1930. Blank: star RS wreath, Tillowitz Silesia Value each: $85.00–100.00.*

Plate 664. Nut cups, 3"w. Blue or cream exteriors, gold or cream with floral decal interior. (unsigned). TM date: 1931–1938 (Mark 16). Blank: none. Value: $65.00–75.00.

Plate 665. Dish, small, perforated handles, 5½"d., EDGERTON 160. (unsigned). TM date: 1928–1938 (Mark 13). Blank: none. Value: $100.00–125.00.

Plate 666. (left) Service plate, 11"d., E212-311. (unsigned). TM date: 1928–1938 (Mark 13). Blank: Pickard. Value: $35.00–45.00. (right) Service plate, 11"d., E232-311. (unsigned). TM date: 1928–1938 (Mark 13). Blank: Pickard. Value: $35.00–45.00.

Plate 667. Consumé cup and saucer, 6"d., E1-61. (unsigned). TM date: 1928–1938 (Mark 13). Blank: Royal Bayreuth coat of arms, Bavaria. Value: $35.00–55.00.

Plate 668. Plates, 9"d. All over rose arrangements. Signed: E. Challinor (Challinor, Edward S.). TM date: 1930–1938. Blank: Rosenthal Selb-Bavaria Value each: $175.00–225.00.

Plate 669. (left) Triangular retailer's display marker, 4½"h., *PICKARD CHINA MADE IN U.S.A. gold on ivory. (unsigned). TM date: 1938–present. Blank: Pickard. Value: $65.00–100.00. (center) Scarf dancer flower frog, 6"h. Plain gold. TM date: 1930–1938. Blank: overpainted. Value: $155.00–195.00. (right center) Triangular retailer's display marker, 4½"h., PICKARD CHINA MADE IN U.S.A. gold with blue-lined border on ivory. TM date: 1938–present. Blank: Pickard. Value: $125.00–135.00. (right) Triangular retailer's display marker 4½"h., PICKARD CHINA MADE IN U.S.A. gold on cream (curly-tongued lion). (unsigned). TM date: 1938–present. Blank: Pickard. Value: $85.00–110.00.*

Plate 671. Plates, souvenir, 8"d., CENTURY OF PROGRESS *(various buildings and exhibits). (unsigned). TM date: 1933. Blank: none. Value each: $35.00–55.00.*

Plate 670. Vase, 7½". Mottled green. (unsigned). TM date: 1930–1938. Blank: crown RS, Germany. Value: $145.00–195.00.*

Plate 673. Leaf-shaped bonbon with perforated handle, 7"l., METALLIC GRAPES. *(unsigned). TM date: 1930–1938. Blank: crown shield P.T. Bavaria Tirschenreuth. Value: $135.00–165.00. (Note the very late date for this pattern which originated about 1908.)*

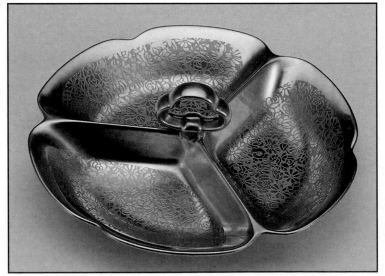

Plate 672. Three-compartment nut dish with center perforated handle, STYLE NO. 749, 6¼"d., ROSE AND DAISY AOG. *(unsigned). TM date: 1930–1938. Blank: Japan. Value: $30.00–45.00.*

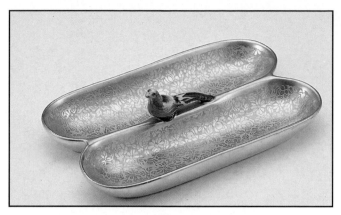

Plate 674. Dual sided cigarette tray with pheasant handle, 6½"l., ROSE AND DAISY AOG with golden pheasant. (unsigned). TM date: 1930–1938. Blank: none. Value: $85.00–125.00.

Plate 677. Bonbon with four rolled handles, 6"d., ROSE AND DAISY AOG. Signed: (unknown). TM date: 1930–1938. Blank: none. Value: $35.00–55.00.

Plate 675. Flower-shaped mayonnaise dish with underplate and ladle, 6¼"d., ROSE AND DAISY AOG. (unsigned). TM date: 1930–1938. Blank: Japan. Value: $125.00–165.00.

Plate 678. Vase, 10½"h. Brown stag on orange and brown ground. Signed: Rhodes (Rhodes, Arnold). TM date: 1930–1938. Blank: Union T CC crown and wreath. Value: $1,300.00–1,400.00.

Plate 676. Scarf dancer flower frog, 6"h. All-over-gold. (unsigned). TM date: 1930–1938. Blank: wreath crown Coronet Registered Germany. Value: $145.00–185.00.

Plate 679. (rear) Charger with perforated tab handles, 10¾"d. Green airbrushed leaf silhouettes on green ground. (unsigned). TM date: 1930–1938. Blank: Hutschenreuther Selb oval lion LHS. Value: $100.00–135.00. (front) Footed bonbon, perforated handles, 6½"d. Gold interior, airbrushed leaves in green on green exterior. (unsigned). TM date: 1930–1938. Blank: star wreath, RS, Germany. Value: $75.00–90.00.

*Plate 680. Vase, 6¾"h. Orange tulips on maroon ground. Signed: Challinor (Challinor, Edward S.). TM date: 1938–present. Blank: Pickard. Value: $265.00–350.00.*

*Plate 681. (left) Plate, rimmed service, 10½"d., YELLOW BOTANY / GLADIOLUS. Signed: Challinor (Challinor, Edward S.). TM date: 1938–present. Blank: Pickard. Value: $85.00–110.00. (right) Plate, 8¼"d., YELLOW BOTANY / MALLOW. Signed: Challinor (Challinor, Edward S.). TM date: 1938–present. Blank: Pickard. Value: $40.00–65.00.*

*Plate 682. (rear) Long-necked vase, style 843, 7¾"h., ROSE AND DAISY AOG. TM date: 1938–present. Blank: Pickard. Value: $50.00–70.00. (left) Oblong, perforated-handle dish, style 241 7"l. TM date: 1938–present. Blank: Pickard. Value: $30.00–45.00. (right) Leaf-shaped celery dish, style 419, 11¼"l. TM date: 1930–1938. Blank: none. Value: $65.00–85.00.*

*Plate 683. Shell-shaped bonbon, 5"l. AOG exterior (no etching), cream interior. TM date: 1938–present. Blank: Pickard. Value: $30.00–50.00.*

*Plate 684. Plate, set of four, 10¾"d., FIRST EDITION FLORAL: PETUNIA, DAHLIA, LILY, TULIP. Signed: E.Challinor (Challinor, Edward S.). TM date: 1938–present. Blank: Pickard. Value each: $165.00–195.00.*

*Note:* The following plates, 684.1 through 684.20 are taken from old Pickard literature wherein pattern names are given, but for which we have found no actual examples.

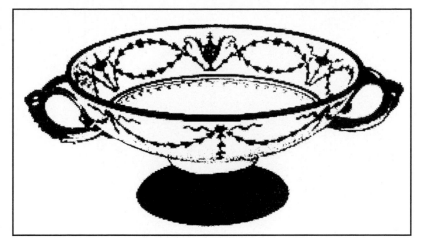

*Plate 684.1.* <u>ADAM</u>.

*Plate 684.2.* <u>ADAM</u> <u>BORDER</u>.

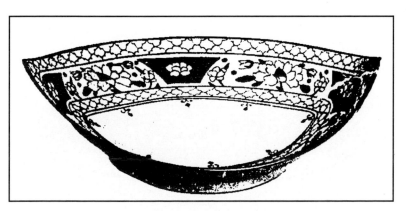

*Plate 684.3.* <u>ATLAN</u> <u>ENAMEL</u>.

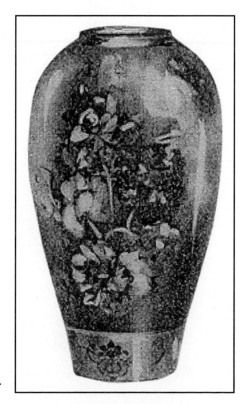

*Plate 684.4.* <u>CHALLINOR</u> <u>GERANIUMS</u>.

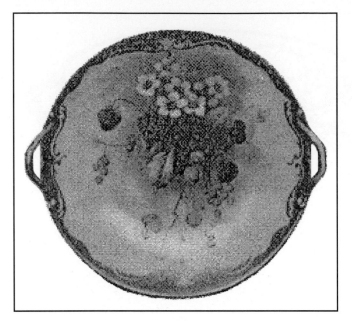

*Plate 684.5.* <u>CHALLINOR</u> <u>MIXED</u> <u>FRUITS</u>.

*Plate 684.5a.* <u>CITRUS</u> <u>FRUITS</u>.

*Plate 684.6.* <u>ENAMELED</u> <u>FLOWERS</u> <u>AND</u> <u>GOLD</u> <u>PANELS</u>.

*Plate 684.7.* <u>FESTOONED</u> <u>FLOWER</u>.

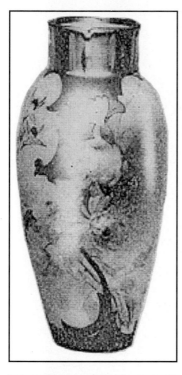

*Plate 684.8.* <u>GR.</u> <u>MUMS</u> <u>AND</u> <u>BIRDS</u>. *(GR. could be Griffiths or Gasper.)*

*Plate 684.11.* <u>PINES</u>.

*Plate 684.9.* <u>M.</u> <u>NASTURTIUM</u> <u>BORDER</u>. *(M. could be Miche, Michel, or Miller.)*

*Plate 684.12.* <u>POINSETTIA</u> <u>AND</u> <u>LUSTRE</u> (2).

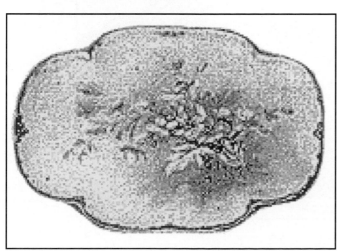

*Plate 684.10.* <u>NATU-RALISTIC</u> <u>BUTTERCUPS</u>.

*Plate 684.13.* POINSETTIAS AND MARGUERITES.

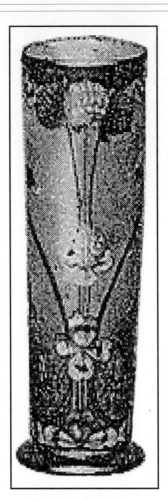

*Plate 684.14.* REURY CLOVER CONVENTIONAL.

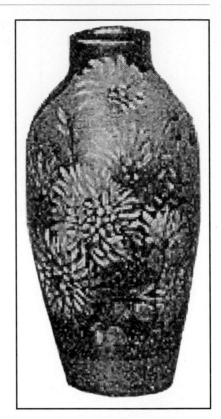

*Plate 684.15.* REURY MUMS.

*Plate 684.16.* SILVER PANSY.

Plate 684.17. <u>TUDOR</u> <u>DESIGN</u>.

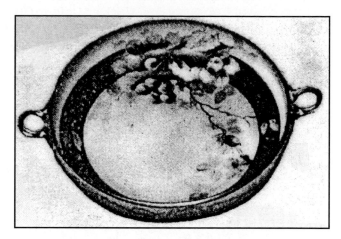

Plate 684.18. <u>VOKRAL</u> <u>CHERRIES</u> <u>IN</u> <u>GOLD</u>.

Plate 684.20. <u>YESCHEK</u> <u>CURRANTS</u> <u>AND</u> <u>PASTE</u>.

Plate 684.19. <u>W</u>. <u>ROSES</u>. *(W. could be Wagner, Walters, or Wight.)*

*Note:* The following plates, 684.21 through 684.32, are etch designs for All-Over-Gold (AOG). These same designs were also used as the etched base for All-Over-Platinum (AOP) ware. They are reproduced here in black and white to facilitate identification. They were applied as the exclusive decoration for chinaware and also in combination with painted panels and borders.

Plate 684.21. ARNICA AOG.

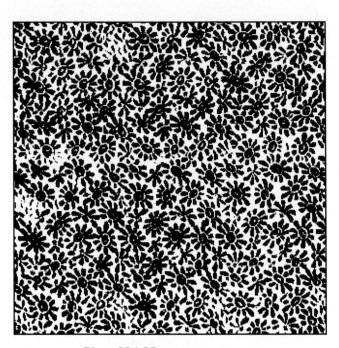

Plate 684.22. ASTER FIELD AOG.

Plate 684.23. DOT AND STAR AOG.

Plate 684.24. FLORAL SCROLL AOG.

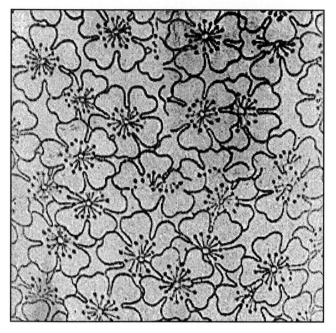

*Plate 684.25.* <u>GOLD</u> <u>TRACERY</u> <u>AOG</u>.

*Plate 684.26.* <u>MORNING</u> <u>GLORY</u> <u>AOG</u>.

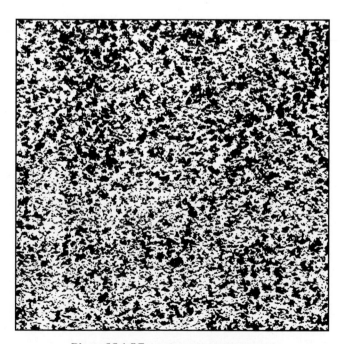

*Plate 684.27.* <u>PLAIN</u> <u>ENCRUSTED</u> <u>AOG</u>.

*Plate 684.28.* PLANETS AOG.

*Plate 684.29.* ROSE AND DAISY AOG.

*Plate 684.30.* ROSE GARDEN AOG.

*Plate 684.31.* SILK MOIRÉ AOG.

*Plate 684.32.* TRAILING VINE AOG.

Index to Pickard Pattern names by plate numbers or advertisement number.

ADAM......684.1
ADAM BORDER......684.2
ALEXANDER ROSES......No example available
AMARYLLIS AND ETCHED GOLD......333, 334
ANTIQUE CHINESE ENAMEL......507, 506
ANTIQUE DAY LILIES......120
ANTIQUE ENAMELS......563, 580, 581
APPLE BLOSSOM BOWER......174
ARABIAN......28, 134, 135, 136
ARNICA AOG......684.21
ARROW MAKER......65
ARROW ROOT ON GREEN LUSTRE......352
ASTER FIELD AOG......684.22
ASTORS (sic) BLUE ENCRUSTED......558.1
ATLAN ENAMEL......684.3
AURA ARGENTA HYACINTHUS......466
AURA ARGENTA LINEAR...347, 348, 349, 350, 351, 425, ......566, 567
AURA MOSAIC......448, 449, 450, 451, 452, 533, 534
AUTUMN ARBOR......357
AUTUMN BIRCHES......477
AUTUMN BLACKBERRIES AND GOLD PASTE......79
AUTUMN BORDER (Pat. No. 37,323)......175, 180
AUTUMN CURRANTS......385, 386, 387
AUTUMN GRAPES AND MATTE GREEN......299
AUTUMN STREAM......474
B.P.O.E.......296
BIRCHES......541
BLACK AND ORANGE CONVENTIONAL......295
BLACKBERRY CONVENTIONAL......148
BLOSSOM TIME......234
BLUE ROSE AND DAISY......621
BLUEBELLS ON GOLD......462
BLUEBELLS......225
BORDER PRIMAVERA......489
BORDURE ANTIQUE......527, 528
BORDURE CHINOISE......482
BOUQUET SATSUMA......583
BROKEN FRET, THE......adv. no. 35
BULL-HEAD LILIES......169
BUMBLEBEES ON ETCHED HONEYCOMB......636
BUTTERCUP CONVENTIONAL......263, 265, 266
BUTTERFLIES AND ETCHED GOLD......613
BUTTERFLY......144, 145
CALLA LILIES......363, 364, 365, 366, 532
CALLA LILY......261, 262
CAMELS AT OASIS......319
CAMPANULA......501, 502, 503
CAPE COD FISHERMAN......67
CAPERCAILZIE......38
CARNATION AND BLACK......377
CARNATION AND PLATINUM......344
CARNATION AND RAISED GOLD...215, 216, 217, 218, 219
CARNATION CONVENTIONAL (Pat. No. 37,170)......89, 90, ......91, 206
CARNATION GARDEN......138, 140
CARNATIONS, LUSTRE, AND MATTE GREEN......446, 447
CARP POOL......71
CASTLE MERE......585
CATTLE BY A HIGHLAND LAKE......57
CELTIC DECORATION......341
CENTURY OF PROGRESS......671
CHALLINOR GERANIUMS......684.4
CHALLINOR HOLLYHOCKS......163, 169
CHALLINOR MIXED FRUITS......684.5
CHALLINOR NASTURTIUMS......196, 390
CHEROKEE ROSE BORDER......442
CHEROKEE ROSE......435
CHERRIES AND GOLD......125
CHERRY BRANCH......109
CHERRY LATTICE (Pat. No. 37,352)......83
CHEVALIER......24
CHINESE PEACOCK......651
CHINESE PHEASANT......604, 605
CHIPPENDALE......adv. no. 40
CHROMA DECO AND PLANETS AOG......643
CHRYSANTHEMUMS, LUSTRE AND GOLD......310
CHRYSANTHEMUMS, LUSTRE AND MATTE RED 307, 308, 309
CHRYSANTHEMUMS, LUSTRE, AND MATTE PEACH......445
CITADEL, THE......68
CITRUS FRUITS......684.5a
CLASSIC RUINS BY MOONLIGHT......596
CLASSIC RUINS......594
CLOVER BLOSSOMS AND HONEY BEE......142
CLOVER CONVENTIONAL......253
COLONIAL DECORATION......484
CONVOLVULVUS......500, 504
CORNFLOWER AND ROYAL BLUE......222
CORNFLOWER CONVENTIONAL (1)......167, 168
CORNFLOWER CONVENTIONAL (1)/pink......167
CORNFLOWER CONVENTIONAL (2)......166, 223, 224, 226
COUFALL GRAPES AND ETCH BORDER......260
CRAB APPLE BLOSSOMS......130, 131
CRAB APPLES IN GOLD ON MATTE GREEN......305
CROCUS CONVENTIONAL......14, 15, 50
CYCLAMEN......157, 158, 159, 160, 161
DAHLIA AND RAISED GOLD WITH LUSTRE......430
DAHLIA RUBRA......455, 456
DAISIES IN GOLD PASTE ON GREEN LUSTRE......251
DAISY AOG......647, 648
DAISY CONVENTIONAL......512

DAISY MULTIFLORA .......................................................418

DESERTED GARDEN.........549, 550, 551, 552, 553, 561

DOT AND STAR AOG ..............................................684.23

DUCHESS OF DEVONSHIRE.....................................608

DUTCH DECORATION.....................................485, 486

(also THE DUTCH BISQUE)

DUTCH WINDMILL.......................................................321

EASTER LILY ..............................183, 184, 284, 285

EGYPTIAN DESIGN .....................................................392

EGYPTIAN PAPYRUS AND LUSTRE ......................86

ENAMEL CHRYSANTHEMUMS ...............................460

(also CHRYSANTHEMUM IN ENAMEL and
CONVENTIONALIZED CHRYSANTHEMUM)

ENAMEL GRAPES AND LEAVES ...............336, 337

ENAMELED FLORAL MEDALLION .......................582

ENAMELED FLOWERS AND GOLD PANELS ....684.6; pcs. 66,
.......................................................67, 68 in adv. no. 8

ENAMELED PEONIES AND PHEASANT....................505, 508

ENCHANTED FOREST .................................................542

ENCRUSTED FRUIT .....................................................556

ENCRUSTED HONEYSUCKLE ...............526, 529, 646

ENCRUSTED LINEAR, ROSE AND DAISY AOG.................616

ENCRUSTED LINEAR .....................453, 454, 530, 531

ETCHED GOLD PEACOCK ON BLUE ....................610

ETCHED PANEL AND ROSES.........................adv. no. 33

ETCHED PEACOCK AND GOLD TRACERY OVER GREEN..652, 657

EVENING SPREADS HER MANTLE ..........................25

EVERGLADES.................................................................475

FALSTAFF .......................................................................318

FESTOONED FLOWER .........................................684.7

FIRST EDITION FLORAL: PETUNIA, DAHLIA, LILY, TULIP....684

FISHER PANSIES AND RAISED GOLD .........................233

FISHING BOAT, HOLLAND 1909.............................316

FLORA GEOMETRICA .................................................255

FLORA GOLD AND WHITE .......................................343

FLORA LINEAR............................................................428

FLORA POLYCHROME..............................................421

FLORA PRIMAVERA....................................................432

FLORAL SCROLL AOG .........................................684.24

FLORAL SCROLL .........................................................598

FLORENTINE ................................................................359

FLORIDA LAGOON......................................................545

FLORIDA MOONLIGHT .........................472, 596, 597

FORGET-ME-NOTS .....................................................423

FRUIT BASKET .............................................................633

FRUIT PANELS ....................................................555, 562

FRUITS LINEAR ...................................................555, 564

FUCHS POPPIES ...........................................................373

GIBSON IRIS...................................................................241

GIBSON NARCISSUS...................................................191

GIBSON PANSIES ...........................................................87

GIFFORD POPPIES ............................................281, 282

GIFFORD SHOOTING STARS....................155, 156

GIFFORD TULIPS ........................................................395

GINKHO [sic] LEAF ...............................................181, 182

GOLD TRACERY AOG................................656, 684.25

GOLDEN CLOVER......................................443, 513

GOLDEN PHEASANT with ROSE AND DAISY AOG ...........627

GOLDEN PHEASANT ....................626, 628, 640

GOOSEBERRY CONVENTIONAL ..........................124

GR. MUMS AND BIRDS .......................................684.8

GRAPE ARBOR ............................................................565

GRAPES IN PANEL......................................................444

GRAPES IN PLATINUM AND GOLD.....................405

HARVEST IN RAISED GOLD AND WHITE.................338, 340

HAWTHORNE ...............................................................548

HAZELNUT CONVENTIONAL................................177

HAZELNUTS.........................................................178, 179

HENRY VI AS A CHILD.............................................58

HESSLER VIOLET BOUQUET....................88, 188

HIGHLANDS, THE ......................................................629

HILLSIDE EDEN PARK .............................................544

HONEYSUCKLE DESIGN .........................................294

HOPS IN LUSTRE AND MATTE GREEN .............300, 302

HUMMING BIRD AND GOLD .................................619

HYACINTHUS.......................................................464, 465

IDEALISTIC, THE ..........................................adv. no.51

INDIAN TREE ...............................................................637

IRIS AND RAISED GOLD WITH LUSTRE.........242, 243, 244

IRIS CONVENTIONAL ...............................30, 33, 45, 92

IRIS LINEAR .................................................................415

ITALIAN GARDEN ............................................584, 638

JAPANESE WOMAN WITH COMB .........................66

JELINEK MORNING GLORIES ...............................203

JELINEK ROSES............................................................77

JEWELED FLORA IN RAISED GOLD ....................342

LAKES OF KILLARNEY ................................adv. no.32

LEON POPPIES ............................................................202

LILIUM ORNATUM .....................416, 417, 518, 519

(also LILY ORNATUM)

LILY PALMATE..................................................297, 298

LION.................................................................................56

LOUIS XIV......................................................................572

LUSTRE GRAPES AND LEAVES ...................381, 383, 384

(also LUSTRE GRAPES)

M. NASTURTIUM BORDER....................................684.9

MARIGOLDS .........................................209, 210, 211

METALLIC GRAPES.....................................382, 673

MICHEL TULIPS CONVENTIONAL .....................194

MIDNIGHT.....................................................................470

MODERN CONVENTIONAL.......................173, 360, 361

MOOR WITH TIGER...................................................54

MOORISH DESIGN.....................276, 277, 278, 279

MORNING GLORY AOG...........................634, 684.26

MORNING GLORY TRELLIS............................................74
NASTURTIUM CONVENTIONAL .............................17, 126
NATURALISTIC BUTTERCUPS...............................684.10
NATURALISTIC PEACHES .......................................116
NAVAJO .................................................................406
NEW ARABIAN .......................................................212
NEW IRIS CONVENTIONAL .................31, 93, 97, 98, 100
NUT HARVEST ........................................................272
OLD DUTCH MILL ..................................................322
OLD FASHIONED FLOWERS ....................................560
ON THE NILE AT BENI HASSEN - EGYPT - 1909 .............313
ORANGE TREE CONVENTIONAL ..........................355, 461
(also ORANGE TREE DECORATION and ORANGE TREE ENAMEL)
ORANGE TREE PANELS............................................111
ORANGES AND ROCOCO GOLD PASTE......................114
ORCHIDS AND GOLD PASTE ....................................213
ORIENTAL BIRD......................................................623
ORNAMENTAL MOSAIC BORDER .......No example available
PANEL DRESDEN AND RAISED GOLD..........................498
PASTEL ROSE AND SILVER......................................431
PASTEL ROSES.......................................................569
PATRICIAN WOMAN..................................................59
PEACHES LINEAR ...........................................232, 441
PEACOCK AND ROSE AND DAISY AOG.......................631
PEACOCK ON GOLD AND BLACK ..............................632
PEACOCK ......................................................630, 631
PEONY CONVENTIONAL ...........................................467
PERSIAN DECORATION ..............................................27
PHEASANT MEDALLION ON WHITE ...........................639
PHEASANT ON BLACK AND GOLD ENCRUSTED ...............559
PHEASANT ..............................................................39
PILGRIM DECORATION..............................................487
PINE CONE ...........................................................259
PINES .................................................................684.11
PINK ENAMEL FLOWERS................................adv. no. 29
PINK TWIN POPPY...........................401, 402, 403, 404
PLAIN ENCRUSTED AOG......................................684.27
PLANETS AOG.............................................658, 684.28
PLATINUM ROSE AND DAISY WITH GOLD BORDER ..........653
PLOVER ..................................................................40
PLUM BRANCH......................................................110
POINSETTIA AND LUSTRE (2) ...........................684.12
POINSETTIA AND LUSTRE........................141, 164, 367
POINSETTIA CONVENTIONAL ...................................439
POINSETTIA PENDANT............................................468
POINSETTIAS AND MARGUERITES ........................684.13
POND LILY AND LUSTRE ........................................283
POND LILY.......................................................76, 220
POPPIES IN GOLD..................................................199
POPPIES LINEAR ...................................................440
POPPIES .................................................................599
POPPY....................................................................19

POPPY AND BLACK .........................................200, 201
POPPY AND DAISY .................368, 369, 370, 409, 410
POPPY AND SERPENTINE PASTE .............................514
POPPY CONVENTIONAL AND BLACK...........................376
POPPY CONVENTIONAL ...........................................371
POPPY IRIDESCENT .................................................372
PRAYING MOHAMMEDAN...........................................52
PURPLE GRAPES AND ETCHED GOLD BORDER................80
PURPLE GRAPES AND MATTE GREEN....pc. 49 in adv. no. 7
PURPLE GRAPES AND POMEGRANATES........................557
RAISED GOLD DAISY ..............................................346
RASPBERRIES AND ETCHED GOLD.............................129
RASPBERRY NOUVEAU (Pat. No. 37,322).................127
REAN CARNATIONS AND GOLD .................................407
REAN PEARS ...................................................122, 123
REAN PINK MUMS...........................................102, 137
REAN PLUMS.........................................................258
RED AND BLUE PARAKEETS ON MATTE GREEN...............311
RED AND GOLD POINSETTIAS AND LUSTRE....................245
REGENCY WATER LILIES .........................................190
REURY CLOVER CONVENTIONAL..........................684.14
REURY LILY CONVENTIONAL ....................................171
REURY MUMS.....................................................684.15
ROCOCO SCROLLS AND ETCHED BORDER..........adv. no. 34
ROSA EMERALDUS ...............................303, 304, 306
ROSE AND DAISY AOG ....614, 647, 648, 654, 659, 662,
...................................672, 675, 677, 682, 684.29
ROSE AND DAISY AOG /P ......................................655
ROSE AND DAISY AOP............................................622
ROSE BASKET .......................................................571
ROSE BASKET/ TRAILING VINE AOG .........................625
ROSE BOWER ........................................................133
ROSE FESTOONS .....................................................11
ROSE GARDEN AOG...........................................684.30
ROSE GARLAND ROCOCO ..........................................34
ROSE MEDALLION ON MORNING GLORY AOG................641
ROSELAND..............................................................554
RUSSIAN DESIGN ...................................................420
RUSSIAN FLOWERS .................................................570
SAILBOATS IN VENICE HARBOR ................................315
SALSIFY.................................................................331
SANTA MARIA DELLA SALUTE...................................317
SCHONER LEMONS...................................................115
SCILLA CAMPANULA ................................................326
SCOTCH ...............................................412, 413, 414
SEASONS, THE........................................................323
SEIDEL PURPLE GRAPES .........................................205
SEVILLE...............................No example available
SHAMROCK.....................................................570, 573
SHERATON, THE......................................................571
SILK MOIRÉ AOG.............................................663, 684.31
SILVER PANSY.............................................434, 684.16

| | |
|---|---|
| *SOUVENIR OF FLORIDA* | 543 |
| <u>SPRING</u> <u>BLOSSOMS</u> | No example available |
| *SPRINGTIME* | 249 |
| *SUMMER MEADOW* | 154 |
| *THISTLES IN PASTE* | 358 |
| *TOMASCHEKO EDELWEISS BORDER* | 227 |
| *TOMASCHEKO* <u>FLORAL</u> *BORDER* | 147 |
| *TOMASCHEKO POPPY BORDER* | 228, 229, 230 |
| *TORCELLO <u>CANAL</u> <u>AND</u> <u>CHURCH</u>* | 314 |
| *TRACERY AND BLUE LUSTRE* | 609, 611 |
| <u>TRAILING</u> <u>VINE</u> <u>AOG</u> | 684.32 |
| <u>TRIPLE</u> <u>TULIP</u> (<u>YELLOW</u> & <u>RED</u>) | 510 |
| <u>TRIPLE</u> <u>TULIP</u> (<u>YELLOW</u> & <u>WHITE</u>) | 419, 509 |
| *TRUMPET FLOWERS AND TRELLIS* | 238, 239 |
| <u>TUDOR</u> <u>DESIGN</u> | 684.17 |
| <u>TULIP</u> <u>CONVENTIONAL</u> | 32, 94, 95, 96, 97, 99, 254 |
| *TULIP GARDEN* | 139 |
| <u>TULIP</u> <u>IN</u> <u>LUSTRE</u> | 235, 236, 424 |
| *TULIP MODERNE* | 4 |
| *TWILIGHT* | 547, 606 |
| *TWIN LILIES* | 438, 539 |
| <u>TWIN</u> <u>POPPY</u> | 373, 374 |
| *TWIN TULIP* | 286, 287, 288, 289, 290 |
| *VENETIAN <u>RENAISSANCE</u>* | 491, 492 |
| *VENICE* | 315 |
| *VERSAILLES <u>GARDEN</u>* | 638 |
| *VIOLET BORDER* | 538 |
| *VIOLET NOUVEAU* | 339 |
| <u>VIOLET</u> <u>SUPREME</u> | 522, 523, 524, 525 |
| *VIOLETS AND LUSTRE* | 280 |
| <u>VIOLETS</u> <u>IN</u> <u>PANEL</u> | 422 |
| *VOBORNIK CHRYSANTHEMUMS* | 101 |
| <u>VOKRAL</u> <u>CHERRIES</u> <u>IN</u> <u>GOLD</u> | 684.18 |
| *W. ROSES* | 684.19 |
| <u>WALLED</u> <u>GARDEN</u> | 546, 595 |
| *WATER LILY CONVENTIONAL* | 426, 427, 520 |
| *WATERLILIES AND ENCRUSTED GOLD* | 617 |
| <u>WEIGELAS</u> (<u>GREEN</u>) | 221 |
| <u>WEIGELAS</u> (<u>PINK</u>) | 221, 463 |
| *WHITE DAY LILIES* | 328 |
| <u>WHITE</u> <u>MORNING</u> <u>GLORIES</u> | pcs. 57, 58 in adv. no. 8 |
| *WHITE POPPY AND DAISY* | 408, 511, 515, 516, 517 |
| *WHITE VIOLETS LINEAR* | 521 |
| <u>WIGHT</u> <u>TULIPS</u> | 207 |
| <u>WILD</u> <u>FLOWERS</u> <u>OF</u> <u>AMERICA</u>: <u>FIELD</u> <u>POPPIES</u>, <u>FORGET-ME-NOTS</u>, <u>WHEAT</u> | 437 |
| <u>WILD</u> <u>FLOWERS</u> <u>OF</u> <u>AMERICA</u>: <u>DAISIES</u>, <u>BUTTERCUPS</u>, <u>FORGET-ME-NOTS</u> | 436 |
| <u>WILD</u> <u>FLOWERS</u> <u>OF</u> <u>AMERICA</u>: <u>VIOLETS</u> | 327 |
| <u>WILDWOOD</u> | 473, 476, 588 |
| <u>WISCONSIN</u> <u>DELLS</u> | 586 |
| <u>YELLOW</u> <u>BOTANY</u> / <u>GLADIOLUS</u> | 681 |
| <u>YELLOW</u> <u>BOTANY</u> / <u>MALLOW</u> | 681 |
| <u>YELLOW</u> <u>CHERRIES</u> <u>AND</u> <u>MATTE</u> <u>GREEN</u> | 301 |
| *YELLOW IRIS CONVENTIONAL* | 264 |
| <u>YELLOW</u> <u>ROSE</u> | 237 |
| <u>YESCHEK</u> <u>CURRANTS</u> <u>AND</u> <u>PASTE</u> | 684.20 |
| <u>YESCHEK</u> <u>CURRANTS</u> <u>IN</u> <u>GOLD</u> | 353 |
| *YESCHEK RASPBERRIES* | 48, 49 |
| *YESCHEK STRAWBERRIES IN GOLD* | 271 |
| <u>YOSEMITE</u> <u>FALLS</u> | 589, 593, 594 |
| *ZINNIAS AND BLUE ON ENCRUSTED GOLD* | 624 |

# JULIUS H. BRAUER STUDIO, 1903–1926

## Kay-Bee China Works 1922–1928

Julius H. Brauer was born in Germany in 1870. He emigrated to the United States in 1890, settling initially in New Jersey where in 1892, he married a girl two years his junior. Marie Brauer had also come from Germany in 1890, so it is possible that their friendship could have begun before they arrived in New Jersey. No record of his employment in Trenton has been found; however, it seems likely that Brauer worked for one of the potteries there, thus becoming aware of Pickard's solicitations for china artists.

At any event, Brauer was an early respondent, and by 1902 he was in Chicago decorating china for Pickard. But Pickard had not yet taken possession of the carriage barn, so Brauer decorated Pickard's china blanks in his home. Pickard then collected the decorated pieces, fired them, and sold them. Compelled by this arrangement to establish a limited home studio, Brauer was not long in perceiving the potential in a complete studio of his own; his stay with Pickard lasted only about 18 months.

By 1903 he was advertising his own studio at 1570 Lill Street, which was also his home. Marie was also a skillful china artist, so the two of them probably accounted for all of the studio's output for a number of years. Julius probably split his time between decorating and selling, while Marie would have been occupied with both decorating and raising their ten-year old son. Both husband and wife employed a conservative, naturalistic style with their designs, insuring a modest growth for the studio's early years. Marie's violets were very well executed (Plate 688) and far beyond the trite renditions of her contemporaries. Julius had a superior talent for making the features of the china blank and his painted designs reinforce each other; a fine example of this is the covered casserole shown in Plate 708.

Without a sales organization such as Pickard's, however, Brauer's studio grew much more slowly and remained a home operation for its first seven years. Nevertheless, by about 1906 Brauer's business had grown to include a number of additional artists. These artists worked as outside cottage workers in much the same manner as Brauer had worked for Pickard, and because of the constant pick-up and delivery required by this arrangement, they often took residence near the studio, just as Pickard's artists had done prior to 1905. Among them were some of Pickard's best artists: Edward Challinor, Harry Griffiths, Joseph Beitler, Carl Koenig, and Max Bachmann.

Joseph Beitler had worked for Pickard and had also operated his own studio in the Chicago Loop; he worked for Brauer a short time, producing some of the very few figural designs known to have the Brauer mark (Plate 701).

Max Bachmann was an early Brauer recruit, and was the only artist to remain with Brauer for the rest of the studio's existence. Both Brauer and Bachmann brought Arabian designs with them from Pickard and these designs were popular for many years. In 1910 Brauer turned his Hamilton Court residence completely into studio facilities, and moved about two miles northwest to live at 3812 N. Hamlin Avenue. Julius Brauer died in 1925, but the studio continued to operate for one more year, probably under the guidance of Marie Brauer and her son, Walter.

Bachmann moved close to the Brauer studios in 1911, and was employed there through the balance of its existence and then continued with the surviving studio, the Kay-Bee China Company.

It is evident that Bachmann suffered the same pressures on his income that other china decorators experienced from the 1920s onward. After working all day at Kay-Bee, he would come home and work evenings making additional pieces. Much of this china included etched designs so his family had to endure the disagreeable odor of asphaltum along with turpentine and linseed oil. Bachmann had no kiln of his own, and the kitchen stove was often pressed into service to speed the paint-drying process. On the weekends he would make the long trip to the South Side of Chicago with these pieces where he would

Photo courtesy R. Koenig.

*Figure 44. Carl Koenig at work in Brauer studio with Max Bachmann (possibly) in background.*

work for Carl Koenig after Koenig left Brauer.

"China decorators in those days had strong bonds to each other and their families," recalled Evelyn Bachmann. "On some Sundays they would go out to Budlong Woods or elsewhere to do still-life sketching, mainly for recreation."

Bachmann did much freelancing, selling individual pieces to the china wholesalers in downtown Chicago. He was still decorating china when he died March 21, 1941, at the age of 65.

Kay-Bee China Works originated in 1922 with Frederick Kammermayer as president, Julius Brauer as secretary, and a civil engineer who operated a chimney company, Heinrich Heine as the treasurer. Frederick "Fritz" Kammermayer had joined the Brauer studio about 1908, and had produced a considerable amount of good commercial work in those years. The precise arrangement of this parallel venture is not known, but it was possibly intended as an outlet for Brauer's production since it was always advertised as a wholesaler. In 1925 and 1926 Kay-Bee boasted a display room in the Chicago Loop at 111 West Washington Boulevard and a factory at 5210 Northwest Highway. It ceased operation in 1928, probably as a result of Julius Brauer's demise. Only one piece of Kay-Bee china has been discovered to date.

## Artists associated with the Brauer Studio

| | |
|---|---|
| Max L. Bachmann* | F. R. Gross |
| Edward C. Barges* | Frederick "Fritz" |
| Joseph C. Beitler* | Kammermayer |
| Walter Bitterly* | Carl F. Koenig* |
| Boch | Max |
| Julius H. Brauer* | Arnold Rhodes* |
| Marie Brauer | Ritter |
| A. Burton* | Rold |
| Edward S. Challinor* | C. Roy |
| Chevalier | George B. St. Clair |
| Cowan | George W. Stahl* |
| Harry R. Griffiths* | |

*Also a Pickard artist.*

## Brauer Trademarks
*(Dates are approximations.)*

Compared with Pickard and Stouffer, the population of surviving Brauer china pieces is quite small, and it is therefore difficult to date Brauer's trademarks with much accuracy. The dating is further complicated by Brauer's use of a rubber stamp which he appeared to use after about 1910 whenever a supply of decals ran out. The red rubber stamp therefore appears with green and black decals. For a short period of time he used gold under his black mark to obliterate the country of origin mark. Somewhat later, he mixed a black rubber stamp with black decals, but in a few instances, both black and red ink are evident in the same mark.

> BRAUER'S
> HAND PAINTED
> CHINA

Mark 1. 1903–1904, ¾", red stamp.

Mark 4. 1910–1916, ⅝"w., red decal and stamp.

> JUL. H. BRAUER
> HAND PAINTED
> CHICAGO

Mark 2. 1904–1905, ¾", red stamp.

Mark 3. 1905–1910, ⅝"w., green decal.

Mark 5. 1911–1926, ⅝"w., black decal and stamp.

## Brauer Plates

Plate 685. Plate, 8½"d. Three orange poppies in three clusters, gold border and gold center. Signed: Rhodes (Rhodes, Arnold). TM date: 1910–1916. Blank: Haviland, France. Value: $85.00–95.00.

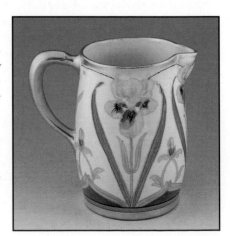

Plate 686. Milk pitcher, 6"h. Three yellow irises with green leaves and pink stems. Signed: B. (Bachmann, Max L.). TM date: 1911–1924. Blank: GDA, France. Value: $135.00–155.00.

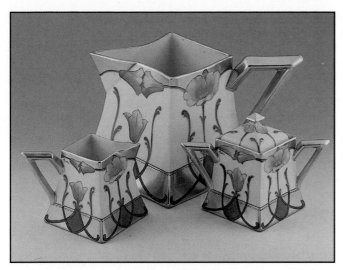

Plate 687. Pitcher, lidded sugar and creamer. Orange Poppies on gold border, red shield, green stems. Signed: Rhodes. (Rhodes, Arnold). TM date: 1910–1916. Blank: D&Co., France. Value: $325.00–365.00.

Plate 690. Small bowl, open-handled, 5¼"d. Blackberries on beige ground with gold outlining. Signed: Grifs. (Griffiths, Harry R.). TM date: 1905–1910. Blank: T&V rectangle, Limoges, France Déposé. Value: $85.00–100.00.

Plate 688. Relish, oblong, perforated handles and side rims, 9"l. Violet clusters on cream, pale green center, gilt edges. Signed: MBRAUER (Brauer, Marie). TM date: 1905–1910. Blank: R.C. crown, crossed swords, Bavaria. Value: $35.00–55.00.

Plate 691. Plate, 8½"d. Three blackberry sprays on pale green/brown leaves, white blossoms. Signed: F.Kammer. (Kammermayer, Fritz). TM date: 1910–1916. Blank: crown H&Co., Bavaria. Value: $55.00–65.00.

Plate 689. Syrup with lid and underplate, 3½"h. Holly with red berries on cream ground. Signed: JEC (unknown). TM date: 1905–1910. Blank: T&V Limoges, France. Value: $85.00–110.00.

*Plate 692. Desert plate, scalloped, Louise, 6"d. Violet cluster on green/cream ground, gold rim, white border. Signed: MBRAUER (Brauer, Marie). TM date: 1905–1910. Blank: J&C Louise Bavaria. Value: $10.00–18.00.*

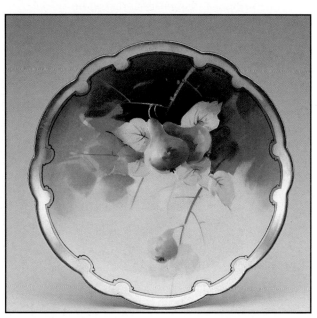

*Plate 693. Plate, 8¾"d. Red/orange tulips with butterfly on inner gold ring, lustre ground. Signed: F.R. Gross (Gross, F. R.). TM date: 1905–1910. Blank: Haviland, France. Value: $45.00–65.00.*

*Plate 694. Plate, scalloped, 7"d. Pear tree branch on orange ground. Signed: Stahl (Stahl, George W.). TM date: 1905–1910. Blank: Limoges, France. Value: $35.00–45.00.*

*Plate 695. (rear) Desert plate, 6½"d. Medium blue border with gold scrolls, red and gold center scrolls. (unsigned). TM date: 1910–1916. Blank: none. Value: $10.00–15.00. (front) Muffineer, straight-sided, 4½"h. Medium blue border with gold and red scrolls, white base. (unsigned). TM date: 1910–1916. Blank: crowned shield HC Royal Bavaria Patent Applied For. Value: $75.00–95.00.*

Plate 696. (rear) Plate, 8½"d. Arabian-decorated gold border, green, red, gold scrolls inner border. Signed: B. (Bachmann, Max L.). TM date: 1910–1916. Blank: Haviland, France. Value: $45.00–65.00. (front) Stein, 6"h. Arabian-style embellished gold border above embellished maroon ground. Signed: Bachman (Bachmann, Max L.). TM date: 1905–1910. Blank: none. Value: $130.00–155.00.

Plate 697. Bowl, turned-in perforated handles, 5"d. Platinum band with white flowers, gold stems, cream ground. Signed: MB (Bachmann, Max L.). TM date: 1911–1924. Blank: none. Value: $40.00–65.00.

Plate 698. Lidded cream and sugar, small Poinsettias on dark green border, green leaves, gold banding, cream ground. Signed: AB. (Burton, A.). TM date: 1910–1916. Blank: none. Value: $125.00–145.00.

Plate 700. Vase, 7"h. Poinsettias, green stylized leaves, black base border. Signed: B (Bachmann, Max L.). TM date: 1910–1916. Blank: none. Value: $375.00–475.00.

Plate 699. Plate, scalloped edges, 8½"d. Five radiused poinsettias on green leaves, gold border. Signed: BRAUER (Brauer, Julius H.). TM date: 1905–1910. Blank: crossed flowers, J&C Louise. Value: $95.00–125.00.

Plate 701. Vase, canteen shaped with arched handles and narrow mouth, 8"h. Art Nouveau woman's portrait, double sided. Signed: JCBeitler (Beitler, Joseph C.). TM date: 1910–1916. Blank: Haviland, France. Value: $250.00–325.00.

Plate 702. Ring-based bowl, regency-style, 9¼"d. Strawberry spray, variegated leaves on red/brown ground. Signed: EChallinor. (Challinor, Edward S.). TM date: 1910–1916. Blank: T&V rectangle, Limoges, France. Value: $395.00–495.00.

Plate 703. Plate, scalloped edge, 8½"d. Three strawberry clusters on green leaves radiused to center, cream ground. Signed: JBRAUER (Brauer, Julius H.). TM date: 1905–1910. Blank: none. Value: $75.00–95.00.

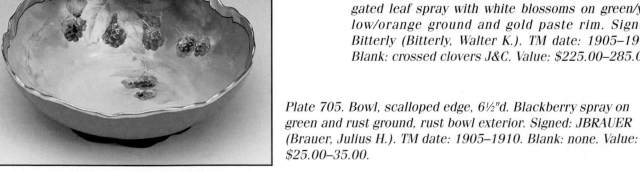

Plate 704. ROMA jug, 6½"h. Blackberries on variegated leaf spray with white blossoms on green/yellow/orange ground and gold paste rim. Signed: Bitterly (Bitterly, Walter K.). TM date: 1905–1910. Blank: crossed clovers J&C. Value: $225.00–285.00.

Plate 705. Bowl, scalloped edge, 6½"d. Blackberry spray on green and rust ground, rust bowl exterior. Signed: JBRAUER (Brauer, Julius H.). TM date: 1905–1910. Blank: none. Value: $25.00–35.00.

*Plate 706. Nappy, hex-scalloped, 5¼"d. Strawberry spray on red and green ground; gold edge with black outlining. Signed: A. Burton (Burton, A.). TM date: 1905–1910. Blank: T&V Limoges, France. Value: $65.00–90.00.*

*Plate 707. PEERLESS cup and saucer. Violet and white violet clusters on lavender border. Signed: Max (Max). TM date: 1910–1916. Blank: bowman on horse Peerless, crossed clovers J&C Bavaria green (2 marks). Value: $25.00–35.00.*

*Plate 708. Covered casserole, open handles, ornate, 8"d. Pink and red poppies on cream ground, green leaves; feathered, French-style gold trim. Signed: JBrauer (Brauer, Julius H.). TM date: 1905–1910. Blank: GDA, France. Value: $350.00–425.00.*

*Plate 709. Plate, 9½"d. Moorish geometric. Signed: JB (Brauer, Julius H.). TM date: 1905–1910. Blank: BMdeM Limoges, France. Value: $65.00–85.00.*

*Plate 710. (left) Plate, 8¼"d. Six red and pink orchids with green leaves on gold border with stems radiused to center. Signed: M.B. (Bonn, M.). TM date: 1905–1910. Blank: none. Value: $75.00–95.00. (right) Muffineer, 4½"h. Red and pink orchids on cream ground, gold top. Signed: MBonn (Bonn, M.). TM date: 1905–1910. Blank: none. Value: $75.00–95.00.*

Plate 711. Whiskey jug with porcelain/cork stopper and shot cup, 6"h. Corn cobs on russet ground. Signed: F.K. (Kammermayer, Fritz). TM date: 1910–1916. Blank: T&V rectangle, Limoges, France. Value: $300.00–375.00.

Plate 713. Muffineer, 4¼"h. Three clusters of purple, lavender, and white pansies with trailing green stems and gold tendrils on cream ground with gold top. Signed: B (Brauer, Julius H.). TM date: 1905–1910. Blank: none. Value: $100.00–145.00.

Plate 712. Hatpin holder, 4½"h. Gladiolus on gold border with pink-green ground and leaf pendants. Signed: Rhodes (Rhodes, Arnold). TM date: 1910–1916. Blank: GDA, France. Value: $200.00–275.00.

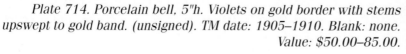

Plate 714. Porcelain bell, 5"h. Violets on gold border with stems upswept to gold band. (unsigned). TM date: 1905–1910. Blank: none. Value: $50.00–85.00.

*Plate 715. Small vase with open handles, 2½"h. Gold floral border with blue medallion of red and yellow conventionalized flower. (unsigned). TM date: 1911–1924. Blank: Limoges scrolls W.G.&Co., France. Value: $45.00–65.00.*

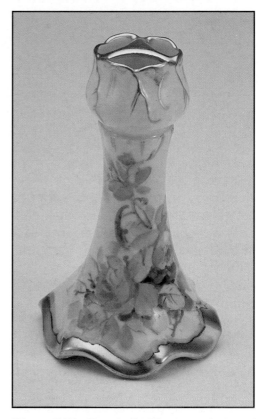

*Plate 717. Hatpin holder, swirled and fluted body with flower blossom top, 4"h. Pink rosebud cluster on cream ground, gold French detailing on top. (unsigned). TM date: 1911–1924. Blank: PL Limoges, France. Value: $235.00–265.00.*

*Plate 716. Plate, 9"d. Tripart design of two blue cornflowers with gold center on white ground. (unsigned). TM date: 1910–1916. Blank: Nippon. Value: $75.00–100.00.*

*Plate 718. Compote with scalloped rim and base, 3¾"h x 6"d. Blue and red raspberries amid green leaves and gold whiplash streamers. Signed: Stahl (Stahl, George W.). TM date: 1905–1910. Blank: none. Value: $125.00–150.00.*

# DOMINICK CAMPANA STUDIO, 1903–1915

## D.M. Campana Art Company 1914–1928+

Dominick M. Campana straddled the broadest range of talents in the spectrum of china decoration. Artist, teacher, supplier, he embodied the dream of every artist-immigrant. Born in Venice, Italy, he worked first as decorator for the Ceramic Art Company (later to become Lenox) in Trenton, New Jersey, from 1899 through 1901. In 1902 he moved to Chicago and decorated china for Pickard for a little more than a year. By 1903 he had set up his own studio in the Auditorium Building, home of many Atlan artists as well as the ceramic historian Edwin Atlee Barber; by 1905 he was selling his own brand of mineral paints.

As an artist he was capable of a wide range of subjects—animals, florals, and conventionalized designs. He taught china painting—the D. M. Campana Art School—at his studio in the Auditorium Building through 1915. Under the name of the D. M. Campana Art Company, he brought out a line of art supplies and wrote at least ten instruction booklets on design and china decorating, all of which he sold by mail through *Keramic Studio* magazine. During this time he also taught a seminar in china painting at the Art Institute, and continued to paint, winning a gold medal at the 1906 Lewis and Clark Exhibition in Portland for a conventionalized Florentine design.

In 1914 the D. M. Campana Art Company opened as an art supply store at 431 South Wabash, and by 1916 he had closed his studio in the Auditorium Building and moved his art school in with his art supply company. Among his instruction books, *The Teacher of China Painting*, though long out of print, is still a viable source of instruction in the art. Campana continued to write instruction books, published many sample designs, and wrote articles for *Keramic Studio*.

By 1930 he had merged his company into the Maurer-Campana Art Company. His contribution as a teacher and supplier to china decorating was significant. His decorations are rarely found today and are prized as much for their historic value as their artistic merit.

# EDWARD W. DONATH STUDIO, 1897–1903, 1905–1928

## American Hand-Painted China Company 1915–1917

Photo courtesy C. Donath.

*Figure 45. Edward W. Donath 1871–1938.*

Edward W. Donath was born in Selb, Bavaria, Germany, in September of 1871. His father was a china decorator at a large factory (both Hutschenreuther and Rosenthal were located in Selb), and at least two of his brothers, Hermann and William, learned china decorating there as well. Edward's high level of proficiency, even in his earliest work (Plate 719), would argue strongly that he too, became a skilled decorator while still in Germany. (The Donath & Company porcelain factory was established in Dresden, Saxony, in 1872 and was later merged into the Hutschenreuther group of factories,[37] but no family connection is known.)

There were six children in the family, and times

were extremely hard. With little to eat and conscription into the German army an imminent threat for the boys, the Donath children emigrated to North America in 1893. Two of the boys went to Mexico and the other two boys and their two sisters settled in Chicago.

Edward Donath married Minnie Todtleben in 1896, and went to work as one of Wilder Pickard's cottage workers at about the same time. (Any of Donath's work from this period would have borne the Edgerton Studios paper label which in all probability would have been washed or worn off, making them unidentifiable today.) He was not content to be just another artist, however, and he wasted little time in making his presence known on the Chicago china decorating scene.

Although most entrants in china exhibitions at that time were women, a few outstanding male artists also participated. The 1896 Central Arts Association Exhibition included such well-known independent china artists as Emil Aulich, Marshall Fry, Jr., and Peter Beuttgen. It also included Edward Donath.[38]

By the spring of 1897 he had gone into business for himself. Little is known of this first attempt except that he opened a studio in the Chicago Loop in the same building tenanted by other china decorators. He became a member of the Chicago Ceramic Arts Association in 1899, and thus continued to widen his circle of contacts in the china decorating community. In 1900 he entered ten items in the CCAA Exhibit at the Art Institute and advertised himself as a teacher of china painting. He also taught at the Chicago Art Institute for a time.

By 1901 he had moved his studio to North Clark Street and was living next door to Max Rost, a decorator who worked for him at that time. In 1903, however, Donath closed his studio and went back to work with Pickard, this time at the carriage barn. Max Rost also went to work for Pickard in 1903.

Donath stayed at Pickard until 1905 and then, at age 33, he again launched out on his own. About this time, he also produced hand-painted china for the large Chicago retailer and mail order house, Pitkin & Brooks (Plate 927). Many of the firms that did both retail and institutional jobbing, not only maintained their own china decorating rooms, but also bought finished product from individual artists. Donath may have used Pitkin & Brooks as an outlet for some of his initial produc-

tion. He worked out of his home for two years and then established a separate studio at 243 West North Avenue. His sister, Mrs. Elizabeth Koplien helped him with the business and also did some decorating (Plate 721). Donath's brother, William, also seems to have been a decorator for him in 1907 and 1908.

Adolph J. Heidrich (Also spelled Heidrick, see separate section.) worked for Donath for just a short time: 1910 through 1912. During this time he followed in his talented father's footsteps in creating many wildlife (Plate 725) and figural (Plate 722) decorations. He signed his work A.H. and A. Heidrich.

Joseph R. Kittler (See separate section.) was a manager for Donath in 1914 and thereafter was a decorator. He did florals and some fruit subjects. About 1920, he left to form his own studio. He signed his work Kitt and Kittler.

Miss Myrtle Peplow worked for Donath in 1916 and 1917. She did poinsettias and other florals, signed Pep and Peplow.

Max Rost was Donath's closest friend and the two families lived in proximity to each other for more than 20 years. Rost worked for Donath both before and after Donath's second period of work with Pickard. Rost operated his own studio from 1910 through 1916, but moved his studio in with Donath's in 1922. Max Rost and former Pickard artist, M. Rost LeRoy, both decorated china for Donath in the 1905–1910 period. (It seems highly probable that these two artists were related, given the great similarity in their names and occupations, but efforts to find further details have been unsuccessful.) During this time, Donath, like Pickard, was plagued with rumors of his use of decals. For a short time he replaced his trademark with a paper label offering a $1,000.00 reward for any of his work not strictly hand-painted (Mark 4). Later pieces often bore both the label and a red stamp.

Throughout its history, much of the studio's output was Edward Donath's own work, and his concentration on the decorating side of the business probably accounted for his scant penetration of the commercial market. That as many of his pieces have survived today is a tribute to his skill as an artist rather than as a businessman. His work was largely confined to naturalistic fruits and flowers (Plate 734 and 736) with just a little stylization occasionally thrown in. But within this realm, he produced outstanding work. He was meticulous with his borders and detailing which always gave his work a finished, commercial quality.

The details are sketchy, but in 1915 he appears to have made an attempt at retailing with the addition of a sales room on State Street in Chicago's Loop under the name of the American Hand Painted China Company. The sales room only lasted for about a year, although he did maintain the "American" name at his North Avenue studio for another two years.

In 1918 Donath moved his studio to 2923 North Lincoln Avenue where he remained for the balance of his career (there was a speak-easy across the street during Prohibition.) Even at its height, the studio probably never employed more than four or five non-family artists at any time. By 1920, artists Max Rost, Joseph R. Kittler, and Adolph Heidrich had all left Donath to form their own studios. The increasing costs of hand painting together with the shift to simpler, more modern designs reduced Donath's small market still further. His son, Charles, had started decorating for him in 1914 at the age of 18, and a younger son, Max, also decorated for him in the 1920s; this use of family talent probably allowed the studio to survive longer than it normally would have. Although both sons claimed commercial art or china decoration as a profession through the late 1920s, Charles contributed more to the business end of the studio, while Max continued to decorate.

Donath's last classified listing under "China Decorators" appeared in January of 1928. By 1930, the Donath studio had ceased decorating china entirely. The Great Depression was deepening, and the market for naturalistic, hand-painted china was gone. In place of china, Donath switched to oil paintings. Like his china, the oils were well executed, but he often had to content himself with no more market for his work than a Sunday display in a downtown park.

He worked to the very end of his life; his son, Charles, helped him in his studio until 1936. His last work was decorating oil cloth covers for kitchen cleanser cans which he sold to a Chicago department store. He died of a heart attack in 1938 while seated in his rocking chair.

*Artists associated with the Donath studio:*

| | |
|---|---|
| F. Beulet* | William Donath |
| Edward Donath* | Harry R. Griffiths* |
| Max Donath | Adolph J. Heidrich |

| | |
|---|---|
| J. Heinz* | Miss Helen D. Miller |
| E. Hoff. | Miss Myrtle Peplow |
| C. King | Wenzel Pfohl |
| Joseph R. Kittler | Rech. |
| Kline | Max Rost* |
| Carl Koenig* | J. René. |
| Fred Kriesche* | R. ST. |
| Elizabeth Koplien | George W. Stahl* |
| M. Rost LeRoy* | |

*\*Also a Pickard artist*

## Donath Trademarks
*(Dates are approximations.)*

Donath's earliest work bears only the signature "Ed. Donath" on the face of the piece. Some of these pieces may have borne the Edgerton/Pickard paper label or perhaps an early Donath studio paper label, but without such labels, one can only assign an 1896–1899 range to them. On later trademarked pieces, Donath signed only his last name; there are just six trademarks that have come to light thus far.

*Mark 1. 1905, ½"l., red stamp.*

*Mark 2. 1905–1906, ¾"d., red double circle stamp.*

*Mark 3. 1906–1910, ⅞"d., paper label (blue on white and white on blue).*

*Mark 4. 1906–1928, ⁹⁄₁₆"d., circular text in red and (very rarely) green stamp.*

Mark 5. 1910–1915, ⅝"
x ⁵⁄₁₆", small rectangle,
red or black stamp.

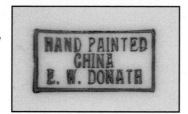

Mark 6.
1910–1915, ½" x
⅞", large rectan-
gle, red or black
stamp.

## Donath Plates

Plate 719. Punch bowl, 13"d, underplate, 17½"d.
Multicolored grape clusters on variegated leaves.
Signed: Ed. Donath (Donath, Edward W.). TM date:
No TM (est: 1897–1901). Blank: Limoges three
stars, France. Value: $1,400.00–1,600.00.

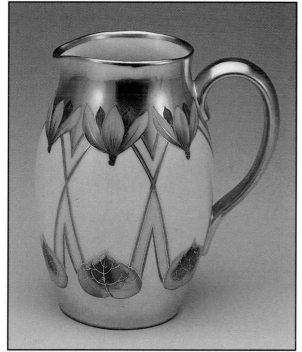

Plate 720. Small milk pitcher, 6"h., Cyclamen.
(unsigned). TM date: 1910–1915. Blank: Hohenzollern China, Germany. Value: $170.00–190.00.

Plate 721. Bonbon, elaborate leaf-edged, 8"l. Currants
and green leaves on cream ground. Signed: Koplien
(Koplien, Elizabeth). TM date: 1910–1915. Blank: none.
Value: $25.00–30.00.

*Plate 722. Liquor jug with handle and lipped spout, 6"h. Monk/distiller drinking. Signed: A. Heidrich (Heidrich, Adolph J.). TM date: 1910–1915. Blank: crown Vienna design Austria. Value: $160.00–225.00.*

*Plate 723. Tankard, 3 plain-handled mugs, 3 dragon-handled mugs, 14"h. Falstaff, and six different monks. Signed: A. Heidrich (Heidrich, Adolph J.). TM date: 1906–1928. Blank: J.P.L., France. Value: $1,800.00–2,200.00.*

*Plate 724. Plate, 8½"d. Spray of pink apple blossoms, dot and scallop border. Signed: Kitt. (Kittler, Joseph R.). TM date: 1906–1928. Blank: crossed clover, J&C Louise Bavaria. Value: $55.00–65.00.*

*Plate 725. Plate, molded scrolls along edge, 9¾"d. Two hunting dogs at point in autumn woods. Signed: A. Heidrich (Heidrich, Adolph J.). TM date: 1906–1928. Blank: Patd Jan 23rd, 1906, J.P.L., France. Value: $135.00–185.00.*

Plate 727. Cake plate, perforated handles, 10½"d. Currant spray on cream ground, gold border. Signed: M. Rost LeRoy (LeRoy, M. Rost). TM date: 1906–1928. Blank: Limoges, Limoges in star France. Value: $45.00–65.00.

Plate 726. Vase, 13½"h. Elk bellowing across canyon with mountain stream and waterfall. Signed: A. Heidrich (Heidrich, Adolph J.). TM date: 1910–1915. Blank: none. Value: $625.00–745.00.

Plate 728. Plate, scalloped edged, 8"d. Yellow and orange tulips, blue and green leaves on gold border. Signed: Heinz (Heinz, J.). TM date: 1906–1928. Blank: 1634 (incised). Value: $85.00–100.00.

Plate 729. Berry dish, scalloped, 5¼"d. Blackberries on green leaves, white blossom. (unsigned). TM date: 1905–1906. Blank: none. Value: $18.00–$25.00.

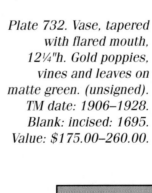

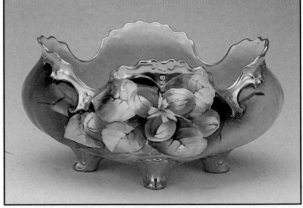

*Plate 730. Cream and sugar. Violet bachelor buttons with maroon centers on cream ground. Signed: J. Rene (Rene, J.). TM date: 1906–1928. Blank: none. Value: $75.00–95.00.*

*Plate 731. Plate, 9"d. Three sets of two white apple blossoms on decorated gold border. Signed: Kitt (Kittler, Joseph R.). TM date: 1906–1928. Blank: Titanic Austria crown and crossed hammers. Value: $25.00–35.00.*

*Plate 732. Vase, tapered with flared mouth, 12¼"h. Gold poppies, vines and leaves on matte green. (unsigned). TM date: 1906–1928. Blank: incised: 1695. Value: $175.00–260.00.*

*Plate 733. Plate, scalloped edge, 7½"d. Variegated leaves and apples on stem border, cream ground. Signed: Donath (Donath, Edward W.). TM date: 1910–1915. Blank: M.Z. double eagle Austria. Value: $20.00–25.00.*

*Plate 734. Bowl, footed bulbous sided, deep-scalloped rim, 8"d. Orange Japanese lanterns on green, blue/green leaves, green ground. Signed: Donath (Donath, Edward W.). TM date: No TM. Blank: none. Value: $110.00–165.00.*

*Plate 735. Toothpick holder, 2¼"h. Two clusters of two white apple blossoms on embellished gold border, green leaves, cream ground. (unsigned). TM date: 1906–1928. Blank: none. Value: $65.00–85.00.*

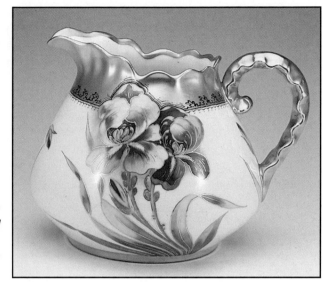

*Plate 736. ROMA jug, 7½"d. Purple irises with long green leaves, French-style with gold outlining, on cream ground with embellished gold border. Signed: Donath (Donath, Edward W.). TM date: 1910–1915. Blank: Hohenzollern China, Germany. Value: $475.00–595.00.*

*Plate 737. Plate, sculpted scrolls on rim, 9¾"d. Yellow peach spray, wide gold border, large, embellished gold virgule. Signed: M. Rost LeRoy (LeRoy, M. Rost). TM date: 1906–1928. Blank: Jan 23, 1906, J.P.L., France. Value: $95.00–120.00.*

*Plate 738. Tea set: ornate, 12"l. tray, lidded teapot, lidded sugar, and creamer. Pink rose clusters on green leaves and brown vines, cream ground. (unsigned). TM date: 1910–1915. Blank: GDA, France. Value: $725.00–795.00.*

# FRANCE STUDIOS,

## 1906–1916

Born in New York in 1870, Robert W. France formed the France Studios in 1906. There is no evidence of his having worked for any other studio prior to that time. His designs were largely conservative, but the quality of his work is among the best of that period. He produced most of the studio's output himself, and he did not sign his own work, electing to simply hand-letter France, Robert W. France, or France Studios on the base of his pieces. Only four other artists are known to have worked for him: George W. Stahl and Harry R. Griffiths, both of whom had worked for Pickard, Elsie W. Bieg, who later founded the Humboldt Studio, and Charles Heyn.

## France Trademarks

Mark 1. 1906–1916, black or colored handscript.

Mark 2. 1906–1916, black or colored handscript.

## France Plates

Plate 739. Plate, 8½"d. Orchid spray on serpentine-embellished gold band. Signed: Griff (Griffiths, Harry R.). TM date: 1906–1916. Blank: T&V rectangle, Limoges, France. Value: $85.00–70.00.

Plate 740. Tankard and 4 mugs, 12"h. Blackberries on variegated leaves, green/yellow ground. Signed: C.Heyn (Heyn, Charles). TM date: 1906–1916. Blank: J.P.L., France. Value: $700.00–900.00.

# A. HEIDRICH STUDIOS, c.1915–c.1922

Adolph J. Heidrich was the son of Anton C. Heidrich (also spelled Heidrick), a well-known china artist from the Trenton Pottery. Anton and his wife had emigrated from Austria in 1880, living successively in Texas—where Adolph was born in 1882—New Jersey, Indiana, Pennsylvania, and finally back to New Jersey. It was here that young Adolph learned the art, and by age 16, he was decorating professionally.

Adolph came west to Chicago about 1905, and there is some question as to whether he is the "Mr. Hardwick" referred to as one of Pickard's initial Ravenswood artists.

He tried his hand at operating a saloon in 1909, but by 1910 he had gone back to decorating china, working for the Donath Studio. His work both for Donath and himself was largely pictorial: monks, seascapes, hunting dogs, and various wild life subjects. The elk subject in Plate 726 is very reminiscent of an elk plate done by his father for the Trenton Pottery Company in the late 1880s and which is currently in the collection of the New Jersey State Museum.

Adolph Heidrich was in all probability a one-man studio. Only two trademarks are associated with this studio.

## Heidrich Trademarks
*(Dates are approximations.)*

Mark 1. 1915–1918, ¹³⁄₁₆"d., circular text red stamp.

Mark 2. 1918–1922, ⅝"d., circular text red stamp.

### Heidrich Plates

Plate 741. Plate, desert, 6"d. Setting sun over green breakers, sea gulls. Signed: A. Heidrich (Heidrich, Adolph J.). TM date: 1918–1922. Blank: hammer, Bavaria. Value: $15.00–20.00.

Plate 742. Plate, pie crust rim, 9¾"d. Moose overlooking lake, mountains, pines in foreground. Signed: A. Heidrich (Heidrich, Adolph J.). TM date: 1915–1918. Blank: none. Value: $165.00–225.00.

Plate 743. Plate, plain rim, 9⅜"d. Rainbow trout on line over lake, waterfall in foreground. Signed: A. Heidrich (Heidrich, Adolph J.). TM date: 1918–1922. Blank: crown over shield HC Royal Bavaria Patent applied for. Value: $165.00–225.00.

# HUMBOLDT ART STUDIO, *1916–1928*

The Humboldt Art Studio was operated by Elsie W. Bieg, the wife of a Chicago attorney. A resident of suburban Oak Park and River Forest, Bieg probably obtained some of her commercial training during her employment at the France Studios. She opened her own business at 3351 West North Avenue in 1915. By 1922 she had added a retail outlet, the Madison Art and Gift Shop on West Madison Street, and by 1924 she had added a third location on Crawford Avenue at which she made and sold candles.

Her designs were commercially adequate and included many banal floral renditions of that time: clusters of forget-me-nots and garlands of rosebuds.

Her signature, generally found on the back of the piece, was large and crude, and detracts substantially from the value of her work. Like Osborne, however, she is best remembered for her emulations of Pickard designs (Plate 744). These emulations are so skillfully done that without an examination of the underside, they are indistinguishable from the Pickard originals. They show her to have been technically very talented, and her signature on these pieces was small and neatly lettered. No trademarks are associated with her studios.

## *Bieg Plate*

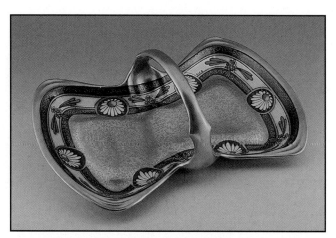

Plate 744. Candy, relish dish, bow-shaped with handle, 9¾"l. ENCRUSTED LINEAR. Signed: Bieg (Bieg, Elsie W.). Blank: none. Value: $75.00–95.00.

# INTERNATIONAL ART STUDIOS, 1910–1911

In 1910, Alfred Keates, Curtis Marker, and Edward Gibson left Pickard and formed the International Art Studios. It was located at 2035 West Giddings, just four blocks west of the Pickard studios. Gibson was president, Keates was treasurer, and Marker was secretary. As might be expected, the few pieces that have come to light, are very well executed and identical in style to the work that these three artists produced while at Pickard. Despite their efforts, the International Art Studio only lasted for two years. From then on, Keates continued under his own name at the same location (see Keates Art Studio), Gibson went into business as an art supply dealer and china painting instructor, while only Marker returned to work for Pickard.

## *International Art Studio Trademark*

*Trademark 1910–1911, green decal. (Caution. Decal not always "fired" and may wash off.)*

## *International Art Studio Plates*

Plate 745. Plate, 8¼"d. Three Easter lilies, green ground, gold outlined leaves, scallop and dot rim. Signed: E. Gibson (Gibson, Edward). TM date: 1910–1911. Blank: circle JHR Bavaria Favorite. Value: $125.00–165.00.

Plate 746. Cream and sugar. Poinsettia on gold band on cream ground. Signed: Marker (Marker, Curtis H.). TM date: 1910–1911. Blank: Royal Bayreuth coat of arms PRIV 1794 Bavaria. Value: $75.00–85.00.

*Plate 747. Syrup pitcher, 4½"h. Three apple blossoms on gold border. Signed: Marker (Marker, Curtis H.). TM date: 1910–1911. Blank: Favorite Bavaria. Value: $165.00–185.00.*

# KALITA STUDIO,
## 1944–1955

Waclaw A. Kalita was born on February 28, 1891, in Cmielow (shmay`-lov), Poland. At the start of World War I in 1914, he left his homeland and emigrated to Chicago via Canada. He married Bronislava Jaworski, the daughter of a Polish count, and she bore him two sons, Bronislaw and Zenon. Kalita initially found work in a Firestone tire factory, but shortly went to work in a succession of china decorating studios that included Stouffer, Osborne, Tolpin, and Pickard. He worked for Pickard during the early 1930s; by the late 1930s he was operating a one-man studio in his home on Henderson Avenue. By 1944 he had hired other artists and was operating a much larger studio out of a ten room home at 4238 North Keystone. This studio included two kilns (in the basement), a separate acid room, and some other rooms set aside for the artists.

Kalita's major talent was in gilding. This was fortuitous since the popular taste demanded gold-etched borders on service plates, decorated trays, and other shapes. Kalita made master drawings, transferred them to etched steel plates, and from these he could repeatedly transfer the designs to the china. Some of the gold borders were also applied over color with a rubber stamp upon which a delicate design had been reproduced. A third form of border decoration utilized the earliest method of etched pattern application: the free-hand painting of designs on china with asphaltic resist, followed by the usual etching process. At this new location, he now employed additional talent from the outside, but like most others, the studio continued to utilize the family in its operation, with Kalita's wife and sons doing the acid dipping and the subsequent kerosene and hot water rinses.

In 1946, the studio moved to a double address at 4413–17 North Central Avenue. Kalita knocked out part of the wall on the north side of the building to provide good north light windows for his artists. At its height, Kalita Studio numbered ten people, eight of whom were decorators. Among them were former Pickard artists Ernest V. Hauptmann (and his artist-wife), Otto Podlaha, Gustav Weissflog, Louis P. Grumieau, and Maxwell R. Klipphahn. The studio boasted five large kilns plus a smaller kiln that was used to heat the building. Kalita continued to do the gold work while the other artists produced the color work. Kalita's largest customer was the Taubé China Company in Philadelphia for whom he produced lamp bases. The studio would ship ten to fifteen barrels of decorated bases every four to five weeks, accounting for almost ninety percent of the output. In addition to decorated china, Kalita also produced pre-etched white china which the amateur could gild and fire; he also made transfer sheets bearing full-color designs in mineral paint which could be applied to china blanks by the less talented hobbyist. He wholesaled both of these products to the large china art supply houses in downtown Chicago; D. M. Maurer and Dominick Campana were two such companies. Despite this transfer sheet business, Kalita never used decals for his own color work.

Max Klipphahn decorated china for Kalita until his death at 81. Kalita's son, Zenon, recalls that, "Klipphahn's hands were unsteady in those last years, yet when his brush touched the china, his shaking would cease long enough to make the stroke, and then the shaking would resume. He signed his work Rean, Klipp, or M.K., but when he was having a bad day, he would sign other artists' names—upon occasion, he even signed my name, 'ZEN.'"

After Kalita closed his studio, he went back to work for Pickard for several years. He had acquired a driver's license at 65, and he made the roundtrip to Antioch every day at 80 miles an hour! Waclaw Kalita died in 1971 at 80 years of age.

## Kalita Trademark

*Trademark 1944–1955, 17/32"w., brown, black, or gold stamp.*

## Kalita Plates

*Plate 748. Tray, 12½"d. Red flowers, daisies in center medallion, wide floral etched border. Signed: Klipp (Klipphahn, Maxwell Rean). TM date: 1944–1955. Blank: none. Value: $155.00–195.00.*

*Plate 749. Salad bowl with fluted, ruffled rim and decorated porcelain serving spoon and fork, 9¾"d. Currant cluster with green leaves and brown/yellow ground. Signed: Klipp (Klipphahn, Maxwell Rean). TM date: 1944–1955. Blank: none. Value: $275.00–350.00.*

# KEATES ART STUDIO,
## 1912–1937

Alfred Keates was born in England in 1861[39], and emigrated to America in 1902 with his wife, son, daughter, sister, and sister-in-law. He decorated for Pickard at the carriage barn and then at Ravenswood. His daughter, Madeline, also decorated for Pickard late in the 1905–1910 period. After his short partnership with Marker and Gibson in the International Art Studio, Keates formed his own studio on North Giddings Avenue in 1912, possibly with the assistance of his daughter. He supplemented the sale of his own decorated china with a firing service for those artists without a kiln. An advertisement in the Art Institute's Atlan Exhibition Catalog proclaimed: "China fired twice daily…Special care taken of outside work." By 1922 he had moved to the far West Side where he operated an art and gift shop through 1928. The Great Depression probably forced him into other lines of art as it did with other artists, for by 1937 he was listed as a lamp manufacturer. "Louis F." and "Adams" are the only other artists known to have worked for this studio. The earliest pieces from this studio had no trademark and bore only Keates' signature on the front.

## Keates Trademarks
### (Dates are approximations.)

*Mark 1. 1914–1920, 1"w., oval black, red, or gold stamp.*

*Mark 2. 1920–1937, ⅞"w., oval black or red stamp.*

# J.R. KITTLER
## 1922–1943

Joseph R. Kittler was born in 1880 in Austria and emigrated to the United States in 1904. He first appears as a decorator for Jacob H. Stouffer in 1908. From there he moved to the Donath studio where he was termed manager in 1914. As an artist he produced good commercial work. In 1922 he established his own studio selling "Hand painted china in all its lines. Wholesale only....We sell to and decorate for department stores, jewelry stores, and jobbers."

Most of his surviving work as an independent studio is either etched all-over-gold or a platinum etch for which he claimed a patent. This platinum has a "steely" appearance which nevertheless was quite popular. The studio was also his home and endured through 1943.

Kittler's trademark was a rectangle which read: *"J.R. Kittler (signature), Platinum China, Reg.U.S.Pat.Office."*

# C.F. KOENIG STUDIOS, 1915–1966

Carl F. Koenig decorated china for Pickard in the 1905–1912 trademark periods. Between 1913 and 1915 he worked for the Brauer studio and also the Donath studio. In 1915 he established his own studio at 3421 West Fullerton. In 1917 he moved to the South Side and remained in business there through the late thirties, operating an art store along with his studio. At least one Pickard/Brauer artist, Max Bachmann, worked for him. Bachmann would work for Brauer throughout the week but would produce freelance pieces in the evenings and take them to Koenig on Saturdays to be fired.

Koenig's work was mostly traditional and conservative with an occasional excursion into Arabian motifs. Although some of his pieces incorporated gold etched borders (Plate 751), he does not seem to have followed Pickard into all-over-gold as many of the other studios did. For the most part, his output was good quality, which accounts for a fair amount of it surviving today. As with other china artists, the Great Depression created substantial hardship; the family lost their home and were forced to move west on 63rd Street.

Koenig's wife Stefanaie handled much of the business end of the studio. She succeeded in renting "Millie's Gift Shop" (the name seemed to attract better than "art studio"), but Koenig was forced to take his porcelain to other studios for firing because he was prohibited from using a kiln on the rented premises.

In 1937 he closed his South Side studio and returned to the North Side where he worked for Yeschek's Ceramic Artcraft Studios and also continued to decorate out of a home studio. After Ceramic Artcraft closed in 1953, he continued his home studio operation at 4371 North Elston until his death in February of 1969. His earliest (and a few later pieces) bear no trademark and are identified only by his signature on the face of the piece.

## Koenig Trademark
### (Date is approximate.)

*Trademark 1917–1938, 1⅛"w., oval as a red or black stamp.*

## Koenig Plates

*Plate 750. Plate with "pie-crust" scalloped rim, 9½"d. Four clusters of gold acorns on maroon and orange oak leaves. Signed: Koenig (Koenig). TM date: No TM. Blank: AK D, France. Value: $155.00–170.00.*

Plate 751. Lemonade set: 6 signed cups, pitcher, and 11" x 15" tray. Blackberry sprays beneath hand-etched blackberry border. Signed: Koenig (Koenig, Carl F.). TM date: No TM. Blank: Z.S.&Co., Bavaria. Value: $425.00–475.00.

# LEROY ART STUDIOS,
## 1925–1946

The LeRoy Art Studio was not a major factor in hand-painted china, but it is included here to avoid any confusion in identity with Pickard artist M. Rost LeRoy. The signatures are quite different.

The LeRoy studios operated from 1925 through 1946, first at 2500 West Chicago Avenue and later just west of the Loop on North DesPlaines Avenue. LeRoy produced some hand-painted china in simple, tasteful designs, but the studio's primary output was all-over-gold etched china. The studio's first mark was a red stamped ¾" dia. circle with "LEROY ART STUDIO" in it. A later mark was simply the name "LeRoy" stamped in gold.

### LeRoy Trademarks
*(Dates are approximations.)*

*Mark 1. 1925–1946, ⅝"l., text as a red or gold stamp.*

*Mark 2. 1925–1946, ¾"d., circle as a red stamp.*

## LeRoy Plate

Plate 752. Salt and pepper, handled 2½"h., ROSE AND DAISY AOG. (unsigned). TM date: 1925–1946. Blank: none. Value: $25.00–35.00.

# LUKEN ART STUDIOS,
## 1895–1926

Minnie A. Luken was born in Ohio, in December of 1867. In 1895 she opened a china decorating studio in her home at 747 West Harrison Street which endured in one form or another at various South Side locations through 1937. Her father was a commercial traveler and her two brothers, Norbert and Alfred, were clerks at the Board of Trade; Norbert eventually became a grain dealer, and the family became affluent enough to afford a Swedish servant girl.

Minnie Luken was a prolific producer of unimaginative florals, floral borders, and a few scenics. She produced complete dinner settings, dresser sets, tea and coffee sets, and a variety of vases, bowls, and chargers, She also produced some of these same products for Pickard for approximately a year—about 1912. (See page 37.)

Despite the unimaginative aspect of her work, it was of sufficient commercial quality to retain a modest market segment for four decades! All evidence indicates that she was a one-woman studio for her entire career, but brother Alfred did operate the Luken "Gift Shop" in 1928, presumably as an outlet for her china. Today, some collectors specialize in her work; it is usually (or should be) modestly priced, and almost every antique show of any magnitude in the Midwest contains some of her work. Other than her signature on the face of the piece, no other mark has been discovered.

# OSBORNE ART STUDIO,
## 1910-1973

Osborne was the only Chicago china artist of any stature to use his first name for his studio name and signature. He was born in Illinois of Norwegian parents in 1884 as Asbjorn T. Olsen. He Anglicized his first name early in his career, and by age 18 (1902) he was already decorating china professionally. In 1908 he married a girl his own age and they had two children, a boy and a girl.

During the first seven or eight years of his career, he probably worked for one or more of the decorator/wholesalers such as Pitkin & Brooks. Several antique dealers have insisted that he received his early training at Pickard. While not discounting these claims, diligent searches at antique shows and auctions and among private collections have turned up no example. Certainly, he was not one of Pickard's top artists nor was he ever Pickard's art director as a few dealers have claimed. By the time of the 1910 Census he describes himself as "working on his own account," that is, he had his own china-decorating business in his home, and by 1914 he had opened a separate studio at 2520 North Milwaukee Avenue.

Osborne did not use a backstamp on much of his product, being content to sign his name on the face of the piece, or in the case of all-over-gold pieces, to scribe his signature on the bottom. In other cases, he used gummed foil labels that were easily removed after purchase. Therefore, although he did employ other artists, one cannot distinguish between unstamped pieces signed by an artist while working for Osborne and pieces which that artist may have made on a freelance basis. He does not seem to have encouraged—or perhaps even permitted—other artists to sign their work for him. The Red Poppy dinner set shown in Plate 758, for instance, includes some unsigned saucers that were obviously painted by another artist. An Osborne piece signed by anyone other than Osborne has yet to be found.

Although he seems to have been devoted primarily to decorated china, he always characterized his studio as an "art studio" and himself as simply an "artist." The studio was not a large one, and inasmuch as Osborne sold art supplies as well as decorated china from a store at the front of the building, he probably employed no more than six or eight china decorators at the studio's height. Nevertheless, he did employ some very good artists. In 1922—the one year in which he claimed a double address for his business—Joseph Blaha, Otto Podlaha, and Arnold Rhodes—each associated with Pickard at one time or another—identify Osborne as their employer. Waclaw Kalita also worked for Osborne later in several different instances.

Osborne is most noted for his emulations of many of Pickard's designs including Gasper's POPPY AND DAISY and Hessler's ENCRUSTED LINEAR. This has led to the erroneous identification of some of his work as unmarked Pickard. His version of the poppy design, for example, differs from the original in that two stems cross over the lowest poppy petal instead of all the stems running behind all the poppies. In other cases, the designs are appear to be exact copies.

His penchant for emulating Pickard designs notwithstanding, Osborne was capable of producing good, commercial designs of his own, including some outstanding figure work (Plates 760, 777, 763). His styles went through much the same progression as Pickard and Stouffer: naturalistic florals, vellum scenics, and all-over-gold. His later offerings included decal art that was often hand blended into the background, and the less expensive "bright gold" took the place of the richer golds of earlier years.

From 1922 until 1933 his business assumed a very low profile and he virtually disappeared. The studio reappeared in the classified listings in 1933; this was curious in that this was the depth of the Great Depression and advertising funds were scarce, as was the money to buy such nonessentials as decorated china. He continued to describe himself as an artist and the business as an art studio. In 1943 the studio moved farther up Milwaukee Avenue to 4150. In 1950 the studio moved farther out of the city to its final location at 6039 Northwest Highway. Osborne T. Olsen died about 1969. Waclaw Kalita was the studio's only artist in those later years and did all of the gold etching until his (Kalita's) death in 1971. Osborne's widow, Augusta, and son, Perry, continued to operate the business until it ceased operation in 1973.

# Osborne Trademarks
### *(Dates are approximations.)*

*Mark 1. 1914–1918, ¹⁵⁄₃₂" dia., red circle over gold square.*

*Mark 5. 1925–1935, ¹¹⁄₁₆" dia., platinum circle.*

*Mark 2. 1917–1924, ⅝" dia., red circle.*

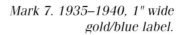

*Mark 6. 1928–1940, ¹¹⁄₁₆" dia., platinum circle.*

*Mark 3. 1917–1940, scribed signature on base.*

*Mark 7. 1935–1940, 1" wide gold/blue label.*

*Mark 4. 1918–1924, ¹⁵⁄₃₂" dia., red circle.*

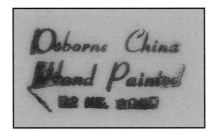

*Mark 8. 1940–1973, ¹³⁄₁₆" wide platinum stamped script.*

# Osborne Plates

*Plate 753. (rear) Narrow bonbon with over-folded sides, perforated handles, 10½"l., ENCRUSTED LINEAR. Signed: Osborne (Olsen, Osborne T.). TM date: No TM (c.1913–1918). Blank: T&V rectangle, Limoges, France. Value: $120.00–145.00. (front) Candlesticks, pair, 6¾"h. Signed: Osborne (Olsen, Osborne T.). TM date: No TM (c.1913–1918). Blank: overpainted. Value: $235.00–295.00.*

Plate 754. Bread tray with perforated handles, 17¼"lg., ENCRUSTED LINEAR. Signed: OSBORNE (Olsen, Osborne T.). TM date: No TM (c.1913–1918). Blank: Made In Japan. Value: $140.00–165.00.

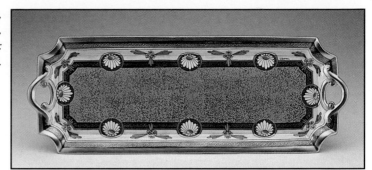

Plate 755. Plate, deeply scalloped and embossed edges, 8½"d., ENCRUSTED LINEAR. Signed: Osborne (Olsen, Osborne T.). TM date: No TM (c.1913–1918). Blank: overpainted. Value: $45.00–65.00.

Plate 756. Lidded coffee, lidded sugar, creamer, 6 cups and saucers, 10½"h., ENCRUSTED LINEAR. Signed: Osborne (Olsen, Osborne T.). TM date: No TM (c.1913–1918). Blank: Germany. Value: $625.00–750.00.

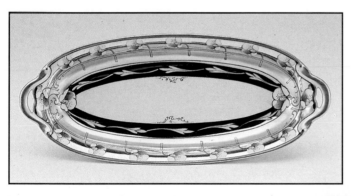

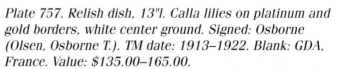

Plate 757. Relish dish, 13"l. Calla lilies on platinum and gold borders, white center ground. Signed: Osborne (Olsen, Osborne T.). TM date: 1913–1922. Blank: GDA, France. Value: $135.00–165.00.

Plate 758. (rear) Charger, handled. 12"d., POPPY AND DAISY. Signed: Osborne (Olsen, Osborne T.). TM date: 1913–1922. Blank: Vignaud Limoges. Value: $125.00–185.00. (front) Dinner set (38 pieces), POPPY AND DAISY. Signed: Osborne. (Olsen, Osborne T.). TM date: No TM (c.1913–1918). Blank: Various. Value: $1,150.00–1,275.00.

Plate 759. Plate, 8½"d. Vellum: lake, moon, and palm trees. Signed: OSBORNE (Olsen, Osborne T.). TM date: 1917–1924. Blank: Thomas shield Bavaria. Value: $120.00–145.00.

Plate 760. Vase, oval, scalloped mouth, 6"h. Vellum: rust leaves and birches foreground, lavender ground, and lake. Signed: Osborne (Olsen, Osborne T.). TM date: 1917–1924. Blank: crown Imperial oval PL Austria. Value: $225.00–275.00.

Plate 761. Plate, 10"d. Vellum: birches beside lake at sunset. Signed: Osborne (Olsen, Osborne T.). TM date: 1917–1924. Blank: shield Thomas Sevres Bavaria. Value: $125.00–160.00.

Plate 763. Vase, 14½"h. Nude with white scarf in woodland scene. Signed: Osborne (Olsen, Osborne T.). TM date: 1913–1922. Blank: T&V rectangle, Limoges, France. Value: $850.00–1,200.00.

Plate 762. Plate, 9"d. Vellum: hawthorn foreground, green foliage, and lake in background. Signed: Osborne (Olsen, Osborne T.). TM date: 1917–1924. Blank: crossed shamrocks J&C Bavaria. Value: $150.00–195.00.

Plate 764. Cream and sugar, POPPIES AOG. TM date: 1928–1940. Blank: none. Value: $35.00–50.00.

Plate 765. Shallow dish with perforated handles and scalloped, perforated rim, 8"d., ROSE AND DAISY AOG. TM date: 1940–1973. Blank: none. Value: $45.00–60.00.

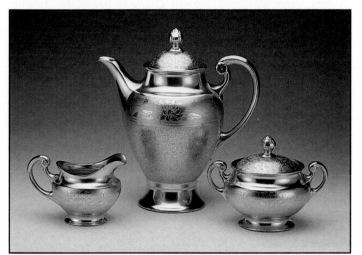

Plate 766. Coffee pot, 11"h., cream and sugar, ROSE AND DAISY AOG with etched water lily border. Signed: Osborne (Olsen, Osborne T.). TM date: 1917–1940. Blank: none. Value: $200.00–250.00.

Plate 767. Teacup and saucer, DESERTED GARDEN. Signed: Osborne (Olsen, Osborne T.). TM date:. Blank: overpainted. Value: $65.00–85.00.

Plate 768. Vase, square, tapered with four perforated handles, 17¾"h. Sailboat panels on encrusted gold. Signed: Osborne (Olsen, Osborne T.). TM date: No TM (c.1913–1918). Blank: overpainted. Value: $900.00–1,200.00.

Plate 769. Ferner, oblong, extended scrolled handles, 13"l. Water lilies border above ROSE AND DAISY AOG. Signed: Osborne (Olsen, Osborne T.). TM date: 1917–1940. Blank: overpainted. Value: $125.00–165.00.

Plate 771. Lidded teapot, lidded sugar, creamer, ROSE AND DAISY AOG . (unsigned). TM date: 1928–1940. Blank: Golden Crown, E&R Made In Western Germany. Value: $145.00–185.00.

Plate 770. Wide mouth vase or urn, 8"h., TRAILING VINE AOG with green band of pink water lilies and gold leaves. (unsigned). TM date: 1917–1940. Blank: overpainted. Value: $120.00–150.00.

Plate 773. Vase, hexagonal, 10"h. Gentleman and maid pastoral, lotus borders with ROSE AND DAISY AOG. (unsigned). TM date: 1925–1935. Blank: (2) Made In Bavaria; P.S. over scales with A.A. in circle. Value: $80.00–95.00.

Plate 772. SYLVIA plate, 8"d., POPPY AND FORGET-ME-NOT AOG. (unsigned). TM date: 1928–1940. Blank: Hutschenreuther Selb circle lion LHS Bavaria Germany Sylvia. Value: $55.00–65.00.

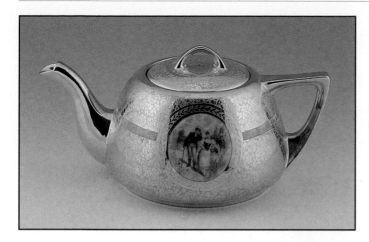

Plate 774. Teapot, 8½"d. Gentleman and maid pastoral inset, pale green band, <u>ROSE</u> <u>AND</u> <u>DAISY</u> <u>AOG</u>. (unsigned). TM date: 1928–1940. Blank: none. Value: $25.00–35.00.

Plate 776. Relish, oblong with perforated handles, 11"l. Lavender, pink, and white blossom spray on pale green, gold banding. Signed: Osborne (Olsen, Osborne T.). TM date: No TM. Blank: M&Z eagles, Austria. Value: $35.00–50.00.

Plate 775. Candlestick, 4½"h. Water lilies on green ground, DAISY SPRAYS AOG. Signed: Osborne (Olsen, Osborne T.). TM date: No TM. Blank: overpainted. Value: $55.00–75.00.

Plate 777. Cache, oval, footed, 12¼"h. Pink and white mums on green leaves. Signed: Osborne (Olsen, Osborne T.). TM date: No TM. Blank: Limoges scroll W.G.&Co., France. Value: $450.00–495.00.

# PARSCHE STUDIOS,
## 1903–1926
### *(as china decorators)*

Parsche (par-shay) Studios was only marginally engaged in china decorating, but it did employ two fine artists and persisted as a china decorator for almost 20 years, hence it has both historical and artistic significance. The studio's primary business was fine cut glass for which it was nationally famous. Franz X. Parsche was born in Bohemia in 1842, and emigrated to America in 1873. A master glass cutter and engraver, he went to work in Burley & Tyrrell's glass department in 1875 and then founded his own company in 1876. At its height in 1903, the studio employed 50 cutters plus all the necessary support staff.

The glass business gradually declined from that point on until by 1918, as Pickard discovered when he tried his hand at etched glass, the market for glass of all descriptions had shrunk appreciably and was saturated with the offerings of amateurs and professionals alike. Having made a furtive start at china decorating in 1911, Parsche now added hand-painted china to his offerings. The timing for this new entry was poor; simpler patterns were more popular and the role of the china artist was diminishing. This is supported by Parsche's grandson Donald's statement that the studio never employed more than one regular china artist at a time. Former Pickard artists Otto Podlaha and Frank H. Hanisch (Platt's "Mr. Hamische") were two such artists.

There was kiln space available, however, and Parsche, like many other studios added to its revenues by firing china for independent artists. The studio sold some of this output under its own name. Former Pickard artist Frank Haase was one of these freelancers and produced some superb work (Plate 778). Initially, because of its low volume, the studio identification was hand lettered; later pieces bore the Cameo Art China mark.

The studio produced a line of all-over-gold etched china, similar to Pickard's. Parsche prepared his own gold which he sold to studios as far away as Tokyo. Chicago customers included the Osborne, Tolpin, and Yeschek studios.

Franz Parsche died in 1929, and the business passed on through his son and grandson. Despite its scant china sales, Parsche Studios continued to sell hand-painted china through 1939; examples of Parsche china are quite rare. A modest glass business endured into the 1970s.

## Parsche Trademarks
### *(Dates are approximations.)*

*Mark 1. 1916–1920 1" dia., hand-lettered black circle.*

*Mark 2. 1925–1938 1" dia., black circle stamp.*

## Parsche Plate

*Plate 778. Plate, coupe, 9"d. Autumn oak leaves, maroon center, black rim with gold acorns. Signed: F. HAASE (Haase, Frank). TM date: 1916–1920. Blank: none. Value: $200.00–275.00.*

# ROGERS-MARTINI
## 1913–1916

### Rogers China Company
### 1915

### E. D. Rogers Company
### 1917

Rogers-Martini began business in 1913 as a china wholesaler. The following year the company changed its focus to decorated china for the retail trade. In 1915, the company expanded with a wholesale outlet, the Rogers China Company, operating out of the same address at 215 Superior Street. Rogers-Martini ceased operation in 1917, but Edward D. Rogers re-entered the wholesale business with the E. D. Rogers Company. It only lasted the year. Only former Pickard artist, George Leach, and an unidentified artist with the initials RED are associated with any of these business combinations. Though listed as china decorators, their primary focus was the wholesale trade. They probably acted as jobbers and distributors for independent decorators. Offerings included floral borders, simple garlands, and some all-over-gold designs.

## Rogers/Rogers-Martini Trademarks

Mark 1. 1915–1917, ¹³/₁₆" dia., red stamped circle.

Mark 2. 1917, ½" dia., black stamped circle.

## Rogers-Martini Plates

Plate 779. Plate, 8½"d. Daisies on wide green border. Signed: Blake (Blake). TM date: 1917. Blank: T&V rectangle, Limoges, France. Value: $15.00–25.00.

Plate 780. Side plate, 6"d. Blue border, blackberries and leaves. (unsigned). TM date: 1915. Blank: JHR circle Hutschenreuther Selb Bavaria. Value: $10.00–15.00.

Plate 781. Cream & sugar, Donatello style. Three-daisy border above gold linears on white ground. Signed: RED (unknown). TM date: 1913–1916. Blank: Z.S.&Co., Bavaria. Value: $35.00–55.00.

# SEIDEL STUDIO,
## 1904–1907

## Marmorstein & Seidel
## 1908

## H. Marmorstein's Art Studio
## 1909–1931

Erhardt Seidel was born in Germany in May of 1863. He served a four-year apprenticeship as a china decorator beginning when he was 14 years old. He emigrated to the United States in 1888, and worked for companies in New York and then New Jersey where he married.

In 1896 he came to Chicago and went to work for Pickard under Pickard's cottage labor arrangement. This was the Edgerton Studios/paper label period and no examples of Seidel's work from this period have come to light.

Seidel stayed with Pickard until 1907 when he opened a studio in the Chicago Loop at 41 Randolph Street. Sales were handled by Anna Seidel while also raising two small children—an arrangement not unlike that of Marie Brauer's.

The downtown studio lasted only a year and Seidel then went into partnership with former Pickard artist, Henry Marmorstein in Marmorstein's home at 244 North Clybourn Avenue. Henry Marmorstein had decorated for Pickard at the carriage barn and also at Ravenswood. Marmorstein & Seidel also lasted only one year; Seidel moved to Seattle in 1909 where he lived till his death in 1916.

Marmorstein continued under the name of H. Marmorstein's Art Studio through 1931. Throughout this time, his studio remained in his home, but eventually employed all of his family—Ernest, Frank, Max, and his wife Martha—as china artists. No examples of Marmorstein's work outside of Pickard have been discovered.

Seidel was a very important Pickard artist, and despite his short, independent existence in Chicago, his work was of the highest quality. He does not seem to have used a backstamp and therefore blank pieces signed by Seidel should be dated in the 1907–1909 period.

Seidel was a master of the art. His subjects ranged through figures, animals, fruits, flowers and even included the turn-of-the-century novelty of "ceramic photography," the kiln-transfer of photographs to china with gilt and painted borders. What has mainly survived however, are his deeply colored fruits and flowers with their rich, decorated borders. His style was unmistakable and no collection should be without at least one example of his work. No trademark is associated with any of these studios.

# J.H. STOUFFER
## COMPANY, 1905–1952

*Photo courtesy P. Burchfield.*

*Figure 46. Jacob H. Stouffer, 1866–1912.*

Jacob H. Stouffer was the seventh of nine children; he was born to William and Frances Stouffer in Adeline, Ogle County, Illinois, on February 5, 1866. He first appeared in Chicago in 1892, living at a boarding house on Lincoln Avenue and working as a bookkeeper at an unidentified company on South May Street. A year later he became manager of the George F. Kimball Company, a window and plate glass wholesaler on South Wabash where he remained through 1899; the following two years he was manager of an unidentified company on Monroe Street.

In 1902 Jacob Stouffer went into business for himself as the J. H. Stouffer Co., China and Glass Wholesalers. Curiously, for the next several years he is listed as western manager of his own company. The explanation for this is given by his address: room 617 at 185 Dearborn. This same street address was home to a number of china brokerages (French, Mulford, Ohio, Oliver) with many other china brokers in the vicinity. Stouffer was undoubtedly brokering for one or more out-of-state china manufacturers.

In 1905, while Wilder Pickard was opening his Ravenswood Studio on the North Side of Chicago, Jacob Stouffer opened his first china decorating studio on the South Side of Chicago at 3000 Lake Park Avenue. He moved adjacent to the new studio at 2956 Lake Park Avenue and former Pickard artist, Jacob Kiefus, moved in at 2950. Jacob Stouffer was president of the new company, and a relative, Milan D. Stouffer, was secretary. (Note: Stouffer descendants have no recollection of a "Milan" Stouffer, and while we would ordinarily discount the name on this basis, "Milan" does appear both in personal and company listings for three years. We include it here for the record in the hope that others may shed some light on the circumstance.)

The company was advertised as the J. H. Stouffer Manufacturing Company which was something of a misnomer. Stouffer never actually *manufactured* china; like all Chicago china decorating studios, he imported French and German blanks and decorated them. But it is clear that this was the year in which he first employed a china decorating staff, fired his own designs, and sold them through some of the channels that he had established in the last few years as a china broker. During this time, Jacob concentrated on the operation of the studio, while Charles P. Stouffer, his younger brother by almost seven years, directed the sales.

"Manufacturing" was dropped from the company's name in 1907 and never used again. Also this year, Stouffer transferred his classified listing to "China and Glass, Retail." This lasted until 1910, when the listing reverted to wholesale. Retailing would have pitted him against potential customers such as Marshall Field's and other large stores; he probably sampled this opportunity without ever really abandoning his wholesale business. In 1915, the company listing appeared under "China Decorators" and remained there for the balance of its existence.

Jacob H. Stouffer died on March 4, 1912, leaving his wife, Marietta, and two small children; he was only 46 years old. By then the family had moved to a fashionable address at 6140 South Woodlawn, and the company was operating at 3225 South Calumet Avenue. Upon Jacob's death, Mary D. Stouffer became president.

Finley Drummond became president in 1915. Drummond had emigrated from England in 1892, and had been both the credit manager and a silversmith with the Towle Manufacturing Company through 1910; he apparently worked for Stouffer between 1911 and 1914 in other capacities before becoming president. Jacob Kiefus became secretary. They held these positions through 1917, but by 1923 Jacob Stouffer's brother, Charles P. Stouffer, was president, his wife, Grace, was secretary-treasurer, and James A. Kennedy was vice president.

The company moved to 2619 South Prairie Avenue in 1922, where it remained through 1932. By 1928, Kennedy was no longer listed as an officer, but Grace and Charles Stouffer continued in their respective positions. In 1932 the company moved to 2611 South Calumet Avenue, and in 1943 it re-located to 902 South Wabash Avenue.

The high period of Stouffer's hand-painted china appears to have spanned no more than 15 or 20 years: 1905 to 1920–25. During this time, however, the company employed some of the best decorators in the business, at least 17 of whom worked for Pickard at one time or another.

One top artist who was never a Pickard artist was Ernest Feix. This very accomplished decorator appears to have worked for Stouffer from 1908 through 1911. Although he worked for Stouffer but a short time, he produced some of the studio's finest pieces. The designs were both original and colorful, essentially in a stylized format (Plates 790, 805). Feix does not seem to have worked for any other Chicago studio, nor did he ever originate his own studio.

In a period when many studios unhesitatingly copied each other's designs—sometimes with no modification, but often with just sufficient change to avoid prosecution—no examples have been discovered to date that would indicate that Stouffer ever followed this practice.

Along with the hand-painted china, Stouffer began to produce all-over-gold etched designs beginning about 1913–1915. The ready acceptance of the gold signified the beginning of a new era in china designs. The gold also proved effective in hiding the blemishes on poor-quality Japanese blanks when the French and German blanks were unobtainable during the last years of the war. Following the move into the new Prairie Avenue studios, another etching room was added early in 1923 to allow the production of all-over-platinum designs.

As tastes in hand-painted china continued to change through the twenties, plainer, simpler designs requiring less labor (and for the most part, less talent) left diminishing opportunities for employment and income for the professional decorator. Those china-decorating studios whose management were themselves artists—White, Brauer, Donath, and a host of lesser decorators—clung obstinately to their traditional designs and consequently began to fade and disappear. Stouffer was second only to Pickard in size and volume, and like Pickard, its competitive strength was a strong market focus. Stouffer was not the least reluctant to accommodate its customers' changing preferences.

New competitors arose as many hand decorators went out of business. These competitors tended to produce mainly gold- and platinum-etched ware. The Great Depression took most of Stouffer's competitors, old and new, out of the picture, and by 1933, only Stouffer and seven other companies remained in the china decorating business. Stouffer's hand-painted china was now much simpler in its designs, and Otto Podlaha's GOLDEN ORCHID (Plate 843), for which he earned $15 per week, was a good example. All-over-gold etching was still generating sales, but Stouffer also began increasing the quantity of its imported finished wares.

Stouffer probably always had a strong focus on institutional wholesaling, and this as much as anything kept the company alive in the lean years. As the 1933 advertisement (Fig. 47) indicates, Stouffer also developed a strong presence with the smaller mail order houses. This enabled the company's eventual return to the form of business with which Jacob Stouffer had started: the importation and wholesaling of finished wares. One piece (Plate 851, Mark 12.1) provides interesting confirmation. It bears the stamp of the Italian manufacturer of the finished ware (Ginori), Stouffer Mark 12, and a Sterling & Welch Co. stamp. Stouffer had obviously imported the finished piece, applied the Stouffer mark, and then "private-labeled" it for a major customer.

The company was sold to others just before America entered World War II—probably 1943 when it moved to the south edge of the Loop. Stouffer finally ceased operation in 1952.

### *Artists associated with the J. H. Stouffer Co.*

| | |
|---|---|
| Edith Arno* | F. Loba* |
| Isadore Bardos* | Marcius |
| Baret | Kate McBride |
| B. Betleis | Harry E. Michel* |
| Joseph Blaha* | Anton Miller* |
| Bullin | George Morley** (G. Morley) |
| Carl Buschbeck* | Nell |
| Ernest Feix (E. Feix) | Wenzel Pfohl |
| Nathan R. Gifford* | A. Piron |
| Harry R. Griffiths* | Otto Podlaha* |
| Halens | POL |
| Samuel Heap* | Regina |
| Ethel R. Honey (Hon)* | Arnold Rhodes* |
| Hovis | Carl Roessler* |
| Hull | K. Ryba |
| Thomas M. Jelinek* | Scot |
| Jacob I. Kiefus* | Shaw |
| Kind | Joseph Simek (J. Simek, J. Sim) |
| Waclaw Kalita* | W. Stens (W. Stens, W. Sten, W.S.) |
| Joseph R. Kittler (Kitt) | Jacob H. Stouffer (Stouffer, J. S.) |
| Marion Lawrence | R. Swartz |
| (M. Lawrence, M.L.) | A. Wall. (A. Wall., A.W.) |
| George P. Leach* | Gustav Weissflog (Gust)* |

*Also worked for Pickard*
**Morley did not work for Stouffer; he was a very prominent decorator for Lenox and like most artists, he also did some freelance work. As Pickard had done with Lebrun's work, Stouffer picked up some of Morley's pieces and resold them under his own mark.*

### *Unidentified initials:*

| | |
|---|---|
| ALF | FK. |
| B.o | JEC |
| C.B. or G.B. | M.R. |
| ESP | VEL |

## *Stouffer Trademarks*
*(Dates are approximations.)*

*Mark 1. 1905, ⅝" wide, red stamp.*

*Mark 2. 1905–1906, ½" wide, red stamp.*

*Mark 3. 1905–1907, ¾" x ⁷⁄₁₆", black stamp.*

*Mark 4. 1906–1914, ⅝" wide, red stamp.*

*Mark 5. 1912–1913, ⅞" wide, red stamp.*

*Mark 6. 1912–1916, ¹³⁄₁₆" wide, red stamp.*

*Mark 7. 1913–1914, ⅞" x ½", red stamp.*

*Mark 8. 1914–1918, ¾" x ⁷⁄₁₆", black stamp.*

*Mark 9. 1918–1922, ¹⁷⁄₃₂" dia., red, black stamp.*

*Mark 10. 1920–1924, ⁹⁄₁₆" dia., red stamp.*

*Mark 11, 11.1. 1925–1938, ½", ¹⁵⁄₁₆", black, silver stamp.*

*Mark 12. 1930–1942, ½" dia., black, gold stamp.*

*Mark 12.1. 1930–1942, same as mark 12 with private label mark added.*

*Mark 13. 1938–1946, ¾" wide, black, gold, silver stamp. (Also over gold circle.)*

*Marks 14, 14.1. 1938–1946, ⁹⁄₁₆" wide, black/gold stamp.*

Stouffer's Fine China
272E64
548E30
897E8
230E30
851E98
157E30
903E55
745E8
531E8
289E30
510E8
596E8
702E33
548E30 Coffee pot, sugar and creamer 24K all over encrusted gold Poppy and Forget-me-not pattern. Capacity 2½ pts.............................Per set $55.10
230E30 After dinner cup and saucer, 24K all over encrusted gold Poppy and Forget-me-not..Per doz. $76.20
272E64 Salt and Pepper, 24K gold top, handles and base, pink roses on Ivory background. Height 4½ in. ....................................Per pair $6.35
897E8 Salt and Pepper, 24K all over encrusted gold. Height 3 in.........................Per pair $2.80
851E98 Flower-bowl, Meissen green color, 24K gold lining. Diameter 9 in. Figure flower holder 24K gold, height 6¼ in....................Per set $26.85
157E30 Cake or sandwich plate, 24K all over encrusted gold Poppy and Forget-me-not. Diameter 10¾ in. .....................................Each $15.55
903E55 Mayonnaise, plate and ladle, 24K all over gold. Plate 5¾ in. diameter, bowl 4¼ in. high..Per set $13.40
745E8 Bon Bon, three compartment. 24K all over encrusted gold with handle................Each $13.40
531E8 Sugar and Creamer, 24K all over encrusted gold. ...................................Per set $13.40
289E30 Vase, 24K all over encrusted gold Poppy and Forget-me-not, Gold handles. Height 9½ in. .....................................Each $28.25
510E8 Sugar and Creamer, 24K all over encrusted gold. ...................................Per set $16.20
596E8 Tray, 24K all over encrusted gold. 6¼ in. by 14 in....................................Each $17.00
702E33 Pitcher or Lemonade jug, 24K all over encrusted gold Rambler rose. Height 8½ in. Capacity 4 pts. .....................................Each $26.85

Author's Collection.

*Figure 47. Stouffer wholesale catalog advertisement from 1932 and 1933.*

## Stouffer Plates

*Plate 782. Plate with scalloped rim, 8¼"d. Red flowers on green, stylized leaves with pale blue rococo border and lattice. Signed: Griff (Griffiths, Harry R.). TM date: 1905–1906. Blank: T&V rectangle, Limoges, France. Value: $90.00–120.00.*

*Plate 784. Plate with scalloped rim, 8¾"d. Three black-berry clusters, variegated leaves, vines to center. Signed: Arno (Arno, Edith). TM date: 1906–1914. Blank: J.P.L., France. Value: $80.00–110.00.*

*Plate 783. Plate, 8½"d. Red-orange day lilies on green leaves, scalloped gold border. Signed: Arno (Arno, Edith). TM date: 1905–1906. Blank: GDA, France. Value: $75.00–90.00.*

*Plate 785. Plate with scalloped rim, 8½"d. Spray of purple plums on green leaves and green/yellow ground. Signed: MJ or MT (MJ or MT). TM date: 1905–1906. Blank: Limoges, France. Value: $95.00–125.00.*

*Plate 786. Plate, 8½"d. White and purple peonies on green and russet ground. Signed: F. Zolty (Zolty, F.). TM date: 1906–1914. Blank: J.P.L., France. Value: $30.00–45.00.*

*Plate 787. Plate, scalloped rim, 8½"d. Triad of large white blossoms, green leaves, stems radiating to gold center, purple flower profiles between. (unsigned). TM date: 1906–1914. Blank: J.P.L., France. Value: $100.00–140.00.*

*Plate 788. Charger, rococo rim, perforated handles, 11¾"d. Three white lilies radiating from gold border, yellow and pale blue ground. Signed: Michel (Michel, Harry E.). TM date: 1906–1914. Blank: arc Patd Jan 23rd, 1906, J.P.L., France. Value: $165.00–195.00.*

*Plate 789. Small plate with scalloped rim, 7¾"d. Lavender flowers with green leaves and stems. Signed: POL (POL). TM date: 1906–1914. Blank: J.P.L., France. Value: $65.00–80.00.*

*Plate 791. Plate, 8½"d. Decorated gold border with alternate geometrics and red and blue florals. Signed: Hon. (Honey, Ethel R.). TM date: 1906–1914. Blank: Haviland, France. Value: $25.00–35.00.*

*Plate 790. Plate, scalloped edges, 8½"d. Lavender asters on gold/brown vines and leaves, green center, cream ground. Signed: E. Feix (Feix, Ernest). TM date: 1906–1914. Blank: J.P.L., France. Value: $110.00–130.00.*

Plate 792. Plate, 8¼"d. Purple clover on nouveau stems on blue and gold border, cream center. Signed: JELINEK (Jelinek, Thomas M.). TM date: 1906–1914. Blank: Haviland, France. Value: $60.00–85.00.

Plate 793. Plate, desert, 7½"d. LARGE POPPIES AOG, hand-painted center medallion of blackberries. Signed: A. Rhodes (Rhodes, Arnold). TM date: 1938–1946. Blank: none. Value: $30.00–45.00.

Plate 794. Plate, scalloped, 8½"d. Three red poppies radiating to center poppy medallion, blue-green leaves. Signed: A.W. (Wall., A.). TM date: 1906–1914. Blank: Haviland, France. Value: $35.00–50.00.

Plate 795. Berry dish, scalloped rim, 6"d. Three clusters of pink apple blossoms on dark green border, gold edged. (unsigned). TM date: 1905–1906. Blank: Limoges, France. Value: $18.00–$25.00.

Plate 796. Plate, 8½"d. Six maroon and orange tulips radiating to scalloped gold border, cream ground. Signed: Michel (Michel, Harry E.). TM date: 1906–1914. Blank: GDA, France. Value: $100.00–135.00.

Plate 798. Plate, scalloped rim, 8½"d. White water lily in colorful pond scene with three gold lily buds inserted from gold border. Signed: A. Piron (Piron, A.). TM date: 1906–1914. Blank: Haviland, France. Value: $95.00–135.00.

Plate 797. Bowl with scalloped edges, 10"d. Cherry spray, green leaves on green/maroon ground. Signed: A. Piron (Piron, A.). TM date: 1906–1914. Blank: T&V rectangle, Limoges, France. Value: $85.00–125.00.

Plate 799. Plate, 8½"d. Strawberry spray on olive ground, gold border. Signed: S. Heap (Heap, Samuel). TM date: 1906–1914. Blank: Haviland, France. Value: $85.00–120.00.

Plate 800. Cup and saucer. Red poppies with green leaves, embellished gold border. Signed: Michel (Michel, Harry E.). TM date: 1906–1914. Blank: Limoges, France. Value: $85.00–110.00.

Plate 801. Cream and sugar. Border panel: single poppy, cream embellished panels, lustre inside and out. Signed: J. Simek (Simek, Joseph). TM date: 1938–1946. Blank: crown Schlacken wer shield PL Austria. Value: $55.00–75.00.

*Plate 802. ISOLDE lidded coffee pot, 4 demi-tasse and saucers, 6.75 Poppies, blue-green leaves on variegated lustre, embellished gold border. Signed: A. Wall. (Wall., A.). TM date: 1906–1914. Blank: PL Limoges, France. Value: $225.00–285.00.*

*Plate 803. Vase, 4¾"h. Poppies on embellished gold border, with blue-green leaves on cream ground. (unsigned). TM date: 1906–1914. Blank: none. Value: $90.00–110.00.*

*Plate 805. Charger, scalloped, perforated handles, 10"d. Lavender and red irises on cream ground, gold border. Signed: E. Feix (Feix, Ernest). TM date: 1906–1914. Blank: Patd JAN 23rd, 1906, J.P.L., France. Value: $145.00–180.00.*

*Plate 806. Cup and saucer. Lavender and red irises on gold border, three stems radiating to ochre center. Signed: E. Feix (Feix, Ernest). TM date: 1906–1914. Blank: Limoges, France. Value: $85.00–100.00.*

*Plate 804. (left) Muffineer, 4½"h. Lavender and red irises out of gold top, cream ground. Signed: E. Feix (Feix, Ernest). TM date: No TM. Blank: none. Value: $125.00–150.00. (right) Demi-tasse cup and saucer. Lavender and red irises on cream ground, three stems to ochre center. Signed: E. Feix (Feix, Ernest). No TM. Blank: GDA, France. Value: $85.00–125.00. Note: Stouffer did not mark muffineers.*

Plate 807. TOURAINE lidded cracker jar, 7"d. Red nasturtiums, green leaves on cream, gold border. Signed: Michel (Michel, Harry E.). TM date: 1906–1914. Blank: Déposé Touraine T&V France. Value: $125.00–150.00.

Plate 808. Powder box, 6"d. Red nasturtiums on green leaves around rim, gold center, cream ground. Signed: Michel (Michel, Harry E.). TM date: 1906–1914. Blank: T&V rectangle, Limoges, France. Value: $100.00–125.00.

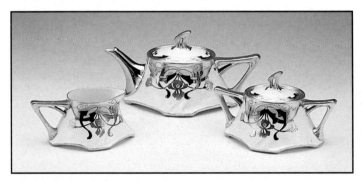

Plate 809. Lidded teapot, lidded sugar, and creamer. Gold and platinum scrolls with floral pendant. Signed: Bardos (Bardos, Isadore). TM date: 1906–1914. Blank: Patd April 2d, 1907, J.P.L., France. Value: $275.00–340.00.

Plate 810. Lidded condensed milk holder with open handles and underplate, 5"h. Gold border with platinum escutcheons bearing red poppy with green leaves descending into white ground. Signed: Leach (Leach, George P.). TM date: 1912–1916. Blank: circle JHR Hutschenreuther Selb Bavaria Favorite. Value: $185.00–225.00.

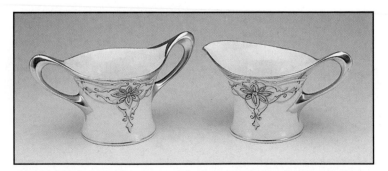

Plate 811. FAVORITE cream and sugar. Platinum-petaled flower surrounded by black-embellished gold scrolling on white ground. Signed: Bardos (Bardos, Isadore). TM date: 1906–1914. Blank: Favorite Bavaria. Value: $100.00–135.00.

*Plate 812. ISOLDE demi-tasse cup and saucer. Blue forget-me-nots with green leaves on gold border and pale blue and pale pink ground. Signed: Michel, HM (Michel, Harry E.). TM date: 1906–1914. Blank: crossed clovers J&C Isolde. Value: $60.00–75.00.*

*Plate 813. (left) Plate, 8½"d. Gold embellished border with alternating pink clover blossoms and green shamrocks. Signed: W.S. (Stens, W.). TM date: 1906–1914. Blank: GDA, France. Value: $40.00–55.00. (right) Bonbon with upswept open handles, 6½"d. Pink clover and leaves on embellished gold border, white ground. Signed: W. Sten (Stens, W.). TM date: 1906–1914. Blank: none. Value: $35.00–45.00.*

*Plate 814. Vase, bowl-style, 4¼"h. Urn with symmetrical, stylized multicolored sprays, gold border, white ground. Signed: J. Sim. (Simek, Joseph). TM date: 1906–1914. Blank: GDA, France. Value: $35.00–55.00.*

*Plate 815. (rear) Plate, 7½"d. Pink clover on gold columns, cream ground. (unsigned). TM date:1906–1914. Blank: Haviland, France. Value: $20.00–30.00. (front) Cream and sugar. Pink clover on gold columns, cream ground. Signed: FK. (unknown). TM date: 1906–1914. Blank: T&V France incised JA. Value: $40.00–55.00.*

Plate 816. Plate, 8¾"d. Three violet clusters radiating from center, cream ground, green leaves on border. Signed: Michel (Michel, Harry E.). TM date: 1906–1914. Blank: Haviland, France. Value: $75.00–90.00.

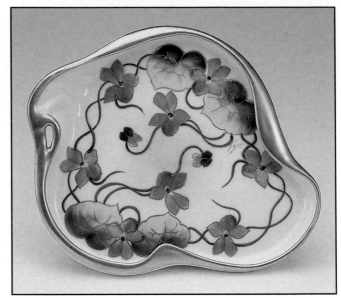

Plate 817. Ring tray, Art Nouveau shape, 6¾"l. Violets on green leaves, gold veining, pale yellow ground. Signed: Gust (Weissflog, Gustav). TM date: 1906–1914. Blank: none. Value: $65.00–80.00.

Plate 818. Lidded mustard boat with attached underplate, 5"l. Violets on blue-green ground and pale yellow ground. Signed: Blaha (Blaha, Joseph). TM date: 1906–1914. Blank: none. Value: $110.00–135.00.

Plate 819. Plate, scalloped edge, 8¾"d. Three pink carnations, blue/green leaves radiating from gold center, gold border. Signed: Kiefus (Kiefus, Jacob I.). TM date: 1906–1914. Blank: AK D, France. Value: $110.00–145.00.

Plate 820. (left) Plate, 8⅝"d. Three red/orange tiger lilies, radiating from center with green leaves and gold border. Signed: J. Sim (Simek, Joseph). TM date: 1906–1914. Blank: Haviland, France. Value: $45.00–60.00. (right) Muffineer, 4½"h. Red/orange tiger lilies, green leaves, cream ground, gold top. Signed: J.Sim (Simek, Joseph). No TM. Blank: none. Value: $170.00–195.00.

*Plate 821. Plate, 8½"d. Three large violets in three rim groups, blue ground, gold/violet center. Signed: C.B. (B., C.). TM date: 1906–1914. Blank: GDA, France. Value: $85.00–95.00.*

*Plate 822. Plate, 8½"d. Tripartite of two pink and yellow blossoms twined out of center, blue ground. Signed: W. Stens (Stens, W.). TM date: 1906–1914. Blank: J.P.L., France. Value: $135.00–165.00.*

*Plate 823. Plate, 8½"d. Three cherry sprays on gold border. Signed: Arno (Arno, Edith). TM date: 1906–1914. Blank: none. Value: $65.00–100.00.*

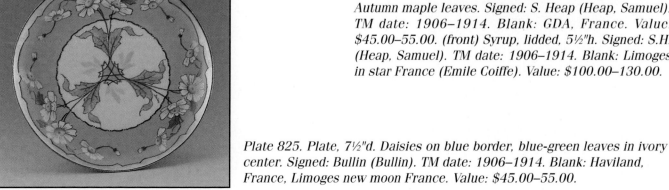

*Plate 824. (rear) Bread & rolls, scalloped, 13½"l. Autumn maple leaves. Signed: S. Heap (Heap, Samuel). TM date: 1906–1914. Blank: GDA, France. Value: $45.00–55.00. (front) Syrup, lidded, 5½"h. Signed: S.H. (Heap, Samuel). TM date: 1906–1914. Blank: Limoges in star France (Emile Coiffe). Value: $100.00–130.00.*

*Plate 825. Plate, 7½"d. Daisies on blue border, blue-green leaves in ivory center. Signed: Bullin (Bullin). TM date: 1906–1914. Blank: Haviland, France, Limoges new moon France. Value: $45.00–55.00.*

Plate 826. Dresser set: tray, hair receiver, pinbox, and jewelry box, 11"w. Pink and blue flowers and buds on gold border on white ground. Signed: W. Stens. (Stens, W.). TM date: 1906–1914. Blank: Limoges, France. Value: $300.00–395.00.

Plate 827. Plate, scalloped rim, 8½"d. Brown sailing ships, steamer in ground, lustre water, sky. Signed: El'ukn(?). TM date: 1906–1914. Blank: Haviland, France. Value: $200.00–260.00.

Plate 828. Vase, tall, 11½"h. Elk bellowing in forest. Signed: K. Ryba (Ryba, K.). TM date: 1906–1914. Blank: GDA, France. Value: $385.00–450.00.

Plate 829. Plate, 8½"d. Vellum: Cranes in lake at sunset. Signed: VEL (unknown). TM date: 1906–1914. Blank: J.P.L., France. Value: $100.00–135.00.

Plate 830. Cream and sugar. Vellum: lavender lagoon. (unsigned). TM date: 1906–1914. Blank: none. Value: $100.00–125.00.

Plate 831. Vase, narrow-mouthed, 7"h. Two hunting dogs at point. Signed: K. Ryba. (Ryba, K.). TM date: 1906–1914. Blank: 3614. Value: $275.00–325.00.

Plate 832. Teapot, 5"h. Pink blossoms on blue-green leaves on pale green border. (unsigned). TM date: 1906–1914. Blank: none. Value: $30.00–40.00.

Plate 833. (left) Lidded powder box, 5"d. Violets with gold-veined leaves, cream ground. (unsigned). TM date: 1906–1914. Blank: T&V rectangle, Limoges, France. Value: $45.00–65.00. (right) Hatpin holder, 3¾"h. Violets with gold-veined leaves, cream ground. Signed: Michel. (Michel, Harry E.). TM date: 1906–1914. Blank: PL Limoges, France. Value: $165.00–200.00.

Plate 834. Ring-holder, fingered, 3½"h. Violets with gold outlines. Signed: J. Simek (Simek, Joseph). TM date: No TM. Blank: Noritake Nippon. Value: $80.00–100.00.

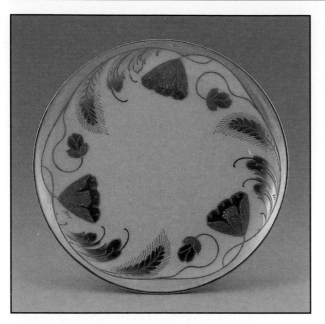

Plate 835. Plate, 7½"d. Poppies and wheat border in raised gold paste. Signed: Bek. (Buschbeck, Carl). TM date: 1906–1914. Blank: Haviland, France. Value: $100.00–135.00.

Plate 836. (rear) Chocolate set: 4 demi-tasse, 4 saucers, lidded pot, 12"h. Gold border with platinum escutcheons descending into white; gold and black embellishments. Signed: Leach (Leach, George P.). TM date: 1906–1914. Blank: T&V Limoges, France Déposé. Value: $325.00–$400.00. (front) Sauce dish, 5½"d. Gold and platinum embellished escutcheons on white ground. Signed: Bardos (Bardos, Isadore). TM date: 1906–1914. Blank: Haviland, France. Value: $40.00–55.00.

Plate 837. Plate, 8¾"d. Platinum and gold geometrics. Signed: Miller (Miller, Anton). TM date: 1906–1914. Blank: Haviland, France. Value: $65.00–100.00.

Plate 838. (left) Plate, 9½"d. Gold encrusted center, three blue medallions with raised lilies and daisies. Signed: J. Simek (Simek, Joseph). TM date: 1938–1946. Blank: crossed flowers J&C Bavaria. Value: $55.00–70.00. (right) Medium pitcher, 7½"h. Gold encrusted body with enameled lily in blue medallion, mother-of-pearl lustre border with scroll and daisy embellishment. Signed: J. Simek (Simek, Joseph). TM date: 1913–1914. Blank: B.&Co. Limoges, France. Value: $115.00–135.00.

*Plate 839. ALEXANDER lidded sugar, teapot, and creamer. Urn with symmetrical stylized multi-colored sprays. Gold border above black body. Signed: J. Sim (Simek, Joseph). TM date: 1906–1914. Blank: T&V rectangle, Limoges, France. Value: $225.00–250.00.*

*Plate 840. Cream and sugar. Cattails, gold with black outline, peach water lilies, green pads, white ground. Signed: MLawrence (Lawrence, Marion). TM date: 1938–1946. Blank: none. Value: $95.00–110.00.*

*Plate 841. Salt and pepper, 3½"h. Pink flowers with gold leaves, stems with black outlines. Signed: ReginA (unknown). TM date: 1938–1946. Blank: none. Value: $15.00–25.00.*

*Plate 842. (left rear) Tray, oval, 9"l., GOLDEN ORCHID. Signed: O Podl (Podlaha, Otto). TM date: 1938–1946. Blank: Overstamped. Value: $40.00–50.00. (right rear) Salt and pepper, 4"h. Signed: OP (Podlaha, Otto). TM date: 1938–1946. Blank: none. Value: $35.00–40.00. Demi-tasse and saucer. Signed: A. Rhodes (Rhodes, Arnold). TM date: 1938–1946. Blank: none. Value: $30.00–45.00. (under demi-tasse) Plate, desert, 7½"d. Signed: ReginA (unknown). TM date: 1938–1946. Blank: none. Value: $10.00–15.00.*

Plate 843. *Lidded teapot, lidded sugar, creamer,* GOLD-EN ORCHID. *Signed: O.Podlaha (Podlaha, Otto). TM date: 1938–1946. Blank: star Girard star 40. Value: $155.00–185.00.*

Plate 844. *(rear) Plate, 8"d. Three radii to alternating gold and platinum flowers, white ground. Signed: Bardos (Bardos, Isadore). TM date: 1906–1914. Blank: Haviland, France. Value: $75.00–95.00. (front) Teapot with upswept handle. Platinum and gold on white, flower and lily of the valley. Signed: Kind. (Kind). TM date: 1906–1914. Blank: T&V rectangle, Limoges, France Déposé. Value: $45.00–55.00.*

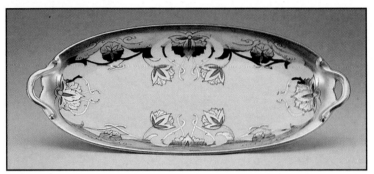

Plate 845. *Tray, relish, handled, 14"l. Gold rim, gold, platinum, and maroon stylized flowers on white ground. (unsigned). TM date: 1912–1916. Blank: GDA, France. Value: $85.00–120.00.*

Plate 846. *Muffineer, 4½"h. Gold top, platinum scrolls with gold lattice and florals on white ground. Signed: Bardos (Bardos, Isadore). No TM. Blank: none. Value: $85.00–125.00.*

Plate 847. *Pedestalled compote with delicate open handles, 8"d. Three etched gold medallions pendent from lattice on narrow etched gold band. (unsigned). TM date: 1906–1914. Blank: T&V rectangle, Limoges, France. Value: $125.00–145.00.*

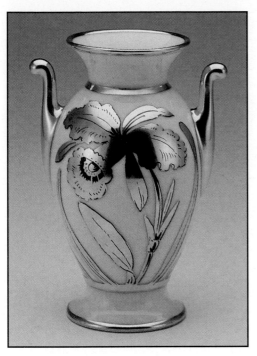

Plate 849. (left) Plate, dinner, 8½"d. Platinum Lily of the Valley sprays above gold circle, platinum linears. Signed: Miller (Miller, Anton). TM date: 1906–1914. Blank: Haviland, France. Value: $75.00–95.00. (right) COLONIAL lidded coffee pot, 11"h. Platinum and gold on white: flower and lily of the valley. Signed: Kind. (Kind). TM date: 1906–1914. Blank: D&Co., France. Value: $100.00–150.00.

Plate 848. Vase with open handles, 6½"h., GOLDEN ORCHID. Signed: A. Rhodes (Rhodes, Arnold). TM date: 1938–1946. Blank: none. Value: $45.00–85.00.

Plate 851. Demitasse and saucer, scalloped rim, 4½"d. Burnished gold. (unsigned). TM date: 1930–1942. Blank: Richard 3 stars Ginori 1-40 Italy, The Sterling & Welch Co. Cleveland. Value: $25.00–35.00.

Plate 850. Bonbon with scalloped rim and one perforated handle, 7"d., POPPY AND FORGET-ME-NOT AOG. (unsigned). TM date: 1930–1942. Blank: none. Value: $45.00–65.00.

Plate 852. Candy dish four perforated fan handles, 7¼"d., FORGET-ME-NOTS AOG. (unsigned). TM date: 1920–1924. Blank: star RS wreath Germany. Value: $40.00–55.00.

Plate 853. Condiment set: tray, salt & pepper, covered mustard pot with spoon, 4¼"ld., AOG encrusted. (unsigned). TM date: 1938–1946. Blank: Made In Japan. Value: $175.00–225.00.

Plate 854. Lidded compote, 6½"d., DAISY FIELD AOG. (unsigned). TM date: 1930–1942. Blank: none. Value: $95.00–135.00.

Plate 855. Three-handled toothpick holder, 1¾"h., DAISIES AND LEAVES AOG. (unsigned). TM date: 1925–1938. Blank: Germany. Value: $65.00–95.00.

Plate 856. Candlesticks, 2¾"h., POPPY. (unsigned). TM date: 1930–1942. Blank: none. Value: $75.00–95.00.

Plate 857. Large tulip bowl, 6½"d., AOG with five cream floral panels. (unsigned). TM date: 1925–1930. Blank: star wreath, RS, Germany. Value: $115.00–135.00.

# TOLPIN STUDIOS,

## *1920–1945*

### Tolpin Art Studio
### 1945–1954

### Illinois China Decorating Company
### 1920–1922

### Progressive China Decorating Company
### 1921–1924

### Rivir Studios
### 1922–1930

### China Decorating Company
### 1923–?

### Roosevelt China Studio
### 1926–1930

### Deluxe China Studios
### 1931

### Tolpin Products Manufacturing Company
### 1950–1954

Much detail is lacking, but the available records suggest that various members of the Tolpin family were responsible for the eventual formation of eight different china decorating studios. The first two family members arrived from Russia in 1907. Subsequent immigrations brought additional relatives to Chicago so that eventually eight china artists were included in the family's ranks. At least two of them, Nesha and Emil, worked for Pickard.

In 1920, Emil Tolpin started a studio under his own name and then in 1925 it became simply, The Tolpin Studios. In 1922 the Rivir Studios opened with Isaac Tolpin as one of its artists; how much more of the family was involved is unknown. Also, in 1923, Louis and Meyer Tolpin opened the China Decorating Company; this had been preceded by the Illinois China Decorating Company in 1920 and the Progressive China Decorating Company in 1921—all at the same address. These studios may have been different names for essentially the same operation, but at any event, none of them survived for long. By 1926, Meyer Tolpin was operating the Roosevelt China Studio, so-named because of its loca-

tion on West Roosevelt Road. All of these studios were located on the Near West Side of Chicago.

No products of the China Decorating Company, the Illinois China Decorating Company, or the Progressive China Decorating Company have been discovered, and what has survived from the other studios is mostly all-over-gold etched pieces. All of the etched work was very good quality, however, with imaginative, original patterns. In 1928 and 1929 the Tolpin Studios boasted a double street address at 2129–31 West Van Buren with a separate warehouse at 2137 West Van Buren. The Studio sold its etched gold china in two of its own exhibits at Chicago's Century of Progress World's Fair in 1933 and 1934. By 1937 the company was also producing lamps. In 1945 the studio moved to 3122 West Lawrence Avenue and was renamed the Tolpin Art Studio where gold refinishing, monogramming, repair, and matching of dinnerware were added. In 1950 a separate company, the Tolpin Products Manufacturing Company, was established at 7244 North Western Avenue to handle the lamp manufacturing trade. Both companies ceased operation in 1954.

*Artists believed to have been associated with one or more of these studios.*

| | |
|---|---|
| Chester Aagaard | Isaac Tolpin |
| Waclaw Kalita* | Isadore Tolpin |
| Anton Miller* | Louis Tolpin |
| Arnold Rhodes* | Meyer Tolpin |
| John Thonander* | Nesha Tolpin* |
| Emil E. Tolpin* | Samuel Tolpin |
| Harry Tolpin | |

*\*Also a Pickard artist*

### Rivir/Tolpin Trademarks
*(Dates are approximations.)*

*1922–1930, red or brown stamp.*

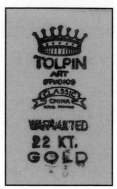

Mark 3.
1945–1954,
gold stamp.

Mark 1. 1925–1938,
¹³⁄₁₆" dia., red stamp
over gold disk and red
stamp only.

Mark 2. 1938–
1945, gold or
black stamp.

## Tolpin Plates

Plate 858. Cream and sugar. Flowered festoon with
alternate blue ribbon festoons on white. Signed: Tol.
(Tolpin). TM date: 1925–1938. Blank: Z.S.&Co.,
Bavaria. Value: $90.00–135.00.

Plate 861. Mayonnaise and underplate, 7"l., STRAW-
BERRY AOG. (unsigned). TM date: 1922–1930. Blank:
none. Value: $45.00–65.00.

Plate 859. Nut or candy
dish, 4½"sq. Modified
rose and daisy AOG
with French lady and
gentleman medallion in
center. (unsigned). TM
date: 1945–1954.
Blank: none. Value:
$35.00–45.00.

Plate 862. Cream and sugar. Floral gold-etched
with lavender lustre border with maroon flower.
Signed: I. Tolpin (Tolpin, Isaac). TM date:
1922–1930. Blank: none. Value: $65.00–85.00.

Plate 860. Creamer, sugar, and tray, ROSE AND DAISY AOG.
(unsigned). TM date: 1938–1945. Blank: Eamag UnShon-
wald, Bavaria. Value: $85.00–100.00.

# WHITE & WHITE

## *1912–1913*

## White's Art Company 1914–1923

There were five children in the White family. Hamilton White, the father, was a teacher and a landscape artist. He was 77 years old when the first company originated in 1912, and probably played only a minor role in its formation. But the three daughters, Ida (55), Sarah (46), and Ellen (?) had all been active artists since the turn of the century. A son, James (47), had also been an artist, but went into sales in 1902.

The initial company, White & White, combined the talents of Ida and Sarah, and their primary business was art supplies. In 1914 however, the company was renamed "White's Art Company" with James as president and Ida as secretary. In March of 1914, *Keramic Studio* carried White's advertisement for Roman gold and offering "...superior china colors used in our studio for years. One of the largest decorators of china in the country. Our matt colors cannot be duplicated [we] teach etching on china and enamel work."

By 1915 the company had changed its identity to that of "china decorators" and grew very rapidly. The growth, however, was largely on the student side, and therefore few examples bearing the red triangle mark have survived. Of these, the quality is mixed, but the better quality predominates and is often equal to Pickard's very best.

The iris chocolate set (Plate 868) in particular, ranks among the finest pieces of hand-painted china from any studio. Other semi-professional artists also contributed to White's collection and probably included a number of women affiliated with the Chicago Ceramic Arts Association and the old National League of Mineral Painters. Bothilde Frank was one such artist.

The few White pieces that have survived betray a good mix of traditional, pictorial, and stylized themes. There was sufficient demand for many designs that, like Pickard, the work was occasionally divided among a number of artists (Plate 872).

The studio operated just north of the Chicago Loop at 201 East Ontario Street for most of its existence. In 1923, the studio moved to Sarah White's residence at 2142 Sedgwick. James, Ida, and Ellen had dropped out of the business, which by then was essentially a one-woman studio, Ellen White. She died at the same address on November 4, 1947.

### Artists associated with White's Art Company

| | |
|---|---|
| Becker | Kenar |
| BEN | Miche* |
| L. Blet | Ney |
| Deon | Osburn (not Osborne) |
| Bothilde Frank | Porreca |
| Charles Hahn* | Howard B. Reury* |
| Heyn | Utwich |
| High | |

*\*Also worked for Pickard*

Unidentified initials:
PGC — PD — EH

## White Trademark

*1914–1923, ⅞" wide, red triangle stamp.*

## White Plates

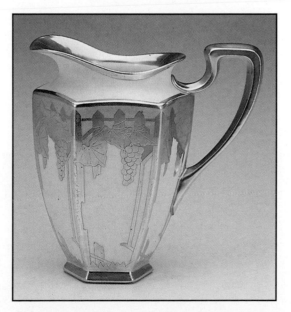

*Plate 863. Pitcher, 8½"h. Grape arbor in etched and incised gold on matte cream ground. (unsigned). TM date: 1914–1923. Blank: B.&Co., France. Value: $225.00–250.00.*

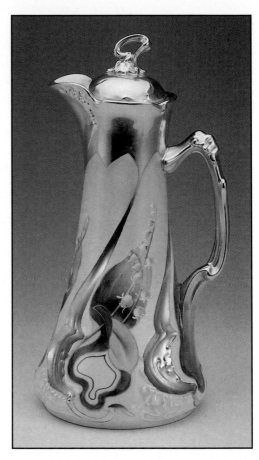

Plate 864. ISOLDE lidded teapot, lidded sugar, creamer, 7"h. Gold grapes on silver, vine and leaves, black ground. Signed: BLET (Blet, L.). TM date: 1914–1923. Blank: crossed clovers J&C Isolde. Value: $225.00–275.00.

Plate 865. ALEXANDER jug, 9"d. Pen-line detailed white, yellow, and pink flowers on Prussian blue band. Signed: Heyn (Heyn). TM date: 1914–1923. Blank: T&V rectangle, Limoges, France. Value: $395.00–450.00.

Plate 867. Lidded chocolate pot, 11½"h. Lilies of the valley on green ground with gold border. Signed: Miche (Miche). TM date: 1914–1923. Blank: J.P.L., France. Value: $325.00–380.00.

Plate 866. Cream and lidded sugar, double perforated handles. Chartreuse cotton blossom border on Prussian blue ground. Signed: Frank (Frank, Bothilde N.). TM date: 1914–1923. Blank: none. Value: $75.00–95.00.

*Plate 868. Lidded coffee, lidded sugar, creamer, (fluted blanks with scalloped feet), 8"h. Lavender/purple irises on green stems, gold lattice on pale blue border. Signed: Blet (Blet, L.). TM date: 1914–1923. Blank: Haviland, France. Value: $475.00–595.00.*

*Plate 869. Plate, drilled for wall mounting, 8"d. Galloping camel in front of pyramids. Signed: Utwich. TM date: 1914–1923. Blank: none. Value: $180.00–225.00.*

*Plate 870. (left) Side plate, 6"d. Medallion of pansies, gold border embellished with colored pansies. Signed: ASB. TM date: 1914–1923. Blank: Haviland, France. Value: $20.00–25.00. (right) Side plate, 6"d. Medallion of carnations, gold border embellished with colored carnations. Signed: ASB. TM date: 1914–1923. Blank: Haviland, France. Value: $20.00–25.00.*

*Plate 871. Tankard, footed, hex, scalloped rim, 10½"h. Lemons on green leaves. Signed: Blet (Blet, L.). TM date: 1914–1923. Blank: none. Value: $295.00–350.00.*

Plate 872. Lidded coffee pot, signed: BLET (Blet, L.). 6 cups and saucers. Open milkweed pods, green leaves, gold trim. Signed: Ney (Ney). TM date: 1914–1923. Blank: Haviland, France. Value: $575.00–650.00.

Plate 873. Pitcher, milk, 4"h. Pink apple blossom on decorated gold border on cream ground. Signed: E.H. (unknown). TM date: 1914–1923. Blank: GDA, France. Value: $35.00–45.00.

Plate 874. Cream and sugar. Violet spray with gold linears. Signed: Blet (Blet, L.). TM date: 1914–1923. Blank: T&V rectangle, Limoges, France, Longchamps. Value: $75.00–125.00.

Plate 875. Lemonade pitcher, 8"h. Orange carp amid seaweed and water lilies. Signed: Blet (Blet, L.). TM date: 1914–1923. Blank: scrolls W.G.&Co., France. Value: $350.00–400.00.

# WIGHT ART STUDIO,
## 1911–1919

Phillip Wight decorated china for Pickard from about 1907 through 1910. In 1911, he formed the Wight Studios Company with himself as secretary and R. Bentley as president. Bentley was an assistant buyer for Mandel Brothers, one of the major downtown department stores (One wonders if there was not a little conflict of interest in this arrangement.) The studio relocated a number of times during its short existence, but was always within a short distance of Pickard.

What little of the studio's output has survived, is conservative florals and Pickard-style simple borders of acceptable commercial quality. Only one other artist is known to have worked for Wight, former Pickard artist, Howard B. Reury. The studio had ceased operation by 1920.

### Wight Trademark

1911–1919, 1⅜" dia., black or maroon stamp.

### Wight Plates

Plate 876. Desert plate, 7½"d. Simple border: scrolls with pink and blue floral harp. (unsigned). TM date: 1911–1919. Blank: crossed clovers J&C, Bavaria. Value: $15.00–20.00.

Plate 877. Cracker jar, lidded, 6¼"d. Blue forget-me-nots sprays with gold scrolls. Signed: Wight (Wight, Phillip). TM date: 1911–1919. Blank: none. Value: $65.00–90.00.

Plate 878. Luncheon set. Apple blossoms on pale green ground. Signed: Wight (Wight, Phillip). TM date: 1911–1919. Blank: Bavaria. Value: $350.00–400.00.

# YESCHEK, INC.
## 1928–1930

### Ceramic Artcraft Studios
### 1940–1953

As foreman of Pickard's etching department, Frank Yeschek had gained much valuable experience in this skill, and in 1928 he decided to go into business for himself. He sold his home on Hermitage Avenue, borrowed $4,500 from artist Otto Podlaha, and purchased a studio from artist August Steiner that Steiner had been operating since 1924. Frank Yeschek was president of the new cor-

*Figure 48. Frank Yeschek in his Ceramic Artcraft Studio.*

Yeschek employed were Pickard artists Paul Nitsche and Louis Grumieaux, the very talented artist from D'Arcy's studio in Kalamazoo, John H. Schindler, and Louis Groskopf. Yeschek then moved his show room to the mezzanine floor of the Palmer House. Whether this move was the proximate cause or not, the business began to decline. The burden of two locations and the on-set of the Great Depression were more than his ambitious enterprise could tolerate, and after a little more than two years of operation the business was forced to close. Yeschek took whatever odd jobs were available and finally moved to Flambeau, Wisconsin, to participate in a family resort business there.

In the fall of 1939 he decided to return to Chicago and china decorating under the name of the Ceramic Artcraft Studios. He moved into a home on Hermitage Avenue and rented a building down the alley at 5003 North Ravenswood, just two blocks north of the old Ravenswood studio. By the middle of the following year Pickard had vacated Ravenswood and moved to Antioch, leaving many Chicago decorators

poration, William McWilliams was vice president, Susan Yeschek was secretary, and her cousin, Clara McWilliams, was treasurer. The enterprise consisted of a studio at 2743 North Sheffield Avenue and a sales room in the Stevens Building on South State Street.

In addition to etched china, Yeschek advertised glassware, hand-painted china, decorated pottery, and terra cotta. His all-over-gold pieces were superb, and he used Pickard's early custom of etching his trademark into the china and firing it in gold, thereby making it as indestructible as the china itself. Very few pieces seem to have survived, however.

Initially, the business went well, and among the artists that

*Figure 49. Ceramic Artcraft Studio.*

available. Yeschek acquired Pauline Fuchs, Louis Grumieaux, Robert Hessler, Frank Nittel, and Arnold Rhodes. (Rhodes did not decorate on the premises; his work was picked up at his home studio in suburban Downers Grove.) Carl Koenig also decorated for Ceramic Artcraft, having closed his studio on the South Side in 1937. Though they were not all employed at the same time, payroll records spanning 1946–1947 list a total of 28 employees, at least eight of whom were artists.

In 1940, a woman whom Susan Yeschek had been nursing died, leaving Mrs. Yeschek a new Buick automobile. The Yescheks sold the car and bought additional kilns with the money—in all, the studio ultimately boasted seven kilns. As it had been in the late 1920s, etched china was again a significant part of Yeschek's product offering and included beautifully patterned service plates and other dinnerware. The studio also acquired contracts for lamp bases from two New York firms and this accounted for much of the studio's volume. The studio did well, the biggest problem was dealing with the temperaments of the artists. Despite this success, Yeschek could not remain content just to decorate. Probably inspired to some degree by Pickard's move into porcelain manufacturing, he attempted to set up a pottery on North Western Avenue. The venture failed almost as soon as it began and brought everything else down with it. Ceramic Artcraft Studios ceased operation in 1953. Broke and understandably discouraged, Yeschek went on to what other jobs he could find, but china decorating was still his passion, and he maintained a tiny basement studio for many years. He died on October 10, 1974.

## Yeschek/Ceramic Artcraft Trademarks

*Mark 1. 1928–1930, ⅝" high, etched gold.*

*Mark 2. 1940–1953, ⁷⁄₁₆" high, gold or black stamp.*

## Yeschek Plates

*Plate 879. Pedestalled tulip bowl compote, 5"h., GRAPEVINE AOG. TM date: 1928–1930. Blank: none. Value: $140.00–185.00.*

*Plate 880. Vase with stanchion handles, 6¼"h. Glossy scenic of poppies and daisies foreground and woods in front of pink sky in background. Signed: (unintelligible). TM date: 1940–1953. Blank: none. Value: $65.00–85.00.*

*Artists associated with one or both of these studios*

| | |
|---|---|
| Charles Clark | Paul Nitsche* |
| Mildred Clark | Frank Nittel* |
| Pauline Fuchs* | Arnold Rhodes* |
| Louis Groskopf | John H. Schindler |
| Louis Grumieaux* | Seraphia Sterling |
| Carl Koenig* | Frank Yeschek* |
| Marie Larson | Joseph Yeschek* |
| Betty Lupinek | |

*\*Former Pickard artist*

# CHINA DECORATING ASSOCIATIONS

## National League of Mineral Painters

The National League of Mineral Painters was organized in 1892 by the Milwaukee artist and entrepreneur, Susan S. Frackleton. Her goal was to provide an association that would advance and coordinate the efforts of the nation's thousands of independent china artists.

The effort was quite successful, with local chapters quickly springing up across the country. These chapters met regularly and included classes of study and instruction, and in the larger metropolitan areas, gave rise to annual exhibitions. While the membership was mostly female, a number of prominent male artists lent significant stature to the organization.

A number of artists held memberships in this association plus the Chicago Ceramic Arts Association and the Atlan Ceramic Arts Association. By 1911, although it continued to be effective on the national scene, competition from local clubs, plus some internal discord, ended the National League of Mineral Painters as a significant organization in Chicago.

## Chicago Ceramic Arts Association

The Chicago Ceramic Arts Association was formed in January of 1892, in anticipation of providing a vehicle for the exhibition of its members' wares at the 1893 Worlds Columbian Exhibition.[40] The association initially numbered 260 members. After the Columbian Exhibition, its popularity continued to grow. At one time or another, it included such notables as Franz B. Aulich, Edward Donath, Dominick Campana, Helen Frazee, Victorine Jenkins, Roxanna Preuszner, Howard Reury, Ione Wheeler, and Abby Pope Walker.

The association conducted its own exhibition at the Chicago Art Institute for many years, and its members were also well represented at the Burley exhibitions. The association disappeared shortly after the end of World War I.

## Atlan Ceramic Arts Club
### 1893–1924

In January of 1893, Florence Pratt Steward conceived the idea of establishing a club for the furtherance of the china decorating art. Although the National League of Mineral Painters and the Chicago Ceramic Association served as a forum for the female china painter, in the estimation of some of its more serious members, it lacked structure and focus. Out of this need grew the Atlan Ceramic Arts Club. The Club derived its name from an Egyptian manuscript on clay baking, and according to Mrs. Steward, "...undoubtedly was transferred by the Atlantians to the country (Egypt)...." (It should be recalled that there was a great fascination with the East at that time, as archeological excavations brought more wonders to light each year. The mystic auras of Atlantis and ancient Egypt thus fit well with the concept of this little club.)

The Club's motto was "Patience, Persistence, Progress" and it appeared on the most prevalent of its many marks in the form of three crossed P's. "ATLAN" frequently appeared below the P's and the artist's name or initials and the date were also often added. Atlan artists came from both ends of Chicago's economic and social spectrum. For some it was a genteel means of fulfilling an artistic bent, but for others, it was their sole means of support.

Four of Chicago's most accomplished pottery and china artists were selected as the club's first officers: Cornie Mann was president, Emma Kittredge was vice president, Florence Pratt Steward was secretary, and Roxanna Preuszner was councilor. The club also recognized its debt to the substantial talents and pioneering efforts of Milwaukee artist and founder of the National League of Mineral Painters, Susan S. Frackelton, by naming her Honorary President. Membership was limited to 18 active artists to avoid competing with the two larger clubs. After the turn of the century, this number was gradually increased so that by 1915, 30 exhibiting members were authorized together with a large group of "associate" members "who may or may not paint." This classification also accommodated original members who had moved to other cities.

The impetus behind the club's organization was the imminent opening of the World's Columbian Exposition on Chicago's South Side in May of 1893. A separate building, "The Women's Building," (designed by 23 year old architect Sophia Hayden[41]), was constructed for the express purpose of exhibiting women's accomplishments in the Arts and Sciences.

The members of the Atlan Club were already advanced artists, and in the space of only six weeks, they produced an array of decorated china in time for entry at the fair. A testimony to their skill was the remarkable number of prizes which this group of 18 artists was awarded: out of a total of 31 prizes, Atlan carried away 18 of them—more than the members of either the long-established Chicago Ceramic Association or the National League of Mineral Painters.

In their first few years, the members were distinguished by their technical proficiency in rendering naturalistic landscapes, portraits, and florals. But in 1898 they embarked on a formal eight week program of education, employing the services of a noted teacher, Mrs. Florence Kohler. Under Mrs. Kohler's tutelage, the members were introduced to a succession of epochs in design: Egyptian, Persian, Arabic, Moorish, East Indian, Japanese, and Chinese. The Atlans diligently pursued their assignments in reading, tracing, and submitting their designs for criticism. This course was so successful that others followed, and Atlan became a prestigious organization, not only by virtue of their unique and technically superlative designs, but also because of the quality of their educational programs.

In rendering their interpretations of these new motifs, their skills in conventionalization were advanced. Subsequent exhibitions of their new work, while they initially did little to displace Cupids and garlands of forget-me-nots in the general public's taste, drew praise and encouragement from art circles across the country.

The goal of the Atlan Club early on, had been the development of an American School of Art, an American style that would be a unique expression of the American porcelain artist. By the close of 1899, their work had evolved into just such a style. Referred to colloquially today as "American Satsuma," it is readily recognized for its conventionalized designs applied in opaque enamels to pottery blanks, most often with a Satsuma crackled glaze. The collector should be aware however, that many, many artists across the country eventually adopted this style. There are thus many "American Satsuma" pieces that become available today—some are very good and many are quite poor. But *very* few Atlan pieces are ever found on the market.

Atlan members agreed in 1899 to limit all exhibition pieces to the conventionalized style. They also agreed never to exhibit the same item in the same exhibition more than once. By 1901, Atlan

had displayed its work in no less than 19 exhibitions, including the Paris World Exhibition and the Paris Exhibit at Tiffany's in New York City. The continual creation of exhibition pieces was a substantial assignment, since each member also did commissioned work, produced decorated china for sale to the general public, and often conducted a studio school as well.

Of the many women associated with Atlan, Helen Frazee was one of its most talented members, and it is she who is credited with the first application of conventionalized design to Satsuma pottery. Her studio was located in the Auditorium Building's tower where such other artists and notables as Franz B. Aulich, Evelyn Beachey, Margaret E. Englehart, Victorine B. Jenkins, Laura Starr, and author/historian Dr. Edwin Atlee Barber were located. Mrs. Frazee had studied painting at the Art Institute and in Atlan's study programs. She was proficient in figural work, landscapes, and floral studies; when she began to conventionalized these subjects, the results were exquisite. Unfortunately surviving pieces of her work are quite rate, as are "Frazee Studio" pieces signed by her students.

Ellen Lovgren and Mabel C. Dibble were two other Atlan artists with superlative skills. Lovgren was the recipient of numerous awards, and when china became scarce during World War I, her application of mineral paints to glass earned high praise from the *Chicago Tribune's* art critic. Mabel Dibble, like Susan Frackelton came from Milwaukee, and also like Mrs. Frackelton, her entrepreneurial efforts included the development of her own line of enamels. Her designs were featured frequently in *Keramic Studio*, and it was her conventionalized Orange Tree design that Emil Tolpin adapted for Pickard's popular *Orange Tree Conventional* design. Miss Dibble received the Boston Society of Arts and Crafts' coveted Master Craftsman award and was subsequently invited to join the Royal Society of Arts in London.

Of all the Atlan artists, Florence Pratt Steward had the vision, the perseverance, and the organizational skills that held the club together for approximately 30 years. In addition to being its founder, Mrs. Steward was the club's historian, writing its account for the Chicago Historical Society in 1902. She conceived the instructional program and taught an extension of it herself, and she was an indefatigable organizer of Atlan's many exhibitions. But beyond this, she too, produced exquisitely conceived and detailed pieces of ceramic art. Her *Conversational Set in Historic Ornament* earned national praise in 1911 for its conventionalized portrayals of ornamental styles in various cultures. In 1917, her spectacular *Meat Course Set*, a 48 piece conventionalization of 12 eras in the history of art, earned her even greater acclaim.

Atlan designs were one-of-a-kind, and the quantity of meticulous labor that went into each piece made volume production out of the question. They were priced for sale at many exhibitions, and they were also sold at a Michigan Avenue store operated by the University of Chicago.

In its three decades of existence, the membership turned over many times and eventually numbered more than 170 artists as past members. Although the by-laws did not prohibit them, no men are known to have been exhibiting members. A number of men did appear as associates or councilors in the exhibition lists and were probably included for their social and financial support.

Atlan seems to have terminated about 1921, although many of its members continued to teach and operate studios well into the 1920s. Its spirit is perpetuated today in its small annuity to the Art Institute of Chicago for the purchase of American pottery and porcelain.

Unlike Pickard, many Atlan pieces do not bear an Atlan club mark since it was only essential that exhibition pieces be so-identified. Absent a mark, only pieces signed by known Atlan artists can be considered as genuine Atlan ware. The Atlan artist list is derived from a reading of almost 30 years of membership rosters, but these rosters did not include associate members, many of whom were quite expert. Associate names have been gathered from Atlan Exhibition catalogs. Additionally there were a few artists who were never affiliated with Atlan, but whose style and quality was indistinguishable from that of Atlan. In order not to leave such fine works of art out of our listings, we have chosen to identify them as "Atlan School."

Of the many non-Atlan artists that undertook conventionalization on their own, Charles L. Wiard was ranked at the top from the start of his career. Described as "that young genius from Waukegan," Wiard won the Atlan Prize at the Atlan Exhibition in 1912, and went on to form his own school in Minneapolis.

## Atlan artists

The following list of Atlan artists includes names derived from exhibition lists, membership lists, and signed pieces of Atlan-marked china. Where appropriate, husband's names are also given since this was often the manner of identification in exhibition catalogs and magazine articles. Dates shown are known periods of Atlan membership, however, most artists maintained studios and/or taught as unaffiliated, CCAA, or NLMP members on either side of these dates. A few "Atlan School" artists are also included in the list and are identified with an asterisk (*).

Abercrombie, A. A., (Mrs. Charles B.) 1907–1911

Adams, Eva E. 1893–1902 Founding member.

Alden, Mary E. 1900–1907

Allfree, Esther L. 1916–1918

Alshuler, Mrs. C. S. 1922

Anderson, Louise. 1893 Founding member.

Atchison, Mrs. Grace 1902–1904

Ayer, Mrs. A. C. 1917–1922

Baird, Mrs. Nannie B. 1902 (K. C., MO resident)

Band, Minnie C. 1918–1922

Banner, Mrs. Shelia 1922

Barothy, Frances A. (Mrs. Arpad M.) 1901–1928 Art studies in Nottingham, England and the Art Institute of Chicago. Member Chicago AG. Juror Art Institute 1914.

Bennett, Bessie 1900 (Honorary member.)

Berglund, Mrs. Axel 1914–1922

Bidwell, Mrs. Charles W. 1921–1922

Biefuss, C. L.* 1908–1920 (Highland Park, IL)

Blair, Margaret 1922

Blomquist, Ruth 1911–1912

Butler, Mrs. John F. 1913

Cherry, Katherine 1922 (St. Louis MO resident. Honorary Member)

Clarke, M. C. (Mrs. Harry H.) 1910–1911

Cole, Lillie E. 1893–1906 Founding member.

Cooper, Helen G. 1909–1911

Coulter, Mrs. Mary L. 1905–1909 Won Atlan prize in 1909.

Crane, Mrs. Anna Brauer 1897

Cremer, Mrs. Harry L. 1911

Cross, Mrs. Nellie A. 1894

Daily, Mrs. Charles T. 1909–1911

Dibble, Mabel C. 1893–1901+ Founding member.

Dickson, Mrs. W. F. 1922

Dudgeon, Edith 1904

Dunham, Mrs. F. S. 1912–1913

Dunne, Mrs. George R. 1911–1915

Dutcher, Mrs. Anna H. 1911

Eichling, Mrs. Philip H. 1921–1922

Emmons, Mrs. George E. 1912–1914

Evans 1914

Farr, Lillian G. 1911–1913

Foster, Belle 1893 Founding member.

Frazee, Helen Inez (Mrs. Abram A.) 1893–1924

Frazer, Beulah L. (Mrs. D. L.) 1899–1906

Freytag, Mrs. Harry Charles 1918–1922

Gale, Grace G. (Mrs. Cosgrove A.) 1914–1922

Girard, Mrs. Laura S. 1902 K. C., MO resident.

Gleason, Mrs. Miriam M. 1918–1922

Gray, Mrs. R. A. 1922

Greenleaf, Mrs. Walter G. 1893 Founding member.

Hadden, Mrs. Herbert T. 1910–1916

Hall, Miss 1897

Hall, Mrs. S. N. 1915–1916

Harner, Elsa Secrest (Mrs. George Warde) 1911–1917 Juror Art Institute 1911.

Hess, Emma 1904

Hewen, Mrs. Sarah C. 1912–1916

Hoelscher, May Brunemeyer (Mrs. Paul G.) 1909–1919

Hoff, M. G.* 1915–1922

Holtgren, Fay Tichnor 1916–1917

Hoyt, Mrs. L. 1893

Hubbard, Florence (Mrs. Charles F.) 1911–1912

Hulbert, Lylian Root 1911

Humphrey, Mrs. Edward L. 1893–1922 Founding member. Life Member. Taught summer classes in Pasadena, CA.

Hutchcraft, Mrs. Edward 1916

Hutchinson, Emma (Mrs. W. B.) 1915–1918

Jack, Edna Dunbar (Mrs. Harry T.) 1909–1911

Jensen, Mrs. Mabel 1921

Jones, Mrs. Edmund 1894

Jones, Mrs. Edwin 1907–1915

Jones, Mrs. Raymond A. 1914–1922

Kelley, Mrs. William Thomas 1922

Kern, June Hibbard 1922

Killham, Ethel Frame (Mrs. Benjamin J.) 1911

Kirchner, Mrs. Julia C. 1911

Kittredge, Emma 1893 Founding member.

Krueger, Mrs. George E. 1913

Kulp, Mrs. Eolah A. 1917–1918

La Bryn, Harriet May 1915–1917

Lathrop, Mrs. William Brown 1917–1921

Lawrence, Charlotte 1904–1906

Lawry, Mrs. Raymond G. 1916

Lawson, Adde (Mrs. V.A.) 1897–1898

Lee, Alice Nugent* 1916

Letz, Mrs. Frank C. 1917–1921

Levedahl, Edith R. 1915–1919

Liebolt, Adelaide M. 1911–1917

Linstedt, Mrs. D.B. 1893 Founding member.

Lockwood, Mrs. J. 1893

Lovgren, Ellen E. 1915–1918

Lowes, Mrs. Francis M. 1917–1922

Lowry, Mrs. Raymond G. 1916

Ludwig, Alma F. 1911–1913

Luman, Mrs. J. R. 1922

Lund, Mrs. Erick 1922

Lytle, Mrs. George A. 1912

Maher, Mrs. Hubert 1906–1907

Mahoney, Margaret L. 1912–1917

Mancl, Mrs. Frank J. 1912

Mann, Cornie H. 1893 Founding member.

Marsh, Mrs. John W. 1895

MaWhinney, Mrs. Elgin 1919–1921

Maxson, Melina, (Mrs. C. M.) 1917–1922

McConnell, Sarah 1904

McCreery, Mrs. R. M. 1894

McCrystle, May (Mrs. James B.) 1899–1906

McDonald, Mrs. Minna S. 1902 K. C., MO resident

McDonald, Mrs. H. C. 1915–1917

McDonald, Mrs. M. 1899

McGarn, Augusta Barton 1911–1917

McGilvray, Flora 1921–1922

McIntyre, Lettie 1893 Founding member.

Mettenet, Mrs. Francis X. 1914

Middleton, Matilda 1900–1915

Milliken, Mrs. J. W. 1893

Miner, Florence H. 1893

Mitchell, Helen 1893

Mosley, Mrs. Glennie 1917–1919

Mosser, Mrs. S. T. 1921–1922

Naper, Mrs. T. Hubert 1906–1908

Nye, Mrs. Laura N. 1906–1908

Odgers, Bertha S. (Mrs. George C.) 1922

O'Hara, Dorthea Warren (Mrs. H. M.) 1922

Oliver, Mrs. N. H. 1922

Park, Bertha J. (Mrs. Ralph Raymond) 1914–1919

Parker, Edythe 1904

Peck, Grace H. 1893–1898 Founding member.

Peterson, Helga Mae 1911–1922

Phillips, Mary A. 1895–1898

Porter, Alice S. 1906

Pratt, Florence, Mrs. E.H. 1893 Founding member. (See Mrs. LeRoy T. Steward.)

Preuszner, Mrs. Roxanna B. 1893 Founding member.

Pruden, Elizabeth M. (Mrs. Alfred J.0) 1916–1918

Pyott, Mrs. D. 1894

Ransom, Katherine 1893

Reece, Mrs. Amelia D. 1911

Riecks, Mrs. Anna M. 1916–1917

Rintoul, Mrs. Robert 1906–1911

Sanford, Mrs. F. E. 1917–1922

Secrest, Madge 1904

Semple, Mrs. Francis H. 1911

Senge, Anna, Mrs. Frank C. 1911–1921

Sessions, Elizabeth Howard (Mrs. Frank M.) 1895–1919

Sexton, Marie A. (Mrs. Stephen William) 1906–1922

Simons, Mrs. G. A. 1921

Smith, Mrs. C. C. 1915–1917

Sower, Mrs. Francis 1917–1921

Sparks, Mrs. Mollie 1912–1917

Sparrow, Martha H. 1912–1913

Steele, E. (Mrs. Fred M.) 1896–1900

Steward, Florence (Mrs. LeRoy T.) 1893–1921 Founding member. (Florence Steward as of 1901; formerly Mrs. E. H. Pratt) Wrote *"Ceramic Decoration."*

Stubbs, Mrs. Minnie Gray 1911

Tichenor, Fay T. 1916

Topping, Helen M. 1895

Umbach, Mrs. E. M. 1922

Van Doren, Mrs. W. E. 1918–1922

Van Hise, Maude 1897

Van Oven, Johanna 1906

Wagner, Mrs. Francis 1893

Ward, Ada, Mrs. 1917–1922

Warner, Mrs. George R. 1917–1921

Weaver, Mrs. Arthur T. 1922

Webster, Cora M. 1915

Wells, Julia 1893 Founding member.

Wiard, Charles Leo* 1895–1928 Won Atlan prize in 1912. Art Institute juror 1913.

Wiese, Eleanor H. 1918–1919

Willets, Florence 1904

Williams, Mrs. Caroline G. 1922

Wilson, Mrs. Grover C. 1917

Wolf, Mrs. Helen 1915–1922

Wright, Jane V. D. (Mrs. E. Scofield) 1906–1917

Wyeth, Lucy S. 1914–1916

Yeomans, Margarite M. 1897–1899

Zeublin, Mrs. J.E 1893–1900

## *Atlan Trademark*

1893–1924, handlettered in various combinations of dates, names, and initials.

## *Atlan Plates*

Plate 883. Fruit stand, hexiform. Ten conventionalized lavender morning glories on buff ground. Signed: crossed Ps, ATLAN, SR or RS (unknown). No TM date. Blank: M&Z crown and eagles, Bavaria. Value: $295.00–375.00.

Plate 881. (left) Soft paste reticulated vase, 5"h. Conventionalized flowers on black ground, blue upper border. Signed: E. Lovgren (Lovgren, Ellen). TM date: No TM. Blank: shield flower RVR. Value: $850.00–1,000.00. (right) Soft paste incense burner, 4¾"h. Conventionalized flower panels with conventionalized floral border. Signed: Ellen Lovgren (Lovgren, Ellen). TM date: No TM. Blank: none. Value: $900.00–1,100.00.

Plate 884. Soft paste ginger jar, 7½"h. Red and blue conventionalized flowers with blue and gold borders. (unsigned). Provenance identifies Ellen Lovgren as the artist. TM date: No TM. Blank: none. Value: $1,300.00–1,600.00.

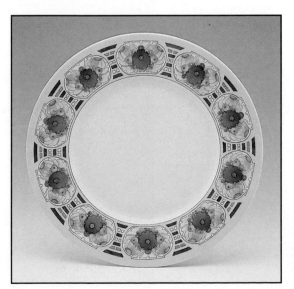

Plate 882. Plate, 10½"d. Blue flower with russet conventionalized daisies in ten border medallions. Signed: E. Lovgren (Lovgren, Ellen). TM date: No TM. Blank: crown H.&Co. Selb, Bavaria. Value: $275.00–350.00.

*Plate 885. Desert cup, pedestalled, 4¾"d. Raised enamel fruit clusters on inner and outer borders. Signed: Mabel C. Dibble (Dibble, Mabel C.). TM date: 1913. Blank: J.P.L., France. Value: $55.00–75.00.*

*Plate 886. (left) Trumpet vase, 3½"h. Conventionalized floral strands on dark blue ground. Signed: Lovgren (Lovgren, Ellen). TM date: No TM. Blank: none. Value: $250.00–335.00. (center) Soft paste round lidded box, 3¾"d. Geometric design in dark blue, green, and orange. Signed: Ellen Lovgren (Lovgren, Ellen). TM date: No TM. Blank: none. Value: $300.00–425.00. (right) Small vase, 3½"h. Conventionalized blue floral medallions on blue and gold ground. (unsigned). Provenance identifies Ellen Lovgren as the artist. TM date: No TM. Blank: none. Value: $300.00–375.00. (front) Miniature salt, 1⅝"h. Conventionalized florals on blue border with gold stem. Signed: Ellen Lovgren (Lovgren, Ellen). TM date: No TM. Blank: Patd Jan 9, 1912. Value: $180.00–225.00.*

*Plate 887. (left) Charger, 13"d. Seven panels of conventionalized apple blossoms on blue and gold. (unsigned). TM date: No TM. Blank: none. Value: $450.00–575.00. (right) Vase, curved taper, 8½"h. Six panels of conventionalized apple blossoms on blue and gold. Signed: crossed P's, ATLAN, SR or RS (unknown). TM date: No date. Blank: none. Value: $400.00–525.00.*

*Plate 889. Vase, cylindrical, 11¼"h. Satsuma-stlye floral on upper border, pendants descending into gray ground. Signed: CL Biefuss (Atlan School). TM date: No TM. Blank: Belleek serpent Willets. Value: $200.00–300.00.*

*Plate 888. Three-tier soft paste pin box, 6½"h. Conventionalized flowers on black ground, gold borders. Signed: Ellen Lovgren (Lovgren, Ellen). TM date: No TM. Blank: none. Value: $600.00–750.00.*

Plate 890. Covered incense burner, 5"w. Conventionalized florals in lavender and green. Signed: crossed P's and ATLAN, '18, A. BERGLUND (Berglund, Mrs. Axel). TM date: 1918. Blank: none. Value: $450.00–625.00.

Plate 891. Decorative dish, covered, 6¾"d. Conventionalized lavender and orange flowers on buff ground. Signed: C L WIARD '08 (Wiard, Charles Leo) (Atlan school). No TM. Date: 1908. Blank: none. Value: $400.00–475.00.

Plate 892. (left) Plate, 9"d. Miniature pastel garlands with blue and gold rim. Signed: E.L. (Lovgren, Ellen). TM date: No TM. Blank: crown RC crossed scepters Bavaria Kronach-Else. Value: $225.00–275.00. (right) Plate, 8¾"d. Conventionalized lavender flowers on gold, green geometric border. Signed: E. Lovgren (Lovgren, Ellen). TM date: No TM. Blank: circle JHR Hutschenreuther Favorite. Value: $225.00–275.00.

Plate 894. Charger with open lattice rim, 12"d. Conventionalized floral garlands. (unsigned) Provenance identifies Ellen Lovgren as the artist. TM date: No TM. Blank: none. Value: $500.00–650.00.

Plate 893. (rear) Tubular vase, 4¾"h Conventionalized purple iris panels on cream ground. (unsigned) Provenance derives from (Lovgren, Ellen). TM date: No TM. Blank: none. Value: $425.00–500.00. (front) Soft paste lidded box, 3¾"d. Conventionalized lavender and green flowers. Signed: Ellen Lovgren (Lovgren, Ellen). TM date: No TM. Blank: none. Value: $400.00–475.00.

Plate 895. Bowl, 7"d. Conventionalized lavender lotus on gold stippled pottery. Signed: Alice Nugent Lee (Lee, Alice Nugent) (Atlan school). No TM. Date: May, 1916. Blank: none. Value: $160.00–195.00.

Plate 896. Small bowl, 5½"d. Beige ground with five repeating scenic panels of castle above brown hills with green-trunked trees. Signed: May B. Hoelscher (Hoelscher, May B). TM date: No TM. Blank: crossed clovers J&C. Value: $180.00–215.00.

Plate 898. Glass lamp base and shade, 13¾"h. Border of conventionalized purple, pink, gold, and yellow flowers. (unsigned). Provenance identifies Ellen Lovgren as the artist. TM date: No TM. Blank: Noritake Nippon. Value: $1,200.00–1,500.00.

Plate 897. Milk pitcher, 6¼"h. Border of conventionalized pink flowers on pale green border, gold outlined, on cream ground. Signed: A. M. L. (Liebolt, Adelaide M.). No TM. Date: 1916. Blank: Belleek serpent Willets. Value: $450.00–575.00.

Plate 899. Shallow dish, 6" x 4½". Miniature green florals in green ground. Signed: F. Steward (Steward, Florence). TM date: No TM. Blank: none. Value: $300.00–375.00.

Plate 900. (left) Octagonal dish, 5"w. Blue flowers on gold border. Signed: E. Lovgren (Lovgren, Ellen). TM date: No TM. Blank: LeSienie Limoges, France Patented F.R. & Co. Chicago. Value: $200.00–250.00. (center) Octagonal plate, 7½"w. Clusters of grapes and pears on green and gold border. Signed: E. Lovgren (Lovgren, Ellen). TM date: No TM. Blank: B&Co. France. Value: $225.00–300.00. (right) Octagonal dish with reticulated rim, 5½"w. Conventionalized orange and blue floral clusters on white ground. Signed: Lovgren (Lovgren, Ellen). TM date: No TM. Blank: shield flower RVR. Value: $225.00–275.00.

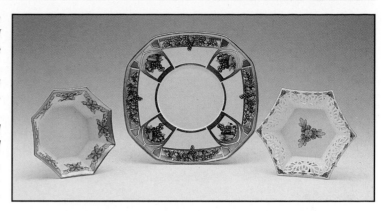

Plate 901. Soft paste lidded box, 4¾"w. Orange and blue geometric pattern with black and white border. Signed: Ellen Lovgren (Lovgren, Ellen). TM date: No TM. Blank: none. Value: $250.00–325.00.

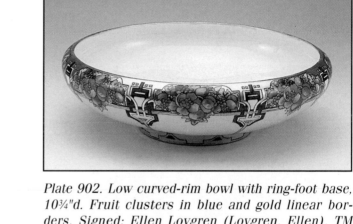

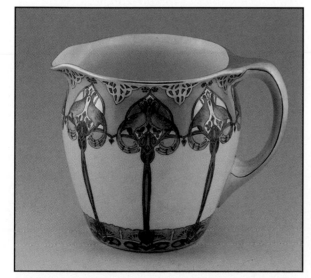

Plate 902. Low curved-rim bowl with ring-foot base, 10¾"d. Fruit clusters in blue and gold linear borders. Signed: Ellen Lovgren (Lovgren, Ellen). TM date: No TM. Blank: none. Value: $600.00–700.00.

Plate 903. Large, simple milk pitcher, 5¾"h. Upper border of peacock pairs stemmed to lower art nouveau border. Signed: L. N. Starr (Starr, Laura N.) (Atlan school). TM date: No TM. Blank: J.P.L., France. Value: $200.00–245.00.

Plate 904. Desk set: ink well, paper weight, blotter holder, pin box, pen tray, blotter corners. Conventionalized blue flower on maroon and gold geometric pattern. Signed: E. Lovgren (Lovgren, Ellen). TM date: No TM. Blank: crown eagles M&Z, Austria (pen tray). Value: $900.00–1,100.00.

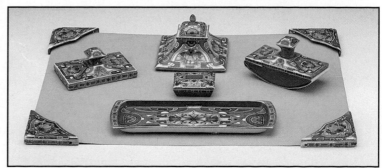

Plate 905. (rear) Serving tray with open handles, 17¼"l. Conventionalized floral border with gold geometric linear border. Signed: E. Lovgren (Lovgren, Ellen). TM date: No TM. Blank: UNO IT Favorite Bavaria. Value: $450.00–525.00. (front) Serving tray with reticulated end aprons, 16¼"l. Floral border. Signed: E. Lovgren (Lovgren, Ellen). TM date: No TM. Blank: Shield flower RVR. Valuc: $450.00–525.00.

Plate 906. Soft paste pitcher, 7¾"h. Conventionalized floral borders on off-white ground. Signed: Ellen Lovgren (Lovgren, Ellen). TM date: No TM. Blank: Lenox palette Belleek. Value: $600.00–750.00.

Plate 907. (left) Vase, 5¾"h. Pink and green geometric border on cream ground. Signed: Ellen Lovgren (Lovgren, Ellen). TM date: No TM. Blank: none. Value: $300.00–375.00. (right) Small plate, 4⅝"d. Conventionalized blue cornflowers on segmented border. Signed: Ellen Lovgren (Lovgren, Ellen). TM date: No TM. Blank: none. Value: $185.00–250.00.

Plate 909. Vase, 7½"h. Satsuma blue flowers, top and base borders with vertical bars. Signed: M.G. Hoff. (Hoff., M.G.) (Atlan school). TM date: No TM. Blank: none. Value: $175.00–225.00.

Plate 908. Large round soft paste covered box on Satsuma blank, 8½"d. Pink and yellow conventionalized cone flowers on gold ground with cobalt banding. Signed: Bertha S. Odgers (Odgers, Bertha S.). TM date: No TM. Blank: none. Value: $490.00–650.00.

*Plate 910. Candlesticks, 8"h. Conventionalized morning glory panels on off-white ground. Signed: Simons (Simons, G. A.). TM date: No TM. Blank: palette L circle Belleek. Value: $225.00–250.00.*

*Plate 911. Heavy-walled circular trivet, 14"d. Five conventionalized pale yellow flowers on pale green leaf border interspersed with five pale lavender iris; conventionalized pale floral center with gold radii. Signed: A. M. Liebolt (Liebolt, Adelaide M.). TM date: 1911–1922. Blank: blank impressed with crown, shield G M JHR. Value: $600.00–750.00.*

*Plate 912. Pin box, 4½"l. Pale flower border, gold trim on cream pottery. (unsigned) (Atlan school). TM date: No TM. Blank: none. Value: $125.00–175.00.*

*Plate 913. Dresser set, child's: hatpin holder, tray, hair receiver, covered dish. Pale yellow and lavender floral on gold band on white ground. Signed: three crossed P's, ATLAN, LCD (unknown). No date. Blank: O&E G Austria. Value: $225.00–265.00.*

*Plate 914. Charger with open handles, 11½"d. Conventionalized russet and pale orange flowers, pale green leaves, geometrically twining stems, beige inner and outer borders. Signed: A. M. L. 1916 (Liebolt, Adelaide M.). No TM. Date: 1916. Blank: none. Value: $400.00–475.00.*

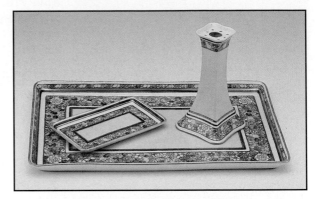

Plate 915. Compote with fluted base and hexagonal, reticulated top, 9"d. Flower garlands on lattice and pedestal base. Signed: Liebolt 5–1–11 (Liebolt, Adelaide M.). No TM. Date: 1911. Blank: obscure shield impressed into blank. Value: $450.00–525.00.

Plate 916. Dresser set: large tray, hatpin holder, pin tray, 12¼"l. Gold band of miniature flowers with blue and gold borders. Signed: A. M. Liebolt (Liebolt, Adelaide M.). No TM. Date: 1912. Blank: Elite L France. Value: $450.00–600.00.

Plate 917. Small tray, 7¾" x 5¼". Border of pale enameled flowers with etched gold geometric floral pattern. Signed. Florence Hubbard (Hubbard, Florence). TM date: 1912. Blank: PL Limoges, France. Value: $150.00–225.00.

Plate 918. Pin box, 4"d. Conventionalized flowers on black circle; gold rimmed. Signed: F. A. Barothy (Barothy, Frances A.). No TM. Date: 1901–1921. Blank: none. Value: $425.00–500.00.

Plate 919. (left) Lidded Satsuma ring box, 2½"d. Flower border. Signed: Mabel C. Dibble (Dibble, Mabel C.). No TM. Date: 1916. Blank: none. Value: $175.00–225.00. (right) Satsuma lidded pin box, 3¼"d. Abstract florals on gold disc. Signed: F.A.Barothy (Barothy, Francis A.). Blank: none. Value: $245.00–300.00.

# THE DECORATOR-WHOLESALERS

There were many jobbers and wholesalers in Chicago that sold both china blanks for decorating and fully decorated imported china. Two of them, however, went a step farther and maintained their own decorating rooms. In this sense, they were competing with some of their own customers. This competitive aspect was "softened" somewhat by their willingness to purchase home-decorated china from some of their artist-customers. Wholesaler exhibitions eventually provided considerable notoriety to individual artists and thereby generated support for the wholesaler's reputation. Art Institute exhibitions later included prizes in various categories by the Burley, A.H. Abbott, and Hasburg companies.

Pickard is not known to have purchased blanks from Pitkin & Brooks, but he did purchase large quantities of blanks from Burley & Co., especially during the Great War when direct import avenues had closed.

## Burley & Co., 1837–1931

### Burley & Tyrrell 1871–1919

*Figure 50. Burley and Company trade card.*

Burley & Co. was established in 1838[42] as A. G. Burley & Co. The first city directory in 1844 advertised that they are "Importers and wholesale and retail dealers in china, glass, earthen, stone ware and looking glasses."

Burley & Tyrrell began business at 46–48 Lake Street in 1871—the year of the Great Chicago Fire—as china, glass, and Queensware wholesalers. By 1873 they had recovered sufficiently to operate a triple address at 274–276–278 Wabash. They moved successively to multiple addresses on State, Lake, and Adams with a warehouse on South Halsted by 1906.

Burley & Co. re-emerged at 83–85 State Street in 1885 as china retailers. They moved successively to multiple addresses on State and on Wabash.

The two companies appeared together for the first time in 1907 at 118–120 Wabash. Despite this combination, Burley & Co. outlived Burley & Tyrrell by many years. Burley & Tyrrell ceased operation after 1919, but Burley & Co. continued to advertise and do business at the same address through 1931.

After the combination, both companies' advertising overlapped each other's retail and wholesale trades while still retaining their original primary focus. The combination boasted two warehouses in 1907 and a large one at 2219–2239 S. Halsted thereafter through 1919

Both companies did a large wholesale crockery trade among the railroads, hotels, restaurants, and other institutions. This form of china was intended for heavy, abusive service, and decoration was most often applied as a decal on a mass-production basis. Hotel logos, railroad insignia, and other private-label designs were fired on blanks imported from French and German factories by the boxcar load.

Of the two businesses, Burley & Co. became more retail oriented after the turn of the century, selling fancy china in its Loop display windows and catering to the individual china decorator as suppliers of white china. To further stimulate this trade, Burley sponsored exhibitions of its own at its Wabash Avenue store and also offered prizes at Art Institute exhibitions of decorated china.

Burley maintained a decorating room above the Wabash Avenue salesroom through the early 1920s, employing students from the Art Institute as Pickard had done, but with less salubrious working conditions. The author's mother was just such an artist, recalling that "...the seats were hard, the light was poor, and the work was very monotonous—nothing but painting little rosebuds all day long."

In addition to its own production, Burley also purchased freelance decorated china from individual artists until it ceased operation.

## Burley Trademark
*(Dates are approximations.)*

*1912–1924, ¹¹⁄₁₆" wide, green decal.*

## Pitkin & Brooks
## 1874–1917 (1939)

Pitkin & Brooks began business as wholesalers of kerosene lamp chimneys, crockery, and other institutional ware. They branched into retail sales and sold large quantities of china through such prestigious stores as Marshall Field's, but also did much direct retailing through advertisements in many midwest small town weekly newspapers.

In addition to maintaining their own decorating rooms, they had much of their product private labeled for them direct from the Limoges factories in France. They also purchased some walk-in decorated china from individual artists. Trademarks are therefore of two styles: a formal mark applied at Limoges (purple was a common color), or a handwritten identification (generally in red).

A number of Pickard artists worked for Pitkin & Brooks, but despite this good talent and the company's wide and prolific distribution, only a small amount of their work has survived. Although the company continued in business through 1939, they did no china decorating after 1917.

*Artists associated with Pitkin & Brooks were:*

Edward W. Donath*          Pascal
J. Heinz*                 Noble Ray*
Imlay**                  Howard B. Reury*

*\* Also a Pickard artist.*
*\*\* No information has been found, but the very high quality of Imlay's work prompts the speculation that this may have been the very accomplished Weller artist, Josephine Imlay.*

## Pitkin & Brooks
## Trademarks
*(Dates are approximate.)*

Mark 1. 1895–1905, ⁷⁄₁₆" dia., black or green decal. Private labeled by others.

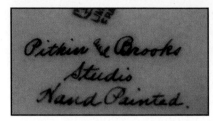

Mark 2. 1903–1910, handscript in red, black, or blue. Used on carry-in pieces.

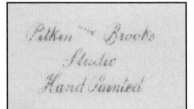

Mark 3. 1903–1910, handscript decal in red or green. Used on in-house decorations.

Mark 4. 1903–1917, private labeled by others.

## Pitkin & Brooks Plates

Plate 920. Plate with elaborate rim embossments, 9¾"d. Cotton blossoms on green ground with purple and russet pods mid-ground and old highlights on rim embossings. Signed: Albere (Albere). TM date: 1895–1905. Blank: Limoges star France. Value: $45.00–70.00.

Plate 921. Plate, 9"d. Variant of Pickard's CARNATION CONVENTIONAL. Signed: Heinz (Heinz, J.). TM date: 1903–1910. Blank: Haviland, France. Value: $125.00–150.00.

Plate 922. Tankard, 9"h. Purple iris between gold Gothic arches on white. Signed: Ray (Ray, Noble). TM date: 1903–1910. Blank: Limoges. Value: $225.00–275.00.

Plate 923. (rear) Plate, 8½"d. Red poppies on gold border with black center with green leaves. Signed: Ross. (Ross). TM date: 1903–1910. Blank: Haviland, France. Value: $130.00–160.00. (front) Creamer and lidded sugar. Poppies on embellished gold border, blue/green stems on black ground. Signed: RAY (Ray, Noble). TM date: 1903–1910. Blank: T&V rectangle, Limoges, France Déposé. Value: $135.00–165.00.

Plate 924. Loving cup, three handled, 5¼"h. Red poppy on embellished gold border with stems and buds painted into dark green base. Signed: N. Ray. (Ray, Noble). TM date: 1903–1910. Blank: T&V rectangle, Limoges, France. Value: $275.00–325.00.

*Plate 925. Tankard, 14¼"h.; tray, 16"d.; and 6 tumblers. Violets on pale green ground. Signed: H. Reury (Reury, Howard B.). TM date: 1903–1910. Blank: T&V rectangle, Limoges, France. Value: $750.00–875.00.*

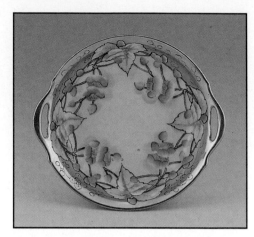

*Plate 928. Dish, perforated handles, 5½"d. Pink blossoms with green and orange leaves, embellished gold border. Signed: Imlay (Imlay). TM date: 1903–1910. Blank: T&V Limoges, France. Value: $15.00–20.00.*

*Plate 926. Candy dish, handled, 5½"d. Violet clusters inside and out, gold rim. Signed: Reury. (Reury, Howard B.). TM date: 1903–1910. Blank: T&V rectangle, Limoges, France. Value: $85.00–95.00.*

*Plate 929. ELITE scalloped plate, 8"d. Conventionalized white flowers, pastel magenta, blue, and peach leaves, wide gold border. Signed: Pascal (Pascal). TM date: 1903–1917. Blank: Elite L France, Hand Painted. Value: $65.00–85.00.*

*Plate 927. Bonbon, round with perforated handles, 6½"d. Pink blossoms on gold scroll, green and gold banded border. Signed: Donath (Donath, Edward W.). TM date: 1903–1910. Blank: T&V rectangle, Limoges, France. Value: $35.00–45.00.*

## Western Decorating Works
## 1865–1896

The Western Decorating Works was founded in 1865 by Frederick Grunewald and Frederick Schmidt and was the forerunner of the larger studio/supplier combinations. These two German immigrants expanded from a base of simple decoration to include china decorating instruction, supplies that ran from mineral paint powders to china blanks, and on-site firing of decorated china.

Western had pioneered the supplier-sponsored exhibition concept prior to 1890, and with the approach of the World's Columbian Exposition, the company coordinated the Columbia Ceramic Association's exhibit.[43] Although many artists utilized Western's services, no marks or signatures are associated with this company which ceased operation just after the Fair in 1895.

# *A*PPENDICES

## A. Chicago China Studios Family Tree

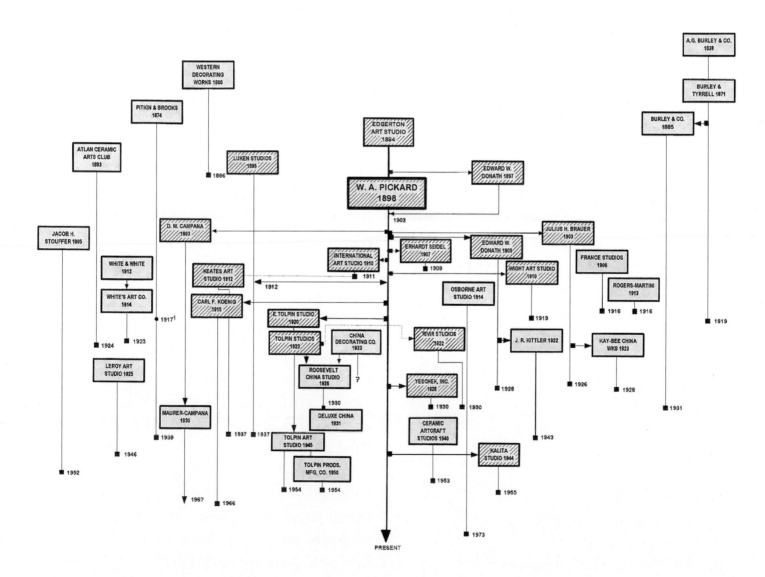

# B. Listing of all listed Chicago China Decorating Studios

The following is a tabulation of all china decorators who appeared in the classified portion of the Chicago City Directories from the time the "China Decorator" heading was first used through the last directory issue in 1928. It also includes later telephone directory listings from 1917 through the late forties. The studios ranged in size from one to fifty or more individuals. Dates given below apply only to years in which directory listings appeared. Caution must therefore be observed in assigning a limit to any individual's full span of china decorating since many decorators worked for other studios before, during, and after their classified listings. **Bold face** indicates an individual studio covered in a separate section of this book. Asterisk denotes a Pickard artist.

Aagaard, Chester S. 1922–1923

Abbott, Annie E. 1914–1917

Adams, Isabella 1914–1916

Adams, Roxa M. 1916

**American Hand Painted China Co.** 1915–1917

Amidei & Dipinto 1916

(Louis Amidei and Elias DiPinto)

Amoges Studios, Inc 1945–1948

(Sunnyside Studios at this location, 1943–1944)

Anderson & Anderson 1915

Anderson & Lee 1913

Apollo Art Studio 1915–1923

Arno, Edith* 1910

Art China Co. 1922–1927

Audy, Zoe 1916

Babcock, George H. 1915–1917

Barnes, Mary O. 1895.00.

Barrett, C. P. 1906

Baton, Jessie 1922

Bavaria China Co. 1931–1932

Becksted, Emily J 1917

Beecher, Mrs. Jennie S. 1908–1912

Beitler, Joseph C.* 1907–1909

Beyers, Mrs. Clara 1911

Biese, Rosebud 1909

Birk, Richard W. 1916–1917

Blanche Studio 1918–1919

Blasche Studio 1916–1917

(Carl Blasche)

Blase, Mrs. Clara M 1904

Blodgett, Caroline 1909–1910

Boetter, Jean 1914–1923

Boyer, Marie (Mrs. Fred) 1912–1917

Brandenburg, Mrs. Beatrice M. 1916

Brandernburg, Mrs. Mae 1915–1917

Breidel, William W.* 1911–1913

Brethener, Elsie B. 1906

Bronson, Della 1906–1907

Brown, Evelyn A. 1912

Brown, Linnie 1913

Brown, Mrs. George H. 1906–1908

Bruce, Caroline 1900 (With Julia M. Cain.)

Buettgen, Peter 1896–1906

Burdette, Helen M. (Mrs. Clark) 1905–1908

Burgeon & Nilsson 1908

Burgeon, Adelbert J. 1889

Burklund, August P. 1907

**Burley & Co.** 1885–1931

Burman, Gertrude 1907–1908

Butler, Carolyn R. 1907–1909

Butler, Gertrude 1907

Cain, Julia M. 1900 (With Caroline Bruce)

Carlsson & Bement Studio 1908.

(Mrs. Beatrice Carlsson and Mrs. Frank Bement.)

Carlsson & Rorabeck Co. 1908–1910

(Mrs. Beatrice Carlsson and Eleanore Rorabeck.)

Carlsson, Olaf A. & Co. 1909–1911

(Same location as Mrs. Beatrice Carlsson)

Carlyle China Art Co. 1908–1912

Carpenter, Mrs. Ruth H. 1911–1913

Carr, Mrs. Catherine 1911–1917

Cashwell, Eloise 1916

Cedarberg, N. O. Co. 1926
(Nels O. Cedarberg, Aurora, IL. Also Sunset Lustre
  Studio.)
Ceramic Art Guild 1904–1905
(Peter Buettgen, manager.)
**Ceramic Artcraft Studios** 1940–1953
("Etchers and decorators of fine chinaware. Serv-
  ing gift, jewelery, and department stores.")
Ceramic Decorating Company 1915–1931
Chase, Mrs. Emily 1906, 1914–1918
Chicago China Decorating Works 1880–1923
Chicago Society of Decorative Art 1877–
(Sold student products in its store at the Art Insti-
  tute.)
Childs, Grace 1910
Clark, Mrs. Laura E. 1914–1917
Clough, Anna 1914
Cole, Lillie E. 1896
(Atlan Member.)
Columbian Ceramic Association 1893–
  (Frederick Grunewald (owner of Western Deco-
  rating Works) organized the Columbian Ceramic
  Association of china decorators for an exhibit at
  the World's Columbian Exposition.)
Conlon, Mrs. Anna 1915
Cook, Mrs. Armetta 1911–1913
Corey, Harriet L.* 1909, 1915
(Also listed under "Art Schools" in 1911.)
Correll, Mrs. Anna 1912–1913
Covvo Studio 1915
Crane, Mrs. Anna Brauer 1909
Crane, Mrs. Delia M. 1911
Cross, Frederick R. 1914
Cross, Mrs. Lydia C. 1914–1917, 1936–1938
Curtis, Mrs. M. L. 1902
Custard, Grace 1914–1916
Dahm, Elsie 1906–1912
Davis, Mrs. Sarah E. 1907
Delanty, Mary M. 1914–1917

DeLuxe China Studios 1931
Diederich, Cora A. 1916–1917
Dirksen, Gerriet J. 1913
Dirkson, John 1915–1917
**Donath, Edward W.*** 1899–1928
Drake, Mrs. Jennie B. 1912
Durkee, Mrs. Thomas 1912–1913
Elite Art & China Studio 1915–1917
Epps, Mrs. Margaret E. 1917
Evans, Mrs. Clara 1914–1916
Everett, J. H. 1907
Ewel, Elizabeth C. 1900
Fleischer, G. A. & Co. 1892–1894
Foster, S. E. 1918–1919
Foster's Gift Shop 1917
Fox, Alvira B. 1910–1913
Fox, Susie M. 1908–1910
**France, Robert W.** 1906–1915
Frank, Mrs. Bothilde N. 1915–1917
Frank, Mrs. Edward 1917
Frazee, Helen Inez (Mrs. Abram A.) 1915–1924
  (Atlan member)
Freiberg, Reinhold 1913–1924
(Small studio, but very good quality decoration)
Freund, Joseph 1899–1901
Fricek, Emma 1917
Friis, Amanda 1913
Gay, Mrs. Mary J. 1912
Gerard Company, The 1914–1924
Gerard, Joseph 1897, 1913–1923
Gessner, Elsie D. (Mrs. J. A.) 1913–1916
(Also worked for Burley Studios)
Giles, Mrs. Ada 1903–1906
Girard, Leon D. 1908–1923
Gleason, Mrs. Merian M. 1922
Glowienke, Clara A. 1913–1917
Golden, Abraham 1915–1917
Gorrell, Lida M. 1914–1921
Gorvett, Clara A. 1914–1917

Graham, Mrs. Marion C. 1915–1917

Gray, Mrs. Mary J. 1913–1915

Gray, Peter H. 1915–1916

Greenleaf, Mrs. Walter G. 1895

(Atlan member.)

Grossek, Clara 1910

Grumieau, Louis P.* 1913

Grunewald & Busher 1892–1897

(See Western Decorating Works.)

Grunewald, Mrs. F. L. 1896–1897

Guzman, Zephyrina 1899

Haden, Thomas 1865–1877

Haley-Parker Studio 1912–1913

Hammond, Mrs. Bessie 1914–1917

Hanssen, Hans A. 1915–1922

Harris, Clark L. 1911–1913

Harris, Mrs. Kathleen 1915

Harris, Mrs. Mary 1914–1917

Harrison Studio 1917

(Floyd H Harrison)

Harrison, Floyd H. 1914–1915

Harrison, John W. 1910–1911

Hasburg, John W. 1892–1915

(Primarily produced gold for decorating.)

Hauptmann, Ernest V.* 1922–1923

Heep, Mrs. Ella 1916–1917

(Formerly Ella Ullrich.)

Heimerdinger, Mrs. Ernestine 1912–1913

(Won 2nd prize (behind Challinor) for 1913 Burley
   & Co. naturalistic exhibit.)

Henderson, Mittie 1905, 1910

Herdeg, Clara 1909–1911

Hernshaw, Mrs. Meta 1908–1910

Hesly, Rosa A. 1910–1913

Heyn, Edward M. 1902–1921

Holmes, Mrs. Anna 1915–1917

Howser, Mrs. Ida B. 1909

Howser, Mrs. Frank G. 1904

Hyde, Mrs. Annie N. 1896

**Illinois China Decorating Co.** 1920–1922

International China Company 1915–1916

Irsch, Bertha J. 1910

Janssen, Mrs. Ethel 1912

Jessop, Faye I. 1909

Joppo Studios 1926–1928

Judd, Mrs. Henry S. 1901

**W. Kalita Art Studio** 1944–1956

(Waclaw A. Kalita*)

Karkling, Emma 1909

Karnatz, Freda 1910

**Keates, Alfred*** 1912–1937

(Some gaps in years and occasionally listed under
   "Artists." Last listing under "Lamps.")

Keates, William F. 1909

Keese, F.M. 1924

Keller, Alexander S. 1901–1905

Kelly, Mrs. Rosa 1916–1929

(Also maintained a retail store.)

Kenwood Studios 1915–1916

Killian, Mrs. Sadie 1916–1917

Kimball Art Shop 1916–1917

King, Mrs. Anna 1910

Kinzie, Mrs. Frances 1914–1917

**Kittler, Joseph R.** 1922–1943

Kittredge & Anderson 1893

(Atlan members. Emma Kittredge & Louise Anderson)

Klipphahn, Maxwell R.* 1915–1917

Knight, Hazel M. 1914–1917

Knight, Sadie A. 1909–1913

Knorer, Grace C. 1917

Koehler, Alwin 1911–1912

**Koenig, Carl F.*** 1915–1966

(Some gaps in listings.)

Kranz China Studio 1928

Krauth, Millicent E. 1914

Kritz, Frank M. 1913

Kugler, Joephine 1916–1917

Lanning, Mrs. Clara 1904

Larson, Anna N. 1914–1921

Lauder, Isabel A. 1915–1916

Laufmann, Elsie 1915

Lawrence, Mrs. Emma L. 1904–1909

Lawrence, Jane M. 1909–1911

Leach, George P.* 1916–1924

Leever, Fern L. 1911–1913

Leigh, Mrs. Alice 1914–1915

**LeRoy Art Studio** 1925–1946

Leslie, Nettie 1908

Levy, Mary 1908

Levy, Mrs. Louis H. 1908–1910

Liberty China Decorating Co 1922–1923

Lingquist Art Shop 1915

Lingquist, Mrs. Cora 1916–1917

Lippincott, Florence I. 1911

Luder, Mrs.Emma 1911–1913

Luken, Minnie A.* 1895–1929

**Luken Studio** 1915–1937

(Minnie A. Luken was listed both as an individual and as a studio.)

Lydston, Amelia C. 1909–1911

Lyster, Adelaide L. 1905–1907

Maloney, Mrs Patrick T. 1916

Marbach, Mrs. Anna 1913–1915

Marbach, Mrs. Wm. 1911

Markham, Mrs. D. 1915–1916

**Marmostein & Seidel** 1908

(Henry Marmorstein* and Erhardt Seidel*.)

**Marmorstein's Art Studio** 1909–1931

(Henry Marmorstein*)

Mathurin, R. P. 1920–1926

Matthews, John M. 1910–1912

McBride, Mrs. Kate 1914–1917

McCrystle, May, Mrs. James B. 1906–1908

(Atlan member.)

McDonald, Mrs. William F. 1902–1904

McDyer, Frances 1917–1918 (Zumares & McDyer)

McGinty, Edward V. 1914–1917

Mehle, Chas. J. 1914–1916

Menzel & Gerard 1896 (Joseph Gerard)

Meyer, Carl 1931

Meyer, Jennie 1917

Middleton, Matilda 1902–1913

(Atlan Member.)

Miles, Clara A. 1907

Mitchell, Caroline E. 1910–1912

Moe, Laura C. 1914–1916

Montgomery, Mrs. Viola 1916

Moore, Mrs. Mary 1909–1911

Mueller, Mrs. Christina 1916–1917

Mulvaney, Eugene J. 1911–1915

(With Irene G. Sutton 1909–10; President of Kenwood Studios 1915.)

Mutual Art Shop 1916

Nash & Renning 1905–1910

(Also see Renning & Nash)

National China Decorating Co.(Inc) 1916–1917
   (Jacob Abelson, president; Samuel Ales, secretary)

Olsen, Mrs. Kathleen 1915–1916

**Osborne Art Studio.** 1918–1973

(Osborne T. Olsen)

Olson, Theodore 1907

Ong, Mrs. Helga A. 1914–1916

Orchardson, Mrs. Sara E. 1906–1908

Palmer, Mabel G. 1908

Parker & Violette 1904

(Edythe Parker, Atlan Mamber, and Mrs. Fletcher Violette.)

Paton, Mrs. Jessie 1916–1917

Peterson, Barbara 1915–1917

Peterson, Helga Mae 1910–1913

Pfohl, Wenzel 1914–1917

Phelps, Viola C. 1911–1913

Phillips, Florence L. 1915–1917

Phillips, Joseph 1889

Phillips, Joseph & Co. 1881

Phillips, William 1892

**Pickard Studios** 1898–present.

(No directory listings for Edgerton Studios.)

Pierce, Mrs. Emma 1912

Pietrzykowski, Marcel 1916–1917

Pioneer China Studio 1936–1937

**Pitkin & Brooks** 1872–1938

Poole, Irene E. 1894–1913

Poole Studios 1915–1917

(Irene E. Poole)

Porter, Alice S. 1904–1906

Porter, Mrs. Rose 1911–1913

Progressive China Decorating Co. 1921–1924

Purtill, Margaret 1913

Quality China Co. 1929–1930

Randall, Mrs. Cora A 1905

Ranniger, Mrs. Helen 1906–1909

Reade, Mamle L. 1910–1913

Renning & Nash 1912–1913

(Anthony L. Renning 1915–1917 Also see Nash & Renning and Ceramic Decorating Works.)

Reury, Howard B.* 1915–1916

Reynolds, May 1915–1917

Reynolds, May C. 1915

Ripley, Louise H. 1897–1998

**Rivir Studios Inc.** 1922–1930

Roetsch, Mrs. Celia E. 1912–1914

**Rogers China Company** 1915

**Rogers-Martini Co.** 1913–1916

(See E.D. Rogers Co.)

**Rogers, E. D. Co.** 1917

(Edward D. Rogers, president.)

**Roosevelt China Studio** 1926–1930

Rosenberg, Adeline J. 1905

Rosenstock, Doll 1901

Rost, Max* 1910–1916

Rusch, Gertrude D. 1916–1917

Salter, Clara 1907

Sanby, J. Robert 1922

Schilling, F. W. 1913

Schmidt Ceramic Chemical Company 1915

(Emil Reinbold, President, Anton Schmidt, Vice President.)

Schneider, Blanch Van Court 1905–1906

Scholz, William R. 1914–1916

Scoville, Julia 1904–1909

Shafer, S. Mrs. Inda 1906–1907

Sherborne, Mrs. C. B. 1922–1924

Shipman, Mrs. Alva I. 1901

Silberhorn, Esther C. 1896–1897

Simon, Sr., Adolph G.* 1907–1930

Slyter, Beatrice 1911

Sommer, Ida C. 1915–1918

Starring, L. T. 1874–1875

Steiner, August W.* 1911–1928

Sterling Deposit Manufacturing Co. 1912–1914

Stetson China Co. 1926–1932

Stevens, Belle O. 1896–1897

Stevenson Studio 1918

(William J. Stevenson 1916)

Stewart, Jeanne M. 1896–1897

Stewart, Mrs. Sarah E. 1909–1911

**Stouffer, Jacob H. (& Co.)** 1905–1952

Stringham, E. Helen 1909

Sugg, Florence R. 1916

Sunnyside Studios 1941–1944

Sutton & Mulvaney 1909–1910

(Irene G. Sutton and Eugene J. Mulvaney.)

Sutton, Irene G. 1914–1916

Sweinhart & Patterson 1902

Swenson, Mrs. Mae 1906–1907

Swindella, Mrs. Fanny 1909

Thime, Magdalene 1915–1917

Thonander, John* 1910–1912

**Tolpin Studios** 1920–1954

Topping, Helen M. 1897

Trenear, Irene 1909–1911

Trieber, Benjamin 1903–1905

Tyrell, Edward R. 1906

Ullrich, Ella 1914–1915

(Later Mrs. Ella Heep.)

Underwood, Mrs. Charles H. 1907–1908

United China Co. 1931–1932

Van Stone, Mrs. Maggie A. 1908–1913

Vanderhock, Mrs. Lizzie G. 1918

Van's China Studio 1915–1924 (Arthur R. Van Wicklin. As an individual: 1910–1922)

Varny, Genevieve 1915

Veernon, Mrs. Anna 1913

Vernon Art Store 1916

Violette, Mrs. Fletcher 1905–1906

Waldman Crockery & China Decorating Co. 1920–1930

Wands, William D. 1910–1916

Wayman, Martha R. 1907–1915

Wertheimer, Kate B. 1914

**Western Decorating Works** 1865–1896

(Frederick I. Grunewald and Frederick J. Schmidt.)

Whale, Mrs. Carrie 1907

Wheeler, Mrs. Ione Libby 1906–1907, 1919–1923

**White's Art Co.** 1914–1923

Whitinger, Mrs. Hazel 1912–1913

**Wight Art Studio** 1911–1919

(Phillip Wight.*)

Wilder, Lillian K. 1911–1912

Williamson, Jacob 1892

Williamson, Jacob W. 1905–1917

Wood, Mrs. Virginia N. 1909

Worthington, Ethel 1915–1917

**Yeschek, Inc.** 1928–1929

(Display ad: "Decorators and Etchers of fine china Offices, Studio 2748 Sheffield Ave. Sales Room 119 S State St.")

Zumares & McDyer 1917

(Anna Zumares and Frances McDyer.)

## C. Select Bibliography

*Books, Pamphlets, and Catalogs*

Aiston, Frances. *How to Fire China.* c.1910.

*The Art of Entertaining.* Chicago, IL: Pickard Studios, 1917.

*Atlan Ceramic Arts Club of Chicago, Constitution and By-Laws.* Chicago: (1897?).

Barber, Edwin Atlee. *The Pottery and Porcelain of the United States.* New York City: G. P. Putnam Sons, 1893.

Blasdale, Mary Jean. *Artists of New Bedford.*

Campana, D. M. *Acid Etching on China and Glass.* Chicago, IL: D. M. Campana, c.1910.

—. *Ceramic Photography.* Chicago, IL: D. M. Campana, c.1910.

—. *Details on Firing.* Chicago, IL: D. M. Campana, c.1910.

—. *Enamel Decoration.* Chicago, IL: D. M. Campana, c.1910.

—. *The Teacher of China Painting.* Chicago, IL: D. M. Campana, c.1910.

—. *The Teacher of Conventional Decorations and Designing.* Chicago, IL: D. M. Campana, c.1910.

*China Chats.* Chicago, IL: Pickard Studios, 1916.

Coysh & Henrywood. *Dictionary of Blue and White Printcd Pottery.* Suffolk, England: Antique Collector's Club, Ltd., 1989, 1982.

Cushion, J. P. *Handbook of Pottery and Porcelain Marks.* London, Boston: Faber & Faber, 1980.

*The China Painter.* Chicago, IL: Thayer & Chandler, 1914.

Darling, Sharon S. *Chicago Ceramics and Glass.* Chicago: Chicago Historical Society, 1979.

—*Decorative and Architectural Arts in Chicago 1871–1933.* A guide to the Chicago Historical Society Ceramics and Glass Exhibition. Chicago: The University of Chicago Press, 1982.

Denker, Ellen Paul. *Lenox China Celebrating a Century of Quality 1889–1989.* Trenton: New Jersey State Museum, 1990.

DeBolt, C. Gerald. *Dictionary of American Pottery Marks,* Rutland, Vermont: Charles E. Tuttle Co. Inc, 1988.

Eberlein and Ramsdell. *The Practical Book of Chinaware.* Philadelphia and New York: J. B. Lippincott, 1948.

Farrar, Estell Sinclaire. *H.P. Sinclaire, Jr., Glassmaker.* Garden City, NY: Farrar Books, 1974.

Frackelton, S. S. *Tried By Fire.* New York: D. Appleton & Co., 1885, 1895.

Gaston, Mary Frank. *American Beleek*. Paducah, Kentucky: Collector Books, 1984

—. *The Collector's Encyclopedia of Limoges*. Paducah Kentucky: Collector Books, 1992.

Godden, Geoffry. *Encyclopedia of British Porcelain Manufacturers*. London: Barrie & Jenkins, 1988.

Hasburg, John W. *A Glittering Trail*. Chicago: 1913.

McClinton, Katharine Morrison. "American Hand-Painted China." *Spinning Wheel*, April, 1967.

McLaughlin, Mary Louise. *China Painting: A Manual for the Use of Amateurs on the Decoration of Hard Porcelain*. Cincinnati: 1877.

—. *Suggestions to China Painters*. Cincinnati. . 1877.

Mitchell, Wesley C. *Business Cycles, The Problem and Its Setting*. New York: National Bureau of Economic Research, 1954.

Monachesi, Nicola Di Rienzi. *A Manual for China Painters*. Boston: Lothrop, Lee & Shepard Co., 1907.

O'Hara, Dorathea Warren. *The Art of Enameling on Porcelain*. c.1910.

Osgood, A. H. *Catalog and Price List of Supplies Required for China Decoration*. New York: Osgood Art School, 1903.

—. *How to Apply Royal Worcester Matt, Bronze, LaCroix, and Dresden Colors to China*. New York City: Osgood Art School, c.1895.

Paist, Harriet B. *Design and the Decoration of Porcelain*. c.1910.

*Pickard China*. Marshall Field & Company. Chicago. 1914.

Platt, Dorothy Pickard. *The Story of Pickard China*. Hanover, PA: Everybodys Press, 1970.

Ries, Heinrich & Leighton, Henry. *History of the Clay-Working Industry in the United States*. London: Chapman & Hall Ltd., John Wiley & Sons, 1909.

Robinson. *Robinson's Atlas of the City of Chicago*. 1886.

Robinson, Dorothy & Feeny, Bill. *The Official Price Guide to American Pottery and Porcelain*. Orlando FL: House of Collectibles, 1980.

*Secrets of Correct Table Service*. Compiled by the School of domestic Arts and Science. The Pickard Studios. 1911, 1912, 1913.

Steward, Mrs. LeRoy T. *Atlan Ceramic Arts Club of Chicago. History 1893–1902*. Chicago: 1902 Unpublished typescript produced for the Chicago Historical Society.

—. *Flat Enamel Decoration on China*. Chicago: 1909.

—. *Ceramic Decoration*. Chicago: 1908.

Tischendorf, H. *Photography on China or Glass*. Kittanning, PA: 1895.

Willy, John. *A Day at the Onondaga Pottery*. Syracuse, NY: O.P. Co., Syracuse China, 1925.

Wood, Serry. *China Classics 5. Hand Painted, Hand-Painted China*. Watkins Glen, NY: Century House, 1953.

Vance-Philips, Mrs. L. *Book of the China Painter*. 32 E. 58th St., NY: 1897.

## Articles

Austin, Amelia C. "Correct China Painting." *Ladies' Home Journal*. Nov. 1899 – Feb 1900.

Darling, Sharon S. "Arts and Crafts Shops in the Fine Arts Building." *Chicago History*, p. 79-85 Summer 1977, vol. VI, Number 2. Chicago: The Chicago Historical Society, 1977.

Stuart, Evelyn Marie. "America as a Ceramic Art Center" *Fine Arts Journal, May 1910, Chapt. 11*, p. 254-267, Chicago.

White, Nina. "Home-grown Fine China." *North Shore Magazine*. Dec. 1989.

Additional background articles on china decorating may be found in various issues of the following publications:

*Art for America*. Chicago, IL 1898–1900
*Arts and Decoration*. New York, NY 1910–1925
*Brush and Pencil*. Chicago, IL 1897–1907
*The China Decorator*, New York, NY 1871–c.1900
*Fine Arts Journal*. Chicago, IL 1899–1919
*Keramic Studio*. Syracuse, NY 1899–1924
*The Sketch Book*. Chicago, Il 1902–1907

# *END NOTES*

1   About 128 West Oak Street.
2   About 113 West Oak Street.
3   About 721 North State Street.
4   See Laura Fry p. 366 in Evans, Paul, *Art Pottery of the United States*. Also lost Fry paper reported in the *Nashville Banner*, Oct 5, 1897, p.1. and *The Clay Worker*, Vol. XXVIII, Nov. 1897.
5   Darling, Sharon S., *Chicago Ceramics and Glass, Chicago*, 1979, p. 53, Fig. 55.
6   Jaques, Bertha, *The Sketchbook*, June 1906, Vol. V, No. 8, p. 381.

7   About 124 West Oak Street.

8   Sales for 1891 were $15,000. *The Wisconsin Tobacco Reporter*, March 11, 1892.

9   *1889 Portrait and Biographical Album of Rock County.*

10  Mrs. Morris Hitchcock talk, *The Wisconsin Tobacco Reporter*, February 9, 1939.

11  *The Edgerton Story Official Program, Centennial Week* July 5–12, 1953, p. 52.

12  *The Wisconsin Tobacco Reporter*, May 25, 1894.

13  The American Art Clay Works was founded in 1892 by a former Pauline modeler, Thorwald P. A. Samson, and a molder, Louis Ipson. In 1895 it was purchased by a local attorney, L. H. Towne, and re-named the Edgerton Art Clay Works.

14  In drummer's parlance, "making" meant to canvass all the potential sales opportunities.

15  *A City Comes of Age, Chicago in the 1890's*, Susan E. Hirsch and Robert I. Goler, The Chicago Historical Society, 1990, p. 31.

16  About 944 North LaSalle Street, between Locust and Oak Streets.

17  d'Albis, Jean, *Haviland*, Paris, 1988, p. 65.

18  Denker, Ellen Paul, *Lenox Celebrating a Century of Quality 1889–1989* p. 28

19  Robinson & Feeny, *The Official Price Guide to American Pottery and Porcelain*, pp 38, 60

20  Cushion, J. P., *Handbook of Pottery and Porcelain Marks*

21  Robinson and Feeny, *American Pottery & Porcelain*, p. 359.

22  *Robinson's Atlas of the City of Chicago*

23  Darling, p. 17.

24  Platt p.11.

25  Some artists did take liberties with the original: compare the two versions of FLORIDA LAGOON (Plate 472).

26  The January, 1911 issue of *Keramic Studio* contained a color plate of a design by Mable C. Dibble entitled "Orange Design." Though the colors are identical, the patterns differ slightly. Dibble was one of ATLAN's most original and accomplished artists.

27  The DUTCH DECORATION was essentially a design by F. Dalrymple as illustrated in the December, 1910 issue of *Keramic Studio.*

28  Pickard Studios, *China Chats*, 1916.

29  In addition to the 1912–1919 range, a few Japanese blanks were used in the 1905–1910 and 1910–1912 ranges. These may have been samples or trial pieces; in general, Pickard and his artists held Japanese china in very low esteem, and there was no volume usage of it until the war.

30  *Keramic Studio*, December, 1917, April, 1918.

31  *Keramic Studio*, December, 1910, p. 174.

32  *Keramic Studio*, January, 1916, pp. 124, 128, 129; p. 124 erroneously refers to this as a first prize.

33  *Keramic Studio* Vol. XIX, No. 1 May 1917, p.1.

34  *Correct Table Service*, 1912, p.6

35  Ravenwood china was the product of the H.P. Sinclaire Glass Company in Corning, NY. China decorating may have begun as early as 1897, but was certainly added to glass production by 1900. Operating in a separate building under the name of the Ravenwood Company, Sinclaire produced a wide variety of decorated fancy china. His trademark was a red or black decal of a raven on a branch with "RAVENWOOD" beneath it. Like Pickard at that time, Sinclaire only engaged in decorating white blanks that were purchased from German, French, and American potteries and did not do any manufacturing. The manufacturing pottery's mark was frequently overpainted with a gold rectangle. Unlike Pickard, Sinclaire occasionally used decals for some of his decorating, and he also probably bought much finished product from others which he re-sold after firing his Ravenwood mark on it. While the decals were often mediocre, Sinclaire's half dozen artists produced good naturalistic fruits and florals, along with well-executed Indians, maidens, and monks. D. Walther and M. Ernlé are the only two known artists associated with this studio. The Ravenwood Company probably ceased operation in the late teens; large stocks of decorated china were moved in with Sinclaire's glass inventory out of which it was sold through 1923.

36  Platt, p.11.

37  Kovel, Ralph and Terry, *Kovel's New Dictionary of Marks*, Crown Publishers, Inc., New York, p. 259.

38  *Arts for America*, vol. VII, October 1897, p. 102.

39  Platt states that Keates was the maternal *grandfather* of Curtis Marker, however, this would seem to be an impossibility inasmuch as Keates was only 21 years older than Marker.

40  Darling, p.11.

41  Weimann, Jeanne Madeline, *The Fair Women*, p. 145, 148–153

42  Burley & Tyrrell catalog 1904

43  Darling, P.14.

# INDEX

*Note:* Pickard pattern names, Atlan artists, and Chicago decorating studios are each listed in separate indices.

Aldrich, Grace M. ...........................17, 19, 50, **106, 110**
Alexander, Ruth L........27, 29, 31, 32, 37, 40, **176, 195**
Anthony, Paul B.......................................32, 50, **201**
Arno, Edith .32, 50, 70, **145, 146, 182,** 280, **283, 291**
Art Institute (Chicago) .....12, 13, 16, 20, 24, 34, 36, 40, 53, 63, 254, 255, 266, 308–310, 321
Atkins, Anna.............................9, 13, 16, **23,** 31, 33, 37
Atlan Ceramic Arts Club ..........15, 20, 38, 53, 254, 266, 308–310
Aulich, Emil .................16, 19, 22, 29, 50, 51, **146,** 255
Aulich, Franz B.......................................50, 70, 308, 309
Bachmann, Max L. ...........25, 29, 51, 55, 245, **249,** 267
Baggerly, Frank F.....................................................14
Barber, Dr. Edwin Atlee .........................53, 254, 309
Bardos, Isadore..42, 43, 51, 70, **143,** 280, **288, 294, 296**
Barges, Edward C. ...............................................51, 246
Beitler, Joseph C. .....18, 19, 22, 51, 70, **113, 117,** 245, 246, **250**
Bero, Albert Bernard...................................................45
Beulet, F. ...................22, 32, 51, **170, 187, 202,** 256
Beutlich, Anton B .....16, 19, 22, **24,** 29, **30,** 32, 39, 42– 44, 51, **134, 143, 147, 148, 150, 163, 179, 184, 200, 212**
Bieg, Elsie W..................................262, 263, **264**
Bitterly, Walter ....................19, 51, 70, **101,** 246, **250**
Blaha, Joseph ...16, 19, 24, 40, 52, 70, **99, 104,** 269, **290**
Blazek, John ..................................29, 32, 52, 57, **175**
Boeglig, Peter ...........................................................52
Boehm, B....................................40, 52, **194, 195**
Bohman, Marie.............................37, 42, 43, 52, **223**
Brauer, Julius H. .....18, 19, 25, 29, 32, 34, 52, 70, **102, 103,** 244–246, **249–252**
Brauer, Marie .............................244–246, **247, 248,** 278
Breidel, William W. 27, 29, 52, 70, **156, 157, 160, 168**
Brun...............................................29, 52, **152**
Burgner, V........................................................40, 52
Burton, A..................................19, 52, 70, 246, **249, 251**
Bushbeck, Carl ...............**30,** 32, 51, 52, 70, **144, 166, 181,**280, **294**
Campana, Dominic M...17–19, 34, 35, 52, 70, 254, 265, 308
Castleton China Company...........................................47
Cathanay, F. A. .......................18, 19, 53, **105**
Ceramic Art Company....................17, 18, 52, 254
Challinor, Edward S. ...17–22, **24,** 27, 29, 32, 35, **36,** 37, 40, 42–45, 47, 53, 56, 65, 70, **105, 107, 122, 127, 129, 130, 136, 151, 172–174, 190–192, 204, 205, 207, 209, 213–215, 219–222, 224, 229, 232,** 245, 246, **250**
Cirnacty, F. .........................37, 41–43, 53, **217, 222**
Comyn, Arthur..21, 22, 27, 29, 32, 53, **160–162, 183, 184**

conventionalization..............17, 20, 21, 27, 40, 309, 310
Corey, Harriet L. ................37, **39,** 40, 53, 70, **190, 215**
cottage labor ...................13, 15, 17, 18, 245, 255, 278
Coufall, Anthony............22, 24, 27, 29, 53, 70, **113, 122, 149, 156, 158, 164**
Cumming(s), Arthur .............26, 29, 51, 53, 54, 56, **161**
D'Arcy Studio ................................................29, 61, 306
decals, decalcomania.......17, 24, 27, 29, 38, 44, 45, 72, 246, 255, 265, 269, 321
Dibble, Mable C......................................309, **314**
Dickinson, H. C..............................................18, 19, 54
Donath, Charles......................................................256
Donath, Edward W.........15, 18, 19, 22, 29, 54, 70, **254, 256, 257, 260, 261,** 308, 322, **324**
Donath, Max .....................................................256
Donath, William .........................................254, 255
Donisch, Edward F. .........................29, 31, 32, 54, **188**
Drzewiecki, Frank......................................................32, 54
Duran, L.....................................................22, 54, **100**
Edgerton "seconds" mark .........................43,44, **72,73**
Edgerton Art Studio ...............................12, 13, 61
Edgerton studio mark ............13, 15, **72,** 255, 256, 278
Edgerton, (William O.?) .......................17, 19, 54, **101**
Edward .....................29, 32, 54, **141, 178, 188**
Efdon .......................................(see Donisch, Edward F.)
Erbe ...................................................42, 43, 54, **221**
etched china and glass ....27, **31,** 32–35, 40–44, 46, 47, **238–240,** 268, 269, 276, 279, 280, 299, 301, 305–307
Eustice, John .....................................................18, 47
Falatek, Louis H. .........21, 40, 42, 43, 54, 70, **198, 222**
Falk, Louis F. ...............................(See Falatek, Louis F.)
Farrington ...............19, 22, 27, 29, 54, **101, 108, 110**
Feix, Ernest.....................................280, **284, 287**
Fischer, Emil J. T. ...21, 22, 29, 30, 32, 40, 51, 54, **126, 132, 133, 140, 143, 144, 154, 168, 180, 196, 197, 200, 201**
Fisher, John .............................(see Fischer, Emil J. T.)
Flood, William F.........................................**24,** 55
Flora .......................................................(see Loba, F.)
Fox.....................................................22, 29, 55, **171**
Frackleton, Susan S......................................8, 308, 309
Frazee, Helen ...............................................308, 309
freelance.....................21, 26, 58, 63, 65, 245, 276, 280
Friedrich ...........................................22, 55, **117**
Fritz.............................................................22, 55,
Fry, Laura......................................................10
Fuchs, John..21, 22, **24,** 25–27, 29, **30,** 32, 40, 50, 51, 54–56, 66, **135, 139, 148, 171, 182, 198, 200**
Fuchs, Pauline...........................42, 43, 55, 70, 307
Gasper, Paul P.....17, 18, 22, 27, 29, **30,** 31, 32, 39, 40, 54–56, 70, **115, 136, 161, 170, 171, 174, 178, 195, 198, 199, 212,** 269
Gerts, J. C. ...................................................42, 43, 55
Gibson, Edward........22, **24,** 27, 29, 41, 55, 56, 62, 70, **114, 135, 139, 145, 264,** 266

Gifford, Nathan R........22, 26, 29, 54, 57, 70, **111, 119, 125, 128–130, 154, 160, 167, 175, 177**, 280

glassware (Pickard)................34, 35, 40, 66, **215, 216**

Goess, Otto W. ...22, 29, 51, 56, **112, 144, 146, 174, 175**

Göttlich, J..........................................37, 40, 42, 43, 56

Grane ...........................17, 19, 22, 56, **101, 102, 208**

Griffiths, Harry R........22, 56, 70, **134**, 245, **246, 247, 262**, 280, **283**

Groskopf, Louis ................................................306, 307

Gross, F. R...............................................246, **248**

Grumieau, Louis P. .................40, 56, 70, 265, 306, 307

Guba, Frank............................................................69

Haag............................................................29, 56

Haase, Frank..........................29, 56, 70, **276**

Hahn, Charles.................19, 22, 57, 70, **98, 126**, 301

Half............................................................32, 57

Hanisch, Frank H..........................................19, 57, 276

Hardwick.....................................**24**, 29, 57, 262

Harp, M. ..................................................40, 57

Hartman .......................................32, 57, **186, 202**

Hartwig, William S. ...................................29, 57

Hauptman, Ernest V.........................32, 40, 52, 57

Heap, Samuel ...18, 22, 24, 57, 70, **120**, 280, **286, 291**

Heidrich, Adolph J........29, 57, 70, 255, 256, **258, 259**, 262, **263**

Heinz, J.................29, 57, 70, **167**, 256, **259**, 322, **323**

Hessler, Robert........16, 19, 20, 22, **24**, 29, **30**, 31, 32, 40, **41**, 57, **58**, 70, **100, 114, 115, 127–129, 134, 138, 153, 166, 169, 173, 186–189, 202**, 269, 307

Hiecke, Gustav H. G.............25, **39**, 40, 42, 43, 50, **58, 208, 209**

Hille, Myrtle .................................................32, 39, **181**

Hip..............................................29, 59, **147**

Honey, Ethel R..................................32, 59, 280, **284**

Jacobus, Oscar ....................................................10–12

Jacobus, Pauline....................................................10, 12

James, Florence M. ...22, **27**, 29, 31, 32, 37, 40, 42, 43, 54, 59, **152, 162, 187, 192, 193, 203, 219, 221**

Jelinek, Thomas M........16, 19, 22, 24, 59, 70, **98, 112, 132, 137**, 280, **285**

Jenkins, Victorine .................................................308, 309

Johnson, Mae E.......................................12, 13, **14**, 59

Kalita, Waclaw A.............59, 60, 70, 265, 269, 280, 299

Kammermayer, Frederick ...............245, 246, **247, 252**

Keates, Alfred....22, 29, 59, 62, 70, **139, 164**, 264, 266

Keates, Madeline.................27, 29, 59, **144, 151**, 266

Kiefus, Jacob I. ..19, 22, 24, 59, **106, 120**, 279, 280, **290**

Kittler, Joseph R................70, 255, 256, **258, 260**, 267

Klein, Ingeborg.....................**41**, 42, 43, 60, **222, 223**

Klipphahn, Maxwell R. ....18, 19, 22, **24**, 29, **30**, 32, 39, 40, 42, **43**, 46, 60,70, **117–119, 121, 124, 140, 148, 149, 159, 169, 178, 185, 206, 207, 225**, 265, **266**

Koenig, Carl F. .......29, 32, 60, 70, **141, 142, 168**, 245, 246, **267, 268**, 307

Koep., F.H..............................22, 29, 60, **116**

Koplien, Elizabeth ..........................................255, **257**

Kriesche, F. .19, 22, 29, 60, **111, 121, 148, 162, 176**, 256

Kubasch, Emil...................................22, 60, **108–110**

Kucia ..............................................42, 43, 61

Lawrence, Marion ................................280, **295**

Leach, George P. ........22, 29, 61, 65, 67, 70, **112, 122, 123, 127, 135, 141, 154, 163**, 277, 280, **288, 294**

Lebrun .....................................29, 61, **137**, 280

Lemke, Walter R. .................22, 29, 61, **112, 151, 156**

Lenox, Inc..................................18, 47, 254, 280

Leon ...19, 22, 61, 70, **99, 105, 117, 118, 122, 123, 137**

LeRoy, M. Rost...19, 22, 35, 61,70, **98, 105, 118, 120, 131**, 256, **259, 261**, 268

Limoges (France) ...................................17, 20, 29, 33

Lindner, Frederick J.........17, 19, 22, 29, **30**, 32, 52, 60, 61, 102, **103, 104, 106, 114–116, 139, 157–159, 179, 185**

Loba, F....13, 15, 19, 20, 22, 29, 61,70, **97, 121, 172**, 280

Loh, John.........19, 22, 29, 32, 61, **101, 137, 142, 172**

Lovgren, Ellen..............................309, **313–318**

Luken, Minnie A. ...............37, 38, 40, 62, 70, **195**, 268

Maley, Eva E................32, 37, 40, 62, **192, 215**

Mark...............................19, 40, 62, **99, 194**

Marker, Curtis H........21, 39, 32, 36, **37**, 39–43, 59, 62, 70, **147, 149, 155, 163, 190, 191, 204–206, 213–215, 217, 222, 224, 226, 228, 264, 265**, 266

Marmorstein, Henry...........................22, 62, **132**, 278

Marshall Field & Co..10, 16, 25, 34, 35, 46, 50, 58, 279, 322

Matsuo, Itero N. .....................................................42

McCorkle, Zuie ............19, 21, 25, 27, 29, 62, **144, 152**

Mentges, Edward P.......................29, 32, 62, 71, **177**

Messino ..............................(see Matsuo, Itero N.)

Miche ..............................29, 62, 71, **150**, 301

Michel, Harry E........22, 24, 62, 71, **98, 135, 136**, 280, **284–286, 288–290, 293**

Miller, Anton ...29, 32, 40, 63, 71, **165**, 280, **293, 297**, 299

monogram ware ...**28, 29**, 35, 52, 61, 68, **75, 125, 166**, 299

Monti, H. A. ..........................................................63

Moore, Bertha L. ......................27, 29, 63, **145, 176**

Morgan, Eben C., Jr. ...........................44, 47, 48, **49**

Morley, George.....................................................280

Motzfeldt, Andrew ...................19, 20, 22, 63, **111, 136**

Mt. Washington Glass Co. .....................................26, 69

Mullen.....................................(see Walters, Frederick)

Neitsche, Paul...............................(see Nitshe, Paul)

Nessy, John ..19, 22, 29, **30**, 32, **39**, 40, 63, 68, 71, **98, 122, 126, 134, 178, 189, 208**

Nichols, Bessie ...............................**41**, 42, 63, **220**

Nichols, Maria Longworth.........................................10

Nitsche,Paul R..............................................63, 306

Nittel, Frank ........................32, **63**, 64, 71, **189**, 307

Osborne (Osborne T. Olsen).......21, 27, 37, 52, 65, 264, 269, **270–275**

Osgood School .....................................................50

Pairpoint .............................................26, 69

Parsche, Franz X. ......................35, 41, 64, 276

Passony (also Passoni), Arthur ....29, 32, 40, **156, 165, 169, 170, 179, 193, 194**
Pauline (Art) Pottery.....................................10–12, 15
Petit.............................................................29, 64
Pfiefer, E. ..............................................22, 64, **113**
Pickard, Dorothy ................(see Dorothy Pickard Platt)
Pickard, Henry Austin.......................43–45, **46**, 47, 48
Pickard, Henry Austin, Jr. (Pete)....6, 33, 44, 47, **48**, 49
Pickard, Minnie Verna .......9, 13, 14, 16, 22, **24**, 27, 29, 32, **33**, 45, 55, 64, **113, 176, 177**
Pickard, Wilder A. .........**9**, 10–22, **24**, 25, 27–29, 31–38, 40, 43–46, 50, 67, 244, 255, 262, 264–266, 268, 276, 278, 279
Pickard, William ......................................43, 44
Pietrykaski.................................19, 64, **104**
Platt, Dorothy Pickard.............6, 31, 42, 43, 52, 54–57, 59–61, 63, 67
Podlaha, Otto .....22, 26, 28, **29, 30**, 32, 33, 40, **64**, 71, **166, 167**, 265, 269, 276, 280, **295, 296**, 305
Pohl, C. ...................................22, 65, **109**
Post, F. ...................................22, 65, **175**
Ravenswood mark .................................44, **72**
Ravenswood Studio ...**22, 23**, 24, 37, 38, 41–43, 45, 46, 50, 54–56, 60, 62, 68, 71, 266, 278, 279, 306
Ravenwood mark.............................44, **73**, 333
Ravenwood Company .....................................333
Rawlins, William T. .............29, 31, 32, 40, 65, **193, 213**
Ray, Noble..................29, 61, 65–67, 71, **153**, 322, **323**
Rean...................................(see Klipphahn, Maxwell R.)
Reury, Howard B. .......22, 29, 62, 63, 65, 71, **125, 128, 131, 147**, 301, 305, 308, 322, **324**
Rhodes, Arnold .....32, 43, 65, 71, **231, 246, 247, 252**, 269, 280, **285, 295, 297**, 299, 307
Richter, Anton........29, **30**, 31, 32, 40, 42, 43, 65, **166, 187, 192, 193, 196, 218**
Richter, S. .............................32, 66, **181, 185**
Roden, Harry.............................22, 66, **99, 107**
Roessler, Carl.................32, 35, 40, 66, **186, 202, 215**
Rookwood Studio ...........................................10
Roseville Pottery........................................25, 51, 55
Rosler ...........................................(see Roessler, Carl)
Ross.............................................(see Roessler, Carl)
Rost, Max......................22, 66, 71, **133**, 255, 256
Roy, A.....................................22, 65, 66, **118**
Ryba, K.....................................280, **292, 293**
Samuelson, Ester.............**41**, 42, 43, 60, 66, **222, 223**
Sargeant, John................................................10
Satsuma (style)..38–40, **211, 212**, 309, **314, 315, 318, 320**
Schindler, John H. ..............................26, 63, 306
Schoenig, Antol ..........................................**30**, 66
Schoner, Otto .........21, 22, **24**, 29, 66, **119, 120, 133, 139, 145, 146, 154, 155, 157, 171**
Seagren, Anna A.......................37, 40, 66, **214**
seconds, marking of.......................46, **72, 73**
Seidel, Erhardt ..........15–17, 19, 22, 67, 71, **114, 117, 119, 120, 138**, 278

Shellenbach, Sherry.........................................45
Shoner..........................................(see Schoner, Otto)
Simek, Joseph ..............280, **286, 289, 290, 293–295**
Simon, (Si) Adolph G., Jr. ...........................44, 45, 67
Simon, Adolph G., Sr.......................................45, 67
Sinclair, George.................22, 29, 61, 65, 67, **127, 176**
Smith Bros. Glass Co. ....................................50, 56
Stahl, George W...........22, 67, 71, **112, 131**, 246, **248, 253**, 256, 262
Steiner, August W. ......................................67, 305
Steward, Florence Pratt.....................................308, 309
Stouffer, Charles P..........................................279
Stouffer, Grace...............................................279
Stouffer, J. H. (Mfg.) Co. (also Stouffer Studios) ........13, 21, 24, 29, 34, 37, 50–53, 56, 57, 59, 60–63, 65, 66, 69, 278–280
Stouffer, Jacob H. .........................24, 60, 267, **278**, 279
Stouffer, Mary D. ...........................................279
Stouffer, Milan D...........................................279
Syracuse China ...........................................17
Thonander, John ...........................32, 67, 71, 299
Tiffany & Co.(also Tiffany Studios) ..........10, 31, 48, 309
Tolley, Harry E.........22, 29, 32, 67, 71, **121, 129, 138, 146, 170, 181, 184, 188**
Tolpin, Emil F. .......**30**, 31, 32, 40, 54, 66–68, 71, **180, 194, 197, 207, 208, 212**, 299, **300**, 309
Tolpin, Isaac.................................299, **300**
Tolpin, Nesha .................27, 29, 32, 68, 71, **168**, 299
Tomascheko, Rudolph ..22, 27, 29, 68, **114, 116, 126, 148**
Unger, Anton .................................................29, **30**, 68
Vetter .......................................19, 22, 68, **118**
Vobornik, Franz............22, **30**, 32, 40, **42**, 43, 68, **117, 123, 165, 168, 198, 214, 221**
Vokral, Jeremiah..19, 22, 29, **39**, 40, 42, 68, **100, 152, 174, 179, 204, 206, 208, 209, 219**
Wagner, Albert H........19, 22, 29, 37, 40, 68, **134, 147, 153, 203**
Walker, Abby Pope .........................................308
Walters, Frederick ..29, 32, 40, 61, 68, **121, 138, 139, 155, 163, 174, 182–184, 187, 203**
Weiss, Arthur J. .................19, 22, 27, 50, 69, **108–111**
Weissflog, Gustav ...............69, 71, **226**, 265, 280, **290**
Wheeler, Ione...............................................308
Wheelock Studio ............................................29
White, Ellen.................................................301
Wiard, Charles Leo.........................................310, **315**
Wight, Phillip.........29, 32, 69, 71, **138, 162, 189, 305**
Willets Manufacturing Company.....................17–19, 29
women, employment of .................................15, 27, 38
Yeschek, Frank P. ......29, **31**, 32, **38**, 40, 55, 58, 61, 64, 67–69, 71, **167**, 305, **306**, 307
Yeschek, Joseph T. ..........20–22, **24**, 25, **26**, 29, **30**, 31, 32, 37, **39**, 40, 42, 43, 54–56, 62, 69, 71, **107, 124, 130, 141, 144, 151, 180, 189, 197–200, 206, 212, 223**, 307
Ziologe.......................................................40, 69